PENGUIN CLASSICS

THE HISTORY OF ALEXANDER

ADVISORY EDITOR: BETTY RADICE

QUINTUS CURTIUS RUFUS, the Roman historian, wrote the only life in Latin of Alexander the Great. The *History* originally consisted of ten books, of which, unfortunately, the first and second are entirely lost. The author's identity and the date of composition of this work have been the subject of great debate. However, the evidence of recent years suggests he was a soldier and politician who rose from obscurity to a senatorial career under Tiberius (AD 14–37). But the fall of the emperor's chief minister, Sejanus, brought his political career temporarily to an end. Thus he turned to writing, and in the ten years between the fall of Sejanus and the accession of Claudius (AD 41) he composed the great part of the *History of Alexander*, which he completed in the emperor's early years. He later obtained the proconsulship of Africa and it appears he died in office in AD 53.

JOHN YARDLEY has published extensively on Roman literature, and has provided translations of Justin for the American Philological Association Classical Resources series (1994) and for Oxford University Press's Clarendon Ancient History series (Books 11–12, 1997). He has also translated Livy 31–40 for the Oxford World's Classics (2001). His most recent works are *Justin and Pompeius Trogus: A Study of the Language of Justin's Epitome of Trogus* (Toronto, 2003) and (with Waldemar Heckel) *Alexander the Great: Historical Sources in Translation* (Blackwell, 2003). He is Professor of Classics at the University of Ottawa and a former President of the Classical Association of Canada.

WALDEMAR HECKEL was born in 1949 in Königshofen, Germany. He was educated in Canada at McMaster University (MA) and the University of British Columbia (Ph.D.). He is now Professor at the University of Calgary, Canada. His books include *The Last Days and Testament of Alexander the Great: A Prosopographic Study* (Stuttgart, 1988) and *The Marshals of Alexander's Empire* (London, 1992). He has also published, with John Yardley, a translation and commentary on Justin, Books 11–12, for the Clarendon History Series (Oxford, 1997).

QUINTUS CURTIUS RUFUS

The History of Alexander

Translated by
JOHN YARDLEY
with an Introduction and Notes by
WALDEMAR HECKEL

PENGUIN BOOKS

PENGUIN BOOKS

Published by the Penguin Group
Penguin Books Ltd, 80 Strand, London WC2R ORL, England
Penguin Group (USA) Inc., 375 Hudson Street, New York, New York 10014, USA
Penguin Books Australia Ltd, 250 Camberwell Road, Camberwell, Victoria 3124, Australia
Penguin Books Canada Ltd, 10 Alcorn Avenue, Toronto, Ontario, Canada M4V 3B2
Penguin Books India (P) Ltd, 11 Community Centre, Panchsheel Park, New Delhi – 110 017, India
Penguin Books (NZ) Ltd, Cnr Rosedale and Airborne Roads, Albany, Auckland, New Zealand
Penguin Books (South Africa) (Pty) Ltd, 24 Sturdee Avenue, Rosebank 2196, South Africa

Penguin Books Ltd, Registered Offices: 80 Strand, London WC2R ORL, England

www.penguin.com

First published 1984
Reprinted with revisions 2001
Reprinted with updated Bibliography 2004

045

Translation copyright © John Yardley, 1984, 2001
Introduction, Notes and additional material copyright © Waldemar Heckel, 1984, 2001, 2004
All rights reserved

Printed and bound in Great Britain by Clays Ltd, Elcograf S.p.A.

Filmset in Monophoto Photina

ISBN-13: 978-0-140-44412-4

www.greenpenguin.co.uk

CONTENTS

INTRODUCTION

The only full-length Latin history of the great Macedonian king and conqueror, Alexander III, survives in no fewer than 123 manuscripts,[1] the oldest of which belong to the ninth century A.D. Unfortunately, the majority of these are of poor quality and the single original (now lost), from which all known manuscripts of Curtius are descended, was incomplete. There are a number of *lacunae* – the largest at the end of Book 5, the beginning of Book 6, and in the middle of Book 10 – but most lamentable is the loss of the entire first and second books. Thus we cannot say with certainty what the title of the work was or why it was written; nor can we be entirely sure about the author's name.

The author's name appears as Curtius Rufus in the titles of the major manuscripts, while the praenomen Quintus is added in the colophons of all but one of these. The title of the work, when it appears, is given variously as *Historiae* or *Historiae Alexandri Magni Macedonis* or *Historiae Magni Macedonis Alexandri* ('The History of Alexander the Great of Macedon'). With the possible exception of Hegesippus, no one shows any signs of having known or used Curtius' history until the Middle Ages.[2]

The present translation is based on H. Bardon's Budé text (Paris, 1961, 1965), which, although generally considered inferior to K. Müller's Tusculum edition (Munich, 1954), is the most accessible of the modern editions and also the one followed by J. E. Atkinson in his commentary on Books 3 and 4.[3] A 'List of Variations from the Budé Text' is appended to the translation.

A. THE AUTHOR AND THE DATE

The identity of Q. Curtius Rufus and the date of composition of the *History of Alexander* have been vigorously debated. In the past century Curtius' time of writing has been assigned to the reigns of more than a dozen emperors from Augustus to Constantine. But the prevailing opinion of the last two decades has favoured the principate of Claudius, or possibly of Vespasian.[4]

The *terminus post quem* for the composition of the *History* is certainly the establishment of the empire, as is clear from the short digression at 10.9.1–6:

But destiny was already bringing civil war upon the Macedonian nation; for a throne is not to be shared (*nam et insociabile est regnum*) and several men were aspiring to it.

I

Their forces first came into conflict, then split up, and when they had put more of a burden on the body than it could stand the limbs started to weaken, and an empire that might have stood firm under a single man collapsed while it rested on the shoulders of a number. So it is with justification that the people of Rome acknowledge that they owe their salvation to their emperor (*principi suo*) who shone out as a new star in the night that was almost our last. It was his rising, I declare, and not the sun's, that brought light back to a darkened world (*caliganti mundo*) at a time when its limbs lacked a head and were in chaotic disarray. How many were the torches he then extinguished! How many in the swords he sheathed! How violent the storm he scattered, suddenly clearing the skies! So our empire is not merely recovering, but even flourishes. If I may be forgiven for saying it, the line of this same house will prolong the conditions of these times – forever, I pray, but at least for a long duration.

Who was this *princeps*, 'who shone out as a new star'? The most serious candidates have been Augustus, Claudius, Vespasian and Septimius Severus. Caligula, Nerva, Trajan, Severus Alexander have all been suggested, but they had no rival claimants and deserve little consideration. The arguments for Septimius Severus have always been weak, though his reign predates what has generally been regarded as the *terminus ante quem* of the *History*, the end of the Parthian empire in A.D. 224.[5] Curtius' reference to Tyre, which 'with long peace completely restoring its prosperity, enjoys tranquillity under the merciful protection of Rome' (4.4.21), is hardly the kind of remark to be made between 193 and 224 of a city sacked by Pescennius Niger in 193 and reconstituted in 198 as a Roman colony. Recent discussions of the terms 'Persae' and 'Parthi' have tried to remove the upper terminal date for the composition of the *History*, arguing that writers of the third and fourth centuries A.D. often used the terms loosely, even interchanging them.[6] But the point is purely academic, since Curtius' description of Parthiene (6.2.12) as the 'land of a people little known at that time but now the most important of all regions situated beyond the Euphrates and Tigris and bounded by the Red Sea (i.e., the Persian Gulf)' serves also to define the limits of Roman power. 'So it is virtually certain that he wrote before the time of the Severi, who claimed Mesopotamia as a Roman province; highly probable that he ante-dated Marcus Aurelius, who set up a protectorate there; and probably safe to put him before Trajan, who made the decisive break with the traditional acceptance of the Euphrates as the frontier between the two Empires.'[7] Thus it appears that our Curtius Rufus wrote during the first century of the Roman empire, and that narrows the field to Augustus, Claudius and Vespasian.

Curtius' digression on the unrest at Rome indicates that the new emperor did not establish the principate but rather restored peace to it, averting rather than participating in a civil war. It is a picture that ill suits Augustus, nor can it be said that Vespasian's accession averted civil war. Furthermore, Curtius speaks of the state as 'lacking a head', implying a brief period of uncertainty and anarchy. Vespasian assumed the title of emperor during Vitellius' reign. And so we are left with Claudius.

Up to this point, our arguments have been negative and the choice of Claudius the result of a process of elimination. But, in fact, Claudius offers the strongest case in favour of his identification with the *princeps* of Curtius' little digression. When he wrote about 'the night that was almost our last', Curtius must certainly have been thinking of the night of Gaius' assassination, when no successor was evident until the Praetorians declared for Claudius (24/25 January, A.D. 41). Generally regarded as unfit to rule, Claudius found an obvious parallel in the mentally defective Arrhidaeus, whose condition was serious enough to cause the Macedonian aristocracy to overlook him entirely when Alexander died. Like Arrhidaeus, Claudius was the misfit brother of a young and heroic figure, and if Germanicus did not actively engage in *Alexandri imitatio*, he was soon compared with the Macedonian king. Moreover, Suetonius (*Gaius* 52.3; cf. Dio 59.17.3) relates that Germanicus' son, Gaius (Caligula), would parade in the breast-plate of Alexander, which he took from the sarcophagus in Alexandria. It served Curtius' interests, of course, to modify his portrait of Arrhidaeus, whom virtually all other writers depicted as severely epileptic or mentally retarded.[8] Thus he appears as a reluctant and somewhat bewildered participant in the succession-struggle of 323 B.C. (10.7.1ff.). Pithon, one of Alexander's bodyguard, is said to have been 'opposed to the young man' (Arrhidaeus was at least thirty-four years old!) and to have made 'derogatory remarks' (*probra*) which 'generated more animosity against himself than disdain for Arrhidaeus' (10.7.5), but we are not told what the substance of these remarks was. And, in general, it is youth and inexperience which make Arrhidaeus indecisive and easily manipulated, rather than mental retardation which renders him incompetent.

Whether Curtius is punning on the name Caligula when he speaks of the 'darkened world' (*caliganti mundo*) cannot be determined with certainty and is, in itself, inconclusive. But the *History* contains other possible contemporary allusions: the degeneration of Alexander, reminiscent of Gaius' character, and the feigned reluctance of Perdiccas to accept the crown (10.6.18–19), recalling the tactics of Tiberius. There is also the remarkable similarity between the speech of Amyntas, son of Andromenes, defending his friendship with the condemned Philotas (7.1.19–40), and M. Terentius' appeal against the charge of *Seiani amicitia* (Dio 58.19.3–4; Tacitus, *Annales* 6.8.1–6).[9] All of which become more easily understood in the light of the career of Q. Curtius Rufus.

The author of the *History of Alexander* may be identical with either or both of the known Curtii Rufi of the early empire. The first of these is a Quintus Curtius Rufus named in the Index of Suetonius' *De Grammaticis et Rhetoribus*. Although his dates are not given, they can be deduced from his relative position in the list, which runs: L. Cestius Pius, M. Porcius Latro, Q. Curtius Rufus, L. Valerius Primanus, Verginius Flavus. About L. Valerius Primanus we know nothing at all, but L. Cestius Pius was active around 13 B.C. and M. Porcius Latro died in 4 B.C.; Verginius Flavus belonged to the age of

Claudius and Nero. Thus it is quite possible that the Curtius of this list was active during the reigns of Augustus, Tiberius, Gaius and Claudius. It is, of course, particularly tempting to identify the rhetorician with the author of the *History*, since the work is so highly rhetorical in character.

Then there is Curtius Rufus, the soldier and politician of Tacitus (*Annales* 1.20.3–21.3) and the Younger Pliny (*Epistulae* 7.27.2–3) who rose from obscurity – rumour held that he was a gladiator's son, or something even worse – to a senatorial career. It is said that, as a young man, he saw a vision in Hadrumetum, a woman larger than life predicting that he would go to Rome and later return as proconsul of Africa, where he would die. This man may have held the quaestorship before Augustus' death,[10] and he attained the praetorship as *candidatus Caesaris* under Tiberius, who made light of Curtius' origins ('*Curtius Rufus videtur mihi ex se natus*'; Tacitus, *Annales* 11.21.2). Then, after a long interval, he reappeared as suffect consul in October of A.D. 43; the epigraphic evidence confirms that his praenomen was Quintus.[11] As consular legate (or governor) of Upper Germany he received the triumphal insignia in 47 or 48, and later he obtained the proconsulship of Africa. It appears that he died in office in A.D. 53.[12]

It is difficult to resist the view[13] that the consul and the rhetorician are one and the same. By this argument, Curtius' praetorship brought him into contact with Sejanus, and, when the latter was at the height of his power (A.D. 26–31), Curtius was virtually forced to cultivate his favour, thereby gaining a reputation for 'surly flattery' (*tristis adulatio*). But Sejanus' fall meant the end of Curtius' political career under Tiberius and his successor, Gaius. Thus, he turned to rhetoric, and during the ten years between the fall of Sejanus and the accession of Claudius, he composed the greater part of the *History of Alexander*, which he completed in the emperor's early years, before his own consulship. Hence the work exhibits a strong rhetorical flavour and the spice of a bitter-sweet senatorial career.

B. THE SOURCES

Although the achievements of Alexander the Great were a popular source of historical inspiration in the late fourth and early third centuries B.C., no contemporary account survives except in fragments.[14] The five major extant works were composed between three and five hundred years after the king's death in 323 B.C., but these are based on the lost primary sources. The earliest surviving account, the seventeenth book of the *Universal History* of Diodorus Siculus, dates to the second half of the first century B.C. Pompeius Trogus, a Romanized Gaul writing in the Augustan age, discussed Alexander in two books of his *Historiae Philippicae*, but this survives only in its 'Prologues' and in the work of a third-century epitomator, M. Junianus Justinus (Justin). Together with Curtius, whom we have assigned to the Claudian period,

Plutarch's *Life of Alexander*, written at the beginning of the second century A.D., rounds out the so-called 'vulgate' tradition, which is uniform in its treatment of Alexander and based on the same primary source. Apart from these stands the *Alexandri Anabasis* of Flavius Arrianus Xenophon (Arrian), a governor of Bithynia and Cappadocia under Hadrian.[15] Modern scholars have generally preferred not only Arrian to the other extant sources, but also his primary sources, Ptolemy and Aristobulus, to the remainder of the lost historians. But this attitude towards Arrian and the vulgate is beginning to change in the light of recent studies into Arrian's method.[16]

The chief primary sources used by all the above-mentioned authors go back, ultimately, to the 'official history' composed by Callisthenes of Olynthus, reputed to be the nephew of Aristotle. Callisthenes accompanied Alexander in order to record his exploits and send favourable reports, apparently published in instalments, to the Greek mainland. But in 327 he was executed for his alleged involvement in Hermolaus' conspiracy (8.6.7ff.; 8.8.21), and it is possible that his account did not continue beyond the Iaxartes (Tanais) campaign of 329 B.C.[17] Up to this point, he provided primary (written) information for subsequent Alexander-historians, notably Ptolemy, Cleitarchus and Aristobulus.

What the precise relationship of these three authors was is far from certain; though we can be reasonably confident in assigning Aristobulus to the third century B.C. It used to be thought that Ptolemy, who was king of Egypt (305–283 B.C.), composed his account of Alexander in his old age. Recently, however, it has been argued that Ptolemy deliberately misrepresented or suppressed the activities of his political enemies – particularly Perdiccas, his supporter Aristonous, and Antigonus the One-Eyed – and that his work was published not long after the settlement at Triparadeisus in 321 B.C.[18] It is, of course, possible that Ptolemy wrote during the 300s, but his history, although clearly biased against certain individuals, exhibits a certain pettiness (perhaps the 'sour grapes' of old age?) rather than the sting of effective propaganda. Furthermore, it is difficult to argue that he wrote before the appearance of Cleitarchus' book, which he seems, on at least one occasion (9.5.21), to have corrected.

Cleitarchus, unlike the other chief historians of Alexander, did not take part in the events he described.[19] The son of an accomplished historian, Dinon, he was a Greek writing in Alexandria sometime after 310 B.C. Although he recorded Cassander's restoration of Thebes and his crimes against the Macedonian royal house, he did not know of Cassander's own death in 297 (Diod. 17.118.2; Curt. 10.10.19), and, unlike Aristobulus (*F.Gr.Hist.*, 139 F54),* he seems to have been ignorant of the outcome of the battle of Ipsus in 301 B.C.[20] Probably, he began his research into the subject soon after the death of Alexander, whose funeral carriage Ptolemy had successfully diverted to Egypt in 321. In addition to the half-finished work of Callisthenes, Cleitarchus

* Abbreviations are listed on p. 265.

probably read and used the accounts of Onesicritus and Nearchus for information on India. The former had been the helmsman of Alexander's own ship
on the Indus river – he falsely claimed to have been the admiral of the whole
fleet (Arr. 6.2.3) – and was the author of a work entitled *How Alexander Was
Educated*, although the main focus of this was, apparently, India. Nearchus,
the admiral, wrote in part to counter Onesicritus' mendacity but also to give
an account of the progress of the fleet from the descent of the Indus to the
rendezvous with Alexander in the West.

Cleitarchus supplemented these contemporary Alexander-historians with
the eye-witness reports of Macedonians and Greeks, many of the latter having
served as mercenaries of the Great King. Hence the work had a strong Greek
flavour: the generalship of Memnon, the advice of Charidemus and Thimodes
(Thymondas), the loyalty of Patron, and the courage and plight of Dioxippus
the boxer, all can be traced to Cleitarchus.[21] We are also given glimpses of
the Persian camp and Darius' councils, and of the wealth of Persia's royal
cities. The former again derive from eye-witness sources, the latter element
was in some cases coloured by information from the *Persica* of Cleitarchus'
father, Dinon.[22] The so-called 'good sources' used by Arrian in his *Alexandri
Anabasis* form a sharp contrast to the Cleitarchean vulgate, represented by
Diodorus and Curtius (and to a lesser extent by Justin and Plutarch): Ptolemy
appears to have written a rather barren military narrative from the Macedonian viewpoint; Aristobulus lent some colour but his history was, far too
often, thinly-veiled *apologia*.

On the other hand, Cleitarchus was prone to exaggerate Alexander's vices,
to credit the incredible, to sacrifice historical accuracy for rhetorical effect.
Clitarchi probatur ingenium, fides infamatur, writes Quintilian (*Institutio
Oratoria* 10.1.74), though even his style was objectionable to Demetrius (*de
Elocutione* 304 = *F.Gr.Hist.*, 137 T10). Strabo too was critical of Cleitarchus'
details about the Amazons, but the important fact is that he was read and
he was the most popular of the Alexander-historians in Rome during
the late republic and early empire.[23] It is not surprising that his colourful
account, with its emphasis on the role of *Tyche* and the degeneration of
Alexander's character, should have attracted the interest of Curtius the
rhetorician.

C. CURTIUS' SOURCES AND MODELS

A comparison of the texts of Curtius and Diodorus' seventeenth book reveals
that, for much of their narratives, these authors followed the same primary
source, and that source was long ago recognized as Cleitarchus.[24] Attempts
to prove that Diodorus did not use Cleitarchus directly, or as his only source,
have met with limited success. F. Schachermeyr's recent methodological
arguments point back to the traditional view that Diodorus was essentially
abbreviating Cleitarchus.[25] Since the argument that Curtius read, and

occasionally mistranslated or corrupted, Diodorus' account will not stand,[26] then it follows that Curtius too relied heavily on Cleitarchus' original. The initial reaction of the reader may well be that there are vast differences between the histories of Curtius and Diodorus, but he must bear in mind the methods, the backgrounds and the intentions of the authors. Diodorus included Alexander in the course of his universal history, reducing Cleitarchus to about one-tenth of the original; Curtius, writing a monograph on the Macedonian king, kept closer to Cleitarchus and added information from his own experience and other sources. Nevertheless, one cannot help but be impressed by the striking similarities in the sequence of events and the phraseology, in spite of the fact that one author writes Greek, the other Latin. The corresponding passages of Diodorus are provided in the notes to the present translation and need not be detailed here.

The internal evidence for Curtius' sources is disappointing. Cleitarchus alone is mentioned more than once (9.5.21; 9.8.15), and the only other primary sources named are Ptolemy and Timagenes (both at 9.5.21). About Timagenes, who came to Rome from Alexandria in 55 B.C., we know very little: Curtius' is our only reference to his discussion of Alexander, although it has been argued that Livy took from Timagenes the view that the Romans would have been no match for Alexander (*id vero periculum erat, quod levissimi ex Graecis, qui Parthorum quoque contra nomen Romanum gloriae favent, dictitare solent, ne maiestatem nominis Alexandri, quem ne fama quidem illis notum arbitror fuisse, sustinere non potuerit populus Romanus*, 9.18.6 = *F.Gr.Hist.*, 88 T9). We know too little about Timagenes to go beyond the conclusion that Curtius may have read his work or knew him through an intermediary, possibly Trogus. On the other hand, Curtius' direct use of Ptolemy will no doubt account for the numerous instances when his history coincides closely with that of Arrian. And it may be that Curtius drew upon Ptolemy for official information: battle order, arrivals of reinforcements, appointments, arrests and executions.

In order to understand Curtius' method of composition, we need to consider not only his historical sources but also his stylistic and literary models. That he read the *Historiae Philippicae* of Pompeius Trogus is virtually certain. But Trogus relied, perhaps indirectly, on Cleitarchus' book, and Curtius will have used him for stylistic reasons rather than for information. Indeed, the most impressive parallel comes from a section of Trogus' work which does not even deal with Alexander (Justin 28.4.2; cf. Curt. 6.1.7–8), though both authors treat a battle between the Spartans and the Macedonians.[27] Arguments have also been advanced for Curtius' use of Vergil (cf., for example, *Aeneid* 2.385 with 3.8.20; *Aeneid* 4.407 with 4.13.18), and the courage of Charus and Alexander at Aornus (8.11.10–17) is clearly modelled on Vergil's story of Nisus and Euryalus (*Aeneid* 9.176ff.).

Curtius' greatest debt, however, was to Livy, echoes of whom can be found throughout his work. Curtius employs Livian modes of expressing his own opinions, of referring to observations he made earlier (*sicut paulo ante dictum est* or *ut supra dictum est*). His statement about the Egyptians' attitude towards the Persians repeats, almost verbatim, Livy's description of the Carthaginians (21.1.3, *superbe avareque crederent imperitatum victis esse*; cf. Curt. 4.7.1: *quippe avare et superbe imperitatum sibi esse credebant*). Alexander (9.2.28) is described in terms similar to Hannibal (Livy 21.43.18; cf. also Curt. 4.16.3 and Livy 30.20.1); like Hannibal, who knows how to conquer but not how to use victory (Livy 22.51.3–4), Alexander is described as a more illustrious man in war than after a victory (8.9.1); characters or incidents not found in other extant Alexander-historians (e.g., the death of Hypsides, 7.7.36–7) find parallels in Livy (27.49.4); and dust-clouds of similar description obscure the soldier's vision at Gaugamela (4.15.32) and at Cannae (Livy 22.46.9). Furthermore, it is doubtful that Clitus knew that Alexander of Epirus was reputed to have said that he encountered men in Italy while his nephew, Alexander the Great, had faced women (8.1.37); this statement very likely comes directly from Livy (9.19.10–11). The list of parallels collected by R. B. Steele is overwhelming, leaving little doubt of his conclusion that Curtius 'borrows material freely, retouches it, and so gives us an Alexander whose history is permeated with Roman colouring'.[28]

This Roman colouring is further enhanced by Curtius' own experience of Imperial Roman politics. Cloak-and-dagger scenes abound (e.g., the framing of Sisenes and the prosecution of Philotas, 3.7.11–15; 6.7.1ff.);[29] free speech is punishable by death (Charidemus, Clitus; but cf. Meleager, 8.12.17–18); and influential courtiers connive to ruin men of worth (Bagoas and Orsines, 10.1.22ff.; cf. Philotas: *vicit ... bonitatem tuam, rex, inimicorum meorum acerbitas*, 6.8.22). Amyntas, son of Andromenes, defends himself with arguments that recall the defence of M. Terentius, and Perdiccas declines the throne in the fashion of Tiberius. Clitus' appointment to the satrapy of Artabazus (8.1.19) amounts to *honor exilii* or *otium cum dignitate*. There are, of course, other Roman elements: the night is divided into four watches (3.8.22; 5.4.17; 6.8.17; 7.2.19); the *testudo* appears on a number of occasions (5.3.9,21,23; 7.9.3); the *jugerum* is used as the equivalent of the Greek *plethron* (5.1.26); Darius is compared with a general celebrating a triumph (4.1.1) and *opimum decus* (a variant for *opima spolia*) is used in the Roman sense of arms wrested from the enemy general (3.11.7; 7.4.40). The Paphlagonian origin of the Veneti (3.1.22) would have interested few outside of Italy, and it may have been taken directly from Livy (1.1.3).

Finally there is the 'Herodotean' element. At Babylon, Darius enumerates his troops using Xerxes' method (3.2.2–3; cf. Herodotus 7.59ff.), and after the parade of the army, he turns to Charidemus, an Athenian exile, asking him for his impressions (3.2.10). Just as Demaratus, the exiled Spartan, praises the fighting skill of his countrymen (Herodotus 7.101–5), so Charidemus warns Darius that his will be no match for the Macedonians (3.2.11–16). That this was not the real substance of Charidemus' speech, or of the version given by Curtius' source, is clear from Diodorus (17.30.2–3), where Darius is urged to appoint Charidemus as Memnon's successor and not personally to risk his empire on the outcome of a single battle. He should rather give Charidemus 100,000 men, one-third of these Greek mercenaries. Diodorus goes on to say that Darius' courtiers suspected Charidemus of wanting the generalship 'in order to betray the Persian empire to the Macedonians' (17.30.4). These arguments, and the fears they inspire in the Persians, Curtius ascribes to Thimodes' mercenaries (3.8.2ff.), because he has already altered Charidemus' speech in order to make it echo Demaratus' comments. Of course, Curtius does not press the comparison too far: Charidemus is executed while Demaratus was allowed to live.

Like Xerxes, Darius is haunted by dreams (3.3.2–7; cf. Herodotus 7.12ff.), and the Macedonians captured at Issus are treated very much like the Greek spies in 481 B.C.: apart from the fact that they were mutilated (cf. Arr. 2.7.1), they too were shown the size of the Persian army and ordered to report what they saw to their countrymen (3.8.13–15; cf. Herodotus 7.146–7). The description of these Macedonian prisoners draws on Livy (30.29.2f.), but the story itself derives from Herodotus.[30] And there are numerous other allusions to Herodotean material. The camp of Cyrus, which Arrian rightly identifies as that of the younger Cyrus (Arr. 2.4.3; cf. Xenophon, *Anabasis* 1.2.20–21), is transformed into the camp of Cyrus the Great, when he campaigned against Croesus (3.4.1). There are constant reminders of the past crimes of the Persians against the Greeks (3.10.8; 4.1.10–11; 4.14.21; 5.6.1); the battle at the Persian Gates is reminiscent of Thermopylae (5.3.17ff.; esp. the Lycian herdsman, 5.4.10ff.); and the destruction of Persepolis at the instigation of the Athenian courtesan Thais is the culmination of the great struggle between East and West (5.7.3ff.). Now, much of the 'vengeance motif' comes originally from Cleitarchus, or perhaps even from Callisthenes, who doubtless emphasized Alexander's role as *Graeciae ultor*. But the clearest Herodotean parallels and allusions (3.2.2, 11–16; 3.3.2–7; 3.4.1; 3.8.13–15) are, apparently, Curtius' own work.[31]

D. THE HISTORY OF ALEXANDER

At a time when contemporary Roman themes, or else universal histories, were popular, Curtius' semi-biographical account of a Macedonian conqueror from the remote past must have seemed somewhat of an oddity. This will perhaps account for Quintilian's failure to mention the *History of Alexander* and its author. He was, after all, not compiling a complete list (*sunt et alii scriptores boni, sed nos genera degustamus non bibliothecas excutimus*, 10.1.104), and it may be that he considered Curtius' work biography instead of history.[32]

What then are the characteristics of the work? To begin with, Curtius writes as a Roman of the senatorial class, and a hypocritical one at that. His condemnation of flattery (8.5.8) hardly suits one who was himself reviled for his *tristis adulatio* (Tacitus, *Annales* 11.21.3), and his scornful attitude towards Bolon ('a man of no refinement or cultivation, an older soldier who had risen from the ranks to his present position', 6.11.1) shows little thought for his own circumstances.

Curtius makes frequent racial comments: the Persians are depicted as effeminate (3.3.14, 18; 3.10.10.; 8.1.37), they do not despise eunuchs as the Romans do (3.3.23), and, in general, their women (notably Sisigambis, Darius' mother) are more courageous than their men (cf. Sisimithres' shame to see women more concerned than men about liberty, 8.2.28). The Scythians get a slightly better press – they have a certain amount of intelligence and 'some of them are even said to have a capacity for philosophy' (7.8.10) – but the Egyptians are 'a volatile people, more inclined to foment unrest then to get things done themselves' (4.1.30). Even the Greeks are 'political trimmers by temperament' (4.5.11), wavering in their loyalty until the outcome of fortune is clear (4.5.12). The Cretans are chastised for supporting both sides (4.1.40), and Curtius writes of the Sicilian Cleon that his 'penchant for flattery was a national as much as a personal defect' (8.5.8). Like Livy he criticizes the fickleness and superstition of the multitude (4.10.7; cf. 9.4.22); thus it is not surprising to find Arrhidaeus' kingship supported by a common soldier (*quidam plerisque Macedonum ignotus ex infima plebe*, 10.7.1).

Secondly, Curtius writes as a rhetorician, sensational and emotive. There is a fondness for the remote and the exotic, there is preoccupation with crowd and panic scenes. The news of Alexander's approach throws the Persian army into utter confusion (3.8.25ff.); panic ensues when Darius flees the battlefield at Issus (3.11.12), when Parmenion appears before Damascus (3.13.9), when the Macedonian troops experience the perils of the Tigris river (4.9.20). And panic sends the Indians headlong to their deaths at Aornus (8.11.22–3). In the same vein, we are shown the sufferings of the army on the journey to Siwah (4.7.6), in the Persian winter (5.6.12ff.) and in the Gedrosian desert (9.10.11ff.).

Hesitations and deliberations are frequent: Alexander debates with himself whether he should take the medicine of Philip the physician (3.6.5–7) and reflects anxiously on the fickleness of fortune before the battle of Issus (3.8.20–21); Darius is torn between flight and an honourable death at Gaugamela (4.15.30). But, better than deliberations, Curtius loves contrasts and ironic reversals. For example, we have Alexander fearing that he will not die in battle but from taking a bath (3.5.5), Arsames devastating the territory he was supposed to protect from devastation (3.4.5), Charidemus avenged by the man against whom he gave the advice that caused his death (3.2.18). Darius leaves his treasures and the noble women and children of Persia in the hands of a traitor 'as though in an impregnable citadel' (3.13.6), and Alexander Lyncestes, although he has rehearsed his defence during three years of imprisonment, is at a loss for words when he is finally put on trial (7.1.8).

Another feature of the work is the character-sketch. Charidemus is introduced as 'an experienced soldier with a grudge against Alexander because of his exile' (3.2.10). Thimodes is 'a young man of great energy' (3.3.1). Medates is 'no political trimmer' (5.3.4) and Betis 'a man of impeccable loyalty to his king' (4.6.7). Nicanor and Hegesimachus have 'a reputation for daring and rashness' and are 'encouraged by the continuing success of their countrymen to disregard any danger' (8.13.13). And the list goes on. In some cases these statements are exaggerated or false, particularly the various comments on Parmenion: 'the most faithful' and 'the best tactician of Alexander's generals' (3.6.4; 4.13.4); 'his loyalty to Alexander himself was such that the latter was not willing to use anybody else's services to kill Attalus' (7.1.3); and especially the brief encomium of Parmenion at 7.2.33, where, among other things, Curtius claims that he 'had gained many successes without Alexander, while Alexander had achieved nothing of significance without him'. This type of characterization is used, as we have seen, of peoples and also of places (mythical sites, 3.4.10; Tyre, 4.4.20–21; Arbela, 4.9.9; Persepolis, 5.7.9; Ecbatana, 5.8.1).

Speeches are, of course, the rhetorician's *forte*, and Curtius has more of them than all the other extant Alexander-historians combined. There are the usual exhortations before battle (3.10.4ff.; 4.14.1ff.) and arguments for pushing on into unknown territory (6.3.1–18; 7.7.10ff.; 9.2.12). Then there are speeches that give opposing viewpoints. Parmenion and Alexander debate the merits of accepting Darius' peace-offer (4.11.10ff.); Euctemon and Theaetetus debate whether the mutilated Greeks should return to their homeland or remain in Asia (5.5.10–16; 5.5.17–20); and Alexander's speech at the Hyphasis is countered by Coenus, the spokesman of the soldiers (9.2.12ff.). And in the great episodes at the Court – the affairs of Philotas, Clitus and Hermolaus – Curtius uses speeches effectively to illustrate Alexander's change of character and the Macedonian reaction to it.

Thirdly, Curtius writes as a moralist. He condemns the avarice of the Macedonian soldiers (3.11.20; 3.13.11), the shameless behaviour of the Babylonians (which he blushes to describe, 5.1.37–8), and the perfidy of Amyntas, son of Antiochus ('such was the penalty Amyntas paid to both kings, for he was no more loyal to the one to whom he had defected than to the one whom he had deserted', 4.1.33). And there are numerous moralizing observations: 'when one's first hopes are thwarted by fortune the future looks better than the present' (4.1.29); and Darius explains to his men that 'in times of adversity the course to follow was not that which sounded impressive but the one that was practical' (5.1.8). Panic 'engenders fear even of the things that help' (3.11.12); fear 'usurps the leader's authority' in times of confusion (8.14.20); and 'often one shows less presence of mind in an embarrassing situation than when really guilty' (9.7.25).

In addition to Curtius' often tedious moral judgements, *fortuna* is omnipresent. *Fortuna* generally corrupts *natura*, as is clear from Darius' treatment of Charidemus (3.2.17–18), and from the actions of Alexander throughout the work. Fortune surprises Alexander in Cilicia at a critical point (3.5.12), and her fickleness is a cause for anxiety (3.8.20); she shatters Darius' careful strategy at Issus, because fear prevents the Persians from carrying out their orders (3.8.29–30), and she saves the Macedonians at the Tigris, as she did earlier at the Granicus and the Cilician Gates (4.9.22; elsewhere *felicitas* is used, 3.4.11; cf. 5.3.22). Thus Alexander trusts his good luck (7.7.28), 'which never tired of indulging him' (8.3.1; cf. 3.6.18); but he was also the only mortal who had *fortuna* in his power (10.5.36).

E. CHARACTERIZATION

Curtius' portrait of Alexander is consistent with the vulgate picture of the young king who was corrupted by his constant good fortune. This view finds first expression at 3.12.18–20:

Had he been able to maintain this degree of moderation to the end of his life, I would certainly consider him to have enjoyed more good fortune than appeared to be his when he was emulating Father Liber's triumph on his victorious march through all the nations from the Hellespont right to the Ocean. For then he would surely have overcome the defects he failed to overcome, his pride and his temper; he would have stopped short of killing his friends at dinner, and he would have been reluctant to execute without trial men who had distinguished themselves in battle and had conquered so many nations along with him. But good fortune had not as yet overwhelmed him: while it was on the increase, he bore it with self-restraint and abstinence, but eventually he failed to control it when it reached its peak.

Curtius goes on in each book to illustrate the deterioration of Alexander's character. In Book 4 it is after the response of the priest of Ammon that Alexander not only allows himself to be addressed as Jupiter's son but actually orders it, since fortune has given him a desire for glory greater than his capacity to handle it (4.7.29–30). In Book 5 we begin to see the correlation between the king's assumption of oriental customs and his steady degeneration: the lengthy stay in Babylon corrupts the soldiers in general (5.1.36), but Alexander is not placed in a bad light until Persepolis, where his fondness for drinking excessively is first highlighted (5.7.4; 5.7.10–11). Book 6 finds Alexander, relieved of the worry of dealing with Darius, abandoning himself to the pleasures of banquets and concubines, and generally giving himself over to foreign customs (6.2.1–5). He is vulnerable to the charms of the eunuch Bagoas (6.5.23); he abandons his policy of sexual restraint and sleeps with Thalestris, the Amazon queen (6.5.29–32); he assumes Persian dress and adopts the practices of the Persian court (6.6.1ff.; the reference to *proskynesis* is anachronistic, 6.6.3). In Book 7 he arranges the death of Parmenion (7.2.11–34) and massacres the Branchidae (7.5.28–35); in Book

8 he murders Clitus (8.1.19–52) and executes Callisthenes (8.8.21). The ninth book depicts him as deceiving posterity with altars and couches, larger than life, erected at the eastern limits of his march (9.3.19), and at the beginning of Book 10 he allows Bagoas to ruin the noble Orsines (10.1.22–38).

Yet, despite this progressive deterioration, Curtius' Alexander continues to have his good points: he is genuinely grieved by the death of Darius' wife (4.10.23–4); he continues to show respect to Sisigambis (5.2.18–22) and compassion for the mutilated Greeks (5.5.5ff.); and in the later books, Curtius emphasizes his fear that Spitamenes' wife might have a bad influence on the Greek camp (8.3.15) and describes at length his bravery (9.4.30ff.). And, in his final estimate, Curtius judges Alexander favourably without attempting to white-wash him:

To be sure it is obvious to anyone who makes a fair assessment of the king that his strengths were attributable to his nature and his weaknesses to fortune or his youth. His natural qualities were as follows: incredible mental energy and an almost excessive tolerance of fatigue; courage exemplary not just in comparison with kings but even with men possessing this virtue and no other; generosity such that he often granted greater gifts than even the gods are asked for; clemency towards the defeated, returning kingdoms to men from whom he had taken them, or giving them as gifts; continuous disregard for death, which frightens others out of their minds; a lust for glory and fame reaching a degree which exceeded due proportion but was yet pardonable in view of his youth and great achievements. Then there was his devotion to his parents (he had taken the decision to deify Olympias and he had avenged Philip); then, too, his kindness towards almost all his friends, goodwill towards the men, powers of discernment equalling his magnanimity and an ingenuity barely possible at his age; control over immoderate urges, a sex-life limited to fulfilment of natural desire; and indulgence only in pleasures which were socially sanctioned.

The following are attributable to fortune: putting himself on a par with the gods and assuming divine honours; giving credence to oracles which recommended such conduct and reacting with excessive anger to any who refused to worship him; assuming foreign dress and aping the customs of the defeated races, for whom he had had only contempt before his victory. But as far as his irascibility and fondness for drink were concerned, these had been quickened by youth and could as easily have been tempered by increasing age. However, it must be admitted that, much though he owed to his own virtues, he owed more to fortune, which he alone in the entire world had under his control. How often she rescued him from death! How often did she shield him with unbroken good fortune when he had recklessly ridden into danger! She also decided that his life and his glory should have the same end (10.5.26–36).

The apparent inconsistency in Alexander's character was not Curtius' own creation but existed already in the sources of the vulgate. Hence Tarn thought that he could detect two main sources in Diodorus, one favourable, the other unfavourable. But the contradictions in the portrait may well have existed in the personality of Alexander himself, and they were exploited by rhetorical historians like Cleitarchus and Quintus Curtius Rufus. In the final analysis, the subject of the work had to take on those admirable qualities which induced the writer to record his achievements in the first place. The literary achievement of Curtius is clear: his is an Alexander who comes to life even more than the one in Plutarch's biography. And we might do well to conclude with E. I. McQueen's judgement: 'Curtius' achievement ... is to create a personality who, without quite being the Alexander of history, nevertheless attains the stature of the real Alexander ...'[33]

F. THE HISTORICAL VALUE OF CURTIUS' WORK

'The famous dictum, *plura transcribo quam credo* (IX 1, 34), is held to typify Curtius' entire approach to history, and his work is dismissed as an artificial collage of anecdotes, selected for their sensational value and strung together to produce the maximum rhetorical effect.'[34] Thus A. B. Bosworth summarizes the prevailing opinion about Curtius' historical contribution. W. W. Tarn, for example, criticized him for 'his complete lack of historical principle', and said of him that 'he seems to have no interest in his subject, save that it enables him to show what a clever man Q. Curtius Rufus was ...'[35] But Tarn, it may be argued, was inclined to discredit Curtius – indeed the vulgate in general – because Curtius discredited Alexander. So much for historical principle. Not all scholars damned Curtius, of course, but few, since Alfonso V of Aragon was purportedly cured of illness by reading the *Historiae Alexandri*, have been enthusiastic about the quality of his work.

It is impossible to assess Curtius' value as an historian without reference to his sources and his method. Hence the casual reader will find it easier to enumerate his weaknesses than to isolate his virtues. It is almost a cliché to remark that Curtius' geography was erratic (e.g., 3.1.13; 7.3.4; 9.7.14) or that his military narrative was poor, especially for one who had served as a consular legate in Germany. And, of course, there are those cases in which he contradicts himself (e.g., compare 5.4.17 and 5.4.22 with 5.4.29; cf. 6.10.37 and 6.11.8; 8.5.2 and 8.5.22; but 5.6.20 need not necessarily contradict 5.6.9). Sometimes he has stories that are simply corruptions of episodes found in other sources, good and bad (e.g., Sisenes, 3.7.11–15; the purple cloth and garments from Macedonia, 5.2.18–22; the speech of Amyntas, an otherwise unknown *regius praetor*, 6.9.28–9; Polyperchon and *proskynesis*, 8.5.22–6.1). But, although we may fairly say of Curtius that the literary surpasses the historical achievement, that should not blind us to the fact that he is a valuable source. Certainly he was himself not a first-rate historian, nor was Cleitarchus, and his conception of Alexander's character is of limited value. He cared little for the causes of the events he described, or even for their impact on the course of history. Perhaps surprisingly, for one trained in the rhetorical schools of the early empire and so familiar with Livy's work, he did not tackle the insoluble question of whether Alexander could have conquered Rome – unless he dealt with the matter in his opening book.

On the other hand, it is to Curtius' credit that he consulted sources other than Cleitarchus, that he used Ptolemy as a useful supplement for official (military and administrative) information. And this argues strongly against the view that he did not care if he got his details right. About his chief source, Cleitarchus, there is little in ancient or modern writers that is favourable.[36] But, despite his dramatic touches and his frequent disregard for accuracy, Cleitarchus often gave information from sources not used by Ptolemy or Aristobulus, and he had no reason, as Ptolemy clearly did, to misrepresent the activities and achievements of some of Alexander's commanders. Thus we learn from Curtius alone the significant contributions of Antigonus the One-Eyed (4.1.35; 4.5.13), the heroism of Aristonus in the city of the Sudracae (9.5.15–18) and Leonnatus' role in bringing the conspiracy of Hermolaus to Alexander's attention (8.6.22). Most of all, we are particularly well informed about the events that immediately followed Alexander's death, events which Ptolemy and Aristobulus did not bother to describe.

Then, too, the literary (i.e., entertaining) character of Curtius' work has generally detracted from our appreciation of it as a historical source. In fact, we ought to approach it as a source rather than a history, to value its information instead of its ideas. The portrait of Alexander, which Curtius shares with the other writers of the vulgate, is as distorted as the apologetic tradition represented by Arrian, and his picture of the Persian court, or of the roles of the Greek mercenaries, is at best uneven. So it is ironic that the writer who is criticized for his lack of attention to detail is especially useful for detailed information. Most of all – though this is not his only strong point – Curtius is informative about individuals: their backgrounds, their appointments, their involvement in conspiracies, their very existence. For example, Curtius alone tells us of Parmenion's capture of Tarsus (3.4.14–15); the details of those taken at Damascus (3.13.12–15); the appointment of Andromachus to the satrapy of Coele-Syria (4.5.9) and his death by fire (4.8.9); the names of the chiliarchs (or, more probably, pentacosiarchs) appointed in Sittacene (5.2.5); the death of Ariobarzanes (5.4.34); the list of Dymnus' fellow-conspirators (6.7.15); the conspiracy of Hegelochus (6.11.22ff.); and the satrapal appointment of Clitus (8.1.19). And this is just a random selection. Unfortunately, Curtius' evidence must be used with caution, since the manuscripts are poor and especially bad at preserving the correct forms of names.

In the final analysis, each of Curtius' statements must stand on its own merits, and it is only through careful comparison with other sources and consideration of Curtius' stylistic and historical sources that the value of each passage in its context can be determined. We must draw back from the temptation to characterize his work – or the work of any ancient author, for that matter – as 'good' or 'bad', for in a work like the *History of Alexander* the 'very good' and the 'very bad' will often be found to exist side by side. Ultimately, this approach will do as much to improve Curtius' image among modern scholars as it will to shake the traditional faith in Arrian as the only reliable source for the study of Alexander.

Acknowledgements

The final work on the Introduction, Notes and Appendices was completed during a sabbatical leave in Germany. In addition to those mentioned by John Yardley, below, I would like to thank Mr Doug Skrainka, who spent many hours with me verifying references, and my wife Lois, who helped with the indices. I also thank Prof. Dr W. Schmitthenner and his colleagues in the Seminar für Alte Geschichte, Albert-Ludwigs-Universität, for their kind hospitality. Most of all, I thank John Yardley, who added textual notes of his own and gave some semblance of order to many of my cryptic entries.

Waldemar Heckel
Freiburg i. Br.
3 December 1983

I must thank the many friends and colleagues who have aided me at various stages in the preparation of this translation. Professor P. G. Walsh read and criticized my first draft of Book 3 and encouraged me to continue. The wording of the entire work has been improved and much 'woodenness' removed thanks to suggestions made by my collaborator Waldemar Heckel, by my wife Norah Yardley and by Betty Radice, whose expertise did much to polish my final draft. The translation was begun in 1979/80 when I was a fellow of the Calgary Institute for the Humanities, which gave me much-appreciated release time from teaching in the Classics Department of the University of Calgary. Finally, and above all, I owe an immense debt of gratitude to my dear friend, Elaine Fantham, for devoting so much time to reading and criticizing the entire work, saving me from error and proferring alternative interpretations or renderings which were almost invariably improvements.

John Yardley

QUINTUS CURTIUS RUFUS

THE HISTORY OF ALEXANDER

SUMMARY OF THE LOST BOOKS
ONE AND TWO[1]*

When Pythodelus was archon in Athens (336/5 B.C.), Philip, son of Amyntas, was murdered by Pausanias, a member of his bodyguard. Pausanias was pursued and executed (cf. Diod. 16.94.2–4)† and, when Alexander succeeded to the throne, he punished the sons of Aëropus, Arrhabaeus and Heromenes, for complicity in the plot against his father (Diod. 17.2.1; cf. Justin 11.2.1–2); their brother Alexander Lyncestes was spared, ostensibly because he had been the first to hail his namesake as the new king (Justin 11.2.2) but, in reality, because he was Antipater's son-in-law (Curt. 7.1.6–7; Justin 11.7.1; cf. Diod. 17.80.2[2]). Alexander gave immediate attention to his father's funeral (Diod. 17.2.1; Justin 11.2.1) and proclaimed that 'only the name of the king had been changed' (Diod. 17.2.2). He was only twenty years old when he ascended the throne of Macedon (Plut. *Alex.* 11.1).

The Greek states and the neighbouring barbarians wrongly equated Alexander's youth with weakness, and the new king moved quickly to crush opposition at home and abroad. First he eliminated his political rivals, especially Attalus, the uncle of Cleopatra. This woman had been the last of Philip's wives, and the source of disgrace and vexation for Alexander's mother, Olympias, who had left the court and joined her brother, the king of Epirus. Furthermore, Attalus had insinuated that Alexander was a bastard by expressing publicly the hope that Cleopatra would bear legitimate heirs to the Macedonian throne (cf. Plut. *Alex.* 9.7; Justin 9.7.3). The only child from this marriage turned out to be a girl, Europa, born only a few days before Philip's death (Diod. 17.2.3; cf. Justin 9.7.12; Athenaeus 13.557e). But Alexander nevertheless feared and resented Attalus, whom Philip had sent ahead with Parmenion to prepare the way for the expedition against the Great King (Diod. 17.2.4; Justin 9.5.9; cf. Curt. 7.1.3). Therefore, he sent a certain Hecataeus to Parmenion to arrange Attalus' arrest or execution (Diod. 17.2.5–6); for Attalus had been in secret communication with Demosthenes, the Athenian orator who was a bitter opponent of Macedon, and had urged many Greek cities to rebel (Diod. 17.3.2). Hecataeus acted quickly, and with Parmenion's acquiescence (Curt. 7.1.3) murdered Attalus (Diod. 17.5.2).

* This summary of the two lost books is by Waldemar Heckel.
† Abbreviations are listed on p. 265.

19

Alexander meanwhile dealt swiftly with the unrest in Greece – not only did the Athenians rejoice at Philip's death, but the Aetolians, the Thebans, as well as the Spartans and other Peloponnesians, were ready to throw off the Macedonian yoke (Diod. 17.3.3–5) – and he marched south into Thessaly, demanding the loyalty of its people in the name of their common ancestor, Achilles (Justin 11.3.1–2; cf. Diod. 17.4.1³). And with speed and diplomacy Alexander brought the Thebans and Athenians into submission (Diod. 17.4.4–6). The latter sent ambassadors to Alexander in Boeotia but Demosthenes, who was one of them, did not venture past Mt Cithaeron, fearing Alexander's wrath on account of his long-time opposition to Macedon and because, as Aeschines alleged, he had accepted money from the king of Persia (Diod. 17.4.8–9; Aeschines 3.173).

Alexander also summoned the delegates of the League of Corinth in order to have himself declared its *hegemon* and, when he had obtained their support for his expedition against Persia, he returned to Macedonia (Diod. 17.4.9).

The government of Persia had undergone a number of changes since Philip II first organized the Greek crusade against the East. At that time, Artaxerxes Ochus ruled in a most oppressive way (Diod. 17.5.3); for it was said that he feared conspiracies (Justin 10.3.1). Nevertheless, he was poisoned by his chamberlain, Bagoas, a eunuch who lusted for power (Diod. 17.5.3). He now placed on the throne Arses, the youngest of Ochus' sons, but he too soon fell victim to Bagoas' treachery (Diod. 17.5.3–4).⁴ Thereafter, Darius, who was not in the direct line of descent from Ochus, ascended the throne through the efforts of Bagoas and because of his reputation for courage (Diod. 17.5.5, 6.1; Justin 10.3.5; Curt. 6.3.12); for it is recorded that Darius once slew the champion of the Cadusians in single combat (Diod. 17.6.1). But, when Darius also became the object of Bagoas' intrigues, he forced the latter to drink his own poison (Diod. 17.5.6; Curt. 6.4.10). This Darius, then, was the man with whom Alexander would contend for world-domination.

When Darius inherited the Persian throne, he found that Alexander's father, Philip, was preparing to march against him, and it is believed by some that he sent a large sum of money to Macedonia to buy Philip's assassins (Curt. 4.1.12; cf. Arr. 2.14.5). Darius' relief was short-lived and, when he saw Alexander intent upon following in his father's footsteps, he sent a force under Memnon the Rhodian to oppose those Macedonians who had established themselves on the Asian side of the Hellespont (Diod. 17.7.1ff.). Memnon had been chosen for the command because of his military skill and because he was related to Artabazus, having married his daughter Barsine (Plut. *Alex.* 21.8–9). The family of Artabazus had long ruled Hellespontine Phrygia for the Great King and, although Artabazus himself had once taken refuge at Philip's court, he was among Darius' most devoted courtiers (Curt. 5.9.1; 6.5.2; cf. Diod. 16.52.3).

Memnon attempted unsuccessfully to capture Cyzicus, but Alexander's general countered by capturing Grynium and enslaving its population. Yet

Memnon was subsequently able to prevent Parmenion from capturing Pitane, and later he held Calas in check (Diod. 17.7.8–10).

Alexander meanwhile, having settled affairs in Greece, campaigned in Thrace, Paeonia and Illyria, in order to secure the borders of Macedonia before departing for Asia (Diod. 17.8.1–2). While he was thus occupied, Demosthenes suborned a messenger to report to the Greeks that the Macedonian army had been annihilated in the north, and that Alexander himself had fallen in battle (Justin 11.2.7–8; cf. Arr. 1.7.2–3). This false report inspired the Thebans to rebel, and they attacked the Macedonian garrison on the Cadmeia (Diod. 17.8.3ff.). But when Alexander heard of the uprising, he came with amazing speed and encamped before the city. Demosthenes, who had incited the revolt and aroused the support of the Athenians, sent arms to the Thebans; the Athenians and the Peloponnesians did not venture to oppose Alexander in battle, but waited instead to see how fortune would treat the Thebans.

Alexander did not move on Thebes immediately, being anxious for a peaceful settlement, since he was eager to get on with the business of Persia (Diod. 17.9.4). But, when Thebes made no move to surrender, he resolved to bring about its destruction. While the rest of Greece awaited the outcome of the struggle, the Thebans were both frightened and perplexed by prophecies and portents and, although many of these foretold certain disaster for the city, the Thebans entered the battle with courage, mindful of their great victory at Leuctra (Diod. 17.10). The Thebans put up a gallant defence until Perdiccas and his battalion forced their way into the city and the besieged garrison on the Cadmeia broke out (Diod. 17.12.3–5). And now the battle within the city turned to slaughter, with not only Macedonians but even Boeotians once subject to Thebes sating their anger with Theban blood; for the men of Plataea, Thespiae and Orchomenus campaigned with Alexander (Diod. 17.13.5; cf. Justin 11.3.8). The rage of the victors knew neither pity nor respect for sacred places and, in the end, more than 6,000 Thebans were killed, with 30,000 taken prisoner; the Macedonian dead numbered more than 500 (Diod. 17.13.6–14.1).

Although Thebes was now entirely in his power, Alexander nevertheless referred the question of her fate to the representatives of the Greek council. These recommended harsh punishment; for Thebes, it was recalled, had medized during Xerxes' war, and even to that day Theban ambassadors received royal treatment at the Persian court (Diod. 17.14.1–2). It was decided to raze the city to the ground as a lesson to all Greek states which contemplated rebellion (Diod. 17.14.3). Some have recorded that Alexander left standing the home of the poet Pindar (Arr. 1.9.10; cf. Plut. *Alex.* 11.12). We have it on the authority of Cleitarchus (*F.Gr.Hist.*, 137 F1 = Athenaeus 4.148d–e) that the sale of the Theban captives brought in 440 talents (cf. Diod. 17.14.4).[5]

Alexander now turned his attention to the Athenians, demanding the surrender of those orators and generals who had fomented the rebellion: these were Demosthenes, Lycurgus, Hypereides, Polyeuctas, Chares, Charidemus, Ephialtes, Diotimus, Moerocles and Thrasybulus (Arr. 1.10.4; Suidas s.v. 'Antipatros'). But the Athenians sent Demades to Alexander to plead for these men and the king relented, demanding only the exile of Charidemus (Diod. 17.15.3ff.; Arr. 1.10.6). Charidemus went to the court of Darius (Curt. 3.2.10; Diod. 17.30.2), while Ephialtes and Thrasybulus also fled to Asia (Diod. 17.25.6; cf. Justin 11.4.10–12).

The king now returned to Macedonia to prepare for the expedition against Persia. His political enemies at home had been silenced by swift action; for Attalus, as we have noted above, had been eliminated and Amyntas, son of Perdiccas, the king's cousin, had been accused of plotting against him and executed before the Theban campaign (Curt. 6.9.17; Arrian, *History of the Successors* 1.22; cf. Arr. 1.5.4; Justin 12.6.14). Nevertheless, his senior commanders, Antipater and Parmenion, advised him to marry and produce an heir before crossing into Asia. Alexander, however, rejected their advice, saying it would be shameful to remain at home for sake of producing children when the forces of the League of Corinth awaited his leadership against Persia (Diod. 17.16.2).

Thus, having held a festival at Dium in Macedonia – this lasted nine days, with one day dedicated to each of the Muses – he made ready for the crossing to Asia (Diod. 17.16.3–4). Antipater was left behind to rule Macedon in his absence; Alexander marched to the Hellespont (Diod. 17.17.1; cf. Arr. 1.11.3).

BOOK 2?

When Alexander reached Sestos, he left Parmenion in charge of taking the army across to Abydos (Arr. 1.11.6). He himself took sixty ships and sailed to the Troad, where he cast his spear into the shore, thus claiming all Asia as his 'spear-won' prize (Diod. 17.17.2; Justin 11.5.10). Some have recorded that the king had earlier sacrificed to Protesilaus, the first man with Agamemnon to touch Asian soil, in the hope of a safer landing (Arr. 1.11.5). Later he visited the tombs of the Homeric heroes, especially honouring that of Achilles, from whom he claimed descent (Diod. 17.17.3; Arr. 1.12.1; Justin 11.5.12; Plut. *Alex.* 15.8; cf. Curt. 4.6.29; 8.4.26).

Returning to the army, he held a review of his troops. The infantry numbered 32,000 (cf. Justin 11.6.2). Of these, 12,000 Macedonians, 7,000 allies, and 5,000 mercenaries were placed under Parmenion's command. Next came the Odrysians, Triballians and Illyrians, 7,000 strong, followed by 1,000 archers and Agrianes (Diod. 17.17.4). Parmenion's son, Philotas, led the 1,800 Macedonian cavalry (cf. Curt. 4.13.26) and Calas, son of Harpalus, the 1,800 Thessalian horse, while Erigyius commanded 600 allied cavalry; Cassander[6] was placed in charge of 900 scouts from Thrace and Paeonia. The cavalry numbered 4,500 in all (Diod. 17.17.4; cf. Justin 11.6.2). Antipater was left to govern Europe with 12,000 infantry and 1,500 horse (Diod. 17.17.5).

As Alexander prepared to leave the Troad, he came upon the temple of Minerva at Ilium (Diod. 17.17.6; Arr. 1.11.7; Plut. *Alex.* 15.7). Here he found that the statue of Ariobarzanes had fallen to the ground. He therefore summoned the seer Aristander, who proclaimed that, since Ariobarzanes had once been satrap of Phrygia,[7] the fallen statue portended a great cavalry victory for Alexander in Phrygian territory. Furthermore, the seer added, Alexander would slay one of the enemy's commanders with his own hand (Diod. 17.17.6). Alexander was pleased with this good omen at the outset of his campaign and he trusted in the good will of Minerva Victoria (cf. Curt. 3.12.27). To this goddess he made sacrifice and dedicated his own armour, taking for himself the most splendid of the suits of armour in the temple. This armour he wore into battle when he first encountered the enemy (Diod. 17.18.1).[8]

The Persian commanders, having missed their opportunity of preventing Alexander's crossing at the Hellespont, held a council of war. Memnon the Rhodian strongly urged that the Persians adopt a scorched-earth policy (Arr. 1.12.9; cf. Curt. 3.4.3) in order to leave desolate the territory which the Macedonians would have to cross, and at the same time, he suggested, they should conduct the war at sea and attack Macedonia (Diod. 17.18.2). But this policy aroused the indignation of the Persians who, jealous of Memnon's influence with Darius (Arr. 1.12.10), argued that they would not destroy their own territory and flee from the invader. Instead they decided to move the army to the Adrastean plain and occupy the banks of the river Granicus, which flows through Hellespontine Phrygia (Diod. 17.18.3–4; Justin 11.6.10; Plut. *Alex.* 16.1).

When Alexander reached the river, he found the Persians well established on the far bank. Parmenion advised against crossing in the face of this opposition, but Alexander replied that, having crossed the Hellespont, he would not be stopped by a mere trickle such as the Granicus (Arr. 1.13.2–6; Plut. *Alex.* 16.3). The Persians were arranged as follows: Memnon and Arsames, satrap of Cilicia, commanded the left wing; Arsites, who ruled Hellespontine Phrygia, was positioned next to them with the horsemen from Paphlagonia; after him came Spithridates, satrap of Ionia, with the Hyrcanian cavalry. Rheomithres led the right wing. In total, there were over 10,000 Persian horse and at least 100,000 infantry (Diod. 17.19.3–5).

The king immediately made his charge with thirteen cavalry squadrons (Plut. *Alex.* 16.3). Parmenion and the Thessalian cavalry attacked on the left, while on the right Alexander inflicted heavy casualties on the enemy (Diod. 17.19.6). Now, indeed, Fortune gathered into one place the best fighters to contest the victory. Spithridates, the satrap of Ionia, was a Persian by race and Darius' son-in-law.[9] He led forty of the so-called kinsmen in a fierce attack on the enemy, catching the eye of Alexander, who quickly moved against him (Diod. 17.20.2). In the duel that followed the barbarian first hurled his javelin, which passed through Alexander's shield and lodged in his breast-plate (Diod. 17.20.3). And now, as each army shouted in support of its respective champion, Alexander drove his *sarissa* into the barbarian's chest, breaking off the point of the weapon. Then, when Spithridates drew his sword, the king thrust the *sarissa* into his face and felled him (Diod. 17.20.4–5).

Just at that point, Rhosaces, the dead man's brother, charged Alexander from behind, striking him on the head with his sword. The king's helmet split in two and fell from his head, and the Persian would have delivered a fatal wound, had not Clitus the Black arrived in time to cut off his hand as he directed the second blow (Diod. 17.20.6–7; Curt. 8.1.20).[10] As it turned out, Alexander suffered only a superficial scalp-wound in the incident. Neverthe-less, during the battle he was exposed to many dangers and withstood two blows to his breast-plate and one to his helmet; three other blows were absorbed by the shield which he had taken from Minerva's temple (Diod. 17.21.2).

It is generally believed that the battle was won chiefly through the king's courage and the skill of the Thessalian cavalry (Diod. 17.21.4). On the Persian side more than 10,000 infantrymen and at least 2,000 of the cavalry were killed (Diod. 17.21.6), among them Pharnaces, the brother of Darius' wife, and Mithrobuzanes, the commander of the Cappadocians (Diod. 17.21.3). More than 20,000 Persians were taken alive.

The Macedonian casualties included nine infantrymen and one hundred and twenty cavalry (Justin 11.6.12), twenty-five of these from the Com-panions, for whom Alexander had bronze statues made by Lysippus and erected at Dium (Arr. 1.16.4; Plut. *Alex.* 16.17; cf. Justin 11.6.13).When Alexander had performed the obsequies to the dead, he marched through Lydia to Sardis, which was surrendered to him by Mithrenes (Diod. 17.21.7; Curt. 3.12.6; 5.1.44).

From Sardis, Alexander marched to Miletus, where Memnon and the survivors of the battle at the Granicus had taken refuge. He stormed this city, sparing its inhabitants but selling the captured soldiers into slavery (Diod. 17.22.1–5). Here, too, Alexander decided to disband his naval forces, and some have believed that he did this in order to deprive his own troops of the hope of escape (Diod. 17.22.5–23.1).

The Persians and the mercenaries who had fled from Miletus were now in Halicarnassus, a large and well-fortified city in Caria. From here Memnon sent his wife, Barsine, and his son to Darius (Diod. 17.23.5; cf. Curt. 3.13.14); for he felt that they would be safer with the Great King, and he also hoped that Darius would be more inclined to entrust to him supreme command, if he had his relatives as hostages (Diod. 17.23.6). This was, in fact, what happened.

Alexander moved his army to Halicarnassus, and on his march he was met by Ada, who belonged to the royal house of Caria and sought his help in regaining the throne. Alexander supported her claim and thereby won the loyalty of the Carians (Diod. 17.24.1–3). Some have reported that Ada adopted Alexander as her son (Arr. 1.23.8). For a long time the Macedonians had difficulty in entering the city; for Memnon's forces were numerous, and they would make sorties from the city to set fire to Alexander's siege equipment (Diod. 17.24.5; cf. Arr. 1.20.9). In one of these skirmishes Neoptolemus, son of Arrhabaeus, who had deserted to the Persian king, was killed (Arr. 1.20.10; cf. Diod. 17.25.5). And when two men from Perdiccas' battalion got drunk and attacked the walls, the Persians issued forth from the city, and others from Perdiccas' group came up in support of their men (Arr. 1.21.1). After some heavy fighting the Persians withdrew, and Alexander asked to recover his dead under truce. Memnon granted the request, although Ephialtes and Thrasybulus the Athenians advised against it (Diod. 17.25.5–6). It was in the final battle that Ephialtes perished; for, when the younger Macedonians showed signs of wavering, Atarrhias led the older men into the fray and turned the tide of the battle (Diod. 17.26–7; Curt. 5.2.5; 8.1.36). The Persians again withdrew into the city. After holding a meeting, Memnon and his men abandoned Halicarnassus and fled to Cos (Diod. 17.27.5; cf. Arr. 1.23.3). Since Memnon had left a garrison in the citadel, Alexander ordered the city razed and walled off the citadel (Diod. 17.27.6).

Parmenion was sent to Sardis with most of the foreign troops and ordered to rejoin Alexander in Phrygia in the spring (Arr. 1.24.3). At the same time the king sent home to Macedonia those men who had recently married, telling their leader Coenus to return in the spring with reinforcements; Cleander was also sent to bring reinforcements from the Peloponnesus (Arr. 1.24.1–2; cf. Curt. 3.1.1). Alexander himself subdued the coast as far as Cilicia. On the borders of Lycia, the Marmares, finding themselves besieged by the Macedonians, committed mass suicide, setting fire to their homes (Diod. 17.28).

While Alexander was in Phaselis, Parmenion intercepted a letter from Darius to Alexander Lyncestes. The latter had offered to assassinate Alexander in return for a thousand talents of gold (Arr. 1.25.3). Alexander had also been warned against Lyncestes by his mother Olympias (Diod. 17.32.1), and he therefore had him arrested, although he did not take any action against him because he was Antipater's son-in-law (Justin 11.7.1–2; Curt. 7.1.5–7).

Alexander had another reason for worry: Memnon, whom he had driven out of Halicarnassus, had captured Chios and Lesbos, and was now preparing to cross to Europe with 300 ships (Diod. 17.29.1–2, 31.3). Memnon had also distributed money in Greece in order to foster dissension there (Diod. 17.29.4), but before he could take further action he fell ill and died. His death was a serious blow to the fortunes of King Darius (Diod. 17.29.4; cf. Arr. 2.1.1–3).

BOOK THREE

[1] Cleander had been sent with money to hire soldiers in the Peloponnese;[1] Alexander meanwhile settled matters in Lycia and Pamphylia and then moved his army to the city of Celaenae.[2] [2] At that time the Marsyas used to flow right through the middle of its walls, a river made famous by Greek poetry with all its myths. [3] Its source is a mountain peak. From this it comes rushing and tumbling down with a thunderous roar on to a rock at the foot of the mountain, and subsequently provides irrigation for the neighbouring plains as several different streams. At this stage it is clear and bears only its own waters. [4] Hence its colour, like that of a calm sea, has given rise to poetic fantasy; for the story goes that nymphs sit on the rock, held fast there by their love for the river.[3] [5] It retains its name, Marsyas, while it flows within the city walls but, when it rolls out beyond them, it moves with increased force and carries a larger volume of water, and people then call it the Lycus.[4]

[6] When Alexander entered the city, it had been deserted by its inhabitants. He proceeded to launch an attack on the citadel, in which they had taken refuge, but he first sent a herald to announce that, if they refused to surrender, they would suffer the extreme penalty. [7] The defenders took the herald to a high tower, which human effort had elevated even beyond its natural position, telling him to observe its height and report to Alexander that he and the Celaenaeans differed in their judgement of the fortifications. He should be aware, they said, that dislodging them was impossible and that they would keep their word to die to the very last man. [8] When they saw that the citadel was completely encircled, however, and that every day their situation became more critical, they negotiated a sixty-day truce, agreeing to surrender the city if Darius himself did not send help within that period. And, when no assistance was forthcoming from him, they surrendered to the king on the appointed day.[5] [9] Next an embassy from the Athenians arrived, requesting the return of the prisoners taken at the river Granicus. Alexander replied that, when the Persian war ended, he would order the restitution to their own people not only of the prisoners in question but of all the other Greeks as well.[6] [10] He also pressed on with the business of Darius who, he had learned, had not yet crossed the Euphrates. He consolidated all his troops from every quarter so as to have his full strength for the decisive engagement of this momentous war.[7]

[11] His army was now being taken through Phrygia, a country of more villages than cities,⁸ but at that time the seat of the once-famous palace of Midas. [12] The name of the city is Gordium. It is on the banks of the river Sangarius, equidistant from the Pontic and Cilician Seas. [13] Between these seas, as we know, the span of Asia is at its narrowest, the two bodies of water compressing it into a constricted isthmus. Asia is attached to the continent, but it is mostly surrounded by water and actually looks like an island. But for the narrow strip separating them, the seas which it now keeps apart would be joined.⁹ [14] Alexander reduced the city and entered the temple of Jupiter. Here he saw the carriage on which they said Midas' father, Gordius, used to ride. In appearance it was little different from quite inexpensive and ordinary carriages, [15] its remarkable feature being the yoke, which was strapped down with several knots all so tightly entangled that it was impossible to see how they were fastened. [16] Since the local people claimed that an oracle had foretold mastery of Asia for the man who untied this impossible knot, the desire to fulfil the prophecy came over Alexander. [17] The king was surrounded by a crowd of Phrygians and Macedonians, the former all in suspense about his attempt at untying it, the latter alarmed at the king's over-confidence – for, in fact, the series of knots was pulled so tight that it was impossible to work out or see where the tangled mass began or ended, and what particularly concerned them about the king's attempt at untying it was that an unsuccessful effort should be taken as an omen. [18] For some time Alexander wrestled unsuccessfully with the hidden knots. Then he said: 'It makes no difference how they're untied,' and cut through all the thongs with his sword, thus evading the oracle's prophecy – or, indeed, fulfilling it.¹⁰

[19] Alexander had now determined to attack Darius wherever he was. To leave everything safe behind him, he gave command of the fleet on the coast of the Hellespont to Amphoterus, and of the land forces to Hegelochus,¹¹ ordering them to free Lesbos, Chios and Cos of their enemy garrisons. [20] They were assigned 500 talents for expenses in the war; 600 talents were sent to Antipater and those in charge of the Greek cities; and ships to guard the Hellespont were levied from the allies under the terms of their treaty.¹² [21] In fact, Alexander had not yet heard of the death of Memnon, on whom he had centred all his concern, for he was well aware that everything would go smoothly if Memnon remained inactive.

[22] They had come now to the city of Ancyra where, after a review of the troops, Alexander entered Paphlagonia. Next to Paphlagonia were the Heneti, from whom some believe the Veneti to be descended. [23] This whole region submitted to Alexander and, by giving him hostages, they were able to avoid the obligation of paying tribute (which, in fact, they had not paid even to the Persians). [24] Calas was given the governorship of this area while Alexander himself made for Cappadocia, taking with him the troops which had recently arrived from Macedonia.¹³

27

2

[1] Darius was duly distressed by the news of Memnon's death.[14] Abandoning hope of any other option, he decided to take to the field in person; for, in fact, he was critical of all the actions of his generals, believing that most lacked military precision and all of them good luck. [2] So he encamped at Babylon and, to enable his forces to start the war with increased confidence, he put on a public display of his entire strength. He encircled with a ditch an area that could hold 10,000 armed soldiers and began a numerical review using Xerxes' method.[15] [3] From sunrise to nightfall columns of armed men entered the enclosure in a prescribed order and, on being discharged from it, took up a position on the Mesopotamian plains, a host of cavalrymen and foot-soldiers almost beyond number and creating the impression of being more than they really were. [4] There were 100,000 Persians, including 30,000 cavalry, while the Medes numbered 10,000 cavalry and 50,000 infantry. [5] There were 2,000 Barcanian horsemen armed with double-headed axes and small shields (closer in appearance to the *cetra*[16] than anything else); and the cavalry were followed by 10,000 Barcanian infantry who were similarly armed. [6] The Armenians had sent 40,000 infantry along with 7,000 cavalry. The Hyrcanians had mustered a total of 6,000 horsemen of excellent quality – by the standards of those peoples, that is – reinforced with 1,000 Tapurian cavalry. [7] The Derbices[17] had 40,000 infantrymen under arms, most of them equipped with bronze- or iron-tipped lances, but a few had just lances of wood hardened by fire. Along with these came 2,000 cavalrymen of the same race. [8] From the Caspian Sea had come 8,000 foot and 200 horse and, with them, other lesser-known tribes who had mustered 2,000 infantry and twice as many cavalry. [9] These forces were supplemented by 30,000 Greek mercenaries, a superb group of young soldiers. As for Bactrians, Sogdians, Indians and others living on the Red Sea (some of whose names were unknown even to Darius), the hurried mobilization precluded their being summoned.[18]

[10] Indeed, the one thing Darius did not lack was military numbers. The sight of this assembly filled him with joy, and his courtiers further inflated his expectations with their usual idle flattery. He turned to the Athenian Charidemus, who was an experienced soldier with a grudge against Alexander because of his exile (it was on Alexander's command that he had been expelled from Athens[19]), and he proceeded to ask whether, in his opinion, he was well enough equipped to crush his enemy. [11] With no thought for his own circumstances and the vanity of royalty, Charidemus answered: 'Perhaps you do not want to be told the truth and yet, if I do not tell it now, it will serve no purpose to admit it at another time. [12] This magnificent army, this conglomeration of so many nations drawn from their homes all over the East, can strike terror into your neighbours. It gleams with purple and gold; it is resplendent with armour and an opulence so great that those

who have not witnessed it simply cannot conceive of it. [13] The Macedonian line is certainly coarse and inelegant, but it protects behind its shields and lances immovable wedges of tough, densely-packed soldiers. The Macedonians call it a phalanx, an infantry column that holds its ground. They stand man next to man, arms interlocked with arms. They wait eagerly for their commander's signal, and they are trained to follow the standards and not break ranks. [14] To a man they obey their orders. Standing ground, encircling manoeuvres, running to the wings, changing formation – the common soldier is no less skilled at all this than the officer. [15] And don't think that what motivates them is the desire for gold and silver; until now such strict discipline has been due to poverty's schooling. When they are tired, the earth is their bed; they are satisfied with food they can prepare while they work; their sleeping time is of shorter duration than the darkness. [16] And now I suppose cavalry from Thessaly, Acarnania, Aetolia – troops that are unbeaten in war – are going to be driven off by slings and by lances hardened in fire! What you need is strength like theirs. You must look for help in the land that produced those men – send off that silver and gold of yours to hire *soldiers*.'[20]

[17] Darius was of a mild and placid disposition, but even natural inclinations are generally corrupted by fortune. Unable to take the truth, he had Charidemus dragged off to execution, guest and suppliant though he was and at a time when he was making very useful recommendations.[21] [18] Even in these circumstances, Charidemus did not forget that he was a free man: 'I have the avenger of my death ready at hand,' he declared. 'You will pay the penalty for rejecting my advice, and pay it to the very man against whom it was given. As for you, so suddenly transformed by your unlimited power, you shall be an example to posterity of how men can forget even their natural inclinations when they have surrendered themselves to fortune.' He was shouting this aloud when those ordered to do so slit his throat. [19] Then, all too late, the king experienced a change of heart and, admitting the truth of Charidemus' words, ordered his burial.[22]

3

[1] Mentor's son Thimodes, a young man of great energy, was ordered by the king to assume from Pharnabazus command of all the foreign troops, in whom the king had most confidence, so that he could use them in the war. To Pharnabazus himself Darius transferred the command which he had previously given to Memnon.[23] [2] Already in a state of anxiety over his immediate concerns, he was further troubled by dreams of impending events, which derived either from his mental agitation or from a genuine premonition of the future. [3] He dreamed that Alexander's camp was alight with a blazing fire. Shortly after this Alexander was brought to him in the same clothes Darius himself had worn, and then rode on horseback

through Babylon before suddenly vanishing along with his horse. [4] The soothsayers had further compounded his worries by offering conflicting interpretations. Some declared the dream was auspicious for the king: the enemy camp had been in flames and Darius had seen Alexander brought before him without his royal robes, in the dress of a Persian commoner. [5] Others disagreed, predicting that his dreaming of the Macedonian camp ablaze portended glory for Alexander; that he was going to seize control even of Asia was perfectly clear, since Darius had worn those very clothes when he was declared king. [6] As generally happens, too, past omens had been brought back to mind by the present worry. They recalled that at the start of his reign Darius had issued orders for the shape of the scabbard of the Persian scimitar to be altered to the shape used by the Greeks, and that the Chaldeans had immediately interpreted this as meaning that rule over the Persians would pass to those people whose arms Darius had copied. [7] However, Darius was very pleased both with the answer of the seers – which was made public – and with the dream that he had had, and he gave orders for camp to be moved to the Euphrates.[24]

[8] It is a tradition among the Persians not to begin a march until after sunrise, and the day was already well advanced when the signal was given by trumpet from the king's tent. Above the tent, so that it would be visible to all, a representation of the sun gleamed in a crystal case. [9] The order of the line of march was as follows: in front, on silver altars, was carried the fire which the Persians called sacred and eternal. Next came the Magi, singing the traditional hymn, [10] and they were followed by 365 young men in scarlet cloaks,[25] their number equalling the days of the year (for, in fact, the Persians divide the year into as many days as we do). [11] Then came the chariot consecrated to Jupiter,[26] drawn by white horses, followed by a horse of extraordinary size, which the Persians called 'the Sun's horse'. [12] Those driving the horses were equipped with golden whips and white robes. Not far behind were ten carts amply decorated with relief carvings in gold and silver, [13] and these were followed by the cavalry of twelve nations of different cultures, variously armed. Next in line were the soldiers whom the Persians called the 'Immortals', some 10,000 in number.[27] No other group were as splendidly bedecked in barbarian opulence: golden necklaces, clothes interwoven with gold, long-sleeved tunics actually studded with jewels. [14] After a short interval came the 15,000 men they call 'the king's kinsmen'. This troop was dressed almost like women, its extravagance rather than its fine arms catching the eye. [15] The column next to these comprised the so-called 'Doryphoroe',[28] the men who usually looked after the king's wardrobe, and these preceded the royal chariot on which rode the king himself, towering above all others. [16] Both sides of the chariot were embossed with gold and silver representations of the gods; the yoke was studded with flashing gems and from it arose two golden images (each a cubit high) of Ninus and Belus

respectively.[29] Between these was a consecrated eagle made of gold and represented with wings outstretched.

[17] The sumptuous attire of the king was especially remarkable. His tunic was purple, interwoven with white at the centre, and his gold-embroidered cloak bore a gilded motif of hawks attacking each other with their beaks. [18] From his gilded belt, which he wore in the style of a woman, he had slung his scimitar, its scabbard made of a precious stone. [19] His royal head-dress, called a 'cidaris' by the Persians, was encircled by a blue ribbon flecked with white. [20] 10,000 spearmen carrying lances chased with silver and tipped with gold followed the king's chariot, [21] and to the right and left he was attended by some 200 of his most noble relatives. At the end of this column came 30,000 foot-soldiers followed by 400 of the king's horses.

[22] Next, at a distance of one stade, came Sisigambis, the mother of Darius, drawn in a carriage, and in another came his wife. A troop of women attended the queens on horseback. [23] Then came the fifteen so-called 'Armamaxae'[30] in which rode the king's children, their nurses and a herd of eunuchs (who are not at all held in contempt by these peoples). [24] Next came the carriages of the 360 royal concubines, these also dressed in royal finery, and behind them 600 mules and 300 camels carried the king's money, with a guard of archers in attendance. [25] After this column rode the wives of the king's relatives and friends, and hordes of camp-followers and servants. At the end, to close up the rear, were the light-armed troops with their respective leaders.

[26] The Macedonian troops, on the other hand, provided a different spectacle: horses and men gleaming not with gold, not with multi-coloured clothes, but with iron and bronze. [27] It was an army ready to stand its ground and follow its leader, and not overloaded with numbers and baggage – an army eagerly watching not just for a signal from Alexander but even for a nod. Any location sufficed for their camp, any food for their provisions. [28] Accordingly Alexander was not deficient in troops in the battle while Darius, king of such a teeming host, was reduced by the confined limits of the battlefield to such small numbers as he had disdained in his enemy.

4

[1] In the meantime Alexander had left Abistamenes[31] in charge of Cappadocia and, making for Cilicia with all his forces, had arrived at the area called 'The Camp of Cyrus'. There Cyrus had maintained a permanent camp when he was on his march into Lydia against Croesus.[32] [2] The area was fifty stades from the pass by which one enters Cilicia. The defile here is very narrow; the local people call it 'The Gates' because the natural formation of the terrain resembles man-made fortifications. [3] Now the governor of Cilicia, Arsames, reflecting upon the strategy advocated by Memnon at the start of the war, decided all too late to follow a course of action that would

earlier have been profitable.[33] He laid waste Cilicia with fire and the sword in order to create a desert for his enemy. Anything that might be of use he destroyed, intending to leave sterile and barren the soil he was unable to protect. [4] In fact, it would have been far more profitable to occupy with a strong force a narrow part of the pass leading to Cilicia and to take up a position on a ridge which opportunely overlooked the road, from which vantage-point he could have held back or crushed an approaching enemy without losses. [5] As it was, he left a few men to guard the mountain passes while he himself retreated, ravaging the land which he should have been protecting from the ravages of the enemy. Consequently, the men left behind felt they had been betrayed and could not even bring themselves to face the enemy, although a force even smaller than theirs could have held the position.

[6] Cilicia is totally enclosed by a continuous range of rugged and precipitously steep mountains.[34] This rises from the sea, forms a sort of curve or bow and then runs back to a different point on the coastline. [7] Through this range, at the spot where it is furthest inland, there are three rugged and extremely narrow passes, one of which is the route into Cilicia. [8] The land levels out towards the sea, its flatness frequently interrupted by streams, including the famous rivers, Pyramus and Cydnus. The Cydnus is notable not for the volume of its water but for its clarity: it runs from its sources with a gentle current and travels over pure soil, with no torrents breaking into its course to disturb its leisurely flow. [9] Accordingly, it remains pure and at the same time it is very cold because of the shade offered it by the very attractive banks, and it enters the sea as clear as it is at its headwaters.[35] [10] In that area there were many monuments popularized in song, which had succumbed to the ravages of time. They were shown the sites of the cities of Lyrnesus and Thebes, the cave of Typhon, the grove of Corycus where saffron grows, and other spots of which nothing had survived but their reputation.

[11] Alexander entered the mountain defile called 'The Gates' and, as he looked at the lie of the land, they say he was never more surprised at his good fortune.[36] For, he observed, he could have been crushed just by rocks, if there had been anyone there to hurl them down on his approaching troops. [12] The road could barely accommodate four armed men abreast, and a mountain ridge overhung a pathway which was not only narrow but at many points ruptured by the numerous streams that flowed over it, emanating from the base of the mountains. [13] Alexander had given instructions for his light-armed Thracian troops to go ahead and reconnoitre the paths, so that no hidden enemy force could surprise his men as they mounted. A company of archers had also taken up a position on the hill-top, keeping their bows strung because they had been warned that it was a battle-manoeuvre, not a march, which they were starting. [14] In this way the army reached the city of Tarsus just at the time when the Persians were putting the torch to it to prevent their enemies falling upon a wealthy town. [15] But Alexander sent Parmenion

ahead with a light-armed detachment to stop the burning and, after he learned that the barbarians had taken to their heels when his men approached, he entered the city which he had saved.[37]

5

[1] The river Cydnus, which was mentioned a moment ago, flows through the centre of the city. It was now summer time, when the blazing sun parches Cilicia with a more searing heat than any other coastline.[38] Furthermore, the hottest part of the day had begun. [2] The king was covered in dust and sweat, and the clear water induced him to have a bath while his body was still overheated. So he undressed and went down into the river before the eyes of his troops, thinking that it would also add to his prestige if he showed his men that he was satisfied with attention to his person which was plain and unelaborate. [3] Scarcely had he entered the water when he suddenly felt his limbs shiver and stiffen. He went pale, and the vital heat all but left his body. [4] When his attendants took hold of him, he appeared to be dying, and he was barely conscious when they took him to his tent. A deep anxiety that bordered on grief descended on the camp. [5] In tears the men complained that, in such a sudden and swift-moving train of events, a king who was the most famous of any period of history had been brought low not even in battle and not by an enemy – had been snatched from them and had lost his life taking a bath! [6] Darius was hard on their heels, they said, a victor before he had seen his enemy, while they had to make their way back to those lands which they had traversed by conquest and where everything had been laid waste by themselves or the enemy. Even if nobody wished to pursue them, they could be defeated by hunger and shortage of supplies as they passed through those endless stretches of desert. [7] Who would command them as they fell back? Who would presume to succeed Alexander? Suppose they *did* reach the Hellespont in their retreat – who would supply a fleet for them to cross it? [8] Then their feelings of pity for the king himself would return and, forgetting their own plight, they would lament that this young man in the prime of his life and with such vitality of spirit, a man at once their king and comrade, was being torn from them, his life-span cut short.[39]

[9] In the meantime Alexander's breath had started to come and go more easily and, lifting his eyes, he had recognized his friends around his sickbed as his consciousness gradually returned. Indeed, the violence of his illness appeared to have abated simply because he realized how serious the situation was. [10] However, his anxiety adversely affected his physical condition, for there were reports that Darius would be in Cilicia in four days. He complained that he was being delivered to Darius bound hand and foot, that a major victory was being snatched out of his hands while he was dying an obscure and inglorious death in his tent. [11] Accordingly, he admitted his friends along with his physicians. 'You can see at what a critical juncture

in my affairs fortune has surprised me,' he said to them. 'I seem to hear the crash of enemy weapons and I, the one who actually commenced hostilities – I am now being challenged. [12] Then did Darius when writing such arrogant letters have my destiny there to advise him? But to no purpose, if I can be cured the way I want! [13] My situation does not admit of tardy remedies and slow doctors. Better for me to die taking an initiative than to recover slowly. So whatever help or skill the physicians can provide, they must realize that the remedy I seek is more for the war than for my life.'

[14] Alexander's sheer foolhardiness had made everyone deeply concerned, and so they all began individually to appeal to him not to increase the risk by his impatience but to put himself in the hands of his physicians. [15] Their suspicions of untested remedies were justified, they said, because the enemy was trying to bribe even Alexander's courtiers to murder him. [16] (In fact, Darius had had it made public that he would give Alexander's assassin a thousand talents.⁴⁰) They therefore believed nobody would risk trying a cure which could come under suspicion through being untested.

6

[1] Among the noted physicians attending the king was Philip, an Acarnanian who had come with him from Macedonia.⁴¹ He was completely devoted to Alexander. When the latter was a boy, Philip had been assigned to him to act as a companion and to look after his health, and now he felt a special affection towards him, not only as his king but also as his foster-child. [2] This Philip promised to produce a remedy that would be efficacious but not drastic, and to reduce the violence of the fever with a drugged potion. His assurance found favour with none but the person at whose risk he made it [3] for Alexander could tolerate anything more readily than delay. His imagination was filled with armed conflict and the line of battle, and he believed that victory depended entirely on his being able to take his position before the standards. What irked him most was that he was not to take the medicine for three days; those had been the doctor's orders.

[4] Meanwhile he received a letter from the most faithful of his officers, Parmenion, in which he was told not to trust his life to Philip who, according to Parmenion, had been bribed by Darius with one thousand talents and the prospect of marrying the king's sister.⁴² [5] The letter had caused Alexander deep concern and he was now secretly calculating and weighing up the divergent courses of action suggested by fear and hope. [6] 'Should I go ahead and drink?' he mused. 'Then, if it turns out that I have been given poison, I shall be thought to have deserved whatever happens. Should I accuse my physician of disloyalty? In that case, am I going to face death in my tent? No, better to be killed by someone else's crime than my own fear.' [7] For a long time he weighed his options. He told no one of the contents of Parmenion's

letter, which he put under the pillow on which he was lying, after sealing it with his own ring.

[8] After two days of such thoughts the day designated by the physician arrived, and Philip entered Alexander's tent with the cup in which he had concocted the potion. [9] When Alexander saw him, he sat up in bed. Holding the letter from Parmenion in his left hand, he took the cup and drank with confidence. Then he told Philip to read the letter and did not take his eyes from his face as he read, believing that he would be able to detect any signs of guilt in his facial expression. [10] After reading the letter Philip demonstrated more outrage than fear. He threw down his cloak and the letter before Alexander's bed. 'Sire,' he said, 'it is a fact that my life has always depended on you, but at this moment it really is true, I think, that my breath is drawn through your sacred and revered lips. [11] The charge of murder that has been brought against me will be repudiated by your recovery; by having *your* life saved by me you will have given me mine. I appeal to you and beseech you: dismiss your fear and let the medicine be drawn into your veins. Let your mind relax for a moment. You are upset and worried at an inopportune time by friends who are certainly loyal but who are only causing trouble by their concern.' These words not only relieved the king's anxiety but actually cheered him up and filled him with hope.

[12] 'Philip,' he said, 'if the gods had granted you the ideal method of testing my feelings towards you, you would certainly have chosen another, but you could not have hoped for one better than this. [13] Even though I received this letter, I still drank the potion you had made up, and now you must believe that I am as concerned about clearing your name as I am for my recovery.' So saying, he offered Philip his right hand.

[14] Such was the strength of the medicine, however, that what happened next lent weight to Parmenion's charges. Alexander's breathing became intermittent and difficult. Philip left nothing untried; he applied poultices to his body, and roused him when he was faint with the smell of food at one time, or wine at another. [15] As soon as he saw Alexander conscious, he would continually remind him of his mother and sisters, or again of the great victory that was coming to him. [16] Then the medication spread into Alexander's veins, and its health-giving properties could be felt throughout his body. First he regained his former mental energy, then his physical strength, and more quickly than had been expected. Three days after being in that condition, he appeared before his men. [17] And the troops showed no less enthusiasm at the sight of Philip than of Alexander. Each of the men grasped his right hand and thanked him as if he were a deity come to help them.

The Macedonians have a natural tendency to venerate their royalty, but even taking that into account, the extent of their admiration, or their burning affection, for this particular king is difficult to describe. [18] First of all, they

35

thought his every enterprise had divine aid. Fortune was with him at every turn and so even his rashness had produced glorious results. [19] His age gave added lustre to all his achievements for, though hardly old enough for undertakings of such magnitude, he was well up to them. Then there are the things generally regarded as rather unimportant but which tend to find greater approval among soldiers: the fact that he exercised with his men, that he made his appearance and dress little different from an ordinary citizen's, that he had the energy of a soldier. [20] These characteristics, whether they were natural or consciously cultivated, had made him in the eyes of his men as much an object of affection as of awe.

7

[1] When he received word of Alexander's illness, Darius marched to the Euphrates as swiftly as his heavily-burdened force would permit. Despite having to build a pontoon bridge over the river he nevertheless managed, in his haste to seize Cilicia, to get his army over in five days.[43] [2] By now Alexander had regained his strength and had reached the city of Soli. This he occupied, levying a 200-talent fine on the population and setting a military garrison on its citadel. [3] He then repaid the vows that had previously been made for his recovery by proclaiming a holiday and a period of games, and he demonstrated the strength of his contempt for the barbarians by celebrating games in honour of Aesculapius and Minerva.[44] [4] He was watching them when the good news arrived from Halicarnassus that the Persians had been beaten in the field by his troops and that the Myndians, Caunians and most of that region had been brought under his control.[45] [5] When the spectacle was over, he moved camp, built a pontoon bridge over the river Pyramus and came to the city of Mallus and, after a further day's march, to the town of Castabalum. [6] There Parmenion met the king. Alexander had sent him ahead to explore the road in the pass through which they were obliged to march to reach the city called Issus. [7] After seizing the narrow part of the road and leaving behind a moderately-sized garrison, Parmenion had captured Issus as well, which had been abandoned by the barbarians. Moving on from there he had dislodged the Persians holding positions within the mountains, secured the whole area with armed detachments and, as mentioned a moment ago, taken possession of the road. Now he came to Alexander to report his own success.

[8] The king then moved his troops ahead to Issus, and here there were deliberations over whether they should continue the advance or wait for the reinforcements that were known to be on their way from Macedonia.[46] Parmenion's view was that there was no place better suited for a fight; [9] the forces of both kings would be numerically equal, he said, since the narrow pass could not accommodate large numbers. In his view, it was imperative for the Macedonians to avoid flat ground and open spaces where it was

possible for them to be surrounded or caught in a pincer-movement. What he was frightened of was that they would be beaten by their own exhaustion rather than the enemy's courage – fresh Persian troops would keep coming to the front if they could take a position which did not restrict their movements. [10] Such soundly-reasoned strategy was readily accepted, and Alexander accordingly decided to await his enemy at the narrowest part of the pass.[47]

[11] There was in the king's army one Sisines, a Persian. He had once been sent to Philip by the satrap of Egypt and, since he was showered with gifts and shown every courtesy, he had chosen exile rather than his native land. Subsequently, he went with Alexander into Asia and was regarded as one of his loyal associates.[48] [12] To Sisines a Cretan soldier handed a letter that had been sealed with a ring, the impress of which was unfamiliar to Sisines. Nabarzanes, an officer of Darius, had sent it, and in it he urged Sisines to perform some act in keeping with his high birth and character – this, Nabarzanes said, would greatly redound to his credit with Darius. [13] Sisines was completely innocent, and he often tried to bring the letter to Alexander but, when he saw the king beset by so many worries about preparations for the coming hostilities, he kept waiting for a more suitable occasion and thus gave rise to the suspicion that he had joined a treacherous plot against him. [14] In fact, the letter had fallen into Alexander's hands before it was given to Sisines. After reading it, Alexander had had it sealed with a ring unknown to Sisines and given to him as a test of the barbarian's loyalty. [15] Because Sisines had not approached the king for several days, it was thought that he had had a treacherous motive for keeping the letter to himself, and he was killed by the Cretans as the army marched on, no doubt on the king's orders.[49]

8

[1] By now the Greek soldiers whom Thimodes had taken over from Pharnabazus had reached Darius. These were his main hope, and virtually his only one. [2] They strongly urged Darius to retreat and head for the plains of Mesopotamia once more, adding that, if he rejected this advice, he should at least split up his innumerable troops and not permit the entire strength of his kingdom to fall beneath a single stroke of fortune.[50] [3] The king found this advice less objectionable than his courtiers did.[51] They observed that the Greeks were of dubious loyalty and could be bought and sold. Treachery was afoot, they claimed, and the only reason the mercenaries wanted the force divided was so that they could hand over to Alexander whatever part was entrusted to them after such a split had been made. [4] The safest course was to surround them with the entire army and wipe them out with a shower of spears to show others that treason did not go unpunished. [5] Darius, however, was a man of justice and clemency. He declared that he would not commit so heinous a crime as to order the slaughter of men who had taken

up his cause and who were his own soldiers. What member of any foreign nation would in future entrust his life to him if he had the blood of so many soldiers on his hands? [6] Nobody's life should be forfeit for making stupid recommendations, he said; if giving advice involved risk he would run out of advisers! If it came to that, the courtiers themselves were summoned to daily meetings with him and proffered conflicting opinions, but the man who gave better advice was not therefore considered more loyal![52]

[7] Accordingly, he ordered a message to be taken to the Greeks to the effect that, while he thanked them for their concern for him, proceeding with a retreat would certainly mean handing his kingdom over to his enemy. Success in warfare depended on one's reputation, he said, and the man who retreated was believed to be on the run. [8] And prolonging the war was hardly justifiable: in a country that was now a desert and had been ravaged alternately by his own forces and the enemy, there would be insufficient provisions for such a large body of men, especially since winter was already coming on. [9] Even splitting the troops meant breaking with tradition, for his ancestors invariably brought their forces *en masse* to a critical battle. [10] Furthermore, he continued, this king who had formerly been a fearsome figure and who had been elated to groundless self-confidence by his enemy's absence – on hearing of Darius' approach, this man's presumption had given way to caution and he had taken to a hiding-place in the narrow parts of a mountain valley, just like the lowly animals that lurk in their woodland lairs at the sound of people passing. [11] Now he was even deceiving his own soldiers with a feigned illness. But he, Darius, was not going to let him put off the fight any longer; he was going to crush the Macedonians as they hung back in that lair into which they had retreated in fear. But there was more show than truth in these boasts of his.

[12] Darius dispatched all his money and most precious treasures to Damascus in Syria with a small military escort, and then he took the rest of his forces into Cilicia, his wife and his mother following the army according to Persian custom.[53] His unmarried daughters and his small son also accompanied their father. [13] It transpired that Alexander reached the pass which affords access to Syria on the same night as Darius reached the place called the Amanic Gates. [14] The Persians had no doubt that the Macedonians had abandoned Issus after taking it and that they were now in retreat, for they had actually taken prisoner a number of wounded and sick Macedonians unable to keep up with the column. [15] Egged on by his courtiers, who succumbed to a frenzy of barbarous ruthlessness, Darius had the hands cut off every one of them and the stumps cauterized. He then gave orders for the men to be taken around so that they could get an impression of his troops and, when they had sufficiently inspected everything, he told them to report what they had seen to their king.[54]

[16] Darius now struck camp and crossed the river Pinarus, intending to stick to the heels of what he believed was an enemy in flight. But the men

whose hands he had amputated reached the Macedonian camp bearing the news that Darius was following them with all the speed he could muster. [17] This was hard to believe; so Alexander sent his scouts ahead with orders to investigate the coastal areas and find out whether Darius was there in person or whether one of his subordinates had been trying to create the impression that the Persian army was coming in its entirety. [18] When the scouts were on their way back, a huge body of men was sighted in the distance. Then fires began to flare up throughout the plains, and the whole area appeared to be alight almost with one continuous blaze; for the Persian hordes were not in formation and were unusually spread out because of the pack-animals. [19] Alexander ordered his men to pitch camp just where they were; he was happy that the issue was to be decided there, in the pass, something he had desired in all his prayers.

[20] However, as usually happens when a critical moment is approaching, his confidence gave way to worry. Fortune itself, whose favour had granted him so much success, he now began to fear. As he considered its past gifts to him, not surprisingly he began to reflect on how changeable it was, and how only a single night now separated him from such a critical event. [21] Then again it would occur to him that the rewards outweighed the risks and that, while his victory might be in doubt, one thing was quite certain, that he would die an honourable death which would bring him great praise. [22] So he ordered his soldiers to refresh themselves and to be ready and under arms at the third watch. Alexander himself climbed to the top of a high ridge and by the light of several torches sacrificed to the tutelary gods of the area in traditional manner.[55]

[23] The men had now been given the specified third trumpet call and they were ready to march as well as to fight. They were instructed to advance briskly and, as day broke, they reached the narrow defile which they had determined to occupy. [24] The advance detachment informed Alexander that Darius was thirty stades away, so at this point he ordered the line to halt and, taking up his arms, arranged the battle-order.

News of his enemy's approach was brought to Darius by terrified peasants, and he could hardly believe that he was really being confronted by the troops he thought were fleeing before him. [25] As a result considerable alarm swept over all the Persians – they were actually better prepared for a march than for a battle – and they hurriedly seized their weapons. However, their feverish haste, as they ran this way and that and calling their comrades to arms, only served to increase their panic. [26] Some had slipped away to a hilltop to get a view of the enemy; most were putting bridles on their horses. Variously occupied and not observing one command, their individual consternation had brought about general confusion. [27] Darius at first decided to occupy a hilltop with a detachment, intending to make an encircling movement around his enemy, both in the front and in the rear, and he was also going to send forward other troops on the side of the sea (which offered protection to his right wing) to press Alexander hard from all directions. [28] In addition he had sent forward a force of 20,000, supplemented by a troop of archers, with orders to cross the river Pinarus (which separated the two armies) and make a stand opposite the Macedonian forces. If they were unable to manage that, they were to fall back on to the hills and, without being detected, encircle the rear of the enemy forces.[56] [29] His sound strategy, however, was shattered by fortune, which is more powerful than any calculation. [30] Some of the Persians were too frightened to carry out their orders, others obeyed them to no effect – for when the parts give out, the entire structure collapses.

9

[1] Darius' army was ordered as follows: Nabarzanes[57] held the right wing with his cavalry and a supplementary force of some 20,000 slingers and archers. [2] On the same wing was Thimodes who was in command of the Greek mercenary infantry, 30,000 strong. This was unquestionably the strongest element of the army, Darius' counterpart to the Macedonian phalanx. [3] On the left wing stood the Thessalian Aristomedes[58] with 20,000 barbarian infantry, and in reserve Darius had placed his most warlike tribes. [4] The king himself intended to fight on this same wing and was accompanied by 3,000 select cavalry (his usual bodyguard) and 40,000 infantry. [5] Then there were the cavalry of the Hyrcanians and Medes, and next to them the cavalry of the other races, positioned beyond them to the right and left. This force, ordered as described, was preceded by 6,000 javelin-throwers and slingers. [6] Every accessible area in the defile was packed with his troops, and the wings stood on the mountains on one side and on the seashore on the other. They had placed the king's wife and mother and a crowd of other women in the centre of the force.[59]

[7] Alexander set his phalanx – the strongest element in the Macedonian army – at the front. Parmenion's son, Nicanor,[60] held the right wing and next to him stood Coenus, Perdiccas, Meleager, Ptolomaeus[61] and Amyntas, all leading their respective units. [8] On the left wing, which reached as far as the sea, were Craterus and Parmenion, but Craterus had been instructed to take orders from Parmenion. The cavalry was deployed on both wings, the Macedonians reinforced by the Thessalians to the right, the Peloponnesians on the left. [9] Before this force Alexander had positioned a company of slingers interspersed with archers, and the Thracians and Cretans, who were also light-armed, preceded the main army as well. [10] Alexander placed the Agrianes who had recently arrived from Thrace[62] opposite those troops which Darius had sent ahead to occupy the hilltop. Parmenion he had ordered to extend his column as far as he could towards the sea so as to separate his line further from the hills held by the barbarians. [11] The latter, in fact, not daring to offer resistance to the Macedonians as they came up or to surround them after they had passed, took to their heels in a panic,

especially at the sight of the slingers. It was this that guaranteed safety to Alexander's flank, which he had feared would be under attack from the high ground.

[12] The Macedonians advanced in rows of thirty-two armed men, for the narrows would not admit a wider line. Then the defiles of the mountain gradually began to widen and open up more room so that the infantry could not only advance in their usual order but could also be given cavalry cover on the flanks.

10

[1] When the two armies were already in sight of each other but still out of javelin-range, the Persian front raised a wild, fierce shout. [2] The Macedonians returned it, the echo from the mountain tops and vast forests making them sound more numerous than they were: surrounding woods and rocks always return any sound they receive with increased volume. [3] Alexander went ahead of his front standards and kept motioning his men back with his hand so that they would not hurry too much in their excitement and be out of breath when they entered battle. [4] Riding up to the line, he would address the soldiers with words that suited their various dispositions. The Macedonians, who had won so many wars in Europe and who had set out to conquer Asia and the furthest lands of the East as much at their own instigation as at his – these he reminded of their long-standing valour. [5] They were the liberators of the world; they would one day traverse the bounds set by Hercules and Father Liber to subdue not only the Persians but all the races of the earth. Bactra and India would be Macedonian provinces.[63] What now lay before their eyes was minimal, he said, but victory gave access to everything. [6] It would not be fruitless labour on the sheer rocks and crags of Illyria and Thrace: they were being offered the spoils of the entire East. And they would scarcely need their swords: the whole enemy line, wavering in panic, could be driven back just by their shields. [7] Alexander also referred to his father, Philip, conqueror of the Athenians, and recalled to their minds the recent conquest of Boeotia and the annihilation of its best-known city.[64] He reminded them of the river Granicus,[65] of all the cities they had stormed or which had capitulated, of the territory that now lay behind them, all of it subdued and trampled beneath their feet. [8] Approaching the Greeks, he would remind them that these were the peoples who had inflicted wars upon Greece, wars occasioned first by Darius and then Xerxes, when they insolently demanded water and earth from them – to deprive them of their drinking fountains and their daily bread when they submitted. [9] He reminded them that these were the men who had demolished and burned their temples, stormed their cities, violated all the laws of gods and men.[66]

Since the Illyrians and Thracians usually made their living by looting, Alexander told them to look at the enemy line agleam with gold and purple –

41

equipped with booty not arms! [10] They were men, he said, so they should advance and seize the gold from this cowardly bunch of women.[67] They should exchange their rugged mountain-tops and barren hill-trails permanently stiff with frost for the rich plains and fields of the Persians.

II

[1] They had now come within javelin-range when the Persian cavalry made a furious charge on the left wing of their enemy – Darius wanted the issue decided in a cavalry engagement since he presumed that the phalanx was the main strength of the Macedonian army. An encircling movement around Alexander's right wing was also in progress. [2] When the Macedonian saw this he ordered two cavalry squadrons to maintain a position on the ridge while he promptly transferred the rest to the heart of the danger. [3] Then he withdrew the Thessalian cavalry from the fighting line, telling their commander to pass unobtrusively behind the Macedonian rear and join Parmenion, whose instructions he was to carry out energetically.

[4] The troops sent forward into the midst of the Persians were now totally surrounded and were stoutly defending themselves. But, being densely packed and virtually locked together, they could not effectively hurl their javelins which, simultaneously discharged, became entangled with one another as they converged on the same targets; so that the few which fell on the enemy did so gently and without inflicting injury, while the majority fell ineffectively to the ground. Thus, obliged to fight hand-to-hand, they swiftly drew their swords. [5] Then the blood really flowed, for the two lines were so closely interlocked that they were striking each other's weapons with their own and driving their blades into their opponents' faces. It was now impossible for the timid or cowardly to remain inactive. Foot against foot, they were virtually engaging in single combat, standing in the same spot until they could make further room for themselves by winning their fight: [6] only by bringing down his opponent could each man advance. But, exhausted as they were, they were continually being met by a fresh adversary, and the wounded could not retire from the battle as on other occasions because the enemy were bearing down on them in front while their own men were pushing them from behind.

[7] Alexander was as much a soldier as a commander, seeking for himself the rich trophy of killing the king.[68] Riding high in his chariot, Darius cut a conspicuous figure, at once providing great incentive to his men to protect him, and to his enemies to attack him. [8] His brother, Oxathres,[69] saw Alexander bearing down on Darius and moved the cavalry under his command right in front of the king's chariot. Oxathres far surpassed his comrades in the splendour of his arms and in physical strength, and very few could match his courage and devotion to Darius. In that engagement especially he won distinction by cutting down some Macedonians who were

recklessly thrusting ahead and by putting others to flight. [9] But the Macedonians fighting next to Alexander, their resolve strengthened by mutual encouragement, burst with Alexander himself into the line of Persian cavalry. Then the carnage truly took on cataclysmic proportions. Around Darius' chariot lay his most famous generals who had succumbed to a glorious death before the eyes of their king, and who now all lay face-down where they had fallen fighting, their wounds on the front of the body. [10] Among them could be recognized Atizyes,[70] Rheomithres and Sabaces, satrap of Egypt[71] – all generals of mighty armies – and heaped around these were a crowd of lesser-known infantrymen and cavalrymen. The Macedonian dead were not numerous, but they were the most courageous of them, and among the wounds received was a sword-graze to Alexander's right thigh.[72]

[11] By this time Darius' horses had been pierced by lances and were distracted with pain; they had begun to toss the yoke and were on the point of hurling the king from his chariot. Frightened that he might fall into his enemy's hands alive, Darius jumped down and mounted a horse which followed his chariot for this very purpose.[73] He even stooped to throwing off his royal insignia so they could not betray his flight. [12] The rest of his men now scattered in fear. They broke out of the fighting wherever they could find an escape-route, throwing down the weapons which shortly before they had taken up to protect themselves – thus does panic engender fear even of the things that help.

[13] Some horsemen whom Parmenion had dispatched were hard on the heels of the fleeing Persians, who by chance had all fled towards that wing. On the right, however, the Persians were pressing hard against the Thessalian cavalry,[74] [14] and one squadron had already been trampled down in the attack. Now the Thessalians wheeled their horses round vigorously, split up and then returned once more to the attack, inflicting great slaughter on the barbarians who, confident of victory, had broken ranks and were in total disarray. [15] The Persian horses as well as their riders were weighed down by their rows of armour-plating, and so they were severely handicapped by this manner of fighting which especially calls for speed.[75] Indeed, the Thessalians had been able to attack them without suffering casualties while they were still wheeling their horses about.

[16] Alexander had not previously ventured to pursue the barbarians, but when he was brought word of this successful engagement and was now victorious on both wings he proceeded to give chase to the fugitives. Not more than 1,000 horsemen accompanied the king, while huge numbers of the enemy were in retreat – [17] but who counts troops at the moment of victory or of flight? So the Persians were driven on like cattle by a mere handful of men, and the fear that drove them to flee also impeded their flight. [18] On the other hand, the Greeks who had fought for Darius (they were led by Amyntas, a lieutenant who had deserted from Alexander[76]) had managed to get away, because they were cut off from the main force, without even

appearing to be in flight. The barbarians took very diverse escape-routes. [19] Some followed a course leading directly into Persia; others, by a more circuitous path, headed for the high ground and sequestered mountain passes; a few made for the camp of Darius. [20] But the camp, filled with all manner of riches, had already been entered by the victors. Alexander's men had made off with a huge quantity of gold and silver (the trappings of luxury, not war) and, since they pillaged more than they could carry, the paths were littered everywhere with the meaner articles which they had greedily cast aside after comparing them with superior goods.

[21] Now they came to the women, and the more these prized their jewels, the more violently they were robbed of them. Not even their persons were spared the violence of lust. [22] They filled the camp with all manner of lamentation and screaming in reaction to their individual misfortunes, and villainy of every shape and form manifested itself as the cruelty and licence of the victor swept through the prisoners irrespective of rank or age. [23] Then a true illustration of fortune's caprice was to be seen. The men who had formerly decorated Darius' tent and fitted it out with all kinds of extravagant and opulent furnishings were now keeping back the very same things for Alexander, as if for their old master. That tent, in fact, was the only thing the Macedonian soldiers had left untouched, it being their tradition to welcome the conqueror in the tent of the conquered king.

[24] However, it was Darius' mother and his wife, prisoners now, who had attracted to themselves everybody's gaze and attention. His mother commanded respect by her age as well as by her royal dignity, his wife by a beauty that even her current misfortune had not marred. The latter had taken to her bosom her young son, who had not yet turned six, a boy born into the expectation of the great fortune his father had just lost. [25] In the lap of their aged grandmother lay Darius' two grown-up but unmarried daughters, grieving for their grandmother as well as themselves. Around her stood a large number of high-born women, their hair torn, their clothes rent and their former gracefulness forgotten. They called upon their 'queens' and 'mistresses', titles formerly appropriate but no longer applicable. [26] They forgot their own plight and kept asking on which wing Darius had stood and how the battle had gone, claiming that they were not captives at all if the king still lived. But Darius' flight had taken him far away with frequent changes of horses.

[27] A hundred thousand Persian infantry and 10,000 cavalry were killed in the action. On Alexander's side about 504 were wounded, a total of 32 infantrymen were lost, and 150 cavalrymen died. At so small a cost was a huge victory secured.[77]

12

[1] The king was exhausted by his long pursuit of Darius and, as night was coming on and there was no hope of overtaking him, he came into the camp

which his men had captured a short time before. [2] He then had invitations issued to his most intimate friends – no mere graze on the thigh could keep him from attending a banquet. [3] Suddenly the diners were alarmed by the sound of lamentation, punctuated by typically barbarian shrieking and howling, coming from the next tent. The company on guard-duty at the king's tent, fearing that this signalled the start of a more dangerous disturbance, had proceeded to arm themselves. [4] The reason for the sudden alarm was the lamentation of Darius' mother and wife and the other noble captives: believing Darius dead, they were raising a loud weeping and wailing in mourning for him. [5] One of the eunuch prisoners had happened to be standing in front of their tent when he recognized Darius' cloak in someone's hands (the man had found it and was now bringing it back) – the cloak which, as was mentioned a short while ago, Darius had cast off so that his identity would not be betrayed by his dress. The eunuch assumed it had been taken from Darius' dead body and so he had brought the false report of his death.

[6] When Alexander learned of the women's misunderstanding, they say he wept for Darius' reversal of fortune and their devotion to him. At first he ordered Mithrenes, the man who had surrendered Sardis, to go and console them, since he knew the Persian language, [7] but then he became concerned that a traitor might only rekindle the captives' anger and sorrow. So he sent Leonnatus, one of his courtiers, instead, instructing him to tell them that their lamentation was unwarranted since Darius still lived.[78] Leonnatus came with a few guards to the tent that housed the captured women and ordered it to be announced that he had been sent by Alexander. [8] The people at the entrance, however, caught sight of their weapons and, thinking their mistresses were finished, ran into the tent shouting that their final hour had come, that men had been sent to kill the prisoners. [9] The women could not keep the soldiers out, nor did they dare admit them and so, making no reply, they silently awaited their victor's will. [10] Leonnatus waited for a long time for someone to let him in but, when no one dared escort him inside, he left his attendants in the entrance and entered the tent. That in itself produced consternation among the women: he had apparently burst in without an invitation. [11] So the mother and wife of Darius fell at his feet and began to beg him to allow them to give Darius' body a traditional burial before they were executed, adding that after paying their last respects to the king they would readily face death. [12] Leonnatus' answer was that Darius was still alive and that they would not only come to no harm but would also retain their royal status with all the dignity of their former positions. Only at that point did Darius' mother allow herself to be raised from the ground.

[13] The following day, Alexander diligently conducted the burial of the soldiers whose bodies he had found, and he also gave instructions for the same honour to be shown to the most noble of the Persians. Darius' mother he allowed to bury whomsoever she wished in traditional Persian fashion. [14] She ordered only a few close relatives to be buried, and those in a manner

befitting their present circumstances, thinking that the elaborate funerals with which Persians paid their last respects to their dead would cause ill-will in view of the simple cremation accorded the victors. [15] When the funeral services had been duly discharged, Alexander sent messengers to the female prisoners to announce his coming and then, leaving the crowd of his attendants outside, he went into their tent with Hephaestion.

[16] Hephaestion was by far the dearest of all the king's friends; he had been brought up with Alexander and shared all his secrets. No other person was privileged to advise the king as candidly as he did, and yet he exercised that privilege in such a way that it seemed granted by Alexander rather than claimed by Hephaestion. While he was the king's age, in stature he was his superior, [17] and so the queens took him to be the king and did obeisance before him after their manner. Whereupon some of the captive eunuchs pointed out the real Alexander, and Sisigambis flung herself at his feet, apologizing for not recognizing him on the ground that she had never before seen him. Raising her with his hand, Alexander said, 'My lady, you made no mistake. This man is Alexander too.'[79]

[18] Had he been able to maintain this degree of moderation to the end of his life, I would certainly consider him to have enjoyed more good fortune than appeared to be his when he was emulating Father Liber's triumph on his victorious march through all the nations from the Hellespont right to the Ocean. [19] For then he would surely have overcome the defects he failed to overcome, his pride and his temper; he would have stopped short of killing his friends at dinner,[80] and he would have been reluctant to execute without trial men who had distinguished themselves in battle and had conquered so many nations along with him.[81] [20] But good fortune had not as yet overwhelmed him: while it was on the increase, he bore it with self-restraint and abstinence, but eventually he failed to control it when it reached its peak. [21] At this particular time, certainly, his actions were such that he outshone all previous kings in self-control and clemency. The unmarried princesses, who were extremely beautiful, he treated with as much respect as if they were his own sisters. [22] As for Darius' wife, who was surpassed by none of her generation in beauty, Alexander was so far from offering her violence that he took the utmost care to prevent anyone from taking advantage of her while she was in captivity. [23] He gave orders for all their finery to be returned to the women, and as captives they lacked none of the magnificence of their former state – only their self-esteem.

[24] Accordingly, Sisigambis said to Alexander: 'Sire, you deserve the same prayers as we made in the past for our king Darius. I can see, too, that you are worthy of them since you have excelled such a great king not only in good fortune but in fair-mindedness as well. [25] I know you call me "my lady" and "your majesty", but I confess that really I am your slave. I can cope with the high position I formerly enjoyed, but I can also endure the yoke of my present situation. As for the extent of your power over us, it is for you

to decide whether you want that demonstrated by clemency rather than cruelty.' [26] The king told them not to worry. He took Darius' son in his arms, and the child, not in the least frightened at the sight of Alexander (although this was the first time he had seen him), put his arms around his neck. Impressed by the boy's fearlessness, the king looked at Hephaestion and said: 'How I could have wished that Darius had acquired something of this character.' Then he left the tent. [27] He consecrated three altars on the banks of the river Pinarus to Jupiter, Hercules and Minerva, and then made for Syria, sending Parmenion ahead to Damascus where the king's treasure was to be found.[82]

13

[1] Parmenion had discovered that a satrap of Darius had also gone ahead, and he feared that his small numbers would be viewed with contempt by the enemy, so he decided to send for reinforcements. [2] It so happened, however, that the scouts sent in advance by him came upon a Mardian and he, when he was brought to Parmenion, handed him a letter sent to Alexander by the governor of Damascus.[83] The Mardian added that the governor now had no reservations about handing over all the king's property along with his money. [3] Ordering the man to be kept in custody, Parmenion opened the letter. In it Alexander was told to send one of his generals quickly with a small detachment so that the governor could surrender to him everything the king had left in his keeping. Parmenion accordingly gave the Mardian an escort and sent him back to the traitor, [4] but the man gave his guards the slip and entered Damascus before dawn.

This event had troubled Parmenion who now feared a plot was afoot; he also felt uneasy about setting out on a strange road without a guide. None the less, he trusted in his king's customary luck and gave orders for peasants to be captured to act as guides. These were quickly found and Parmenion arrived at the city three days later. By now the governor was frightened that he had not been trusted [5] and so, pretending to have little confidence in the town's defences, he ordered the royal money (called *gaza* by the Persians), together with the most valuable objects, to be brought out before sunrise. Although he feigned flight, his real purpose was to offer the treasure as plunder to the enemy. [6] As the governor left the town, thousands of men and women went with him, a crowd that would move to compassion anyone but the man to whose protection they had been entrusted. Indeed, to increase the proceeds of his treachery, he was ready to lay before his enemy booty more welcome than any sum of money – men of noble birth along with the wives and children of Darius' officers, plus the ambassadors to the Greek cities. All these Darius had left in the traitor's hands as though in an impregnable citadel.

[7] The *Gangabae* (which is what the Persians call their porters) were

unable to stand the weather – the wind had brought a sudden snowfall and the ground at the time was frozen hard – so they put on the gold-and-purple-embroidered clothing that they were carrying with the money. Nobody dared stop them: the king's misfortunes meant that even the dregs could flout his authority. [8] As a result, the picture presented to Parmenion was that of an army not to be despised, and so he proceeded with caution. He addressed a few words of encouragement to his men as if for a regular battle, telling them to spur on their horses and briskly charge the enemy. [9] In fact, the men carrying the goods dropped them and took to their heels in fright, while the armed guard escorting them, equally terror-stricken, also proceeded to throw down their arms and make for familiar side-roads. [10] The governor, feigning fright himself, had caused general panic by his pretence. The royal treasure was now littered throughout the plains: the cash accumulated to pay the men (a massive sum), the clothes of so many high-ranking men and so many distinguished women, [11] golden vessels, golden bridles, tents elaborately decorated on a royal scale, and wagons full of enormous wealth, abandoned by their owners. It was a sight to sadden even the looters – if there were anything that could arrest greed! For now a fortune of amazing and unbelievable proportions, which had been hoarded up over many years, was being rooted out by the looters, some of it torn by bramble-bushes, some of it sunk in the mud. The looters did not have enough hands to carry off their booty.

[12] Now they reached those who had been the first to flee. Several women were dragging their little children along with them as they went, and among these were the three unmarried daughters of Ochus, who had been king before Darius.[84] Once before a revolution had brought them down from the lofty station their father enjoyed, but now fortune was more cruelly aggravating their plight. [13] The same group contained the wife of Ochus, the daughter of Darius' brother, Oxathres, and the wife of Artabazus, Darius' chief courtier, as well as Artabazus' son, whose name was Ilioneus.[85] [14] The wife and son of Pharnabazus (the man whom Darius had given supreme command over the coastal area) were also taken, as were the three daughters of Mentor, and the wife and son of the renowned general Memnon.[86] Scarcely any courtier's household was unaffected by the catastrophe. [15] Also captured were the Lacedaemonians and Athenians who had broken their oath of allegiance to Macedon and joined the Persians. By far the best known among the Athenians because of their pedigree and reputation were Aristogiton, Dropides and Iphicrates, and among the Lacedaemonian prisoners were Pasippus and Onomastorides, along with Onomas and Callicratides; these also enjoyed distinction in their home city.[87]

[16] The coined money taken amounted to 2,600 talents, and the weight of wrought silver was equivalent to 500 talents. Thirty thousand men were also captured, together with 7,000 pack-animals and their burdens. [17] However, the man who betrayed his huge fortune was quickly visited by the

avenging deities with a well-deserved punishment. One of his confidants – I suppose out of respect for the king's station, even in these sad circumstances – murdered the traitor and took his head to Darius, providing him with a timely consolation for his betrayal; for now he had both taken revenge on an enemy and was also aware that the memory of his former majesty had not disappeared from the minds of all his subjects.

BOOK FOUR

[1] Darius was the king of an army that had recently been great; he had entered battle riding high in his chariot, more like a general celebrating a triumph than one going to war. But at this point he was in flight, through terrain which he had filled with armies almost beyond number but which was now deserted – to form one vast and solitary wilderness. [2] The king had few followers. Not all had made off in the same direction as he, and those who had done so found that as their horses gave out they could not keep pace with Darius who kept changing his. [3] He reached Onchae, where he was welcomed by 4,000 Greeks, and then he raced to the Euphrates[1] by a more direct course, believing that he would have control only of the territory which his speed would enable him to seize before the enemy.

[4] Parmenion, whose efforts had secured the booty at Damascus, was appointed by Alexander to the command of what is called Coele Syria,[2] with orders to keep a close watch both on the plunder and on the prisoners-of-war. [5] The Syrians, not yet sufficiently cowed by military disasters, refused to recognize the new authority, but they were swiftly reduced and brought to heel. The island of Aradus[3] also surrendered to Alexander. [6] At that time its king, Strato, controlled the mainland coast and large stretches of territory extending some distance inland. Alexander accepted Strato's surrender and advanced his camp to the city of Marathus.[4] [7] There he was brought a letter from Darius, the arrogant tone of which he found extremely offensive. He was especially annoyed at Darius' adding the title 'His Majesty' to his own name but not to Alexander's, [8] but Darius also made the demand (rather than request) that Alexander should accept as much money as the whole of Macedonia could hold in return for Darius' mother, wife and children, and then fight for the kingdom on equal terms with Darius, if he so wished. [9] If Alexander would finally bring himself to listen to good advice, Darius continued, he would be satisfied with his forefathers' realm, leave what belonged to another and enter into an alliance with him. [10] On those points, he said, he was ready to exchange guarantees.

For his part Alexander responded much like this: 'His Majesty Alexander to Darius: Greetings. The Darius whose name you have assumed wrought utter destruction upon the Greek inhabitants of the Hellespontine coast and upon the Greek colonies of Ionia,[5] and then crossed the sea with a mighty army, bringing the war to Macedonia and Greece. [11] On another occasion Xerxes, a member of the same family, came with his savage barbarian troops, and even when beaten in a naval engagement he still left Mardonius in Greece so that he could destroy our cities and burn our fields though absent himself.[6] [12] Everyone knows that my father, Philip, was murdered by assassins whom your people had seduced with the expectation of a huge Persian reward.[7] The wars you Persians undertake are unholy wars. You have weapons and yet you put a price on your enemies' heads – just as you, the king of a great army, recently wished to hire an assassin to kill me for 1,000 talents. [13] Hence I am not the aggressor in this war, but acting in self-defence. Furthermore, the gods support the better cause: I have already brought most of Asia under my control and defeated you in person in the field. You should not expect anything from me in view of your failure to observe the conventions of war towards me, but if you come to me as a suppliant I promise that you shall have your mother, your wife and your children without payment of ransom. [14] I know both how to conquer and how to deal with the conquered. If you are afraid to put yourself in my hands I shall give you my sworn guarantee that you can come without risk. And by the way, when you write to me remember that you are writing not just to a king, but to *your* king.' Thersippus was sent to deliver the letter.

[15] Next Alexander went down into Phoenicia where he accepted the surrender of the town of Byblos,[8] after which he came to Sidon, a city reputed for its antiquity and the fame of its founders. [16] The king in Sidon, Strato,[9] relied on the support of Darius for his position, but because his surrender to Alexander had been prompted by his citizens' wishes rather than his own, he was considered unworthy of his rule, and Hephaestion was authorized to appoint to the throne the Sidonian he considered most deserving of that high office. [17] Hephaestion was the house-guest of two young men who enjoyed some distinction among their fellow-citizens, but when given the opportunity of assuming the throne they said that traditionally nobody was elevated to the position unless he was of royal blood. [18] Hephaestion expressed admiration for their high principles in declining the kind of power that others pillaged and murdered to gain: 'My congratulations to you on being the first to realize how much greater an achievement it is to disdain kingship than to accept it. But name someone of royal blood, a man who will remember that he acquired his power from you.'

[19] They could see that many viewed the prospect of such great power with a hopeful eye and from inordinate ambition for the throne were now flattering individual friends of Alexander. They decided, however, that none had a better claim than one Abdalonymus who, though distantly related to the royal family, was now reduced by poverty to tending a market garden in the suburbs, from which he derived a meagre income. [20] As often happens, the cause of his reduced circumstances was his honesty, and now

he was so preoccupied with his daily work that he failed to hear the clash of arms that had shaken the whole of Asia. [21] So these two noblemen came without notice into his garden, which Abdalonymus happened to be clearing of weeds, carrying the robe with its royal insignia. [22] They saluted him as king. 'These garments which you see in my hands,' said one of them, 'must now replace those dirty rags of yours. Wash from your body its perpetual coating of mud and earth. You must now assume the disposition of a king and carry your characteristic moderation with you into the estate which you merit. And when you take your seat on the throne with power of life and death over all your citizens, see that you do not forget these circumstances in which – no, indeed, because of which – you receive your kingdom.' [23] The whole thing was like a dream to Abdalonymus. Several times he asked if they were out of their minds, to mock him so shamelessly; but as he hesitated, the dirt was washed from him, the purple and gold embroidered robe was placed upon him, and he was reassured by their sworn protestations, so that it was in all seriousness that he came as king in their company to the palace.[10]

[24] Rumour swiftly made its usual sweep of the whole city. Support began to emerge in some quarters, resentment in others, and the rich protested against Abdalonymus' low status and poverty to Alexander's friends. [25] The king immediately had him brought before him, looked at him for some time, and then said: 'Your physical characteristics are not at odds with the reports of your ancestry, but I want to know how well you endured poverty.'

'Oh that I may be able to bear royal authority with the same equanimity!' answered Abdalonymus. 'These hands of mine satisfied my needs. I had nothing, but lacked nothing.' [26] From what Abdalonymus said, Alexander gained an impression of a noble character. Accordingly he not only had Strato's royal appurtenances assigned to him but a large part of the Persian spoils as well, and he also added to his control the area adjoining the city.

[27] In the meantime, Amyntas (who, as we observed above,[11] had defected to the Persians from Alexander) arrived at Tripolis with 4,000 Greeks who had accompanied him in flight from the battle. He embarked his troops on ships, crossed to Cyprus and, believing that in the present circumstances a man could hold whatever he seized as a rightful possession, decided to make for Egypt. He was now on hostile terms with both kings, and constantly on the watch to profit from conditions changing in either's favour. [28] He engendered in his soldiers hope for success in his great enterprise, telling them that Sabaces, the governor of Egypt, had fallen in battle[12] and that the Persian garrison was leaderless and weak while the Egyptians, who were always at odds with their governors, would regard them as allies, not enemies.

[29] Their predicament compelled them to try every option; when one's first hopes are thwarted by fortune the future looks better than the present. With one voice, they shouted that he should lead them where he wished; whereupon Amyntas, thinking he should exploit their enthusiasm while they

were fired with hope, penetrated as far as the harbour-mouth of Pelusium by pretending that he was the advance-guard for Darius. [30] Taking control of Pelusium, he moved his troops forward to Memphis; news of this brought all the Egyptians running from their various villages and cities to wipe out the Persian garrisons – for the Egyptians are a volatile people more inclined to foment unrest than to get things done themselves. Despite their alarm the Persians did not abandon hope of keeping their hold on Egypt, [31] but Amyntas defeated them in battle and drove them into the city. After pitching camp, the victors then sallied forth to plunder the countryside and carried off everything, as if the possessions of their enemy had been put at their disposal.

[32] Mazaces realized that his men were intimidated by the unsuccessful engagement, but pointed out to them that the enemy were in disorder, and careless and over-confident from their victory; thus he induced them to make a determined sortie from the city and to recover what they had lost. [33] The strategy proved as successful in its results as it was sound in reasoning – the enemy were killed to a man, along with their leader. Such was the penalty Amyntas paid to both kings, for he was no more loyal to the one to whom he had defected than to the one whom he had deserted.

[34] The recapture of Lydia was now being attempted by the generals of Darius who had survived the battle of Issus, together with all the troops who had followed them as well as some young Cappadocians and Paphlagonians enlisted for the purpose. [35] Alexander's general, Antigonus, was in command of Lydia[13] and, although he had dispatched to the king most of the soldiers from his garrison, he nevertheless showed his contempt for the barbarians by taking the field with his men. In that theatre, too, the fortune of the two sides remained unaltered: the Persians were defeated in three battles in various locations.

[36] In this same period the Macedonian fleet, which Alexander had summoned from Greece, defeated Aristomenes[14] (who had been sent by Darius to recapture the coast of the Hellespont) either capturing or sinking his ships. [37] Then the Persian admiral Pharnabazus exacted money from the Milesians, set a garrison in the city of Chios and made for Andros and then Siphnos with 100 ships. He also established garrisons on those islands and imposed fines on them.

[38] This great war was being fought by the two richest monarchs of Europe and Asia respectively, each hoping for domination of the world, and it also set the armies of Greece and Crete in motion. [39] The Spartan King Agis[15] opened hostilities with the Macedonian governor Antipater with a levy of 8,000 Greeks who had fled from Cilicia and made their way home. [40] The Cretans had supported both sides on different occasions and were alternately occupied by Spartan and Macedonian garrisons. In fact, the squabbles between these were comparatively insignificant: fortune's attention was focused on the struggle on which all else depended.

2

[1] By now all Syria and all Phoenicia except Tyre were under Macedonian control,[16] and Alexander was encamped on the mainland which was separated from the city of Tyre by a narrow strait. [2] Surpassing all other cities of Syria and Phoenicia in size and renown, Tyre seemed more likely to accept the status of ally with Alexander than subjection to him. Tyrian envoys now brought him a gift of a golden crown, and they had already shown their hospitality by conveying to him a plentiful supply of provisions from the city. Alexander gave orders that the gifts be received as a gesture of friendship, and in a warm address to the envoys he stated his wish to sacrifice to Hercules, a deity especially revered by the people of Tyre. [3] The Macedonian kings, he told them, believed themselves descendants of the god,[17] and furthermore he had been advised by an oracle to make this sacrifice. [4] The envoys replied that there was a temple of Hercules outside the city in the area which they called Palaetyros,[18] and there the king would be able to offer due sacrifice to the god. [5] Alexander lost his temper, which he also failed to control on other occasions. 'You think nothing of this land army,' he said 'because of your confidence in your position, living as you do on an island, but I am soon going to show you that you are really on the mainland. And you can be sure that I shall either enter your city or storm it.'

[6] Dismissed with this message, the envoys began to advise their fellow citizens to let into the city the king who had already been given recognition by Syria and Phoenicia, [7] but the Tyrians had sufficient confidence in their position to decide to withstand a siege. The strait separating the city from the mainland had a width of four stades.[19] It was particularly exposed to the south-westerly wind, which rolled rapid successions of waves on to the shore from the open sea, [8] and nothing represented a greater obstacle to a siege-work – which the Macedonians were contemplating, to join island and mainland – than this wind. In fact, to construct moles here is difficult even when the sea is smooth and calm, but the south-westerly undermines the initial foundations as the sea batters them violently. No mole is strong enough to withstand the corrosive force of the waves as the water seeps through the joints in the construction and, as the wind increases, floods over the very top of the structure. [9] Apart from this there was another difficulty no less serious: the city walls and their turrets were surrounded by especially deep water.[20] This meant that projectiles could be directed at them only from ships and at a distance, that scaling-ladders could not be set against the walls, and that any approach by foot was out of the question since the wall dropped sheer into the sea. The king had no ships, but even if he had been able to bring some up, they could have been kept at bay with missiles because of their instability in the water.

[10] Meanwhile a trivial event boosted the confidence of the Tyrians.

A delegation of Carthaginians had arrived at that time to celebrate an annual religious festival in accordance with their tradition (Carthage having been founded by Tyre, which was always honoured as its parent-city[21]). [11] The Carthaginians began to encourage the Tyrians to face the siege with confidence; help, they said, would soon be coming from Carthage (in those days the seas were to a large extent dominated by Carthaginian fleets). [12] The people of Tyre accordingly decided on war. They deployed their artillery along the walls and turrets, distributed weapons to the younger men, and allocated the city's generous resources of craftsmen to workshops. Tyre re-echoed with the noise of war-preparations. Iron 'hands', called 'harpagones', for throwing on the enemy siege-works, were manufactured in advance, along with 'crows' and other devices used for defending cities.[22] [13] It is said that when the metal that was to be forged had been set in the furnaces and the bellow-blasts were fanning the fire, streams of blood appeared beneath the flames, which the Tyrians interpreted as an omen unfavourable to the Macedonians. [14] On the Macedonian side, too, while some soldiers happened to be breaking bread they noticed drops of blood oozing from it. Alexander was alarmed at this, but their most accomplished soothsayer Aristander claimed it would have been a bad omen for the Macedonians if the blood had run on the outside of the bread, but since it had run from the inside, it actually portended destruction for the city they had determined to besiege.

[15] Since Alexander's navy was a long way off and he could see that a protracted siege would severely impede his other plans, he sent heralds to urge the Tyrians to accept peace terms; but the latter, violating international conventions, killed them and threw their bodies into the sea. Outraged by the disgraceful murder of his men, Alexander now resolved to lay siege to the city.

[16] First, however, a mole had to be constructed to join the city and the mainland, and the sight of the fathomless deep filled the soldiers with despair, for it could scarcely be filled even if they had divine aid. How could rocks big enough be found, or trees tall enough? To make a mound to fill such a void they would have to denude whole regions; the strait was perpetually stormy, and the more constricted the area of its movement between the island and the mainland, the more fierce it became. [17] But Alexander was not inexperienced in dealing with the soldier's temperament: he announced that he had seen in a dream the figure of Hercules extending his right hand to him, and himself entering Tyre as Hercules led him and opened the way. He included a reference to the murdered heralds, and the Tyrians' violation of international conventions, and added that this was the only city that had dared delay his victorious progress. [18] Then the generals were instructed to reprove their men, and when they were all sufficiently aroused he set to work.

Large quantities of rock were available, furnished by old Tyre, while timber to construct rafts and siege-towers was hauled from Mt Libanus. [19] The structure had reached some height from the sea-bed without yet breaking the surface of the water [20] when the Tyrians began to bring up small boats and to hurl insulting taunts at them about 'those famous warriors carrying loads on their backs like pack-animals'. They would ask, too, if Alexander 'had more power than Neptune'. Their jeers actually served to fuel the soldiers' enthusiasm. [21] Little by little the mole now began to rise above the surface and the mound's width increased as it approached the city. The Tyrians, who had hitherto failed to notice the mole's growth, now perceived its size. With their light skiffs they began to encircle the structure, which was not yet joined to the island, attacking with missiles the men standing by the work. [22] Many were wounded without a casualty on the part of the Tyrians, who could both withdraw and bring up their boats without hindrance; and so the Macedonians were diverted from their work to protecting themselves. Furthermore, as the mole proceeded further from shore, the materials piled on it were increasingly sucked into the sea's depths. [23] Alexander, therefore, had hides and sheets of canvas stretched before the workmen to screen them from Tyrian missiles, and he erected two turrets on the top of the mole from which weapons could be directed at approaching boats. [24] The Tyrians, in turn, landed their boats on the coast well out of sight of their enemy, put soldiers ashore, and cut down the Macedonians who were carrying the rocks. On Mt Libanus, too, Arab peasants made an attack on the Macedonians while they were scattered, killing some thirty of them and taking a smaller number prisoner.

3

[1] The incident obliged Alexander to split his forces. Not to appear to be frittering away time in besieging a single city, he gave the operation to Perdiccas and Craterus while he himself made for Arabia with a detachment of light-armed troops.[23] [2] Meanwhile the Tyrians took an enormous ship, loaded its stern with rocks and sand so that its prow stood high out of the water, and daubed it with bitumen and sulphur. Then they rowed out the ship which, after its sails caught a strong wind, quickly came up to the mole. [3] At this point the oarsmen fired the prow and then jumped into boats that had followed the ship expressly for this purpose. The vessel flared up and began to spread the blaze over a large area. Before help could be brought it engulfed the towers and other structures built on the top of the mole. [4] The men who had jumped into the small boats also tossed firebrands and anything else that would fuel the flames on to these buildings; the topmost sections of the turrets, as well as the lower ones, had now caught fire, while the Macedonians on them were either consumed in the conflagration or else threw aside their arms and hurled themselves into the sea. [5] Preferring to take them alive rather than kill them, the Tyrians would beat their hands with

sticks and stones as they swam until they were disabled and could be safely taken on board. [6] Nor was it just a matter of the superstructure being burned down. The same day it so happened that an especially high wind whipped up the sea from its very depths and smashed it against the mole. The joints loosened under the repeated battering of the waves, and water running between the rocks caused the work to rupture in the centre. [7] As a result the mounds of stones supporting the earth heaped on the mole collapsed, and the whole structure crashed into the deep water, so that on his return from Arabia Alexander found scarcely a trace of his huge mole.

There followed what usually happens when things go wrong: they resorted to mutual recrimination when they might have complained with more justice about the violence of the sea. [8] The king set to work on a fresh mole, but now he aimed it directly into the head-wind, instead of side-on to it, so that the front offered protection to the rest of the work which, as it were, sheltered behind it. Alexander also added breadth to the mound so that towers could be raised in the middle out of range of the enemy's missiles. [9] Moreover, the Macedonians threw into the sea entire trees complete with their huge branches on which they set a load of rocks. Then they added another mass of trees to the pile and heaped earth on them; and over this they built up another layer of rocks and trees, thus forming a structure virtually bonded together into a solid whole.

The Tyrians meanwhile applied themselves energetically to any device that might impede the mole. [10] Particularly helpful to their purpose were the swimmers who would submerge out of their enemies' sight and swim unobserved right up to the mole, where they would pull towards them with hooks the projecting branches of the trees. Often these came away, taking much of the building material into the deep water, and the swimmers then had little difficulty managing the logs and tree trunks, once the weight on them had been removed. After that the whole structure, which had been supported by the logs, followed into the deep when its base collapsed.

[11] Alexander was dejected, undecided whether to continue or leave. At this point the fleet arrived from Cyprus, and Cleander simultaneously came with the Greek soldiers who had recently sailed to Asia.[24] Alexander split the 190 ships into two wings:[25] the Cypriot king, Pnytagoras, and Craterus took command of the left, and Alexander himself sailed on the right in the royal quinquereme. [12] The Tyrians had a fleet, but they refused to risk a naval engagement, setting a mere three vessels in the Macedonians' path directly below the city walls. These Alexander rammed and sank.

[13] The next day he brought the fleet up to the city's fortifications. At all points his artillery, especially his battering rams, shook the walls. The Tyrians hurriedly repaired the damage by setting rocks in the breaches and also started an inner wall which would give them protection should the first wall give way. [14] But disaster was closing in on them at every point: the mole was within javelin-range; Alexander's fleet was encircling their walls;

they were facing disaster in a battle waged concurrently on land and sea. The Macedonians had lashed pairs of quadriremes together in such a way that the prows were locked together but the sterns were as far separated as could be managed. [15] The space between the sterns they had filled with yard-arms and stout beams bound together, with decking laid over these to form platforms for infantrymen. After equipping the quadriremes in this manner they moved them up to the city, and from there missiles could be safely discharged on the defenders because the infantrymen were protected by the prows.

[16] At midnight Alexander ordered his fleet, equipped as described above, to encircle the walls and, as the ships closed in on the city at all points, a numbing despair descended on the Tyrians. Then, suddenly, thick clouds shrouded the sky and a layer of fog extinguished such twilight as there was. [17] By degrees the sea began to roughen and swell; a stronger wind whipped it up into waves and the vessels started to collide with each other. The lashings keeping the quadriremes together began to snap and the platforms to shatter with a huge roar, dragging the soldiers with them into the deep. [18] Since the vessels were lashed together, manoeuvring them in the rough water was impossible: infantrymen obstructed oarsmen in the performance of their tasks and oarsmen infantrymen. And as usually happens in such circumstances, the skilled began to obey the unskilled, with helmsmen, who customarily gave orders, now following instructions out of fear for their lives. The sea, lashed by their oars with greater determination, finally surrendered the vessels to the sailors, their rescuers, who brought them to shore, most of them as wrecks.

[19] Thirty ambassadors from Carthage happened to arrive during this period, more to encourage the besieged than to help them – for the Carthaginians, they announced to the Tyrians, were handicapped by a war at home and were fighting not for power but simply for survival. [20] The Syracusans were even then putting the torch to the crops in Africa, and had made camp not far from the walls of Carthage.[26] Though frustrated in their great expectations, the Tyrians did not lose heart; instead they handed over their wives and children for evacuation to Carthage, being ready to face whatever might happen with increased fortitude if they had the most precious part of their community removed from the common peril. [21] One of their fellow citizens had also made it known at an assembly that he had dreamed that Apollo, a deity especially revered by the Tyrians, was leaving the city, and that the mole laid in the sea by the Macedonians turned into a woodland glade. Despite the unreliability of the speaker,[27] [22] the Tyrians in their panic were ready to believe the worst; they bound the statue of Apollo with a golden chain which they attached to the altar of Hercules, the deity to whom they had consecrated their city, in the hope that he would hold Apollo back. The statue had been brought from Syracuse and erected in the land of their forefathers by the Carthaginians, who had not decorated Carthage itself more

lavishly than Tyre with the many spoils taken from cities which they had captured. [23] Some also advocated the revival of a religious rite which had been discontinued for many generations and which I certainly would not have thought to be at all acceptable to the gods – namely the sacrifice of a free-born male child to Saturn. (Such sacrilege – to use a more appropriate word than sacrifice – the Carthaginians inherited from their founders, and they are said to have continued the practice right down to the time of their city's destruction.)[28] Had it not been vetoed by the elders, whose judgement carried weight in all matters, cruel superstition would have triumphed over civilized behaviour.

[24] However, the urgency of the situation (more efficacious than any art) provided some novel means of defence beyond the conventional ones. To hamper the ships that approached the walls they had lashed stout beams to ropes; moving the beams forward with an engine, they would suddenly slacken the ropes and drop them on the ships. [25] Hooks and blades hanging from the beams would also injure either the marines or the actual vessels. Furthermore, they would heat bronze shields in a blazing fire, fill them with hot sand and boiling excrement and suddenly hurl them from the walls. [26] None of their deterrents aroused greater fear than this. The hot sand would make its way between the breastplate and the body; there was no way to shake it out and it would burn through whatever it touched. The soldiers would throw away their weapons, tear off all their protective clothing and thus expose themselves to wounds without being able to retaliate. The 'crows' and 'iron hands' let down from the engines also eliminated a large number of them.

4

[1] At this point a weary Alexander had decided to raise the siege and head for Egypt. After sweeping through Asia at a headlong pace he was now detained before the walls of a single city, with so many magnificent opportunities lost. [2] Yet it was as disgraceful for him to leave a failure as to linger there; he thought, too, that his reputation would suffer – his reputation which had gained him more conquests than military action – if he left Tyre as witness that he could be beaten. To leave nothing untried, he ordered more ships to be brought up and manned with hand-picked infantrymen. [3] Now it also happened that a sea-creature of extraordinary size, its back protruding above the waves, came to rest its huge body on the mole which the Macedonians had laid. Both sides caught sight of it as it parted the water and raised itself up. Then it submerged once more at the head of the mole, [4] and alternately rearing most of its body above the waves and diving beneath the surface it finally went under not far from the city's fortifications. The sight of the creature cheered both sides.[29] [5] According to the Macedonian interpretation, it had pointed out the path the mole should take. According to the

Tyrians, Neptune, exacting vengeance for the occupation of the sea, had snatched the beast away, which meant the mole was sure to collapse shortly. Exhilarated by the omen, they turned to feasting and excessive drinking and at sunrise they unsteadily boarded their vessels which they had decorated with flowers and wreaths – so premature were they not only in seeing an omen of their victory but in actually celebrating it!

[6] Now it so happened that the king had ordered the fleet to be moved in the other direction, leaving thirty smaller vessels on the beach. The Tyrians captured two of these and struck sheer panic into the others until Alexander, hearing the shouts of his men, eventually brought the fleet to the beach from which the commotion had come. [7] The first of the Macedonian ships to appear was a quinquereme superior to the others in speed, and when the Tyrian vessels sighted it two of them charged against its sides from opposite directions. The quinquereme turned on one of these, to find itself rammed by the enemy's prow, but the Macedonian vessel in turn grappled this ship. [8] The other Tyrian ship, which was not caught up and had a free run, began a charge at the quinquereme's other flank, at which point a trireme of Alexander's fleet, arriving very opportunely on the scene, charged into the ship bearing down on the quinquereme with such violence that the Tyrian helmsman was hurled into the sea from the stern. [9] More Macedonian ships then appeared and the king also came up. The Tyrians backed water, with difficulty retrieved their entangled ship, and all their vessels retreated to the harbour together. The king followed up swiftly, and though unable to enter the harbour because projectiles kept him away from the walls, he still managed to sink or capture nearly all the enemy ships.

[10] The men were then given two days' rest, after which they were ordered to bring up the fleet and siege-engines simultaneously so that Alexander could press his advantage at all points against a demoralized enemy. The king himself climbed the highest siege-tower. His courage was great, but the danger greater [11] for, conspicuous in his royal insignia and flashing armour, he was the prime target of enemy missiles. And his actions in the engagement were certainly spectacular. He transfixed with his spear many of the defenders on the walls, and some he threw headlong after striking them in hand-to-hand combat with his sword or shield, for the tower from which he fought practically abutted the enemy walls. [12] By now the repeated battering of the rams had loosened the joints in the stones and the defensive walls had fallen; the fleet had entered the port; and some Macedonians had made their way on to the towers the enemy had abandoned.[30]

The Tyrians were crushed by so many simultaneous reverses. Some sought refuge in the temples as suppliants while others locked their doors and anticipated the enemy by a death of their own choosing. Others again charged into the enemy, determined that their deaths should count for something. But the majority took to the rooftops, showering stones [13] and whatever happened to be to hand on the approaching Macedonians.

Alexander ordered all but those who had fled to the temples to be put to death and the buildings to be set on fire. [14] Although these orders were made public by heralds, no Tyrian under arms deigned to seek protection from the gods. Young boys and girls had filled the temples, but the men all stood in the vestibules of their own homes ready to face the fury of their enemy. [15] Many, however, found safety with the Sidonians among the Macedonian troops. Although these had entered the city with the conquerors, they remained aware that they were related to the Tyrians (they believed Agenor had founded both cities) and so they secretly gave many of them protection and took them to their boats, on which they were hidden and transported to Sidon. [16] Fifteen thousand were rescued from a violent death by such subterfuge.[31] The extent of the bloodshed can be judged from the fact that 6,000 fighting-men were slaughtered within the city's fortifications. [17] It was a sad spectacle that the furious king then provided for the victors: 2,000 Tyrians, who had survived the rage of the tiring Macedonians, now hung nailed to crosses all along the huge expanse of the beach. [18] The Carthaginian ambassadors Alexander spared, but he subjoined a formal declaration of war (a war which the pressures of the moment postponed).

[19] Tyre was captured six months after the start of the siege,[32] a city enjoying much distinction in the eyes of later generations because of its antiquity and its frequent turns of fortune. Founded by Agenor, for a long period it held in subjection not only the adjacent sea but any land visited by its fleets. If the popular tradition is to be believed, its people were the first to teach or to learn the alphabet, and it is a fact that its colonies were scattered almost throughout the entire world (Carthage in Africa, Thebes in Boeotia, Gades on the Ocean). [20] I suppose that since they ranged freely over the sea and made quite frequent visits to lands unknown to other peoples they selected settlements for their overflowing population of younger people, or perhaps their inhabitants grew tired of the frequent earthquakes (this is another traditional explanation) and were compelled to seek by force new homes in foreign lands. [21] After experiencing many disasters and rising again after its destruction, now at last, with long peace completely restoring its prosperity, Tyre enjoys tranquillity under the merciful protection of Rome.[33]

5

[1] It was about this time that a letter arrived from Darius finally addressing Alexander as 'Your Majesty'. Darius requested that Alexander should take his daughter, named Statira, as his wife, saying that all the land between the Hellespont and the river Halys would be her dowry – Darius himself being content to retain the lands to the east.[34] [2] Should Alexander by chance feel hesitant to accept the offer, Darius said, he should remember that fortune never stood still and whatever degree of prosperity men enjoyed, the envy to

which they were exposed was greater. [3] His fear, Darius continued, was that, like the birds wafted up to the sky by their natural lightness, Alexander would also be carried away by the vanity of his youthful mind – nothing was more difficult than keeping control of great fortune at his age. [4] He, Darius, still had many other lands in his power, and he would not always be vulnerable to attack in a narrow pass. Indeed, Alexander would have to cross the Euphrates, the Tigris, the Araxes and the Hydaspes, all providing stout defences for Darius' kingdom; he would have to enter open country (Media, Hyrcania, Bactra) where the small number of his troops would put him to shame. [5] And as for the Indians living next to the Ocean – when would he reach them, not to mention the Sogdians, Arachosians and other tribes stretching as far as the Caucasus and the Tanais? He would grow old in the process of reaching all those territories even if he fought no battles. [6] In fact, he should stop summoning Darius to him – his coming would mean the end of Alexander.

[7] In reply Alexander told the bearers of the letter that Darius was promising him property which was not his to give, and that what he wished to divide was something he had already totally lost. Lydia, Ionia, Aeolia and the Hellespont coast, the dowry offered him, were already his own rewards of victory. Rules, he said, were made by the victors and accepted by the defeated, and if Darius was the only person who failed to recognize which status either king enjoyed, he should take the first opportunity of deciding the question in battle. [8] Furthermore, when he crossed the sea, the empire he had aimed at was not Cilicia or Lydia – slight reward for a war of such proportions – but Darius' capital Persepolis, then Bactra and Ecbatana and the furthest shores of the East. Wherever Darius could run he could follow, and Darius should stop trying to frighten with rivers a man whom he knew to have passed over seas.

[9] Such was the interchange of letters between the kings. Meanwhile, the people of Rhodes were surrendering their cities and harbours to Alexander. The king had awarded the governorship of Cilicia to Socrates, and had ordered Philotas[35] to assume charge of the area around Tyre, while Parmenion had handed over what is called Coele Syria to Andromachus[36] so that he could himself take part in the rest of the campaign. [10] Alexander ordered Hephaestion to skirt the Phoenician coast with his fleet, and he himself came in full force to the city of Gaza.[37]

[11] About this time there took place the traditional Isthmian games,[38] which the whole of Greece gathers to celebrate. At this assembly the Greeks – political trimmers by temperament – determined that fifteen ambassadors be sent to the king to offer him a victory-gift of a golden crown in honour of his achievements on behalf of the security and freedom of Greece. [12] A short while before, the very same people had been straining to catch the fluctuating reports, so that they could follow in whatever direction fortune carried their vacillating loyalties.

[13] Meanwhile not only did Alexander march against the cities still refusing the yoke of domination, but the excellent leaders who served as his generals had also made inroads into several districts. Calas marched into Paphlagonia and Antigonus into Lycaonia; Balacrus defeated Darius' general Idarnes[39] and recaptured Miletus, [14] while Amphoterus and Hegelochus with a fleet 160 strong brought the islands between Achaea and Asia under Alexander's control. They also occupied Tenedos and had decided to seize Chios at the invitation of its inhabitants, [15] but Darius' governor Pharnabazus arrested the Macedonian sympathizers and returned the city, with a fairly small garrison, to Apollonides and Athanagoras, who were supporters of the Persian cause. [16] Alexander's generals persisted with their siege of the city, relying less on their own strength than on the sentiments of the besieged. They were not mistaken. Quarrelling between Apollonides and the officers of the garrison provided them with an opportunity to break into the town. [17] When the gate had been broken down and a Macedonian company had entered, the townspeople, who had previously considered surrendering the town, now joined Amphoterus and Hegelochus. The Persian garrison was slaughtered and Pharnabazus, Apollonides and Athanagoras were handed over in shackles to the Macedonians, [18] along with twelve triremes complete with marines and crews, thirty crewless ships and pirate boats, and 3,000 Greek mercenaries hired by the Persians.[40] The Macedonians distributed the latter among their troops to augment their numbers, executed the pirates and added the captured crews to their fleet.

[19] It so happened that the tyrant of Methymna, Aristonicus, came with some pirate vessels to the harbour boom at the first watch, ignorant of events on Chios. Challenged by the guards, he replied that he was Aristonicus coming to see Pharnabazus. [20] The guards declared that Pharnabazus was sleeping just then and could not be seen for the moment, but the port was open to an ally and a friend, and he could have an audience with Pharnabazus the next day. [21] Without hesitation Aristonicus went right in, and the pirate skiffs followed in his wake.[41] As they brought the vessels up to the harbour quay the guards reset the boom and sent out the alarm to the nearest sentries. None of them dared resist; all were clapped in irons and handed over to Amphoterus and Hegelochus.[42]

[22] From here the Macedonians crossed to Mitylene which had been recently seized by the Athenian Chares, and was now held by him with a garrison of Persians, 2,000 strong. Unable to withstand the siege, Chares surrendered the city on condition that he be allowed to leave in safety, after which he made for Imbros. The Macedonians spared those who surrendered.

6

[1] Losing all hope of the peace which he had expected his letter and ambassadors to gain, Darius now concentrated on rebuilding his strength and

vigorously resuming hostilities. [2] He therefore ordered his generals to meet in Babylonia, and he also told Bessus, the governor of Bactria, to come to him with the largest army he could muster. [3] Of the nations in that part of the world the Bactrians are the most spirited, with a fierce disposition very different from that of the soft-living Persians. Located not far from the belligerent Scythians, who make their living by looting, they were constantly at war. [4] Bessus alarmed the king: his loyalty was suspect and he was restless in his position as a second-in-command; he had regal ambitions, and treason was feared on his part since it was his only way to realize them.⁴³

[5] Alexander meanwhile devoted the utmost care to ascertaining Darius' destination, but he was unable to discover this because of the Persian custom of concealing the secrets of their kings with an amazing degree of loyalty – [6] no intimidation and no hope of reward can elicit a word to betray their confidences. The ancient code, enforced by the kings, had ordained silence in these matters on pain of death, and disclosure meets with more severe punishment than any crime. The Magi, too, believe that no important matter can be dealt with by a person who has difficulty in keeping silent, something which nature has decreed to be very easy for a man. [7] Thus, ignorant of all the enemy's activities, Alexander proceeded to besiege Gaza. The governor of the city, Betis,⁴⁴ a man of impeccable loyalty to his king, had to defend walls of vast compass with a small garrison. [8] After appraising the site, Alexander ordered shafts to be driven into the earth which, being light and easily dug, lent itself to underground operations (a result of the large sand deposits left by the sea, which was close by, and the fact that there were no rocks and stones to hinder excavation). [9] He began the work in an area out of sight of the townspeople and had towers moved up to the walls to divert their attention from it. But the ground was also ill-suited to moving towers because the subsiding sand would retard the wheels. This caused the flooring in the towers to shatter and resulted in many men sustaining wounds without being able to retaliate; for they were exhausted by the effort of moving the towers back, which was as difficult as moving them forward.

[10] So the retreat was signalled. The next day Alexander ordered the city walls to be encircled by his troops, and at sunrise, before moving up his army, he offered a traditional sacrifice, asking for the help of the gods. [11] By chance, a crow which was flying past dropped a clod it was carrying in its claws. Hitting the king on the head, the clod disintegrated and the earth dropped in pieces from him. The crow meanwhile took up a position on the nearest siege-tower. The tower had been smeared with pitch and sulphur; the bird's wings stuck to this and after unsuccessfully attempting to fly off it was caught by some bystanders. [12] The incident appeared to deserve consultation with a soothsayer (and Alexander was not untainted by superstition). Aristander, the prophet who commanded the greatest credibility, declared that while the omen did indeed predict that the city would be destroyed, there was also danger that Alexander would sustain injury, so his advice was that

the king should take no initiative that day. [13] Despite his annoyance that this city was all that stood in the way of secure entry into Egypt, Alexander nonetheless deferred to the prophet and signalled a retreat.

This gave encouragement to the besieged, who now made a sortie from the gate to attack the retreating Macedonians, believing that the enemy's indecision represented an opportunity for themselves. [14] In fact, they began the battle with more bravado than determination, for when they saw the Macedonians facing about they came to a sudden halt. By now the noise of the engagement had reached the king, who came to the front line, dismissing from his mind the danger of which he had been forewarned – though in deference to his friends' pleas he did put on his cuirass, which he rarely wore. [15] Catching sight of him, a certain Arab, who was a soldier of Darius, attempted an exploit too great for his fortune. He covered his sword with his shield and threw himself before the king's knees, pretending to be a deserter. Alexander told the suppliant to rise and ordered that he should be received among his men. [16] The barbarian, however, swiftly transferred the sword to his right hand and lunged at the king's neck. Alexander avoided the blow by a slight movement to the side, and with his sword lopped off the barbarian's hand which had missed its mark, thus ridding himself, he thought, of the peril foretold for that day. [17] But in my opinion fate cannot be circumvented. While Alexander fought courageously in the front rank he was hit by an arrow which passed through his cuirass and stuck in his shoulder, from which it was extracted by Philip, his doctor. [18] Blood began to gush from the wound, to the alarm of all present, for the cuirass prevented them from seeing how deeply the weapon had penetrated. As for Alexander, he did not even lose colour; he ordered the bleeding to be staunched and the wound bandaged. [19] For a long time he remained on his feet before the standards, either concealing or mastering his pain, until the blood which had shortly before been suppressed by the application of a dressing began to flow more copiously and the wound, painless while still warm, swelled up as the blood cooled. [20] He began to faint, his knees buckled, and the men next to him caught him and took him back to camp. Betis, believing him dead, headed back to the city, exulting in his victory.

[21] Before his wound was properly healed, Alexander raised a mound to the level of the city's fortifications and had several tunnels dug beneath the walls. [22] The townspeople for their part built a new defence-work as high as the old walls, but even that could not reach the height of the towers set on the Macedonian mound and so the interior of the city was exposed to enemy projectiles. [23] What finally spelt disaster for the city was the undermining of the city wall: it collapsed and the enemy entered the breach. Alexander himself led the advance troops and, as he approached somewhat recklessly, he was struck on the leg with a rock. [24] He supported himself with his spear and, though the scab had still not formed on his first wound, kept fighting in the front line, goaded also by his anger at having received

two wounds in besieging that particular city. [25] Betis, after a well-fought battle, was exhausted by his many wounds and deserted by his men; nevertheless, he fought on with unflagging determination, though his arms were slippery with blood, his own as much as the enemy's. [26] But when he was attacked by weapons from every direction ...[45]

Betis was brought before the young king, who was elated with haughty satisfaction, although he generally admired courage even in an enemy. 'You shall not have the death you wanted,' he said. 'Instead you can expect to suffer whatever torment can be devised against a prisoner.' [27] Betis gave Alexander a look that was not just fearless, but downright defiant, and uttered not a word in reply to his threats. [28] 'Do you see his obstinate silence?' said Alexander. 'Has he knelt to me? Has he uttered one word of entreaty? But I shall overcome his silence: at the very least I shall punctuate it with groans.' [29] Alexander's anger turned to fury, his recent successes already suggesting to his mind foreign modes of behaviour. Thongs were passed through Betis' ankles while he still breathed, and he was tied to a chariot. Then Alexander's horses dragged him around the city while the king gloated at having followed the example of his ancestor Achilles in punishing his enemy.[46]

[30] Some 10,000 Persians and Arabs fell at Gaza, but for the Macedonians too it was no bloodless victory.[47] Indeed, the siege is celebrated not so much because of the city's fame as because Alexander's life was twice imperilled there. In his haste to reach Egypt Alexander now dispatched Amyntas[48] to Macedonia with ten triremes to levy new recruits, [31] for even in successful engagements there was attrition to the troops, and the king felt less confidence in soldiers drawn from the conquered races than in those from home.

7

[1] The Egyptians had long been opposed to the power of the Persians, believing that their rule had been avaricious and arrogant, and Alexander's prospective arrival had inspired them to hope, for they had gladly welcomed even Amyntas,[49] coming as a deserter with power that had no firm basis. [2] Consequently a huge crowd had gathered at Pelusium, the point at which Alexander seemed likely to enter Egypt; and in fact he arrived in that area of the country now called 'Alexander's Camp' six days after moving his troops from Gaza. [3] He then ordered his infantry to head for Pelusium, and he himself sailed up the Nile with a select troop of light-armed soldiers. The Persians had been thoroughly shaken by the Egyptian uprising and they did not dare to await his arrival. [4] Alexander was now not far from Memphis, command of which had been left to Darius' lieutenant, Mazaces.[50] Mazaces surrendered to him all the gold he had – more than 800 talents – and all the royal furniture. [5] From Memphis Alexander sailed upstream and penetrated into the interior of Egypt where, after settling administrative

matters without tampering with Egyptian traditions, he decided to visit the oracle of Jupiter Ammon.[51] [6] The journey that had to be made could scarcely be managed even by a small band of soldiers lightly armed: land and sky lack moisture; the sands lie flat and barren, and when they are seared by the blazing sun the ground swelters and burns the feet and the heat is intolerable. [7] Apart from the high temperatures and dryness of the terrain one also has to contend with the tenacious quality of the sand which, because of its depth and the fact that it gives way to the tread, is difficult to negotiate on foot.

[8] The Egyptians, in fact, exaggerated these difficulties, but Alexander was nevertheless goaded by an overwhelming desire to visit the temple of Jupiter – dissatisfied with elevation on the mortal level, he either considered, or wanted others to believe, that Jupiter was his ancestor.[52] [9] So he sailed downstream to Lake Mareotis with the men he had decided to take with him, and there ambassadors from Cyrene brought him gifts, asking for peace and requesting that he visit their cities.[53] Alexander accepted the gifts, concluded treaties with them, and resumed his proposed journey. [10] The first and second day the difficulties seemed bearable, for they had yet to reach the vast stretches of naked desert, though even now the earth was barren and lifeless. [11] However, when plains covered with deep sand appeared, it was as if they were entering a vast sea and their eyes vainly looked for land – [12] no tree was to be seen, not a trace of cultivated soil. They had also run out of water, which had been carried in skins by camels, and in the arid soil and burning sand not a drop was to be found. [13] The sun had also parched everything, and their throats were dry and burned, when suddenly – whether it was a gift of the gods or pure chance – clouds shrouded the sky and hid the sun, providing enormous relief for them, exhausted as they were by the heat, even despite the absence of water. [14] In fact, though, high winds now showered down generous quantities of rain, of which each man collected his own supply, some of them, wild with thirst, attempting to catch it with gaping mouths.

[15] After four days in the desert wastes, they found themselves not far from the site of the oracle. Here a number of crows met the column, flying ahead of the front standards at a slow pace, occasionally settling on the ground, when the column's advance was relatively slow, and then again taking off as if they were going ahead to show the way.[54] [16] At last the Macedonians reached the area consecrated to the god which, incredibly, located though it is among the desert wastes, is so well screened on all sides by encircling tree branches that the rays of the sun barely penetrate the shade, and its woods are sustained by a wealth of fresh-water springs. [17] The climate, too, is amazingly temperate, with the mildness of springtime, providing a healthy atmosphere through all the seasons of the year. [18] Next to the shrine to the east are the nearest Ethiopian tribes; to the south they face Arab peoples called Trogodytes, whose territory extends right to the Red Sea; [19] to the west live other Ethiopians called Simui; and to the north are

the Nasamones, a tribe of the Syrtes who make a living by looting ships (they haunt the shore-line and their knowledge of the shallows enables them to seize vessels stranded by the tide).

[20] The people who inhabit the wooded area are called Hammonii; they live in scattered huts, and regard the centre of the wood, which is encircled by three walls, as a citadel. [21] The first rampart surrounded the old palace of their kings; behind the second lived their wives, children and concubines, and the oracle of the god is also in this area; the outermost fortifications were the homes of the palace attendants and bodyguards.[55] [22] There is also a second wood of Ammon with a fountain called 'The Water of the Sun' at its centre. At sunrise it runs lukewarm, and yet at midday, despite the inordinate heat, it is cold, warming up towards evening and growing boiling hot at midnight. Then, as dawn approaches, it loses much of its nocturnal heat until at daybreak it drops back to its original lukewarm temperature.[56] [23] The image worshipped as divine does not have the appearance commonly accorded deities by artists; it most resembles a navel and is composed of an emerald and other jewels. [24] When an oracular response is sought, priests[57] carry this along in a gilded boat from which a large number of silver cups hang on both sides, and married and unmarried women follow singing in traditional fashion some artless song by which they believe an infallible answer is elicited from Jupiter.

[25] On this occasion, as the king approached, he was addressed as 'son' by the oldest of the priests, who claimed that this title was bestowed on him by his father Jupiter. Forgetting his mortal state, Alexander said he accepted and acknowledged the title, [26] and he proceeded to ask whether he was fated to rule over the entire world. The priest, who was as ready as anyone else to flatter him, answered that he was going to rule over all the earth. [27] After this Alexander went on to inquire whether his father's murderers had all received their punishment. The priest's answer was that no harm could come to his father from anybody's wrongdoing, but that as far as Philip was concerned all had paid the penalty; and he added that he would remain undefeated until he went to join the gods. [28] Alexander thereupon offered sacrifice, presented gifts both to the priests and to the god, and also allowed his friends to consult Jupiter on their own account. Their only question was whether the god authorized their according divine honours to their king, and this, too, so the priest replied, would be agreeable to Jupiter.

[29] Someone making a sound and honest judgement of the oracle's reliability might well have found these responses disingenuous, but fortune generally makes those whom she has compelled to put their trust in her alone more thirsty for glory than capable of coping with it. [30] So Alexander did not just permit but actually ordered the title 'Jupiter's son' to be accorded to himself, and while he wanted such a title to add lustre to his achievements he really detracted from them. [31] Furthermore, although it is true that the Macedonians were accustomed to monarchy, they lived in the shadow of

liberty more than other races, and so they rejected his pretensions to immortality with greater obstinacy than was good either for themselves or their king. [32] But we shall return to these matters at the appropriate time; for the present I shall proceed with my narrative.

8

[1] Returning from the shrine of Ammon, Alexander came to Lake Mareotis, not far from the island of Pharos. After an examination of the area's natural features he had at first decided to locate a new city on the island itself, [2] but it then became apparent that it had not the capacity for a large settlement, and so he chose for his city the present site of Alexandria (which draws its name from its founder). Taking in all the land between the lake and the sea he marked out an eighty-stade circuit for the walls, and left men to supervise construction of the city.⁵⁸ He then set out for Memphis, [3] for the desire had come over him (understandable, indeed, but ill-timed) to visit not just the Egyptian interior but Ethiopia as well. In his longing to explore antiquities, the famous palace of Memnon and Tithonus was drawing him almost beyond the boundaries of the sun.

[4] But the war facing him – much the larger burden of which still remained – had eliminated all opportunity for leisurely travel. He gave charge of Egypt to Aeschylus the Rhodian and Peucestes the Macedonian, allotting them 4,000 infantry to garrison the country, and he ordered Polemon to police the mouths of the Nile, giving him thirty triremes for the job. [5] Appollonius was put in charge of the part of Africa adjoining Egypt, and Cleomenes was to exact taxes from that part of Africa and from Egypt. By ordering people to migrate from neighbouring cities to Alexandria, Alexander provided the new city with a large population. [6] There is a report that,⁵⁹ after the king had completed the Macedonian custom of marking out the circular boundary for the future city-walls with barley-meal, flocks of birds flew down and fed on the barley. Many regarded this as an unfavourable omen, but the verdict of the seers was that the city would have a large immigrant population and would provide the means of livelihood to many countries.⁶⁰

[7] While Alexander was sailing downstream, Parmenion's son Hector, a young man in the very prime of his youth who was especially dear to Alexander, wanted to catch up with him, and boarded a small vessel along with a complement of men exceeding the boat's capacity. [8] The boat sank, abandoning to the water all those aboard. Hector struggled with the current for a long time, and although his sodden clothes and tight-fitting shoes were an impediment to his swimming, he still managed to reach the bank in a half-dead condition. He was exhausted, and as soon as he was able to take breath – panic and his peril having repressed his respiration – he expired, with none there to give him attention, since the others had emerged from the water

on the opposite bank. [9] Grief at losing him struck Alexander deeply; he recovered the body and buried it with a magnificent funeral.[61]

This grief was further deepened by news of the death of Andromachus, whom he had put in command of Syria: the Samaritans had burned him alive. [10] Alexander marched with all possible speed to avenge his murder, and on his arrival the perpetrators of the heinous crime were surrendered to him. [11] He appointed Memnon[62] to replace Andromachus, executed the murderers of the former governor, and handed over to their own subjects a number of local rulers, including Aristonicus and Ersilaus of Methymna,[63] whom they tortured and put to death for their crimes. [12] Next he heard embassies from Athens, Rhodes and Chios. The Athenians congratulated him on his victory and begged that the Greek captives should be restored to their own people, while the Rhodians and Chians lodged complaints about the garrisons imposed on them. [13] Their requests seemed reasonable and were all granted. Moreover, as a reward for their exceptional loyalty to him, Alexander reimbursed the people of Mitylene for their war expenses and also added a large area to their territories. [14] Furthermore, appropriate honours were accorded the kings of Cyprus who had defected to him from Darius and sent him a fleet during his assault on Tyre. [15] Amphoterus, the admiral of the fleet, was then sent to liberate Crete, most of which was occupied by both Persian and Spartan armies; and he was especially ordered to rid the sea of pirate fleets, since it had been at the mercy of buccaneers while the two kings were locked in war with each other.[64] [16] After settling these matters Alexander dedicated a gold mixing bowl and thirty cups to Hercules of Tyre and then, pressing on against Darius, had orders given for a march to the Euphrates.

9

[1] When Darius learned that his enemy had turned aside from Egypt into Africa, he wondered whether he should halt in the area of Mesopotamia or make for the interior of his kingdom, for there was no doubt that he could more effectively get the outlying tribes to prosecute the war with vigour if he were there in person, whereas he was now finding it difficult to rouse them through his satraps. [2] Then a report circulated from reliable sources that Alexander intended to pursue him in full force into any area he went and so, well aware of the energy of his adversary, he ordered all the forces coming to his aid from distant nations to muster in Babylonia. After the Bactrians, Scythians and Indians had assembled, forces of the other peoples also arrived to support him. [3] However, since his army was half as large again as it had been in Cilicia, many were without weapons, and procuring these became the highest priority. For the cavalry and their mounts there were protective coverings made of interconnected iron plates; those whom Darius had previously provided only with javelins were now also issued shields and swords;

[4] and herds of horses to be broken in were distributed among the infantry-men, so that his cavalry would be stronger than before. Next came what he believed would strike abject terror into his enemy – 200 chariots armed with scythes, an armament exclusive to those races. [5] From the end of the chariot-pole projected iron-tipped spears, and to the cross-beam on each side they had fixed three sword-blades. Between the wheel-spokes a number of spikes projected outwards, and then scythes were fixed to the wheel-rims, some directed upwards and others pointing down to the ground, their purpose being to cut down anything in the way of the galloping horses.[65]

[6] With his army so ordered and equipped, Darius moved his troops from Babylon, keeping the famous river Tigris on his right while the Euphrates covered his left. His army filled the Mesopotamian plains. [7] He then crossed the Tigris, and on hearing that his enemy was not far distant he sent his cavalry-commander Satropates[66] ahead with 1,000 picked men, while his general Mazaeus was allocated 6,000 others to stop the enemy crossing the river. [8] Mazaeus was also instructed to lay waste and burn the area Alexander was approaching, for Darius believed that as his enemy possessed nothing but what they gained by looting, they could be starved into sub-mission, while he himself had lines of supply both overland and by the Tigris.

[9] He had now reached Arbela, a village which his own disastrous defeat was to make famous.[67] Storing most of his supplies and baggage here, he then bridged the river Lycus and spent five days, as he had previously done at the Euphrates, taking his army across. [10] From there he advanced some eighty stades to pitch camp at a second river, named the Boumelus.[68] The area was suitable for deploying his forces: it was a wide-open plain suitable for riding on, without even a ground covering of shrubs or low bushes, and one could get an unimpeded view even of things a long way off. So Darius gave orders for protrusions in the flat land to be levelled and any higher ground to be completely flattened.

[11] The Macedonians estimated the number of Darius' troops as accurately as could be done at a distance, but they had great difficulty convincing Alexander that after so many thousands had been massacred Darius had reconstituted an even greater force. [12] Alexander, however, was a man who paid no attention to any danger, especially superior numbers, and eleven days later he arrived at the Euphrates. He bridged the river, ordering the cavalry to cross first and the phalanx after them, while Mazaeus, who had swiftly appeared with his 6,000 cavalry to check his crossing, did not dare expose himself to danger.

[13] Alexander gave his men a few days off, not for rest but to build up their morale, and then began a vigorous pursuit of his enemy. He was afraid Darius would make for the interior of his kingdom and would have to be followed through vast stretches of completely desolate land that would furnish no supplies. [14] Three days later, skirting Armenia, he penetrated to the Tigris. The whole area beyond the river was still smoking from recent fires, for

Mazaeus was putting the torch to all the ground he covered, just like an enemy invader. [15] Since the daylight was dimmed by dark blankets of smoke, Alexander at first halted for fear of an ambush, but when advance scouts reported that all was safe, he sent a few cavalrymen ahead to attempt a crossing of the river. At the start the water level reached the top part of the horses' chests; then, at mid-channel, it came up to their necks, [16] and it is a fact that no other eastern river moves with such violence, receiving as it does the waters of many torrents and actually sweeping rocks along. It is from the swiftness of its flow that it has its name, because in Persian *tigris* means 'arrow'.[69]

[17] The infantry was in effect split into two wings flanked by cavalry. Holding their weapons above their heads, they had little difficulty in reaching mid-stream, [18] and the king was the first of the infantry to emerge from the water to the bank. Since his voice could not be heard, he used his hand to point out the shallow spots, but maintaining their balance was almost impossible for the men because at one moment they would lose their footing on the slippery rocks and at another they would be swept off their feet by the speed of the current. [19] Those carrying packs on their shoulders encountered particular difficulty for, since they were unable to keep their balance, their awkward loads would sweep them away into the swift whirlpools; and as they all struggled to keep up with their lost spoils, they found they had a greater struggle against each other than against the river, while the heaps of baggage floating in various places knocked many off their feet. [20] The king told them to be content with holding on to their weapons, that he would make good all other losses, but advice could not be taken nor commands obeyed because his words were drowned by the panic and the general shouting as the men struggled with one another. [21] Finally they came out at a point where the current was slower and revealed some shallow water, and nothing was lost but a few pieces of baggage.

[22] The army could have been annihilated if anyone had had the courage to seize victory at this juncture, but the king's unceasing good fortune kept the enemy at bay. It was this, too, which had enabled him to cross the Granicus while thousands of cavalry and infantry stood on the far bank, and to defeat an enemy of massive numerical superiority in the narrow passes of Cilicia. [23] His recklessness, his predominant characteristic, might be underestimated because the question whether or not he had acted precipitously never had to be asked. If Mazaeus had attacked the Macedonians as they crossed, he would no doubt have defeated them while they were in disorder, but he began to ride towards them only when they were on the bank and already under arms. [24] He had sent only 1,000 cavalry ahead, and so Alexander, discovering and then scorning their small numbers, ordered Ariston, the commander of the Paeonian cavalry, to charge them at full gallop. [25] The cavalry, and especially Ariston, distinguished themselves in that day's engagement. Ariston aimed his spear straight at the throat of the

Persian cavalry commander, Satropates, ran him through, and then followed him as he fled through the thick of the enemy, hurled him from his horse and decapitated him as he struggled. The head he brought back and, to loud applause, laid before the king's feet.

10

[1] Alexander encamped there for two days and had marching orders proclaimed for the third, [2] but at about the first watch there was an eclipse of the moon.[70] First the moon lost its usual brightness, and then became suffused with a blood-red colour which caused a general dimness in the light it shed. Right on the brink of a decisive battle the men were already in a state of anxiety, and this now struck them with a deep religious awe which precipitated a kind of panic. [3] They complained that the gods opposed their being taken to the ends of the earth, that now rivers forbade them access, heavenly bodies did not maintain their erstwhile brightness, and they were met everywhere by desolation and desert. The blood of thousands was paying for the grandiose plans of one man who despised his country, disowned his father Philip, and had deluded ideas about aspiring to heaven.[71]

[4] Mutiny was but a step away when, unperturbed by all this, Alexander summoned a full meeting of his generals and officers in his tent and ordered the Egyptian seers (whom he believed to possess expert knowledge of the sky and the stars) to give their opinion. [5] They were well aware that the annual cycle follows a pattern of changes, that the moon is eclipsed when it passes behind the earth or is blocked by the sun, but they did not give this explanation, which they themselves knew, to the common soldiers. [6] Instead, they declared that the sun represented the Greeks and the moon the Persians, and that an eclipse of the moon predicted disaster and slaughter for those nations. They then listed examples from history of Persian kings whom a lunar eclipse had demonstrated to have fought without divine approval. [7] Nothing exercises greater control over the masses than superstition. Usually ungovernable, cruel and capricious, when they are gripped by superstition they obey prophets more readily than their generals. Thus the dissemination of the Egyptians' responses restored hope and confidence to the dispirited soldiers. [8] The king felt he should exploit this surge of confidence, and at the second watch he moved camp, keeping the Tigris on his right and the so-called Gordyaean Mountains on his left.

[9] He had begun the march when just before dawn scouts brought news that Darius was approaching, so he drew up his troops, arranged his line of battle, and advanced at the head of his army. [10] But it proved to be only some Persian stragglers, about 1,000 strong, who had appeared to be a great army, for when the truth cannot be ascertained fear magnifies falsehoods. [11] On learning this the king took a few of his men and overtook the Persian column, now retreating to the main body, killing some and capturing others.

He also sent ahead some cavalry on a scouting mission, with further orders to extinguish the fires lit in the villages by the Persians; [12] for, as they withdrew, they had hastily set roof-tops and stacks of corn alight, and though the flames had caught the top portions they had not yet reached the bottom. [13] The cavalry extinguished the fires and discovered large quantities of grain, and they also began to find themselves well supplied with other commodities. This in itself generated enthusiasm in the soldiers for pursuing the enemy; for since the Persians were burning and ravaging the land, haste was imperative to prevent everything being consumed before they arrived. [14] Thus what had been done through necessity now became policy. Mazaeus, who previously could take his time burning the villages, now had to be content with making good his escape, and what he left behind to his enemy was mostly undamaged. [15] Alexander had now heard that Darius was no more than 150 stades away and so, having as he did a surfeit of provisions, he halted for four days in the same place.

[16] A letter from Darius was then intercepted in which he tried to suborn the Greek soldiers to murder or betray Alexander. The king wondered whether he should read it aloud in a general assembly since he had sufficient confidence in the good-will and loyalty of the Greeks, [17] but Parmenion deterred him by declaring that such promises as Darius made should not reach the soldiers' ears; for Alexander was vulnerable even if only one man were a traitor, and avarice recognized nothing as a crime. Alexander followed this advice and struck camp.

[18] On the journey one of the captive eunuchs attached to Darius' wife announced to Alexander that her health was failing and that she was scarcely breathing. [19] Exhausted by the unremitting hardships of the journey and her dejected state of mind, she had collapsed in the arms of her mother-in-law and unmarried daughters, and later she died. [20] News of her death was brought to Alexander by a second messenger. The king might have received news of his own mother's demise: with many groans, and tears such as Darius might have shed welling up in his eyes, he entered the tent in which Darius' mother was now sitting beside the corpse. [21] The sight of her prostrate on the ground brought him fresh sorrow. This new misfortune had reminded Darius' mother of her earlier ones; she had taken the grown-up girls to her bosom, a great consolation for the grief they shared, though she should have been consoling them. [22] Before her stood her little grandson, all the more to be pitied because he was not yet aware of the disaster in which he had a greater share than anyone.[72]

[23] One would have thought that Alexander's tears were being shed among his own relatives and that he was in need of receiving consolation rather than giving it. He took no food, and accorded every honour to the funeral ceremony, which was celebrated in traditional Persian fashion, thus showing himself truly worthy of the great reputation which he still enjoys for clemency and self-discipline. [24] He had seen the queen only once, on the day

of her capture, when he had gone to see not her but Darius' mother, and her outstanding beauty had inspired in him not lust but behaviour redounding to his glory.

[25] In the general grief and alarm Tyriotes,[73] one of the eunuchs who had attended the queen, slipped out of a gate which was not heavily guarded because it faced away from the enemy. Arriving at Darius' camp, he was received by the guards and taken to the king's tent groaning and tearing his clothes. [26] The sight of Tyriotes upset Darius, who now expected all kinds of bad news and did not know what to fear most. 'Your expression,' he said, 'indicates some great disaster, but see to it that you do not spare the ears of an unfortunate man. I have learned to live with unhappiness, and often the knowledge of one's fate is a source of consolation in misfortune. [27] You are not going to tell me, are you, what I most suspect and fear to put into words – that members of my family have been violated, something which would be worse than any kind of torture for me and, I think, for them?' [28] 'No, by no means,' replied Tyriotes. 'Whatever respect can be accorded to queens by their subjects was also given them by the victorious king. The truth is, your wife died a short time ago.'

[29] At this not only groans but wailing could be heard throughout the camp. Darius had no doubt that his wife had been put to death for refusing to accept indecent advances, and in a frenzy of grief he shouted out: 'Alexander, what is the great crime I have committed against you? Which of your relations did I kill that my cruelty should merit such punishment? Your hatred of me is unprovoked, but even supposing the war you have started is just, should you have fought it with women?' [30] Tyriotes swore by the gods of his country that no violence had been offered the queen, that Alexander had actually lamented her death and wept as much as Darius was doing then, [31] but these declarations served only to revive an anxious suspicion in the mind of the adoring husband, who inferred that Alexander's grief for a captive must have derived from his having had sexual relations with her. [32] Accordingly, keeping only Tyriotes back and dismissing everybody else, he said to him (without tears now but with a sigh): 'Tyriotes, do you see that lies will not do? The instruments of torture will soon be here, but for heaven's sake don't wait for them if you have any regard for your king. Surely he did not dare to do ... what I want to know yet fear to ask ... he being a young man and her master?' [33] Tyriotes offered to undergo torture, calling the gods to witness that the queen had been treated with propriety and respect. [34] Finally, accepting the truth of the eunuch's words, Darius covered his head and wept for a long time. Then, with tears still streaming from his eyes, he uncovered his face and held his hands up to the sky. 'Gods of my country,' he said, 'before all else make firm my rule; but my next prayer, if my career is at an end, is that Asia find no other ruler than this just enemy, this merciful victor.'[74]

11

[1] Consequently, although after his two failures to gain peace Darius had been focusing entirely on a military solution, he was so overwhelmed by his adversary's restraint that he sent ten ambassadors, his principal 'kinsmen', to carry fresh overtures of peace to Alexander. The latter called a council and had the deputation brought in. [2] 'Darius,' said the eldest, 'has in no way been compelled to petition you a third time for a peace-treaty; it is your fairmindedness and your restraint that has prompted him to do so. [3] We have not felt that his mother, wife and children are prisoners, apart from their being separated from him. You protect the virtue of his surviving relatives just like a father; you accord them the title 'your highness' and permit them to retain the majesty of their former status. [4] The expression I see on your face is similar to that on Darius' when we were sent by him, but he mourns a wife, you a foe. Were you not now delayed by the supervision of her funeral you would at this time be standing in battle-formation. Is it surprising that Darius seeks peace from someone who shows such kindness? What need is there for war when the enmity between the parties is eliminated? [5] Formerly he designated the river Halys, the boundary of Lydia, as the limit of your rule, but he now offers everything between the Hellespont and the Euphrates as dowry for the daughter he gives you in marriage. [6] Keep in your possession his son Ochus as guarantee of his word regarding the peace-terms, but return his mother and the two unmarried daughters – in return for the three he requests that you accept 30,000 talents of gold. [7] I should not tell you now, were I not aware of your moderation, that this is an occasion on which you should not just grant peace but actually seize it yourself. [8] Reflect on how much land you have left behind you and consider how much you have ahead. An oversized empire is fraught with danger because it is difficult to keep secure what one cannot control. Can you see how ships of excessive weight are unmanageable? I rather think the reason why Darius has lost so much is that an excess of possessions invites great losses. [9] Some things are easier to win than to protect – how much easier, indeed, our hands find grasping things than holding them! The death of Darius' wife may also make you realize that your clemency can achieve less now than it did before.'

[10] Alexander ordered the deputation to leave the tent and then put the matter to his council, but for a long while none dared express an opinion because they did not know the king's feelings in the matter. [11] Finally Parmenion stated that his previous recommendation had been that Alexander should return the captives from Damascus for a ransom, since a large sum of money could have been raised for them, whereas guarding them kept many brave Macedonian soldiers busy. [12] Now too, he said, it was his firm opinion that Alexander should take 30,000 talents of gold in exchange for one old woman and two girls who merely retarded the army's progress. [13] A rich kingdom could be acquired by negotiation and without combat, and

no one had ever possessed those lands between the Hister[75] and the Euphrates which were bounded by such distant limits. Alexander should turn his attention back to Macedonia rather than onward to Bactra and India.

[14] Alexander was displeased with Parmenion's words, and said when he finished: 'Yes, I too would prefer money to military glory if I were Parmenion. As it is, I am Alexander. I am not worried about lack of money and I am aware that I am not a merchant but a king. [15] I have nothing to sell and I certainly refuse to peddle my fortune. If we do decide the prisoners should be returned, we shall do the honourable thing and make a gift of them instead of charging a price.'[76] [16] He then brought in the Persian deputation and replied as follows: 'Tell Darius that my acts of clemency and generosity arose from no desire to be his friend but from my natural inclinations. [17] I do not make war on prisoners and women; my antagonist must be armed. [18] Now were he suing for peace in good faith I would perhaps consider granting it, but since in fact he writes letters to incite my soldiers to betray me and tries to bribe my friends to assassinate me, I must pursue him to the end – not as a legitimate enemy but as a poisoning murderer. Accepting the peace-terms you bring makes him victor. [19] He generously gives me the land beyond the Euphrates. That demonstrates that you have forgotten where it is that you are talking to me – I am already across the Euphrates and my camp stands beyond the boundary of the land he generously promises me as dowry! Drive me out of here so that I may know that what you are leaving me is really yours. [20] In the same spirit of generosity he offers me the hand of his daughter, whom I know to be the intended bride of one of his vassals. A great honour he does me if he prefers me to Mazaeus as a son-in-law![77] [21] Go, tell your king that what he has lost and what he still possesses both remain the prizes of war. It is war that will determine the boundaries of our respective empires and each shall have what the fortunes of tomorrow assign to us.'

[22] The ambassadors replied that since Alexander was intent on war, he was being honest in not deceiving them with false hopes of peace. They asked to be sent back to their king as soon as possible, since he too needed to prepare for hostilities, and after they were dismissed they reported to Darius that a battle was imminent.

12

[1] Darius immediately dispatched an advance unit of 3,000 horse under Mazaeus to secure the roads the enemy would take. [2] Alexander, on the completion of the last rites for Darius' wife, left all the more cumbersome appendages to his army in the fortified camp under a small garrison and hastened to meet the enemy. [3] He had split his infantry into two bodies, giving cavalry cover to the flanks on both sides, and the column was followed by the baggage. [4] Then he sent ahead Menidas and 200 horse with orders to determine Darius' whereabouts, but since Mazaeus had taken up a position

close by, Menidas did not dare advance beyond him, reporting to Alexander that he had heard nothing but the noise of men and the neighing of horses. [5] On sighting the scouting party in the distance, Mazaeus also pulled back to the Persian camp with news of the approach of the enemy, and Darius, who wanted to settle the issue in the open plains, accordingly ordered his men to arms and drew up his battle-line.

[6] On the left wing were about 1,000 Bactrian horse, the same number of Dahae and 4,000 Arachosians and Susians. These were followed by 100 scythed chariots, next to which stood Bessus with 8,000 horse, also Bactrian. [7] Two thousand Massagetae completed the cavalry detachment. Alongside these Darius had added the infantry contingents of several races, not indiscriminately mixed but with each contingent attached to the cavalry of its respective race. Then came Persians, Mardians and Sogdians led by Ariobarzanes and Orontobates. [8] These two commanded units of the force, but supreme command rested with Orsines, who was descended from one of the seven Persians and also traced his line back to the renowned King Cyrus.[78] [9] These were followed by other tribes unfamiliar even to their own allies, and then came Phradates with a mighty column of Caspii at the head of fifty chariots. Behind the chariots were Indians and other residents of the Red Sea area, who provided nominal rather than real support, [10] and this detachment was completed by another group of scythed chariots to which Darius had attached his foreign troops. These were followed by the so-called lesser Armenians, themselves followed by Babylonians, and after both came the Belitae and the inhabitants of the Cossaean Mountains. [11] Next were the Gortuae, a people of Euboean stock who had once returned with the Medes[79] and now had degenerated to total ignorance of their original culture. Next to them Darius had positioned the Phrygians and the Cataonians, and the entire column was brought up by the Parthyaei, a race living in the areas which are today populated by Parthians who emigrated from Scythia. Such was the appearance of the left wing.

[12] The right was composed of people from greater Armenia, Cadusia, Cappadocia, Syria and Media, and these also had fifty scythed chariots. [13] The total for the whole army amounted to 45,000 cavalry and 200,000 infantry.[80] Drawn up as described, they advanced ten stades and when the order was given to halt awaited their enemy under arms.

[14] For no apparent reason alarm permeated Alexander's army. The men were panic-stricken as fear swept imperceptibly through all their breasts. Intermittent flashes in the bright sky, of the type seen on hot summer days, had the appearance of fire; the Macedonians believed that they were flames gleaming in Darius' camp, and that they had negligently advanced among enemy outposts. [15] Now if Mazaeus, who was guarding the road, had struck while they were still panicking, a terrible disaster could have been inflicted on the Macedonians, but in fact he sat inactive on the hill he had occupied, content not to be under attack. [16] Alexander, learning of the

consternation among the troops, ordered that a halt be signalled and his men lay down their arms and rest. He told them the sudden panic was completely unjustified, that the enemy still stood a long way off, [17] so, finally pulling themselves together, they simultaneously recovered their confidence and took up their weapons. Even so Alexander believed that in the circumstances the safest plan was to establish a fortified camp on the spot.

[18] Mazaeus had positioned himself with a select cavalry unit on a high hill overlooking the Macedonian camp, but the next day he returned to Darius, either because he panicked or because his mission had been limited to gathering intelligence. [19] The Macedonians then occupied the hill which he had abandoned, for it was safer than the flat ground and it also afforded a view of the enemy battle-line then being deployed on the plain. [20] But the humid atmosphere in the hills had diffused a mist over the area and, while this did not prevent a general view of the enemy, it did render it impossible to see how their forces were divided and organized. The Persian horde had flooded the plains, and the noise from the myriads of soldiers had filled the ears even of those a long way off.

[21] The king began to have second thoughts and to weigh up Parmenion's recommendation against his own strategy – all too late, for they had reached the stage where only victory would allow either army to retire without incurring disaster. [22] Hiding his concern, Alexander therefore ordered the mercenary cavalry from Paeonia to advance. [23] As was observed above, he had already drawn out the phalanx into two bodies, each of which received cavalry protection. Now the mist began to disperse and the brightening daylight revealed the enemy line. The Macedonians, eager for the fight or else tired of waiting, emitted a thundering war-cry; the Persians replied, and the woods and valleys round about rang with a terrifying noise. [24] Restraining the Macedonians from charging the enemy was no longer possible, but Alexander still thought it preferable to fortify his camp there on the hill, and ordered a rampart to be built. This task was quickly finished and he then withdrew into his tent, from which the whole enemy battle-line could be seen.

13

[1] Now a complete picture of the approaching battle arose before Alexander's eyes. Armour gleamed bright on horses and men; all the enemy's diligent preparations were obvious in the tension of the generals as they rode up and down the ranks, [2] and there were a number of other insignificant things, too, that had caused him alarm, already on edge in anticipation as he was: the hubbub of the troops, for instance, horses neighing, weapons flashing here and there. [3] Either in doubt or else wishing to test the mettle of his men, he convened a war-council to ask of them the best course of action. [4] Parmenion, the best tactician of Alexander's generals, was of the opinion that what was required was some ploy rather than pitched battle. The enemy could be

crushed by an attack in the dead of night, he said: they differed among themselves in customs and language, and if thrown into panic by a sudden attack while they were sleeping, how could they form up in the confusion of the night? [5] In the daytime, however, the first thing to meet the Macedonians would be the terrifying sight of Scythians and Bactrians with their shaggy faces and long hair, and their enormous stature – and soldiers, he said, were more prone to groundless and irrational fears than to those having some justification. [6] Furthermore, the huge enemy hordes could surround the smaller Macedonian force, for the battle was being fought not in the narrow and difficult passes of Cilicia but on a flat open plain.

[7] Support for Parmenion was almost unanimous and Polyperchon[81] felt that victory certainly lay in such a plan. [8] It was on the latter that Alexander fixed his gaze, since he was reluctant to criticize Parmenion a second time after recently reproaching him more severely than he had intended. 'The subterfuge you recommend to me is characteristic of brigands and thieves,' he said, 'for deception is their only aim. [9] But I shall not permit Darius' absence, narrow terrain or a furtive attack at night to detract from my glory. My decision is to attack in broad daylight. I prefer to live to regret my bad luck than to be ashamed of my victory. [10] There is also a further consideration: I have it on good authority that the Persians are posting watches and remaining under arms, so that even catching them off-guard would be impossible. So, prepare for combat!' Thus inciting them for battle, he sent them off to refresh themselves.

[11] Darius guessed that his enemy would do just what Parmenion had recommended to Alexander, and had therefore issued orders for the horses to stand bridled, for a large section of the army to remain under arms, and for the watches to be kept more strictly than usual. Consequently his whole camp was lit up with fires. [12] Accompanied by his generals and kinsmen, he did the rounds of the troops personally as they stood under arms, and while doing so he called upon the Sun, Mithras, and the sacred, eternal fire to inspire the men with a courage in keeping with their glory of old and their forefathers' monumental achievements. [13] If the human mind had any ability to divine heaven's aid, he said, the gods were certainly on their side. They had recently struck a sudden panic into the Macedonians, he added, who were still in a state of distracted fear and throwing down their arms – thus were the tutelary gods of the Persian empire exacting from these madmen a well-deserved punishment. [14] Nor was their leader any saner than they: like a beast of the wild he was totally preoccupied with the plunder he was seeking and charging straight into the trap set before it.

Among the Macedonians there was similar apprehension. They passed the night in fear, as if the engagement were appointed for that time. [15] Never more alarmed, Alexander had Aristander summoned to offer vows and prayers. Dressed in white and with sacred boughs in his hand and his head veiled, Aristander led the king in prayers as the latter solicited the aid of

Jupiter and Minerva Victoria. [16] The sacrificial rite completed, Alexander returned to his tent to rest for the remainder of the night. But sleep and relaxation were both impossible: at one moment he considered sending his troops down from the ridge against the Persian right wing, at the next meeting his enemy head on, and then again he would weigh the merits of veering his army towards their left wing. [17] Finally, anxiety brought physical fatigue, and he fell into a deeper sleep than usual.

At daybreak, after assembling to receive their orders, the officers were amazed at the silence surrounding the king's tent.[82] [18] Usually Alexander would send for them, and sometimes there were sharp words for the dawdlers. Now they were astonished that at this crucial juncture he had failed to wake up, and they believed that he was not sleeping but shrinking with fear. [19] None of his bodyguards dared enter the tent, however, even though the moment of decision was at hand, and the men could neither take up arms nor proceed to their ranks without Alexander's command. [20] After a long delay Parmenion took it upon himself to tell the men to eat, and only when it was imperative for them to move out of camp did he finally enter Alexander's tent. After calling him by name several times, he woke him with his hand since he could not with his voice. [21] 'It's broad daylight,' he said. 'The enemy have brought up their army in battle-formation, while your men are still not under arms, waiting for your command. What has happened to your old alertness? Usually you are waking up the watch!' [22] Alexander replied, 'Do you think I could have fallen asleep before easing my mind of the worries that kept me from resting?' Then he ordered the trumpet-signal to be given for battle. And when Parmenion kept on expressing surprise at the king's claim to have enjoyed a carefree sleep, [23] 'It's not a bit surprising,' he said. 'When Darius was burning the land, destroying villages and ruining our food supplies, I was beside myself with despair. [24] But now that he is preparing to decide the issue in battle, what do I have to fear? Good heavens, he has answered my prayers! But you shall receive the justification for my strategy later. All of you go now to your respective commands. I shall join you presently and tell you what I want done.' [25] It was very rarely he wore his cuirass (and then it was at the request of his friends rather than through fear of the danger that had to be faced), but on this occasion he took up this piece of armour before proceeding to the men. Never had they seen their king in such high spirits, and from his undaunted expression they inferred a sure hope of victory on his part.

[26] Alexander had the rampart levelled; then he ordered his troops to march out and drew up his line of battle. On the right wing was placed the cavalry unit called the *agema*, which was led by Clitus.[83] To him Alexander also adjoined Philotas' cavalry squadrons, stationing on his flank the other cavalry commanders, [27] with Meleager's squadron[84] standing last and the phalanx following it. Behind the phalanx were the *Argyraspids*[85] under the command of Parmenion's son, Nicanor. [28] In reserve stood Coenus and his

detachment, and behind him were placed the Orestae and Lyncestae,[86] followed by Polyperchon and then the foreign troops.[87] The latter, in the absence of their general Amyntas, were commanded by Philip, son of Balacrus;[88] only recently had they entered an alliance with the Macedonians. This was how the right wing appeared.

[29] On the left Craterus was in charge of the Peloponnesian cavalry[89] – to which were attached squadrons of Achaeans, Locrians, and Malians – and the rear was brought up by the Thessalian horse under Philip. The infantry-line was given protection by the cavalry. Such was the appearance of the left wing in front.

[30] To prevent an encircling movement by the numerically superior Persians, Alexander had enclosed his rear with a strong division, and he also strengthened his wings with reserves which he faced to the side, not the front, so that the wings would be ready for combat in the event of the enemy trying to encircle them. [31] In this position were the Agrianes, under the command of Attalus, along with the Cretan archers. The rearmost ranks Alexander faced away from the front, so that the circular formation could give protection to the whole army, and here were placed the Illyrians plus the mercenary troops. Alexander had also stationed the Thracian light-armed troops in this position. [32] So flexible was the battle-formation which he arranged that the troops standing at the rear to prevent an encircling movement could still wheel round and be transferred to the front. Consequently the flanks received as much protection as the front line, and the rear as much as the flanks.

[33] After making these troop dispositions Alexander gave instructions to the men. If the Persians shouted as they released their scythed chariots, they were to open ranks and receive the charge in silence – Alexander was sure that meeting no resistance the chariots would pass through the ranks without inflicting damage – but if the enemy did not shout they should strike panic into them with war-cries and stab their frightened horses in the belly from both sides. [34] The wing-commanders were instructed to extend the wings so that they would not be surrounded by being too compressed, but not to weaken the rear in doing so. [35] Baggage and prisoners, including Darius' mother and children, who were kept under guard, he positioned close to the army on high ground, leaving a small force in charge of them. As on other occasions, Parmenion was given command of the left wing; Alexander himself took his position on the right.

[36] Before they were within javelin-range a certain deserter, Bion, came galloping at full speed to Alexander with a report that Darius had dug iron spikes into the ground at the point at which he thought his enemy was going to unleash his cavalry, and he had clearly marked the spot to enable his own men to avoid the trap.[90] [37] Alexander had a guard put on the deserter and assembled his generals. Revealing what had been reported, he warned them to avoid the designated area and to inform the horsemen of the danger.

[38] Alexander's exhortations were inaudible to the troops since the

noise of the two armies prevented them hearing, but he was visible to them all as he rode up and down the ranks addressing the officers and anyone close to him.

14

[1] They had traversed so many lands, Alexander told them, hoping for the victory for which they were now to fight, and this one decisive struggle was all that remained. He reminded them of the river Granicus, of the mountains of Cilicia, of Syria and Egypt conquered while they passed through them – these, he said, should do much to bolster their confidence and inspire them to win glory. [2] The Persians had been overtaken while running away, and would now fight only because escape was impossible. For two days they had been rooted to the spot, pale with fear and burdened under the weight of their own arms, and the clearest sign of their desperation was their burning of their own cities and agricultural land, by which they admitted that anything they did not spoil belonged to their foes. [3] He told them not to harbour unwarranted fears of the names of unknown races: it had no bearing on the outcome of the war who were called Scythians, who Cadusians. The very fact that they were unknown meant they had no worth: [4] brave men were never unknown, while cowards who had been ferreted out of their hiding-places contributed nothing beyond their names. As for the Macedonians, their courage had ensured that there was no place on earth unaware of their quality.

[5] Look at the disorganized army of the Persians, he told them – some armed only with a javelin, others with stones in slings, only a few with regular weapons. There were more men *standing* on the Persian side, but more were going to be *fighting* on the Macedonian. [6] Nor was he asking them to do battle valiantly without providing the rest with an example of bravery himself – he was going to fight before the front standards. All his scars were testimony to his courage, every one of them a decoration for his body, and his men knew that he was almost alone in refusing to share in their collective spoils, that instead he used the rewards of victory to enrich and honour them. [7] His words, he continued, were addressed to brave soldiers, but to men not in that category he would have said this, that they had reached the point from which flight was impossible. They had covered such huge distances and had all those rivers and mountains as a barrier behind them; now they had to fight their way back to their country and their homes. Such were his words to inspire the officers and the soldiers closest to him.

[8] Darius was positioned on the left wing, closely surrounded by a large contingent of his men, hand-picked from his cavalry and infantry. He had been eyeing with contempt his enemy's meagre numbers, believing that Alexander's line had been weakened by his extension of the wings. [9] Seated high in his chariot, he turned his eyes right and left to the troops around him,

and stretching out his arms towards them he said: 'Recently you were the masters of lands washed by the ocean on one side and bounded by the Hellespont on the other. But now it is not glory for which you must fight but for survival, and for what you prize more than survival: freedom. [10] Today will consolidate or terminate an empire greater than any age has seen. At the Granicus we fought the enemy with but a fraction of our strength; defeated in Cilicia we could retreat into Syria, with the Tigris and Euphrates providing strong defences for our empire. [11] We have now reached the point from which, if we are defeated, there is no opportunity even for flight. To our rear everything lies depleted by this long war: cities without inhabitants, land without men to till it. Our wives and children are following the army and are easy pickings for our enemy, unless we place our bodies as a barrier before these, our nearest and dearest.

[12] 'As for my own responsibilities, I have put together an army that plains almost limitless in extent can barely hold: I equipped it with horses and arms, provided supplies enough to meet the needs of such huge numbers, and chose a site in which our line of battle could be fully deployed. [13] The rest is up to you. Just have the courage to win, and pay no attention to your enemy's reputation – that flimsiest of weapons against men of fortitude. The quality you have hitherto feared as bravery is merely recklessness; once its initial impetus is gone, it wilts like certain creatures which have spent their stings. [14] These plains have exposed their numerical inferiority which was hidden by the mountains of Cilicia, and you can see their thin ranks, their elongated wings, their centre weak and depleted. Why, the rearmost ranks he has faced away from us – already starting their flight! They can be trampled down by our horses even if I send nothing but our scythed chariots against them! [15] Winning this battle will mean winning the war. For there is no chance of escape for them either: the Euphrates and Tigris keep them boxed in on both sides.

[16] 'Furthermore, the advantages they formerly enjoyed are now reversed. We have the light and mobile army, theirs is heavy with loot. So we shall slaughter them as they are caught in the toils of the plunder taken from us, and the cause of our victory will also be its reward. [17] Any of you alarmed by the reputation of that nation must realize that Macedonian weapons are over there, but not Macedonian bodies. We have spilt a lot of blood on both sides, and the loss is always more serious when numbers are small. [18] And no matter how great he may appear to the cowardly and timid, Alexander is but a single creature, and a headstrong and crazy one, if you place any trust in my judgement – his success thus far is due more to our fear than his courage. [19] But nothing can last without the support of reason. Though good luck may seem to be on your side, eventually it fails to compensate for recklessness. Besides, everything is of short duration and subject to change – and fortune's blessings are never unmixed. [20] The gods brought the Persian empire through a successful history of 230 years to the absolute

peak of power. Perhaps it will now prove that they have so arranged its fate as to give it a good shock rather than to shatter it, in order to remind us of human frailty which is too often forgotten in times of prosperity. [21] A short time ago we were actually invading the Greeks; now in our own home we are trying to repel an invasion, and we in our turn are storm-tossed by changing fortune. Obviously one nation cannot contain this empire since we both aspire to it in turns.

[22] 'But, even if we had no hope, the emergency of our situation should spur us on. Our backs are to the wall. My mother, my two daughters, Ochus,[91] heir to this empire from birth, princes who are children of royal birth, your generals – these Alexander has in chains like criminals. Unless I can hope for something from you, I am for the most part a prisoner myself. Rescue my own flesh and blood from captivity; restore to me my loved ones, those for whom you are willing to die: my mother and my children – for my wife I have already lost in that prison of his. [23] You must believe that these are all stretching out their hands to you, imploring the aid of our country's gods and calling for your assistance, pity, loyalty, to free them from their shackles, from slavery and a life dependent on others' whims. Do you believe that they can endure to be slaves to people whom they would find it beneath their dignity to rule over?

[24] 'I see the enemy line on the move, but the closer I come to the critical moment the more aware I must feel of the inadequacy of my words. I beg you by our country's gods, by the eternal fire carried before us on the altars, by the bright sun that rises within my empire's boundaries, by the eternal memory of Cyrus who first wrested the empire from the Medes and Lydians and transferred it to Persia[92] – deliver the Persian people and its honour from the depths of disgrace. [25] Go forward in high spirits and charged with confidence, to bequeath to your descendants the glory which you inherited from your ancestors. In your right hands you bear freedom, might and hope for the future. He who despises death escapes it, but death overtakes every coward. [26] I myself ride in my carriage not just because it is our tradition, but also to be seen by my men, and I will welcome it if you emulate my performance, whether my example be one of bravery or cowardice.'

15

[1] Alexander meanwhile gave the order for his line to advance at an angle;[93] he wanted to circumvent the trap revealed to him by the deserter and also to encounter Darius, who commanded a wing. [2] Darius, too, turned his line at the same angle, telling Bessus to order the Massagetan cavalry to charge Alexander's left wing on the flank. [3] Before him Darius kept his scythed chariots which, on a signal, he released *en masse* against the enemy. The charioteers charged at full speed in order to increase the Macedonian casualties by taking them by surprise, [4] and as a result some were killed by the spears that projected well beyond the chariot-poles and others

dismembered by the scythes set on either side. It was no gradual withdrawal that the Macedonians made but a disordered flight, breaking their ranks. [5] Mazaeus struck further panic into them in their consternation by ordering 1,000 cavalry to ride around and plunder the enemy's baggage, thinking the captives who were kept under guard with the baggage would break free when they saw their own people coming.

[6] Parmenion, on the left wing, had not missed this, and he swiftly dispatched Polydamas to advise the king of the danger and ask for his orders. [7] After hearing Polydamas, Alexander said: 'Go, tell Parmenion that if we win this battle we shall not only recover our own baggage but also capture the enemy's. [8] So there is no reason for him to weaken the line in any way. Rather his actions should do credit to me and my father, Philip – let him ignore the loss of the baggage and fight courageously.'[94]

[9] Meanwhile the Persians had been pillaging the baggage. With most of the guards killed, the prisoners broke free, grabbed whatever they came upon that would serve as weapons and, joining forces with their countrymen's cavalry, attacked the Macedonians who were now exposed to danger on two fronts.

[10] Sisigambis' attendants joyfully brought her the message that Darius had won, that the enemy had been routed with great loss of life, and that they had finally even been stripped of their baggage. For the attendants believed the fortunes of the battle to be the same everywhere, and that the victorious Persians had split up to plunder. [11] Though the other prisoners urged her to end her sorrow, Sisigambis retained her former demeanour: not a word left her lips and there was no change in her colour or expression. She sat motionless – afraid, I think, of aggravating fortune by expressing joy prematurely – so that people looking at her could not decide what she would prefer the outcome to be.[95]

[12] In the meantime Alexander's cavalry-commander, Menidas, had arrived with a few squadrons to help defend the baggage (whether this was his own idea or done on Alexander's orders is unknown), but he was unable to hold out against an attack from the Cadusians and Scythians. With no real attempt at fighting he retreated to the king, less a champion of the baggage than a witness to its loss! [13] Indignation had already crushed Alexander's resolve, and he was afraid – not without justification – that concern with recovering the baggage might draw his men from the fight. Accordingly he sent Aretes, the leader of the lancers called the *Sarisophoroi*, against the Scythians.

[14] Meanwhile, after causing havoc in Alexander's front lines, the chariots had now charged the phalanx, and the Macedonians received the charge with a firm resolve, permitting them to penetrate to the middle of the column. [15] Their formation resembled a rampart; after creating an unbroken line of spears, they stabbed the flanks of the horses from both sides as they charged recklessly ahead. Then they began to surround the chariots

and to throw the fighters out of them. [16] Horses and charioteers fell in huge numbers, covering the battlefield. The charioteers could not control the terrified animals which, frequently tossing their necks, had not only thrown off their yokes but also overturned the chariots, and wounded horses were trying to drag along dead ones, unable to stay in one place in their panic and yet too weak to go forward. [17] Even so a few chariots escaped to the back line, inflicting a pitiful death on those they encountered. The ground was littered with the severed limbs of soldiers and, as there was no pain while the wounds were still warm, the men did not in fact drop their weapons, despite the mutilation and their weakness, until they dropped dead from loss of blood.

[18] In the meantime Aretes had killed the leader of the Scythians who were looting the baggage. When they panicked he put greater pressure on them, until on Darius' orders some Bactrians appeared to change the fortunes of the battle. Many Macedonians were crushed in the first onslaught, and more fled back to Alexander. [19] Then, raising a shout as victors do, the Persians made a ferocious rush at their enemy in the belief that they had been crushed in every quarter. Alexander reproached and encouraged his terrified men, single-handedly reviving the flagging battle and then, their confidence finally restored, he ordered them to charge the enemy.

[20] The Persian line was thinner on the right wing, since it was from there that the Bactrians had withdrawn to attack the baggage; Alexander advanced on these weakened ranks, causing great loss of Persian life with his attack. [21] The Persians on the left wing, however, positioned themselves to his rear as he fought, hoping that he could be boxed in. He would have faced terrible danger, pinned in the middle as he was, had not the Agrianian cavalry[96] come galloping to assault the Persians surrounding the king and forced them to turn towards them by cutting into their rear. There was confusion on both sides. Alexander had Persians before and behind him, [22] and those putting pressure on his rear were themselves under attack from the Agrianian cavalry; the Bactrians on their return from looting the enemy baggage could not form up again; and at the same time several detachments broken off from the main body were fighting wherever chance had brought them into contact.

[23] With the main bodies almost together the two kings spurred on their men to battle. There were more Persian dead now, and the number of wounded on each side was about equal. Darius was riding in his chariot, Alexander on horseback, [24] and both had a guard of handpicked men who had no regard for their own lives – with their king lost they had neither the desire nor the opportunity to reach safety, and each man thought it a noble fate to meet his end before the eyes of his king. [25] But the men facing the greatest danger were, in fact, those given the best protection, since each soldier sought for himself the glory of killing the enemy king.

[26] Now whether their eyes were deceiving them or they really did sight it, Alexander's guards believed they saw an eagle gently hovering just above

the king's head, frightened neither by the clash of arms nor the groans of the dying, and for a long time it was observed around Alexander's horse, apparently hanging in the air rather than flying. [27] At all events the prophet Aristander, dressed in white and with a laurel-branch in his right hand, kept pointing out to the soldiers, who were preoccupied with the fight, the bird which he claimed was an infallible omen of victory. [28] The men who had been terrified moments before were now fired with tremendous enthusiasm and confidence for the fight, especially after Darius' charioteer who, seated before the king, drove the horses, was run through by a spear. Persians and Macedonians alike were convinced that it was the king who had been killed, [29] and though the fortunes of the battle were, in fact, still even, Darius' 'kinsmen' and squires caused consternation almost throughout the battlefield with their mournful wailing and wild shouts and groans. The left wing was routed, abandoning the king's chariot which the close-formed ranks on the right received into the middle of their column.

[30] It is said that Darius drew his scimitar and considered avoiding ignominious flight by an honourable death, but highly visible as he was in his chariot, he felt ashamed to abandon his forces when they were not all committed to leaving the battle. [31] While he wavered between hope and despair, the Persians gradually began to give ground and broke ranks.

Alexander changed horses – he had exhausted several – and began to stab at the faces of the Persians still resisting and at the backs of those who ran. [32] It was no longer a battle but a massacre, and Darius also turned his chariot in flight. The victor kept hard on the heels of his fleeing enemy, but a dust-cloud rising into the air obstructed visibility; [33] the Macedonians wandered around like people in the dark, converging only when they recognized a voice or heard a signal. But they could hear the sound of reins time and time again lashing the chariot-horses, the only trace they had of the fleeing king.

16

[1] On the left wing, which (as stated above) was under Parmenion's command, the fortunes of the battle were very different for both sides. Mazaeus exerted pressure on the Macedonian cavalry squadrons by making a violent attack on them with all his horse [2] and, having superior numbers, he had already begun to encircle their infantry when Parmenion ordered some riders to report their critical position to Alexander and tell him that flight was inevitable unless help came quickly. [3] The king had already covered a great distance in his pursuit of the fleeing Persians when the bad news from Parmenion arrived. His mounted men were told to pull up their horses and the infantry column came to a halt. Alexander was furious that victory was being snatched out of his hands and that Darius was more successful in flight than he himself was in pursuit.

[4] Meanwhile news of his king's defeat had reached Mazaeus, and he, alarmed at his side's misfortunes, began to relax his pressure on the dispirited Macedonians despite his superior strength. Although ignorant of why the attack had lost its impetus, Parmenion quickly seized the chance of victory. [5] He had the Thessalian cavalry summoned to him and said: 'Do you see how after making a furious attack on us a moment ago those men are retreating in sudden panic? It must be that our king's good fortune has brought victory for us too. The battlefield is completely covered with Persian dead. [6] What are you waiting for? Aren't you a match even for soldiers in flight?'

His words rang true, and fresh hope revived their drooping spirits. At a gallop they charged their enemy, who started to give ground not just gradually but swiftly, and all that prevented this being termed a flight was the fact that the Persians had not yet turned their backs. However, since he was ignorant of how the king was faring on the right wing, Parmenion checked his men [7] and, given the opportunity to retreat, Mazaeus crossed the Tigris – not taking a direct route but a longer, circuitous one which accordingly offered greater safety – and entered Babylon with the remnants of the defeated army.

[8] With only a few accompanying him in his flight, Darius had sped to the river Lycus.[97] After crossing he considered breaking down the bridge, since reports kept arriving that the enemy would soon be there, but he could see that destroying the bridge would make the thousands of his men who had not yet reached the river an easy prey for his enemy. [9] We have it on good authority that, as he went off leaving the bridge intact, he declared that he would rather leave a road to those chasing him than take one away from the Persian fugitives. Darius himself, covering a huge distance in his flight, reached Arbela about midnight.

[10] Could anyone comprehend or express in words all those tricks of fortune – the wholesale slaughter of officers and troops, the flight of the conquered, the disasters that befell them individually and collectively? Into a single day fortune packed the events almost of an entire era! [11] Some of the fugitives took the shortest route open to them; others made for woods off the beaten track and for paths unknown to their pursuers. Horse and foot were leaderless and indiscriminately mixed – armed and unarmed, wounded and uninjured were all together. [12] Then, as fear replaced compassion, those unable to keep up were abandoned amid mutual lamentation. Thirst parched the throats of the tired and wounded especially, and throughout the countryside they threw themselves down at all the streams, trying to gulp the flowing water with open mouths. [13] The water became muddy and they swallowed it greedily, so that their stomachs quickly became distended under the weight of the mud, and after their limbs had now become relaxed and devoid of feeling, their sensations were aroused again by fresh wounds when the enemy overtook them. [14] Finding the closest streams occupied, some

had gone further off the paths to get any trickle of water hidden anywhere, and no pool was too remote or dried up to escape the thirsty Persians. [15] From the villages closest to the road old men and women could be heard wailing, still calling on Darius as their king in the barbarian fashion.

[16] As observed above, Alexander had checked his men's swift pursuit and had now reached the river Lycus. Here the huge numbers of fleeing Persians had overloaded the bridge. Several had hurled themselves into the river as the enemy bore down on them, and because of the weight of their armour and their exhaustion from running and fighting they were sucked down into the eddies. [17] As the waves of fugitives kept piling blindly on to each other, there was no longer room for them not only on the bridge but even in the river; for when men have begun to panic, their fear is only for the original cause of their terror.

[18] Alexander's men urged him not to abandon pursuit of the enemy who were making good their escape. However, he gave as a pretext for stopping the fact that their weapons were blunt, their hands were tired, they were physically exhausted from so much running, and nightfall was fast approaching; [19] though his real motive was concern for the left wing which he believed to be still in combat. He decided, therefore, to go back there to lend assistance to his men. He had already turned back when the horsemen sent by Parmenion brought news of victory in that quarter as well. [20] In fact, however, the greatest danger Alexander faced that day was when he was leading his troops back to camp. With him was a small group of men who were out of formation and flushed with victory, believing that the enemy had been entirely routed or killed in battle. [21] Suddenly there appeared before him a column of Persian cavalry. At first the Persians halted. Then, seeing the small Macedonian numbers, they unleashed some squadrons against them. [22] Alexander advanced at the head of his men and, concealing the extent of the danger rather than ignoring it, he was not betrayed by the good luck he always enjoyed in times of crisis. [23] He transfixed with his spear the Persian cavalry commander whose eagerness for the fight led him to charge incautiously and, when he was unhorsed, Alexander ran the next man through and several others with the same weapon. [24] His friends also fell on them while they were in confusion. But the Persians did not die without inflicting casualties – the entire armies did not clash with greater violence than these makeshift companies. [25] Finally, when in the fading light running seemed safer than fighting, the Persians split into groups and made their escape and the king, after surviving this extraordinary danger, led his men back to camp in safety.

[26] Forty thousand Persians fell, according to the victor's reckoning, while fewer than 300 Macedonians were lost.[98] [27] This victory, however, the king owed more to his own heroism than to good luck: it was his courage, not the location as before, that won the day. [28] He deployed the troops with consummate skill and he himself fought with great valour. The loss of the

packs and baggage he very wisely disregarded because he saw that the battle would decide the entire issue and, while the outcome of the fight was still undecided, he conducted himself like a conqueror. [29] Subsequently, when he had struck panic into his enemy and routed them, his pursuit of the fugitives was characterized by caution rather than eagerness, which is scarcely to be believed in view of his impulsive nature. [30] Had he continued to pursue the retreating Persians while part of his army was still in combat, he would either have suffered defeat through his own misjudgement or else have owed his victory to another's courage. If he had been intimidated by the large numbers of Persian cavalry that met him, he would in his hour of victory have faced a disgraceful flight or a wretched death.

[31] His officers must not be cheated of their praise either. The wounds each received are testimony to their valour. [32] Hephaestion suffered a spear-wound in the arm; Perdiccas, Coenus and Menidas were almost killed by arrows.[99] [33] If we want a fair assessment of the Macedonians of the day we shall have to say that the king truly deserved such subjects and his subjects so great a king.

BOOK FIVE

I

[1] As for contemporaneous operations in Greece or in Illyria and Thrace under the supreme command of Alexander, if I intended to record these in accordance with strict chronology, I should be obliged to interrupt my Asian narrative. [2] There seems to be good reason for presenting this as a whole, especially up to Darius' flight and death, and for preserving in my work the coherence of the actual events.[1] I shall therefore begin with the occurrences connected with the battle at Arbela.

[3] Around midnight Darius had reached Arbela, where fortune had also driven most of his friends and soldiers in their flight. [4] Calling these to a meeting, he told them that he was sure Alexander's destination would be the most important cities and land which was replete in all commodities, for he and his men were after rich and easily-acquired plunder. [5] In the circumstances, said Darius, this would prove to be his own salvation, since he was going to head for the wastelands with a light-armed detachment – the remote parts of his empire being still intact, he would have no difficulty in raising from them forces for the war. [6] As far as he was concerned, the rapacious Macedonians could seize his treasure and glut themselves with the gold for which they had so long hungered – for they were soon going to be his prey. Experience had taught him that expensive furniture, concubines and troops of eunuchs were no more than deadweight and encumbrances, and with these in tow Alexander would be handicapped by the very things which had previously given him victory.

[7] To everyone his words seemed full of despair. They recognized that the rich city of Babylon was being surrendered to the victor, who would soon occupy Susa and then the other gems of Darius' kingdom which had occasioned the war. [8] Darius went on to say that in times of adversity the course to follow was not that which sounded impressive but the one that was practical: war was fought with iron not gold, and by men not city-buildings, and all things come to the man with the weapons. This, he said, was how his ancestors had, after initial reverses, swiftly recovered their old prosperity. [9] Thus the men's confidence was restored – or else they obeyed his orders without accepting his reasoning – and he crossed the boundaries of Media.[2]

[10] Shortly afterwards Arbela with its store of royal furniture and rich

treasure surrendered to Alexander. There were 4,000 talents plus clothing of great value for, as was noted above, the entire army's wealth had been accumulated in that spot.[3] [11] Then an outbreak of disease spread by the stench of corpses lying all over the fields prompted him to move camp prematurely. As they went on Media was to the left and to the right was Arabia,[4] an area famous for its rich perfumes. [12] In the country between the Tigris and the Euphrates the route lies through the plains, and here the soil is so rich and fertile that animals are purportedly kept from grazing in case they die from over-eating. The fertility results from the moisture which comes from the two rivers, and virtually all the soil in the area oozes water because of the underground springs fed by them. [13] The rivers themselves rise in the Armenian mountains and, after separating from each other in a large arc, they continue on their courses, a measurement of 2,500 stades being given by those who have recorded the widest point between the two in the area of the Armenian mountains. [14] After they have begun to cut through Median and Gordyaean territory, they gradually converge, the spit of land left between them becoming narrower as they progress, [15] and they are closest in the plains the inhabitants call 'Mesopotamia' (for it is enclosed by the rivers on both sides). After this they pass through Babylonian territory and discharge into the Red Sea.[5]

[16] After three days' march Alexander arrived at Mennis.[6] Here there is a cave with a stream that pours forth huge quantities of bitumen,[7] so much in fact that it is generally recognized that the massive walls of Babylon were cemented with bitumen from it.

[17] Moving on to Babylon Alexander was met by Mazaeus, who had taken refuge in the city after the battle. He came as a suppliant with his grown-up children to surrender himself and the city. Alexander was pleased at his coming, for besieging so well-fortified a city would have been an arduous task [18] and, besides, since he was an eminent man and a good soldier who had also won distinction in the recent battle, Mazaeus' example was likely to induce the others to surrender. Accordingly Alexander gave him and his children a courteous welcome. [19] Nevertheless, he put himself at the head of his column, which he formed into a square, and ordered his men to advance into the city as if they were going into battle.

A large number of the Babylonians had taken up a position on the walls, eager to have a view of their new king, but most went out to meet him, [20] including the man in charge of the citadel and royal treasury, Bagophanes. Not to be outdone by Mazaeus in paying his respects to Alexander, Bagophanes had carpeted the whole road with flowers and garlands and set up at intervals on both sides silver altars heaped not just with frankincense but with all manner of perfumes. [21] Following him were his gifts – herds of cattle and horses, and lions, too, and leopards, carried along in cages. [22] Next came the Magi chanting a song in their native fashion, and behind them were the Chaldaeans, then the Babylonians, represented not only by priests but also by musicians equipped with their national instrument. (The role of the latter was to sing the praises of the Persian kings, that of the Chaldaeans to reveal astronomical movements and regular seasonal changes.[8]) [23] At the rear came the Babylonian cavalry, their equipment and that of the horses suggesting extravagance rather than majesty.

Surrounded by an armed guard, the king instructed the townspeople to follow at the rear of his infantry; he then entered the city on a chariot and went into the palace. The next day he made an inspection of Darius' furniture and all his treasure, [24] but it was the city itself, with its beauty and antiquity, that commanded the attention not only of the king, but of all the Macedonians. And with justification. Founded by Semiramis[9] (not, as most have believed, Belus, whose palace is still to be seen there), [25] its wall is constructed of small baked bricks and is cemented together with bitumen. The wall is thirty-two feet wide and it is said that two chariots meeting on it can safely pass each other. [26] Its height is fifty cubits and its towers stand ten feet higher again.[10] The circumference of the whole work is 365 stades, each stade, according to the traditional account, completed in a single day.[11] The buildings of the city are not contiguous to the walls but are about a juger's[12] width from them, [27] and even the city area is not completely built up – the inhabited sector covers only eighty stades – nor do the buildings form a continuous mass, presumably because scattering them in different locations seemed safer. The rest of the land is sown and cultivated so that, in the event of attack from outside, the besieged could be supplied with produce from the soil of the city itself.

[28] The Euphrates passes through the city, its flow confined by great embankments. Large as these structures are, behind all of them are huge pits sunk deep in the ground to take in the water of the river when in spate, for when its level has exceeded the top of the embankment, the flood would sweep away city buildings if there were no drain-shafts and cisterns to siphon it off. [29] These are constructed of baked brick, the entire work cemented with bitumen.

The two parts of the city are connected by a stone bridge over the river, and this is also reckoned among the wonders of the East.[13] For the Euphrates carries along with it a thick layer of mud and, even after digging this out to a great depth to lay the foundations, one can hardly find a solid base for supporting a structure. [30] Moreover, there is a continuous build-up of sand which gathers around the piles supporting the bridge, impeding the flow of water, and this constriction makes the water smash against the bridge with greater violence than if it had an unimpeded passage.

[31] The Babylonians also have a citadel twenty stades in circumference. The foundations of its turrets are sunk thirty feet into the ground and the fortifications rise eighty feet above it at the highest point.[14] [32] On its summit are the hanging gardens, a wonder celebrated by the fables of the Greeks.[15] They are as high as the top of the walls and owe their charm to the shade

of many tall trees. [33] The columns supporting the whole edifice are built of rock, and on top of them is a flat surface of squared stones strong enough to bear the deep layer of earth placed upon it and the water used for irrigating it. So stout are the trees the structure supports that their trunks are eight cubits thick and their height as much as fifty feet; they bear fruit as abundantly as if they were growing in their natural environment. [34] And although time with its gradual decaying process is as destructive to nature's creations as to man's, even so this edifice survives undamaged, despite being subjected to the pressure of so many tree-roots and the strain of bearing the weight of such a huge forest. It has a substructure of walls twenty feet thick at eleven foot intervals, so that from a distance one has the impression of woods overhanging their native mountains. [35] Tradition has it that it is the work of a Syrian king who ruled from Babylon. He built it out of love for his wife who missed the woods and forests in this flat country and persuaded her husband to imitate nature's beauty with a structure of this kind.[16]

[36] Alexander halted in this city longer than anywhere else, and here he undermined military discipline more than in any other place. The moral corruption there is unparalleled; its ability to stimulate and arouse unbridled passions is incomparable. [37] Parents and husbands permit their children and wives to have sex with strangers, as long as this infamy is paid for. All over the Persian empire kings and their courtiers are fond of parties, and the Babylonians are especially addicted to wine and the excesses that go along with drunkenness. [38] Women attend dinner parties. At first they are decently dressed, then they remove all their top-clothing and by degrees disgrace their respectability until (I beg my readers' pardon for saying it) they finally throw off their most intimate garments. This disgusting conduct is characteristic not only of courtesans but also of married women and young girls, who regard such vile prostitution as 'being sociable'.

[39] After thirty-four days of revelling in such dissipation, that army which had conquered Asia would doubtless have been weakened for any subsequent confrontations, if it had had an adversary. To lessen the effects of the damage, however, it was continually refurbished with reinforcements. [40] Amyntas, the son of Andromenes,[17] brought from Antipater 6,000 Macedonian infantry [41] and 500 cavalry, along with 600 Thracian cavalry and 3,500 infantry, and there had also arrived from the Peloponnese some 4,000 mercenary infantry and 380 cavalry. [42] Amyntas had also brought fifty grown-up sons of Macedonian noblemen to serve as a bodyguard. These act as the king's servants at dinner, bring him[18] his horses when he goes into battle, attend him on the hunt and take their turn on guard before his bedroom door. Such was the upbringing and training of those who were to be great generals and leaders.[19]

[43] Alexander ordered Agathon to take command of the citadel in Babylon with 700 Macedonians and 300 mercenary troops, and left Menes and Apollodorus as governors in charge of Babylonia and Cilicia,[20] giving them

2,000 soldiers and 1,000 talents, and ordering both to hire supplementary troops. [44] On the deserter Mazaeus he conferred the satrapy of Babylon, and he instructed Bagophanes, who had surrendered the citadel, to accompany him. Armenia was assigned to Mithrenes, the man who had betrayed Sardis. [45] From the money surrendered to Alexander at Babylon the Macedonian cavalry were each given 600 denarii while the foreign cavalry received 500, the Macedonian infantry 200 and the others three months' pay.[21]

2

[1] With this business settled, Alexander came into the area known as the satrapy of Sittacene. This is fertile country producing rich quantities of provisions of all kinds, and [2] so he extended his stay. To ensure that his men did not grow idle and lose their spirit, he appointed judges and established prizes of a novel kind for a competition based on military courage – [3] those adjudged to possess the greatest valour would win command of individual units of a thousand men and be called 'chiliarchs'. This was the first time the Macedonian troops had been thus divided numerically, for previously there had been companies of 500, and command of them had not been granted as a prize of valour.[22] [4] A huge crowd of soldiers had gathered to participate in this singular competition, both to testify to each competitor's exploits and to give their verdict on the judges – for it was bound to be known whether the honour attributed to each man was justified or not. [5] The first prize of all went to Atarrhias for his bravery;[23] it was he who had done most to revive the battle at Halicarnassus, when the younger men had given up the fight. Antigenes[24] was judged second, Philotas the Augaean[25] gained third place, and fourth went to Amyntas. After these came Antigonus, then Amyntas Lyncestes, with Theodotus[26] gaining seventh and Hellanicus last place.[27]

[6] To traditional military organization Alexander also introduced several very serviceable innovations. Formerly, cavalrymen were enrolled in separate units according to their nationality, but he now abolished tribal distinctions and gave command of the units to men of his own choosing without regard to race. [7] It was previously his practice in moving camp to give the signal on a trumpet, but the noise and commotion that rose from the ranks generally made a trumpet-blast inaudible, so he set on the general's tent a pole which would be visible from every side, and from this went up a signal all the men would see – flame at night and smoke by day.

[8] Just before Alexander reached Susa, the satrap of that region, Abulites, sent his son to meet him,[28] promising that he would surrender the city – a step he may have taken independently or else on Darius' orders, so that Alexander would be delayed by taking plunder. [9] The king gave the young man a courteous welcome and, using him as a guide, came to the river Choaspis,[29] which reputedly carries fine drinking water. At this point Abulites met him with gifts of a regal opulence, [10] which included dromedaries of

outstanding speed and a dozen elephants imported from India by Darius – now an asset to the Macedonians rather than the deterrent the Persians had hoped, as fortune passed on to the conqueror the resources of the conquered. [11] After entering the town Alexander brought out from the treasury an unbelievable quantity of money – 50,000 talents of silver, not coined but in bullion.[30] [12] A succession of kings had amassed this great wealth over a long period of time for their children and descendants, as they thought, but now a single hour brought it all into the hands of a foreign king.

[13] Alexander now sat on the royal throne, but it was too high for him and so, since his feet could not reach the step at the bottom, one of the royal pages set a table under them. [14] Noticing some distress on the part of a eunuch who had belonged to Darius, the king asked him why he was upset. The eunuch declared that it was from this that Darius used to eat, and he could not withhold his tears at the sight of his consecrated table put to such disrespectful use. [15] The king was struck with shame at his offence against the gods of hospitality and was ordering the table's removal when Philotas said: 'No, your majesty, don't do that. Take this as an omen, too – the table from which your foe ate his banquets has been made a stool for your feet.'[31]

[16] When Alexander was almost at the border of Persia, he handed over to Archelaus the city of Susa with a garrison of 3,000 men, leaving Xenophilus in charge of the citadel and ordering 1,000 old veterans to serve as its garrison. [17] Callicrates was given custody of the treasure and Abulites was restored to the satrapy of the region of Susa. Darius' mother and children he also left in the city. [18] As it happened, Alexander had been sent from Macedonia a present of Macedonian clothes and a large quantity of purple material. Since he showed Sisigambis every mark of respect and his regard for her was that of a son, he ordered these to be given to her along with the women who had made the clothes, and [19] he added the message that, if she liked the clothes, she should train her granddaughters to make them and that he was presenting her with women to teach them to do so.[32] At these words tears came to the queen's eyes, signifying her angry rejection of the gift – for to Persian women nothing is more degrading than working with wool. [20] Those who had taken the gifts brought word that Sisigambis was offended, and Alexander thought the matter warranted some expression of apology and consolation. So he came to her in person and said: 'Mother, these clothes I am wearing are not merely a gift from my sisters, but also their handiwork. I was led into error by our own customs. [21] Please do not take offence at my ignorance. I have, I hope, scrupulously observed what I have discovered of your conventions. [22] I know that among you it is not right for a son to sit down in his mother's presence without her permission, so whenever I have come to you I have remained on my feet until you beckoned me to sit. Often you have wanted to show me respect by prostrating yourself before me but I have forbidden it. And the title due to my dear mother Olympias I give to you.'

3

[1] When he had calmed Sisigambis, Alexander arrived after four days' march at the river Tigris, called Pasitigris by the natives.[33] Rising in the mountains of the Uxians, it rushes down-country for fifty stades in a rocky channel between well-treed banks. [2] Received next by the plains, its course through them is calm enough to make it navigable, and it glides smoothly on for 600 stades over gentle terrain before meeting the Persian sea.[34] [3] Alexander crossed the river and arrived in the country of the Uxians with 9,000 infantry, the Agrianes and 3,000 Greek mercenary archers plus 1,000 Thracians. This area borders on Susa and runs as far as the Persian frontier, leaving only a narrow pass between it and the Susians. [4] The satrap of the area was Medates,[35] who was no political trimmer – he had determined to be loyal to the very end. [5] But men who knew the area informed Alexander of the existence of a secret path over the mountain passes at some distance from the city, and they told him that if he sent a few light-armed men they could emerge from it above the enemy.[36] [6] Since Alexander favoured the idea, these same men were made the guides and Tauron,[37] his lieutenant, was given 1,500 mercenaries and about 1,000 Agrianes with orders to set out on the track after sunset.

[7] Alexander himself broke camp at the third watch and at about daybreak he crossed the defile. He then cut wood to make wickerwork coverings and shelters to give protection from missiles to the men bringing up the siege-towers, and proceeded to besiege the town. [8] The whole terrain was sheer crag, with boulders and stones impeding access, and consequently, since they had to battle with the location as well as the enemy, the Macedonians were flung back with many injuries. Even so they came forward again, for the king had placed himself among the leaders and would ask them if they did not feel embarrassment, men who had reduced so many cities, at failing in a blockade of a small fort with no reputation. [9] As he urged them on, projectiles were directed at him at long range and his men, unable to make him retire, were giving him protection with a tortoise-formation of their shields.[38]

[10] Finally Tauron and his detachment appeared above the citadel, a sight which made the enemy falter and the Macedonians enter the fray with increased vigour. [11] An attack from two fronts was a severe blow for the townspeople, and stemming the enemy assault was impossible. A few were disposed to meet their deaths but more were for taking flight, and a large number retreated to the citadel. From there thirty spokesmen were dispatched to beg for mercy, but the grim reply from Alexander was that no pardon could be given. [12] Accordingly, daunted by the added fear of torture, they sent men to Darius' mother Sisigambis, by a secret path unknown to their enemy, to ask her to use her influence to mollify the king, for they realized that she was esteemed and respected like a mother by Alexander. (In addition, Medates had married her sister's daughter and so was closely related to Darius.) [13]

For a long time Sisigambis rejected the suppliants' pleas, claiming that an entreaty by her on their behalf was inappropriate in view of her circumstances. She added that she was afraid she might overtax the conqueror's indulgence, and that she reflected more often on her present status as captive than her former one as queen. [14] But she finally capitulated and begged Alexander in a letter to excuse her intercession in the matter. She was asking for his pardon for the townspeople, she said, but failing that for pardon for her own entreaties, which were made merely for the life of a friend and relative who was no longer Alexander's enemy but his suppliant.

[15] This one episode can illustrate the king's self-control and clemency at that time. Not only did he pardon Medates but he also gave all the others their freedom with full amnesty, those who surrendered and those taken prisoner alike. He left the town intact and permitted the townspeople to cultivate their lands free of taxes. Had Darius been the victor, his mother could not have gained more from him.[39]

[16] Alexander then added the conquered Uxians to the satrapy of Susiana. After this he split his forces between himself and Parmenion and ordered the latter to advance along the route through the plains, while he himself with some light-armed troops took the mountain chain that runs in an unbroken line into Persia. [17] Laying waste this whole area he entered Persia after two days, and after four the narrow pass they call the Susian gates. This pass Ariobarzanes had occupied with 25,000 infantry.[40] It comprises steep cliffs, precipitous on all sides, on top of which stood the Persians, out of weapon-range, deliberately inactive and giving the impression of being fear-stricken, as they waited for the Macedonian force to enter the narrowest part of the defile. [18] When they saw the Macedonians advancing with no regard for their presence, they began to roll massive rocks down the mountain slopes, and these would frequently rebound from rocks lower down and fall with even greater velocity, crushing not only individuals but entire companies. [19] Stones, shot from slings, and arrows were also showered on them from every direction. But the greatest source of anguish for Alexander's courageous men was not this but their inability to strike back, their being caught and slaughtered like animals in a pit. [20] Anger turned to rage. They grasped at the jutting rocks and, one giving another a lift, kept trying to clamber up to their enemy, but with the hands of many simultaneously pulling at them the rocks would break loose and fall back on the men who had dislodged them. [21] Thus they could neither make a stand nor press ahead, nor even gain protection from a tortoise-formation of shields, because of the vast size of the objects hurled down by the barbarians. Alexander suffered agonies, as much of shame as despondency, at his foolhardiness in stranding his army in the gorge. [22] Till that day he had been unbeaten; none of his undertakings had failed. No harm had come to him entering the ravines of Cilicia, or when the sea had provided him with a new route into Pamphylia.[41] But now his good fortune was arrested, stopped dead, [23] and the only remedy

was to go back the way he had come. And so, signalling the retreat, he ordered the men to leave the pass in close formation with shields interlocked above their heads;[42] and they drew back a distance of thirty stades.[43]

4

[1] Alexander then pitched camp in an area open on every side and, besides giving rational consideration to his next move, he was also prompted by his superstition to summon the soothsayers. [2] But in these circumstances what could even Aristander predict, the soothsayer in whom he had most confidence? So Alexander halted the sacrifices on the grounds that the time was unsuitable, and ordered men with a knowledge of the area to be brought to him. These told him of a way through Media that was safe and open, [3] but the king's conscience would not permit him to leave his men unburied, for by Macedonian convention there is hardly any duty in military life as binding as the burial of one's dead.

Accordingly Alexander ordered the recently captured prisoners to be summoned to him.[44] [4] Among them was one who spoke both Greek and Persian. He told Alexander that he was wasting his time trying to take an army into Persia over the mountain-ridge: the paths through the woods barely afforded passage for one man at a time; everything was overgrown with brush and the intertwining tree-branches produced a continuous forest. [5] Persia, in fact, is enclosed on one side by unbroken mountain chains; the range runs from the Caucasus mountains to the Red Sea (and measures 1,600 stades in length and 170 in width), and where the mountains come to an end they are replaced by another barrier, the sea. [6] Beyond the foothills lies an extensive plain, a fertile stretch of land containing numerous villages and cities. [7] Through the fields the river Araxes[45] brings down the water of a large number of torrents into the Medus, and the latter, making a southerly turn, goes on into the sea as a smaller river than its tributary. [8] No river encourages a greater growth of vegetation: it carpets with flowers whatever it flows past and its banks are covered with plane trees and poplars; seen from a distance these give the impression that the woods on the banks are a continuation of the mountains. For the well-shaded river glides along in a bed cut deep into the soil, and is overhung by hills bearing rich foliage themselves because of the moisture that seeps into their base. [9] No area in all Asia is believed to possess a healthier climate; its temperate weather is due to the unbroken mountain chain on one side, which affords a cover of shade and alleviates the heat, and to the sea's proximity on the other, which provides the land with moderate temperatures.

[10] After this description the prisoner was asked by Alexander whether his information derived from hearsay or personal observation. He replied that he had been a shepherd and had travelled over all the paths in question, and

added that he had been twice captured, once by the Persians in Lycia and the second time by Alexander. [11] The king was put in mind of a prophetic statement made by an oracle – the reply to him during a consultation was that his guide on the road to Persia would be a citizen of Lycia.[46] [12] So he heaped on the captive such promises as the exigencies of the situation and the man's fortune in life demanded, told him to arm himself like a Macedonian and, with a prayer for the success of the venture, instructed him to point the way without regard for its difficulty or steepness. For, said Alexander, he and a few men would win through, unless the prisoner believed that Alexander in his pursuit of glory and undying fame could not go where his own sheep had taken him! [13] At the captive's repeated insistence on the difficulty of the path, especially for men in armour, the king said: 'You can take my word for it; none of the men following you will refuse to go anywhere you lead them.'

[14] Alexander now left Craterus in charge of the camp with his regular troops plus the forces under Meleager's command and 1,000 mounted archers, and instructed him to keep up the routine appearance of the camp, deliberately increasing the number of fires so that the Persians would be led to believe that Alexander himself was in the camp.[47] [15] However, should Ariobarzanes discover that he was coming through by means of the winding mountain paths and attempt to block his passage with a detachment of his troops, then Craterus was to give him some cause for alarm to attract his attention, making him divert his troops to the more imminent danger. [16] But if Alexander stole a march on his enemy and gained possession of the woods, then when Craterus heard the confused uproar of the Persians chasing the king, he was to set out without hesitation on the road from which they had been driven the previous day, for with the enemy's attention focused on Alexander he would find it undefended.

[17] At the third watch Alexander himself set out for the mountain path which had been described to him, his troops silent and not even a trumpet-signal being sounded. The men were lightly armed and under orders to take three days' supplies.[48] [18] But even apart from the impossible crags and precipitous rocks that time and again made them lose their footing, their progress was further impeded by snow-drifts, into which they fell as if into pits and, when their comrades tried to lift them, instead of coming out themselves they would pull in their helpers. [19] Night and the unfamiliar landscape also multiplied their fears, as did the guide, whose loyalty was not above suspicion – if he escaped from his captors, they themselves could be trapped like wild animals. The king's safety and their own depended on the loyalty or the life of a single prisoner. [20] At last they reached the top. The path to Ariobarzanes went off to the right, and at this point Alexander left Philotas, Coenus, Amyntas and Polyperchon with a troop of light-armed men. They were told to advance slowly because their force included horsemen

among the infantry and the soil in the area was very rich and productive of fodder; and they were given some of the captives to act as guides.[49]

[21] Alexander himself took his bodyguard and the squadron called the *agema*[50] and advanced with considerable difficulty along a path which was steep but well-removed from the enemy outposts. [22] It was midday, they were tired and they needed sleep, since they had as much of a journey before them as behind them, though it was not so steep and difficult. [23] Alexander therefore refreshed his men with a meal and some sleep, resuming the march at the second watch. Nothing caused him great difficulty on the journey until the point at which the mountain range gradually sloped down to the more level land, where the road was broken by a huge chasm formed by merging mountain streams. [24] In addition, the tree branches at this point intertwined and clung together to bar their way with a continuous hedge. At this, deep despair descended on them, so deep that they could hardly keep from weeping. [25] The darkness especially terrified them, any stars that were out being hidden from sight by the trees with their unbroken covering of foliage. They were not even left their sense of hearing because the woods were shaken by a wind that smashed the branches together and produced a noise greater than its force would warrant. [26] Finally the long-awaited daylight diminished the terrors exaggerated by the night. The ravine could be circumvented by a short detour, and each man had begun to act as his own guide. [27] They emerged on a high peak from which they could see an enemy outpost. They quickly armed themselves and appeared at the rear of the Persians, who had no fear of such an attack. The few who risked a fight were cut down, [28] and the groans of the dying plus the dismayed expressions of the men who ran back to the main body also prompted the fresh troops to flee even before they tasted the danger themselves. [29] The noise penetrated to the camp commanded by Craterus, who now took out his men to seize the defile in which they had been brought to a halt the day before.[51] [30] At the same time further panic was instilled in the Persians by Philotas, Polyperchon, Amyntas and Coenus, who had been told to take a different route. [31] The Persians were under attack from two directions and Macedonian arms were gleaming all around them, but they put up a memorable fight. To my mind, pressure of circumstances can turn even cowardice into courage, and desperation often provides the basis for hope. [32] Unarmed men grappled with men who were armed, dragging them to the ground by virtue of their bodily weight and stabbing many with their own weapons.

[33] Accompanied by a force of some forty cavalry and 5,000 infantry Ariobarzanes broke through the centre of the Macedonian line, causing great loss of Macedonian and Persian blood, as he hurried to occupy the regional capital, the city of Persepolis. [34] But he was shut out from there by the city garrison and vigorously pursued by the enemy. Renewing the battle, he fell with all those who had fled with him.[16] Craterus also came on the scene, driving on his troops at a rapid pace.

5

[1] Alexander built a fortified camp in the place from which he had driven the enemy troops, for although the complete rout of the Persians had declared him the victor, his progress was impeded by the road, which was broken at several points by deep ditches with steep sides. He was obliged to advance slowly and cautiously, wary now of the treacherous nature of the terrain rather than an enemy ambush. [2] On the road he was brought a letter from Tiridates,[53] guardian of the royal moneys, informing him that at the news of his coming the people in the city wanted to pillage the treasury. Since this had been abandoned, he advised Alexander to make haste to seize it, for the road, though crossed by the Araxes, was an easy one. [3] To none of the king's virtues could I give more justified praise than his speed in action. Leaving his infantry behind, he rode all night and arrived at the Araxes at dawn, with his cavalry who were exhausted by the long journey. [4] He demolished the villages in the vicinity, and with the timber from them he swiftly constructed a bridge on stone piles.[54]

[5] When he was not far from the city, the king was met by a pitiful group of men whose misfortune has few parallels in history. They were Greek captives, some 4,000 in number, whom the Persians had subjected to various kinds of torture.[55] [6] Some had had their feet cut off, some their hands and ears. They had been branded with letters from the Persian alphabet by their captors, who had kept them to amuse themselves over a long period by humiliating them. When the Persians realized that they themselves were now in someone else's power, they had not opposed their wish to meet the king. [7] They looked more like outlandish phantoms than men, with no recognizably human characteristic apart from their voices. Thus they occasioned more tears than they had shed themselves. Individually they had experienced diverse and varied fortunes, and their observers saw afflictions that seemed similar and yet were different, so that it was impossible to determine who was to be pitied most. [8] But when the men cried out that Jupiter, the avenger of the Greeks, had finally opened his eyes, all the soldiers felt they were sharing the unfortunates' torments. Alexander wiped away the tears he had shed and told them to take heart, for they would see their cities and their wives. Then he built a fortified camp two stades from the city.

[9] The Greeks left the camp's circumvallation to consider what particular favour they wanted to ask of the king. Some were for requesting a settlement in Asia, others for returning home. Then, it is said, Euctemon of Cyme addressed them in these words: [10] 'Not long ago we were ashamed to emerge from the darkness of our prison even to ask for help. Do we now desire to parade these injuries of ours before all Greece, as if they provide a pleasing spectacle – injuries for which I'm not sure whether we feel more shame or bitterness? [11] Yet people who hide their distress bear it best, and to those suffering misfortune no homeland is as welcome as solitude and being

allowed to forget their former circumstances. For those who set store by the compassion of those closest to them are unaware of how quickly tears can dry. [12] No one can maintain constant affection for what he finds repulsive, for just as misfortune brings complaints so prosperity brings disdain, and everybody has his own circumstances in mind when he considers someone else's. Were we not sharing misfortune, we should long ago have found each other repulsive – so why is it surprising that the fortunate always seek out those like themselves? [13] Since we have long been dead men, please let us look for a place to bury these mangled bodies of ours. Our return will bring great joy indeed to the wives we married when we were young! And our sons in the prime of their youth and at the peak of their success will of course recognize as their fathers these left-overs from the slave-prison! [14] How many of us are up to covering all that territory, anyway? We are cut off far from Europe in the remotest areas of the East, old men and weak with most of our limbs mutilated. Of course we'll be able to endure what has worn out armed and victorious soldiers! [15] Then there are the wives that chance and our dire situation gave to us as our only comfort after our capture – do we drag them and our small children along with us or do we abandon them? [16] If we come with them no one will want to recognize us. So shall we forthwith abandon those who are at the moment dear to us when it is uncertain that we shall ever see those we seek? No, we should hide among people who became acquainted with us *after* our miseries began.'

So said Euctemon. [17] Taking up the debate for the other side the Athenian Theaetetus said that no decent person would judge those dear to him by physical appearance, especially when their injuries came from an enemy's brutality rather than from nature. The man ashamed of what has happened by accident, he said, deserved everything he got – he entertained a poor opinion of human nature and had no hope for compassion because he would himself deny compassion to another. [18] The gods were offering them what they had never dared to hope for: their homeland, wives, children, and everything else that men prize as much as their lives or face death to regain. [19] Why, he asked, did they not break out of their prison? At home they breathed a different air, saw a different daylight. Their customs, their religious observances, their language were sought even by foreigners; these were theirs from birth, and they were going to relinquish them voluntarily, although all that made their condition pitiful was being forcibly deprived of them! [20] He himself was certainly going to return to hearth and home, and take advantage of the king's great kindness. Some might be held back by feelings for their partners and the children whom their slavery had forced them to recognize, but those who loved their country more than anything else should leave.

[21] A few concurred, but for the rest, habit, more forceful than nature,

prevailed. They agreed that the king should be asked to assign them a place to settle, and [22] 100 spokesmen were appointed for this purpose. Alexander thought they were going to ask for what he himself was thinking of awarding them, and so he said to them: 'I have had pack-animals reserved for your transportation and I have ordered a gift of 1,000 denarii to be given to each of you. When you return to Greece, I shall ensure that, this misfortune of yours apart, nobody can consider his condition in life superior to yours.' [23] Tears welled up and they stared at the ground, daring neither to raise their eyes nor say a word. At last when the king asked the reason for their dejection, Euctemon answered much as he had spoken in the meeting. [24] Alexander was moved to compassion not only for their misfortune but also for their feelings about it. He ordered them each to be given 3,000 denarii, and to this gift were added ten pieces of clothing plus cattle, sheep and seed-corn so that the land assigned to them could be tilled and sown.[56]

6

[1] Alexander called a meeting of his generals the next day. He told them that no city was more hateful to the Greeks than Persepolis, the capital of the old kings of Persia, the city from which troops without number had poured forth, from which first Darius and then Xerxes had waged an unholy war on Europe.[57] To appease the spirits of their forefathers they should wipe it out, he said. [2] By now the Persians had abandoned the town, panic scattering them in various directions, and the king led in the phalanx without delay. Alexander had stormed or accepted the surrender of many cities which were full of royal treasure, but the wealth of this city eclipsed everything in the past. [3] Into it the barbarians had packed the riches of all Persia: mounds of gold and silver, huge quantities of clothing, and furniture which was not functional but ostentatiously ornate. [4] This led to armed fighting among the victors; anyone who had taken richer spoils was seen as an enemy and, since the men could not carry everything that came into their possession, goods were no longer indiscriminately pillaged but subjected to prior appraisal![58] [5] They ripped apart royal robes as each man grabbed a piece for himself, and they hacked to pieces with axes vases that were precious works of art. Nothing was left intact, nothing removed in one piece. Statues were dismembered and individuals dragged away the limbs they had broken off. [6] But cruelty as well as avarice ran amok in the captured city: soldiers laden with gold and silver butchered their captives, now of no worth, and cut down people they came across at random anywhere, people who could previously have won mercy by promising to ransom themselves. [7] Many accordingly anticipated the enemy's violence by suicide, putting on their most expensive clothes and hurling themselves down from the walls with their wives and children. Some had set fire to their homes – something which it seemed the enemy would

soon do anyway – to burn themselves alive along with their families. [8] Eventually Alexander issued orders for his men to keep their hands off the women and their dress.

It is reported that the quantity of money captured here was huge almost beyond belief [9] but, unless we are also going to be sceptical about other matters, we must accept that this city's treasure comprised 120,000 talents.[59] To transport this (for he had decided to take it with him for military expenses), Alexander ordered pack-animals and camels to be brought from Susa and Babylon. [10] In addition to this sum, 6,000 talents came from the capture of Parsagada,[60] a city founded by Cyrus which was surrendered to Alexander by its governor Gobares.

[11] The king ordered Nicarchides to assume charge of the citadel of Persepolis, and left him a garrison of 3,000 Macedonians. Tiridates, who had surrendered the treasure, also retained the rank he had held under Darius.[61] Alexander left there a large section of his army and the baggage, under the command of Parmenion and Craterus, [12] while he himself made for the interior of Persia with 1,000 cavalry and a detachment of light-armed infantry. This was at the time of the Pleiades,[62] and though hindered by heavy rains and almost unbearable weather, he nevertheless pressed on towards his goal.

[13] They had reached a road covered with permanent snow which was frozen hard by the intense cold. The desolation of the terrain and the trackless wilderness terrified the exhausted soldiers, who thought they were looking at the limits of the world. They gazed in astonishment at the total desolation with no sign of human cultivation, and they clamoured to go back before daylight and sky also came to an end. [14] The king refrained from reproaching them for their fear. Instead he jumped from his horse and proceeded to make his way on foot through the snow and hard-packed ice. His friends were ashamed not to follow him, and the feeling spread to his officers, and, finally, the men. The king was the first to clear a way for himself, using an axe to break the ice, and then the others followed his example. [15] Eventually, after journeying through virtually impassable forests, they found the odd trace of human cultivation and flocks of animals wandering here and there. The inhabitants, who lived in scattered huts, had believed that the roads were impassable and that this gave them protection; when they saw the enemy column, they killed those unable to go with them and made for some remote, snow-covered mountains. [16] Subsequently they talked to captives of the Macedonians and this gradually calmed them down. They surrendered to Alexander and were not severely punished.

[17] After ravaging Persian territory and bringing several villages into his power, Alexander reached the Mardians, a bellicose people with a culture very different from other Persians: they dig caves in the mountains to provide shelter for themselves, their wives and their children, and their diet consists of the meat of domesticated or wild animals. [18] Even the women are not

of a milder disposition (as nature usually provides). Their hair sticks out in shaggy bunches, their clothes are worn above the knee, and they bind their foreheads with a sling which serves both as a head-dress and a weapon. [19] But this tribe was also brought low by the momentum of Alexander's good fortune. On the thirtieth day after setting out from Persepolis, he returned to it, [20] and then awarded his friends and the other men gifts proportionate to their individual merit, distributing virtually everything he had taken in the city.

7

[1] Alexander had some great natural gifts: a noble disposition surpassing that of all other monarchs; resolution in the face of danger; speed in undertaking and completing projects; integrity in dealing with those who surrendered and mercy towards prisoners; restraint even in those pleasures which are generally acceptable and widely indulged. But all these were marred by his inexcusable fondness for drink. [2] At the very time that his enemy and rival for imperial power was preparing to resume hostilities, and when the conquered nations, only recently subdued, still had scant respect for his authority, he was attending day-time drinking parties at which women were present[63] – not, indeed, such women as it was a crime to violate, but courtesans who had been leading disreputable lives with the soldiers.

[3] One of the latter was Thais.[64] She too had had too much to drink, when she claimed that, if Alexander gave the order to burn the Persian palace, he would earn the deepest gratitude among all the Greeks. This was what the people whose cities the Persians had destroyed were expecting, she said. [4] As the drunken whore gave her opinion on a matter of extreme importance, one or two who were themselves the worse for drink agreed with her. The king, too, was enthusiastic rather than acquiescent. 'Why do we not avenge Greece, then, and put the city to the torch?' he asked.

[5] They were all flushed with wine, and they got up, drunk, to burn a city which they had spared while under arms. Alexander took the lead, setting fire to the palace, to be followed by his drinking companions, his attendants and the courtesans. Large sections of the palace had been made of cedar, so they quickly took flame and spread the conflagration over a large area. [6] The army, encamped not far from the city, caught sight of the fire. Thinking it was accidental, came running in a body to help. [7] But when they reached the palace portico, they saw their king himself still piling on torch-wood, so they dropped the water they had brought and began throwing dry wood into the blaze themselves.

[8] Such was the end of the palace that had ruled all the East. From it in bygone days law had been sought by so many nations; it had been the birthplace of so many kings; it had struck unparalleled terror into the land of Greece, constructing a fleet of 1,000 ships and an army that flooded Europe,

after bridging the sea and digging through mountains to make a marine canal. [9] Not even in the long period following its destruction did it rise again; the Macedonian kings took up residence in other cities, which are now occupied by the Parthians. Of Persepolis there would be no trace were its location not marked by the Araxes.[65] This had flowed close to the walls, and according to people living close by – though it is a matter of belief rather than knowledge – the city was twenty stades from it.

[10] The Macedonians were ashamed that a city of such distinction had been destroyed by their king during a drunken orgy. The whole episode was given a serious explanation and they convinced themselves that this was the most appropriate method of destruction for it. [11] As for Alexander, it is generally agreed that, when sleep had brought him back to his senses after his drunken bout, he regretted his actions and said that the Persians would have suffered a more grievous punishment at the hands of the Greeks had they been forced to see him on Xerxes' throne and in his palace.[66]

[12] The next day he made a gift of thirty talents to the Lycian who had been his guide for the route into Persia. From here he now moved into Media, where he was met by fresh reinforcements from Cilicia: 5,000 infantry and 1,000 cavalry, both under the command of the Athenian Plato.[67] His forces thus augmented, Alexander determined to pursue Darius.

8

[1] By now Darius had reached Ecbatana, the capital city of Media. (This is now inhabited by the Parthians who use it as their summer residence.[68]) He had decided to go from there to Bactra, but his fear of being overtaken by the fast-moving Alexander made him change both his strategy and his route. [2] Alexander was 1,500 stades away, but no distance now seemed a sufficient counterbalance to his speed, and Darius began to prepare for battle rather than retreat.

[3] He had with him 30,000 infantry, including 4,000 Greeks whose loyalty to the king remained unshaken to the end, [4] as well as a force of 4,000 slingers and archers, plus 3,300 cavalry, mainly Parthieni, under the command of Bessus, governor of the province of Bactriana.[69] [5] With this force Darius veered off the military road a little, telling the camp-followers and the men guarding the baggage to go on ahead.[70] [6] He then called a council and said: 'Had fortune set me among cowards and men who considered life at any cost preferable to an honourable death, then I should prefer to be silent and not waste my words. [7] As it is, I have personal experience of both your courage and your loyalty from evidence more compelling than I should have liked, and I ought to strive to prove myself worthy of such friends rather than wonder whether you remain the men you were. [8] Of the many thousands under my command you are the ones who have followed me, twice defeated and twice in flight, [9] and your unflinching loyalty makes me believe that

I am a king. Traitors and deserters are now rulers in my cities, not, indeed, because they are thought to deserve such an office but so that the rewards given to them might tempt your support away from me. Yet it is *my* fortune, not the victor's, which you have chosen to share and you truly deserve to have the gods reward you on my behalf, if I am unable to do so myself. [10] And to be sure, they *will* reward you. No future generation will be so unresponsive nor will public opinion be so grudging as to fail to transport you to the skies with praises which are your due.

'Even had I been considering flight (an idea I find thoroughly unacceptable), I would have been encouraged by your bravery to face the enemy. [11] How long, I ask, am I going to be an exile in my own kingdom and flee through my own empire from a foreign king, when by trying the fortunes of war I can either recover what I have lost or else achieve death with honour? [12] Or perhaps it is preferable to await hopefully the victor's decision, to follow the example of Mazaeus and Mithrenes[71] and govern a single province at another's whim – supposing that now he prefers to indulge his vanity rather than his anger! [13] I pray the gods never grant anyone the power to remove or to place this diadem on my head! I am not going to live to see the loss of this empire: my rule and my life shall end together. [14] If such are your feelings, and such are your principles, not one of you has failed to gain his freedom. None of you will be forced to endure the Macedonians' contempt, none their haughty expressions. For each man his right hand will win either revenge for all his sufferings or an end to them. [15] I am living proof of fortune's capriciousness, and I am justified in looking for a change for the better on her part. But if the gods are opposed to wars that are just and righteous, brave men will still be able to die an honourable death. [16] By the glorious achievements of my forefathers whose rule over all the East won them undying renown, by the men to whom Macedonia once paid tribute, by all the fleets sent to Greece[72] and all the trophies won by your kings, I beg and beseech you: assume the courage appropriate to your reputation and that of your nation [17] to meet whatever fortune has in store for us with the resolute spirit with which you have faced the events of the past. As for me, I shall certainly have perpetual fame conferred on me, whether by a glorious victory or a glorious battle.'

9

[1] As Darius said this, the prospect of the peril at hand sent a numbing chill through the hearts and minds of all alike; they had nothing to suggest, nothing to say. Then Artabazus spoke. He was the oldest of Darius' friends and, as we observed above,[73] he had been a guest at Philip's court. 'We shall follow our king into battle,' he said, 'dressed in our richest robes and equipped with our finest armour, mentally prepared to expect victory but also ready to die.' [2] All applauded these words, apart from Nabarzanes. He attended

the council meeting, but he had joined Bessus in a conspiracy to perpetrate a hitherto unheard-of crime:[74] they had decided to use the troops under their respective commands to seize and imprison Darius. They reasoned that if Alexander overtook them they could ingratiate themselves with the victor by handing over their king alive – he was sure to set great store by the capture of Darius – whereas, if they managed to get away from him, they would kill Darius, seize his kingdom themselves and restart hostilities.

[3] They had long been considering this treason and now Nabarzanes prepared the way for their nefarious plan. 'I realize that the opinion I shall express will not sound good to you at first,' he said, 'but doctors use harsh remedies to cure more serious ailments, and when a captain fears shipwreck he rescues what can be saved of his cargo by jettisoning part. [4] Now I do not urge you to incur loss, only to use a sound plan to save yourself and your kingdom. We have the gods against us in this war, and fortune has not ceased from her relentless hounding of the Persians. What we need is a fresh start with fresh omens. Temporarily transfer your authority and your command to another who can carry the title of king only until the enemy quits Asia and who can then, victorious, return your kingdom to you. [5] That this will happen soon one can reasonably expect: Bactra stands intact, the Indians and Sacae are under your control, and there are so many nations and armies, so many thousands of infantry and cavalry all ready to apply their strength to reversing the current position that greater military resources remain for you than have been expended. [6] Why do we run like wild animals into needless destruction? What distinguishes a brave man is not a hatred of life but his contempt for death. [7] Cowards are often brought to squander their lives when they cannot tolerate hardship, but courage leaves nothing untried and, as death is the end of everything, it is enough to meet it without reluctance. [8] So if Bactra, the safest haven for us, is our goal, let us appoint Bessus, the satrap of the area, as temporary king, and when the issue is settled he will return to you, the legitimate king, the command he has held in trust.'

[9] Not surprisingly Darius lost his temper, though the enormity of the wickedness lurking in Nabarzanes' treacherous words was not apparent. 'You vile slave!' he said. 'So you have found the opportunity you wanted to bring your treachery into the open!' He drew his sword and looked as if he would kill Nabarzanes, [10] but Bessus and some Bactrians swiftly encircled him, ostensibly upset and entreating him to stay his hand, but really in order to clap him in irons if he persisted. [11] Nabarzanes meanwhile slipped away, soon to be followed by Bessus. In order to have a secret meeting, they told the troops under their command to withdraw from the main body of the army.

[12] Artabazus then proceeded to placate Darius with observations appropriate to the circumstances, repeatedly reminding him of their critical position. He told him he should be tolerant of the stupidity or misconceptions of men who, whatever else they were, remained his subjects. At that moment,

he said, Alexander was hard on their heels, a formidable adversary even if Darius had all his people behind him – and what would happen if the men who had followed him in his flight were alienated from their king?

[13] Reluctantly Darius deferred to Artabazus, and in view of the general agitation among the men he remained in the same spot, although he had earlier decided to move camp. However, shaken as he was both by depression and despair, he shut himself away in his tent. [14] As a result the camp was under no one's command, feelings were divided, and they no longer met as before to consult the common interest. [15] Patron,[75] the commander of the Greek troops, told his men to take up arms and be ready to carry out orders; [16] the Persians had withdrawn from the camp; Bessus was with the Bactrians and was attempting to win over the Persians by telling them of Bactra and its wealth, the region being still untouched, and also of the dangers threatening them if they stayed. But among the Persians there was almost unanimous agreement that to desert a king was an act of impiety. [17] In the meantime Artabazus fulfilled all the functions of a commander, constantly visiting the Persians' tents, encouraging and exhorting them both individually and as a body, until it was sufficiently clear that they would do his bidding. He also succeeded, with difficulty, in getting Darius to take food and apply his attention to the situation.

10

[1] Inflamed with greed for kingship, Bessus and Nabarzanes now decided to carry out the plan they had long been hatching. With Darius still alive, however, there could be no hope of gaining such power, [2] for among those peoples the king commands extraordinary respect: his name itself is enough to make them assemble, and the veneration he enjoys in prosperity remains with him in adversity. [3] What inflated the wicked ambitions of the two was the area under their control which in terms of arms, fighting men and area ranked second to none belonging to those peoples: it comprised a third of Asia and possessed a population of young men equal in number to the armies Darius had lost. [4] They had scant respect not merely for Darius but for Alexander, too; for from this area they expected to recover the full strength of the empire – if Darius fell into their clutches. [5] After long considering all the options they decided to use the Bactrian soldiers (whose obedience to them was abject) to seize the king, and a messenger would also be sent to Alexander to inform him that Darius was alive and in their custody. [6] If, as they feared, Alexander rejected their treacherous overtures, they would murder Darius and head for Bactra with the troops of their own people. [7] However, open arrest of Darius was impossible because the Persians, many thousand strong, would come to the aid of their king, and the loyalty of the Greeks also caused apprehension. [8] They therefore resorted to cunning to accomplish what they could not by force: they decided to feign remorse over their withdrawal,

making the excuse to Darius that they had panicked. Meanwhile men were sent to subvert the Persians; [9] they played on the soldiers' hopes and fears to win them over, telling them that they were exposing their lives to complete catastrophe and were being dragged to destruction while Bactria was accessible to them, all set to welcome them with its possessions and an opulence they could not possibly imagine.

[10] While they were thus engaged, Artabazus arrived, perhaps on Darius' orders or perhaps of his own accord. He brought word that Darius had been mollified and that the degree of friendship they had previously enjoyed with the king was still open to them. [11] They wept and made excuses for their behaviour, begging Artabazus to plead their cause with Darius and take their entreaties to him, [12] and after spending the night in this manner Bessus, Nabarzanes and the Bactrian soldiers appeared at the entrance to the king's tent just before dawn, masking their secret treachery with the guise of solemn duty. Darius gave the signal to march and climbed into his chariot in his usual manner. [13] Nabarzanes and the other traitors fell to the ground and actually paid homage to a man they would put in irons shortly afterwards, even shedding tears as evidence of their remorse – so ready to deceive is the human character! [14] When they entreated him as suppliants Darius, by nature an ingenuous and sympathetic person, was persuaded not only to believe what they said but to weep as well. [15] Even now, however, they experienced no pangs of conscience about the crime they had plotted, although they could see the qualities of the person they were deceiving, both as king and as a man. As for Darius, he had no worries about the impending danger as he hurried to escape the hands of Alexander, his only fear.

11

[1] Patron, the Greek commander, told his men to equip themselves with the arms which were hitherto being transported in the baggage and to be ready and on the alert for any order he might give. [2] He himself followed the king's carriage, looking out for a chance to talk to him, for he had sensed treachery on Bessus' part. Bessus, however, feared just such a move from Patron and would not step away from the carriage, acting more like a guard than a companion. [3] Thus Patron hesitated for a long while, often drawing back when on the point of speaking, and did no more than look at the king, wavering between loyalty and fear. [4] At last Darius' eyes fell on him. He told the eunuch, Bubaces, who was one of those closest to his carriage, to ask Patron if he had anything to tell him. Patron answered that he *did* want to talk to him but only in the absence of others, and he was then told to step forward without an interpreter (for Darius had some knowledge of Greek).

[5] 'Your Majesty,' said Patron, 'we few are all that remain of 50,000 Greeks. We were all with you in your more fortunate days, and in your present situation we remain as we were when you were prospering, ready to make for and to accept as our country and our home any lands you choose.

[6] We and you have been drawn together both by your prosperity and your adversity. By this inviolable loyalty of ours I beg and beseech you: pitch your tent in our area of the camp and let us be your bodyguards. We have left Greece behind; for us there is no Bactra; our hope rests entirely in you – I wish that were true of the others also! Further talk serves no purpose. As a foreigner born of another race I should not be asking for the responsibility of guarding your person if I thought anyone else could do it.'

[7] Bessus knew no Greek, but a guilty conscience prompted him to believe that Patron had given him away, and the fact that Darius' conversation with the Greek was being kept from the interpreters made him absolutely certain of it. Darius, however, was not in the least alarmed, as far as one could tell from his expression, and he proceeded to ask Patron his reasons for giving the advice he brought. [8] Patron, believing further procrastination ill-advised, said to him: 'Bessus and Nabarzanes are plotting against you. Your fortunes and your life are in extreme danger, and this day will be the last either for the traitors or for you.' [9] In fact Patron might have earned the credit and distinction of saving the king's life. [10] Naturally, this would be ridiculed by those who feel certain that the affairs of mankind are governed by chance rather than that each person is destined by an immutable law to a life-cycle governed by an interconnected series of invisible causes pre-ordained long in advance. [11] At all events Darius answered that, although he was well aware of the loyalty of the Greek troops, he would never leave his compatriots, and that it would be more difficult for him to condemn them than to be duped by them. He preferred to endure among his men anything that fortune brought him rather than to become a deserter, he said, and if his soldiers did not wish him to be saved, his death was coming too late. [12] Patron now despaired of the king's life and returned to the men under his command, ready to resort to any means to prove his loyalty.

12

[1] Bessus had felt a violent urge to kill Darius immediately, but the fear that he would be unable to ingratiate himself with Alexander unless he surrendered the king alive made him postpone the crime he was planning to the following night. He now began to congratulate Darius on having avoided with prudence and caution the scheming of a traitor who already had his eyes on Alexander's wealth, for he would have made the enemy a gift of the king's head. [2] It was not surprising, said Bessus, that a man who was himself on hire should put a price on everything; a man without immediate family and without a home, an exile the whole world over, he was a dangerous enemy passed from one to another at the nod of the bidders. [3] As Bessus tried to clear himself and invoked the gods of his country as witnesses to his loyalty, Darius gave him a look which signified his acceptance, though in fact he was certain of the truth of the charges made by the Greeks. Things had gone so

far that not to show confidence in his own men was as dangerous as being deceived by them. [4] The number of men feared to be unreliable and disposed to treachery was 30,000; Patron had 4,000.[76] If Darius entrusted his life to the latter and showed no trust in his compatriots' loyalty, he saw that he was offering an excuse for treason; and so he preferred to remain an innocent rather than a deserving victim. [5] But when Bessus disclaimed any treacherous plot, Darius answered that he had as much evidence of Alexander's sense of justice as of his courage, and any who expected a reward for betrayal from him were mistaken – none would be a more severe avenger or punisher of treason than Alexander.

[6] Night was already coming on when the Persians, following their usual practice, laid down their arms and hurried off in groups to fetch supplies from the nearest village. The Bactrians, however, remained under arms, as they had been instructed by Bessus.

[7] Meanwhile, Darius ordered Artabazus to be summoned, and acquainted him with the charges made by Patron. Artabazus was sure that Darius ought to go over to the Greek camp, and said that the Persians would also follow him when news of his peril spread. [8] But Darius was now consigned to his fate and would no longer listen to advice that could save him. Artabazus, his sole comfort in his misfortune, he embraced as if he were to see him no more and, bathed in their mutual tears, he ordered him to be taken away by force as he still clung to the king. Then, covering his head so as not to witness the grief of Artabazus, who left as though from a funeral pyre, he prostrated himself on the ground. [9] At this point the men forming his customary bodyguard slipped away (men who ought to have risked even their lives to protect their king) because they thought they would be no match for all the armed men they believed to be already approaching. A deep solitude fell on the tent: only a few eunuchs stood around the king, because they had nowhere else to go. [10] Darius, however, dismissed all those present and for a long time mulled over one plan after another. Then, beginning to feel oppressed by the isolation he had shortly before sought for comfort, he ordered Bubaces to be called to him. [11] With his eyes on Bubaces he said: 'Go, all of you – look after yourselves. You have acted properly, demonstrating your loyalty to your king right to the end. As for me, I am waiting here for what is ordained by my fate. If by chance you are wondering why I do not end my own life, it is because I prefer my death to come from another's wrongdoing, not my own.'

[12] After these words from Darius the eunuchs' mournful cries filled not only the tent but the entire camp; then others burst in and themselves began a lament for the king, tearing their clothes and wailing lugubriously in the barbarian manner. [13] When the noise reached the Persians they were panic-stricken: they dared neither take up weapons, for fear of meeting the Bactrians, nor remain inactive, in case they appeared guilty of impious

desertion of their king. [14] The whole camp, bereft of its leader and his authority, rang with a confused and dissonant clamour.

Misinterpreting the lamentations, their soldiers had brought a report to Bessus and Nabarzanes that the king had died by his own hand, [15] and the two rushed up at a gallop at the head of a group of men they had hand-picked to execute the crime. On entering the tent they were informed by the eunuchs that the king still lived; they ordered him to be arrested and bound. [16] The king who a short time ago had ridden in a chariot and received divine honours from his people was now, with no interference from without, made a captive of his own slaves and set in a squalid wagon. [17] His money and his furniture were looted, as though the act was sanctioned by the conventions of war, and the conspirators made off in flight, laden with the spoils they had acquired by this final piece of villainy. [18] Artabazus headed for Parthiene with those under his command plus the Greek troops; anything provided more security than remaining in the sight of murderers, he thought. [19] After having promises heaped on them by Bessus, and largely because they had no one else's lead to follow, the Persians attached themselves to the Bactrians whose column they overtook two days later. [20] To allow the king some mark of respect, however, they bound him with fetters of gold, for fortune kept on devising new kinds of insult for him; and to prevent his being recognized by his royal trappings they had covered the wagon with dirty skins. Men unacquainted with Darius were set to drive the animals, so that he could not be pointed out to the more inquisitive soldiers on the march. Guards followed at a distance.[77]

13

[1] On hearing that Darius had moved from Ecbatana, Alexander left the road leading into Media and proceeded in vigorous pursuit of the fleeing king. [2] He arrived at Tabae, a town in the remotest part of Paraetacene, to be informed by deserters that Darius was making for Bactra in headlong flight.[78] [3] Subsequently he received more reliable intelligence from the Babylonian Bagistanes, who claimed that, while Darius was not actually a prisoner, he was in danger of being murdered or put in irons.[79]

[4] Alexander summoned his generals and said: 'The task that remains is of great importance but the effort will be brief. Darius is not far off, deserted by his troops or overthrown by them. In his person lies our victory, and speed will reward us with this great prize.' [5] With one voice they shouted that they were ready to follow him, bidding him to consider neither the hardship nor the risk involved. Alexander, therefore, led his force on speedily, racing rather than marching and not even resting at night to compensate for the day's exertions. [6] After advancing 500 stades, they reached the village where Bessus had seized Darius. [7] There Melon, the interpreter of Darius,

was captured.[80] Poor health had made him unable to keep pace with the Persian force and, when he was overtaken by the swiftly moving Alexander, he posed as a deserter. From him Alexander learned the facts. [8] But as his men were tired and needing rest, he combined with his select force of 6,000 cavalry the so-called *dimachae*,[81] 300 strong. (These carried heavier body-armour but rode horses, and when circumstances and the terrain required it they fought as infantry.)

[9] While Alexander was thus engaged, he was approached by Orsilos and Mithracenes who had deserted out of disgust at Bessus' treachery.[82] They reported that the Persians were 500 stades away but that they would reveal a short-cut to Alexander. [10] The king was pleased that the deserters had come, and early in the evening he took some light-armed cavalry and set off under their guidance on the road they showed him, ordering the phalanx to follow with all the speed they could manage. Alexander himself advanced with his troops in square formation, regulating the pace so as to allow front and rear to remain in contact.

[11] After advancing 300 stades they were met by Mazaeus' son Brochubelus,[83] a former satrap of Syria. He had also deserted, and now brought the news that Bessus was no more than 200 stades distant and that his army, taking no precautions, was marching in a disordered manner, out of formation, apparently heading for Hyrcania. If Alexander accelerated his pursuit, he would overtake them while they were in disarray. Darius, he added, was still alive. [12] Alexander was ever a man of action, but the deserter now fired him with an obsessive desire to catch Bessus. His men put spurs to their horses and went on at a gallop. At this point one could hear the noise of the enemy marching along, but a dust-cloud hid them from sight. Alexander checked his speed momentarily to allow the dust to settle. [13] They had by now been spotted by the barbarians and had themselves caught sight of the retreating enemy column. The Macedonians would have been no match for them whatsoever if Bessus had shown as much enthusiasm for battle as for murder, for the barbarians enjoyed a superiority both in numbers and strength and would, moreover, have entered battle fresh while their enemy were exhausted. [14] But Alexander's name and reputation, extremely important factors in warfare, turned them to panic-stricken flight.

[15] Bessus and his fellow-conspirators came to Darius' wagon and started urging him to mount a horse and flee to escape his enemy. [16] Darius, however, declared that the gods had come to avenge him and, calling for Alexander's protection, refused to go along with the traitors. At this they were furious. They hurled their spears at the king and left him there, run through many times. [17] They also maimed his animals to prevent them advancing any further, and killed the two slaves accompanying the king. [18] After this crime, to scatter the traces of their flight, Nabarzanes made for Hyrcania and Bessus, with a small retinue of cavalry, for Bactra. Deprived of their leaders, the barbarians dispersed wherever hope or panic directed them, and a mere

500 cavalry remained massed together, still unsure whether resistance or flight was the better idea.

[19] When Alexander discovered that his enemy was terrified, he sent Nicanor on with some cavalrymen to check their flight and he himself followed with the rest. Some 3,000 who offered resistance were cut down and the others were now being herded along like cattle, but without injury since the king's orders were to avoid bloodshed. [20] None of the captives was able to identify Darius' cart and, though the wagons were individually searched as the Macedonians overtook them, there was no indication of where the king had fled. [21] As Alexander sped along, barely 3,000 of the cavalry kept up with him,[84] but into the hands of those following him at a slower pace fell whole columns of fleeing Persians. [22] It is an incredible fact that the captives outnumbered their captors – so completely had their misfortune deprived these terrified men of their senses that they had no clear perception of the enemy's small numbers and their own multitude.

[23] Meanwhile, since they lacked a driver, the animals pulling Darius had left the main road and after wandering around for four stades had come to a stop in a certain valley, exhausted as much by the heat as by their wounds. [24] There was a spring close by. This had been pointed out to the Macedonian Polystratus by people who knew the area, and he now came to it because he was tormented with thirst. While he drank the water from his helmet, he caught sight of the spears stuck in the bodies of the dying animals [25] and, surprised at their being wounded rather than driven off ... [was shocked by the cries] of a man only half alive ...[85]*

---

* The text breaks off at this point, and the remainder of Book 5 and the first pages of Book 6 are lost. See Notes, pp. 282–3.

BOOK SIX[1]

[1] He threw himself into the thick of the fighting and, cutting down those putting up any determined resistance, drove most of the enemy before him. [2] The winning side now began to run and, until they brought their over-enthusiastic pursuers down to level ground, they were falling without striking back; but the moment they reached a position where they could make a stand they fought on equal terms. [3] Among all the Spartans their king was conspicuous not only for his fine physique and weapons but even more for his magnificent and unsurpassable courage. [4] He was under attack from all directions, both at long and short range. For a long time he kept up the fight on different sides, parrying missiles with his shield or avoiding them with an agile movement, until his thighs, transfixed by a spear and bleeding heavily, gave way as he fought. [5] His attendants placed him on his shield and swiftly carried him back to camp, scarcely able to bear the violent jarring of his wounds.

[6] The Lacedaemonians did not abandon the fight, however. As soon as they could gain a position which favoured them more than the foe, they closed ranks and withstood the assault of the enemy line which came at them like a flood. [7] That there never was a more violent conflict is a matter of record: the armies of the two nations with the greatest military reputations were fighting an evenly matched battle. [8] The Spartans reflected on their prestige of old, the Macedonians on their prestige of the present, the former fighting for liberty and the latter for power, the Spartans lacking a leader and the Macedonians fighting space. [9] Moreover, the constant change of fortunes on that day alternately increased the confidence and anxieties of each side, as if Fortune deliberately kept even the clash between these men of supreme valour. [10] However, the narrow terrain to which the fighting had been confined would not permit a full-scale engagement of the two forces, so there were more spectators than combatants and those beyond the range of missiles shouted encouragement to their respective sides.

[11] Eventually the Spartan line began to tire, the men hardly able to hold their weapons which were slippery with sweat, and then to give ground. [12] When an enemy thrust made the Spartan retreat more pronounced, the victor started exerting pressure on his disordered foe and, swiftly covering all

the ground previously occupied by the Spartans, started pursuit of Agis. [13] The latter, seeing his men on the run and the enemy vanguard approaching, gave orders that he be put down. He tried his limbs to see if they could respond to his inner determination, [14] but found that they failed him. He sank to his knees, swiftly put on his helmet and, using his shield to cover his body, started brandishing his spear in his right hand, actually daring any of the enemy to strip the spoils from him as he lay there. [15] No one would risk hand-to-hand combat with him. They attacked him at long range with spears, which he flung back at his enemy until a lance lodged in his exposed chest. He pulled it from the wound, momentarily rested his bowed and failing head on his shield, and then collapsed dead upon his arms, blood and breath flowing from him together.[2] [16] Five thousand three hundred Lacedaemonians fell, and no more than 1,000 Macedonians,[3] but hardly anyone returned to camp unwounded.

The victory shattered the spirit not only of Sparta and her allies but of all who had kept a speculative eye on the war's fortunes. [17] Nor was Antipater unaware that the expression of those congratulating him belied their true feelings, but his desire to finish the war obliged him to tolerate such deception. Though pleased with the success of the campaign, he nonetheless feared an envious reaction because in his achievements he had exceeded the scope of a subordinate officer. [18] In fact, though Alexander wanted his enemies defeated, he actually expressed his displeasure that the victory had gone to Antipater, for he felt that anything redounding to another's credit detracted from his own.[4] [19] Accordingly Antipater, being well acquainted with Alexander's vanity, did not presume to arrange the terms of the victory himself but left them to the discretion of the Greek council. [20] This only granted the Lacedaemonians permission to send ambassadors to the king, while the Tegeans, with the exception of the ringleaders, won pardon for their rebellion, and orders were issued for the Achaeans and Eleans to give 120 talents to the people of Megalopolis, whose city had been under siege from the rebels.

[21] So ended the war. It had started suddenly, but it was concluded before Darius' defeat by Alexander at Arbela.[5]

2

[1] Alexander could better cope with warfare than peace and leisure. As soon as he was free of the worries that beset him, he yielded to dissipation, and the man whom the arms of Persia had failed to crush fell before its vices. [2] There were parties early in the day; drinking and mad revelry throughout the night; games; women by the score. It was a general decline into the ways of the foreigner. By affecting these, as though they were superior to those of his own country, Alexander so offended the sensibilities and eyes of his people that most of his friends began to regard him as an enemy. [3] For the

Macedonians clung tenaciously to their own practices and were used to satisfying their natural requirements with a diet that was sparing and easily accessible; and these he had now driven into the depraved customs of foreigners and conquered nations. [4] This explains the increase in the plots against his life, the mutiny of his men and the more-public displays of resentment and mutual recrimination among them; it explains why Alexander subsequently oscillated between anger and suspicion which arose from groundless fears, and it explains other similar problems which will be recounted later.

[5] Since he was spending his days as well as his nights on these protracted banquets, Alexander would use entertainments to relieve the tedium of feasting. But he was not content with the large number of performers he had requisitioned from Greece; instead, female captives would be ordered to sing in their native manner their artless songs which grated on the ears of foreigners. [6] The king himself noticed one of these women more downcast than the others and out of shyness resisting those trying to bring her forward. She was exceptionally beautiful, and her modesty lent further charm to her beauty. With eyes fixed on the ground and her face veiled as far as was allowed, she made the king suspect that she was too highly born to appear among such dinner-table displays. [7] So she was asked who she was, and answered that she was the granddaughter of Ochus, the former king of Persia,[6] being the daughter of his son; and that she had been the wife of Hystaspes (who had been related to Darius and who had himself commanded a powerful army).

[8] There yet lingered in the king's heart slight traces of his former qualities. He felt respect for a woman of royal stock who had suffered a reversal of fortune and for so eminent a name as that of Ochus. [9] He not only ordered the captive released but he also had her possessions returned to her and a search instituted for her husband so that he could return his wife to him if he were found. The following day he instructed Hephaestion to have all the prisoners brought to the royal quarters and there he verified the lineage of each of them, separating from the common people those of noble birth. The latter numbered 1,000 and included Oxathres, brother of Darius, who was as distinguished for his nobility of character as for his brother's station in life. [11] Oxydates, a Persian nobleman kept in shackles because he had been condemned to execution by Darius, was freed and given the satrapy of Media by Alexander.[7] The king also admitted Darius' brother to his circle of friends, allowing him to retain all the honour due his ancient and distinguished lineage.[8] [10] Twenty-six thousand talents had accumulated in booty from the most recent engagement, 12,000 of which were disbursed as bonuses for the men while a similar sum was embezzled by the scandalous dishonesty of those in charge of it.[9]

[12] From here they marched into Parthiene, land of a people little known at that time but now the most important of all regions situated beyond the

Euphrates and Tigris and bounded by the Red Sea. [13] This level and fertile area was occupied by the Scythians, who remain today troublesome neighbours, with settlements both in Europe and Asia. Those living across the Bosphorus are considered Asiatic, the Europeans being those whose territory extends from the west of Thrace to the river Borysthenes and from there in a straight line to the Tanais,[10] [14] the river which separates Europe and Asia. There is no doubt that the Scythians, the ancestors of the Parthians, made their incursions from the area of Europe, not from the Bosphorus.

[15] In those days the famous city of Hecatompylos still stood, a Greek foundation, and here the king established a long-term camp, drawing supplies from the country all around.[11] Thus the rumour spread, on no authority – rumour being a vice to which idle soldiers are prone – that Alexander was satisfied with his achievements thus far and had decided on an immediate return to Macedonia. The soldiers scattered to their tents like madmen and prepared their baggage for the journey – [16] one might have thought a signal had been given for general packing-up of the camp – and the bustle of men looking for their tent-mates or loading wagons came to the king's ears. [17] That the Greek troops had been ordered home had lent credibility to the rumour and, since Alexander had given the cavalry 6,000 denarii each and the infantry 1,000, they all thought the time for discharge was coming for them too.

[18] Alexander was justifiably alarmed, for he had decided on an expedition to India and the furthest parts of the East. He assembled his generals in his tent and, with tears in his eyes, complained that he was being brought to a halt in the middle of a brilliant career, to return home more like a defeated man than a conqueror; [19] that the obstacle he faced was not his men's cowardice but the ill-will of the gods who had instilled in soldiers of the highest courage a sudden pining for home – though they would have returned there shortly with increased glory and fame. [20] At this point each of the officers offered his support. Each demanded for himself all the most difficult tasks and also promised the loyal service of his men, if Alexander were prepared to calm them down with some conciliatory words appropriate to the occasion. [21] The men, they said, had never withdrawn disheartened and dispirited when they had been able to tap his reserve of vitality and stout-hearted resolve. Alexander answered that he would act on this advice, but that the officers were to prepare the crowd to listen to him. When all the arrangements that seemed appropriate had been made, Alexander had the troops summoned to a meeting and delivered before them the following speech.[12]

3

[1] 'Men! If you consider the scale of our achievements, your longing for peace and your weariness of brilliant campaigns are not at all surprising. [2] Let me pass over the Illyrians, the Triballians, Boeotia, Thrace, Sparta, the

Achaeans, the Peloponnese – all of them subdued under my direct leadership or by campaigns conducted under my orders and instructions. [3] Just look! Beginning the war at the Hellespont, we have delivered Ionia and Aeolis from subjection to the insolent barbarian, and we have in our power Caria, Lydia, Cappadocia, Phrygia, Paphlagonia, Pamphylia, Pisidia, Cilicia, Syria, Phoenicia, Armenia, Persia, the Medes and Parthiene. [4] I have subjugated more provinces than others have captured cities, and in my calculations I may have forgotten some because of the very numbers involved!

[5] 'Consequently, men, if I believed that our grip on the lands we have so swiftly conquered were sufficiently firm, I would certainly break loose from here, even if you tried to detain me, back to my home, to my mother and sisters[13] and the rest of our countrymen, so that there especially I could enjoy the reputation and glory I have won with you, in that place where the richest of our rewards for victory are waiting for us – joyful children, wives and parents, peace and quiet, the carefree possession of what our valour has won. [6] But our empire is new and, if we are prepared to admit the truth, insecure; the barbarians still hold their necks stiff beneath the yoke. We need time, men, for them to develop more pliant dispositions and for civilization to moderate their wildness. [7] Even crops await a fixed time to ripen: it is a fact that even inanimate things take their own time to grow mellow. [8] All these races were accustomed to the rule and authority of another and they have no affinity to us in religion, culture or language. Do you really think that the battle that conquered them subdued them as well? No, it is your military strength that checks them, not their own disposition; fearing us while we are here, they will be our enemies when we are gone. What we are dealing with is a pack of wild animals; they are naturally intractable, and even captured and confined they will only be tamed by the passage of time.

[9] 'I have proceeded so far on the assumption that everything previously under Darius' rule has submitted to our arms, whereas in fact Nabarzanes has occupied Hyrcania and the murderer Bessus is not only in possession of Bactra but is even threatening us,[14] while the Sogdians, Dahae, Massagetae, Sacae and Indians remain independent. The moment they see our backs turned they will all be after us; [10] for they are all of the same stock, while we are foreigners and racially different. Everybody finds it easier to be governed by his own people, even if the man in charge is more to be feared. [11] So we must either let go what we have taken or seize what we do not yet hold. Men, surgeons who treat sick bodies leave behind nothing that will harm the patient; just so we must cut away whatever is an obstacle to our rule. A small spark overlooked often starts a big fire. Where the enemy is concerned, nothing can be safely underestimated: treat a man with contempt and you strengthen him by your indifference. [12] Even Darius did not inherit his rule of the Persians; he owed his succession to the throne of Cyrus to the benefaction of the eunuch Bagoas.[15] So do not think that Bessus will have a difficult task seizing a vacant throne. [13] We really have made a mistake,

men, if we conquered Darius only to transfer his power to his vassal – to a man who committed the most heinous crime by keeping his own king in irons like a captive at a time when he stood in need of external assistance (a king whom we, his conquerors, would certainly have spared) and finally killing him so that he could not be rescued by us.

[14] 'Are you going to permit a man like that to take the throne? Personally I cannot wait to see him nailed to a cross, paying a fitting penalty to all monarchs, all peoples and to the loyalty which he violated. [15] But just suppose you receive word soon that this very man is devastating the cities of Greece or the Hellespont. What pangs of regret will you feel then that Bessus deprived you of the rewards of your victory? Then you will hasten to recover your losses; then you will take up your weapons! But what better strategy it is to smash him while he is still panicking and barely in control of himself!

[16] 'A four days' march remains for us,[16] for men who have trodden so many snows, forded so many rivers, crossed so many mountain ranges. Our progress is not impeded by a sea that covers the road with a surging tide or stopped by the cramping defiles of Cilicia – everything before us is flat and easy. We stand on the threshold of victory. [17] There remain for us a mere handful of runaways and murderers of their own master. It is a noble undertaking, I can tell you, that you will transmit to posterity to augment your fame, one that will be counted among your most glorious achievements – that you avenged even your enemy Darius, letting your hostility towards him end with his death, by executing his murderer, and that you allowed no criminal to slip through your fingers. [18] If you do this, how much greater do you think the Persians' obedience to you will be, when they realize that yours are righteous wars and that your anger is directed against the crime of Bessus and not against the Persian race?'

4

[1] His words were received with great enthusiasm by the soldiers, who told him to lead them wherever he wished. [2] The king did not check their momentum, and two days later he was pressing ahead through Parthiene towards the Hyrcanian border. To protect Parthiene against a barbarian incursion, he had left Craterus[17] behind with the troops that were under his command and the contingent led by Amyntas, to which were added 600 horse and as many archers. [3] He now gave Erigyius a small escort and told him to take the baggage by a route through the plains, while he himself took the phalanx and the cavalry, covering a distance of 150 stades before establishing a fortified camp in the valley leading into Hyrcania.

Here there is a dense, shady grove of tall trees, the valley's fertile soil watered by streams that flow from the cliffs above it. [4] The river Ziobetis has its source right at the foot of the mountains. It flows as a single stream over a distance of some three stades and then, deflected by a rock which blocks its tiny bed, its waters divide and form two channels. [5] Then it becomes a torrent, its violence increased by the rugged rocks over which it runs, and suddenly it drops beneath the ground. For 300 stades it glides along on an invisible course before reappearing as if produced from a separate source.[18] Forming a new channel it now flows with greater volume than before, [6] for it widens to thirteen stades, and then it contracts once more, compressing its flow between narrower banks until it eventually joins another river called the Rhidagnus. [7] According to the local people, anything thrown into the aperture closer to the original source re-emerges at the second opening where the river reappears. Therefore Alexander gave orders for two horses to be thrown in where the waters drop under the ground, and the men sent to retrieve them saw their carcasses discharged where the river re-emerges.

[8] Alexander had already given the men four days' rest in the same place when he received a letter from Nabarzanes, the man who had joined Bessus in taking Darius prisoner. The drift of the letter was that Nabarzanes had not been Darius' enemy; that he had, in fact, made to him what he had believed were useful recommendations – and had almost been killed by him because of the loyal advice he had given his king. [9] Darius had contemplated transferring the custody of his own person to the foreign troops, he said, a contravention of all that was lawful and right, and an indictment of his own people's loyalty, which they had maintained unblemished towards their monarchs for 230 years. [10] He (Nabarzanes) had been on a steep and slippery path, and had been guided by the pressures of the situation. Darius, too, he continued, after killing Bagoas, had satisfied the people with the explanation that he had executed him for plotting treason.[19] [11] To poor mortals nothing is dearer than life, and it was love of life that drove him to extreme measures – but he had been a follower, not one who desired the actual outcome, [12] and when a general calamity strikes, everyone follows the path of his own good. If Alexander told him to come, he would come without anxiety, he said, unafraid that so great a king would break an assurance he had given, for a god does not usually cheat fellow gods. [13] If, on the other hand, Nabarzanes was thought undeserving of his assurance of protection, then he could take flight to many places of exile, for a brave man's home was where he chose to settle. [14] Alexander did not hesitate to give Nabarzanes an assurance, using the Persian conventions, that he would be unharmed if he came.

Even so, Alexander advanced with his troops in square formation and tight order, and repeatedly sent scouts ahead to explore the area. [15] The light-armed headed the line, the phalanx came next and the baggage followed the infantry. The king's anxiety had been aggravated both by the belligerent temper of the natives and the lie of the land which made access difficult. [16] A continuous open valley extends as far as the Caspian sea where two spits of land jut out from it like arms and, bending slightly in the middle, form a curved shape which more than anything resembles the moon while it is still a crescent, before it has reached its full orb. [17] To the left lie the Cercetae, Mossyni and Chalybes; on the opposite side are the Leucosyri and the plains of the Amazons (the former to the north of the valley, the latter where it turns to the west).

[18] The Caspian, which is less salty than other seas, has a population of huge serpents and its fish are very differently coloured from other fish. Some call it the Caspian sea, others the Hyrcanian.[20] There are also some who believe that the Palus Maeotis[21] drains into it, claiming that the water is less saline than in other seas because of the tempering effect of the marsh water flowing into it. [19] To the north the sea has a great swell and covers the coastal area, sending waves far inland and swamping most of the country with stagnant pools. Again, in different weather conditions, the sea recedes, retreating with as much ferocity as it surged forward and restoring the land to its natural condition. Some have entertained the belief that these waters are not the Caspian sea but that they flow from India into Hyrcania, the high ground of which slopes down into a continuous valley, as was observed above.

[20] From here the king advanced twenty stades along a virtually impassable track overhung by forest, his progress hindered further by torrents and floods. Meeting with no enemy, however, he pressed on and finally arrived in a more cultivated area [21] which produces plentiful quantities of all provisions and, in particular, bears fruit in great abundance (and the soil is particularly suited to viticulture). [22] A tree common in the region resembles an oak and has leaves thickly coated with a honey, but if the local people fail to gather it before sunrise this sap evaporates even at moderate temperatures.[22]

[23] Advancing thirty stades from here Alexander was met by Phrataphernes, who surrendered both himself and the men who had fled after Darius' death. The king received them courteously and then went on to the town of Arvae,[23] where he was met by Craterus and Erigyius. [24] They had brought with them Phradates,[24] the governor of the Tapuri, who also was given a guarantee of immunity; his example encouraged many to put Alexander's clemency to the test. [25] Then Alexander awarded the satrapy of Hyrcania to Manapis,[25] who had come to Philip as an exile during Ochus' reign, and he also restored the Tapuri to the rule of Phradates.

5

[1] Alexander had already penetrated the furthest reaches of Hyrcania when he was met by Artabazus, Darius' most loyal supporter, as was noted above,[26] together with his children, Darius' relatives and a small contingent of Greek soldiers. [2] As Artazabus approached, the king offered him his right hand, for the Persian had been Philip's guest during his exile when Ochus was king, and the loyalty which he had displayed towards his king right to the end drew

Alexander to him even more than the obligations of guest-friendship. [3] Given a friendly welcome, Artabazus said: 'Your majesty, I pray to heaven you may prosper with unending good fortune. Everything here brings me happiness but I am tortured by this one thought, that my declining years make long enjoyment of your kindness impossible for me.' He was in his ninety-fifth year, [4] and accompanying him were nine young men, all sons of his by the one mother.[27] These Artabazus brought to Alexander's right hand, with a prayer that they might live only as long as they would be of service to him. [5] The king, who generally travelled on foot, on this occasion had horses brought up for himself and Artabazus so that the old man would not feel embarrassed to ride while Alexander walked.

[6] After pitching camp, Alexander called a meeting of the Greeks whom Artabazus had brought; but they replied that, unless the Spartans and the men of Sinope were also given guarantees of safety, they would have to consider what to do next. [7] The people in question had been sent as a Spartan delegation to Darius, and after his defeat they had attached themselves to the Greek mercenaries in the Persian force. [8] With no promises or guarantees of immunity the king told them to come and accept whatever decision he made about them, and after long hesitation and much vacillation they did finally agree to come. [9] Democrates the Athenian,[28] however, who had always been a strong opponent of Macedonian power, despaired of pardon and fell on his sword. The rest, abiding by their decision, put themselves in Alexander's hands. [10] They numbered 1,500 soldiers and there were also ninety who had been dispatched as envoys to Darius.[29] The soldiers were apportioned as reinforcements to the army while the others were sent home, except for the Lacedaemonians, whom Alexander ordered kept under guard.

[11] Only the Mardians – a culturally backward race on the borders of Hyrcania who lived by pillaging – had failed to send ambassadors, and they alone appeared unlikely to do Alexander's bidding. Indignant that one people could prevent his being invincible, the king left the baggage under guard and went ahead with a light-armed unit. [12] He had made the journey at night and by dawn the enemy were in sight. It was a débâcle rather than a battle. Dislodged from the hills they had occupied, the barbarians took to flight, and the first villages, deserted by their inhabitants, fell to the Macedonians. [13] However, the interior of the country could be penetrated by the army only at great cost in fatigue: it was enclosed by mountain ridges, tall forests and impassable cliffs. What open spaces there were the barbarians had barricaded with defences of a novel kind. [14] Trees were purposely planted close together. When their branches are still supple the natives bend them by hand, twist them together and plant them in the earth once more. From them, as if from a new root, fresh stems grow with even greater vigour, [15] and the people do not allow these to grow in the direction they would naturally take but weave them together like latticework. When covered with thick foliage

they hide the ground, so that the road is blocked by a continuous hedge of the branches, which act as invisible snares. [16] The only way to make an entrance was by hacking at them, but this too involved great effort since the tree-branches had been toughened with a large number of knots while the pliant shoots of the intertwining branches, which hung like suspended hoops, absorbed the force of the axe-blows.

[17] Now the local people, practised in crawling through the undergrowth like animals, had on this occasion also entered the wood, and were harassing their enemies with missiles from their hiding places. Like a hunter, Alexander explored their lairs and killed several of them. Finally he ordered his men to surround the wood so that they could burst in wherever an opening was to be found. [18] In their ignorance of the area, however, many lost their way and some were captured, and the captured included the king's horse, whom they called Bucephalas,[30] prized above all other animals by Alexander. (The horse would not allow another man to sit on him and, when the king wished to mount, he would of his own accord bend his knees to receive him, so it was thought that he was aware of his rider's identity.) [19] Alexander's anger and grief surpassed the bounds of propriety. He ordered that the horse be traced and a proclamation issued through an interpreter that failure to return him would result in no Mardian being left alive. Terrified by this warning, the Mardians brought up the horse and other gifts, too, [20] but even this failed to appease Alexander. He gave orders for the woods to be felled and for earth to be hauled from the mountains and heaped on the flat ground where the branches formed the barrier. [21] When the work had reached a considerable height the barbarians abandoned hope of holding their position and capitulated. The king took hostages from them and put them under Phradates.

[22] Four days later Alexander returned to camp. He now sent home Artabazus, doubling the honours Darius had conferred on him. Arriving then at the city in Hyrcania where the palace of Darius stood, he was met by Nabarzanes, who had been given a safe conduct and who now brought Alexander lavish gifts, [23] including Bagoas, an exceptionally good-looking eunuch in the very flower of his youth. Darius had had a sexual relationship with him and presently Alexander did, too. It was Bagoas' pleas that did most to influence Alexander to pardon Nabarzanes.[31]

[24] On the border of Hyrcania, as was observed above, lived a tribe of Amazons. They inhabited the plains of Themiscyra in the area of the river Thermodon, [25] and their queen, Thalestris, held sway over all those between the Caucasus and the river Phasis. Passionately eager to meet Alexander, she journeyed from her realm and when she was not far off she sent messengers ahead to announce that a queen had come who was longing to see him and make his acquaintance. [26] Granted an immediate audience, she ordered her company to halt while she went forward attended by 300 women; as soon as she caught sight of the king she leaped unaided from her

horse, carrying two spears in her right hand. [27] The dress of Amazons does not entirely cover the body: the left side is bare to the breast but clothed beyond that, while the skirt of the garment, which is gathered into a knot, stops above the knee. [28] One breast is kept whole for feeding children of female sex and the right is cauterized to facilitate bending the bow and handling weapons.

[29] Thalestris looked at the king, no sign of fear on her face. Her eyes surveyed a physique that in no way matched his illustrious record -- for all barbarians have respect for physical presence, believing that only those on whom nature has thought fit to confer extraordinary appearance are capable of great achievements. [30] When asked if she had a request to make she unhesitatingly declared that she had come in order to share children with the king, since she was a fitting person on whom to beget heirs for his empire. A child of the female sex she would keep, she said, but a male she would give to his father. [31] Alexander asked if Thalestris wished to accompany him on his campaigns, but she declined on the grounds that she had left her kingdom unprotected, and she kept asking him not to let her leave disappointed in her hopes. [32] The woman's enthusiasm for sex was keener than Alexander's and she pressed him to stop there a few days. Thirteen days were devoted to serving her passion, after which Thalestris headed for her kingdom and Alexander for Parthiene.[32]

6

[1] It was at this point that Alexander relinquished control of his appetites. His self-restraint and continence, supreme qualities at the height of good fortune, degenerated into arrogance and dissipation. [2] The traditional ways of his people, the healthy, sober discipline and unassuming demeanour of the Macedonian kings he considered beneath his eminent position and he began to ape the Persian royalty with its quasi-divine status. [3] Men who had conquered scores of nations he wished to lie prostrate on the ground to venerate him, and he sought gradually to inure them to servile duties and to bring them down to the level of captives. [4] Accordingly he wore on his head a purple head-band interwoven with white, like the one Darius had once had, and he assumed Persian dress -- without fearing the omen implicit in his moving from victor's insignia to the garb of the conquered. [5] His claim was that he was wearing Persian spoils, but the fact was that with the clothes he had also adopted Persian habits, and a contemptuous demeanour accompanied the ostentatious dress. [6] Furthermore, he sealed letters sent to Europe with the stone of his old ring, but on those written to Asia was set the seal of Darius' ring -- apparently one man's mind could not cope with the fortunes of two.[33] [7] He had also forced Persian clothing on his friends and on the cavalry, the élite of the troops. They found it distasteful, but did not dare refuse to wear it. [8] The royal quarters had a complement of 365 concu-

bines,[34] the number Darius had possessed, and along with them were hordes of eunuchs practised in playing the woman's part.

[9] Towards all this, smacking as it did of extravagance and foreign habits, the veterans of Philip, a group inexperienced in sensuality, displayed open revulsion. Throughout the camp one sentiment and one view found expression, that they had lost more by victory than they had gained by war, [10] and that at that very moment they were experiencing defeat, surrendering to the ways of aliens and foreigners. How could they face people, they asked, returning home dressed like captives? They felt ashamed of themselves now, they said, and their king resembled one of the conquered rather than a conqueror – demoted from king of Macedon to satrap of Darius.

[11] Alexander was aware that his chief friends and the troops were grossly offended, so he attempted to regain their favour with generous gifts. But in my opinion free men find the wages of servility to be distasteful. [12] To forestall mutiny, then, the general inactivity needed to be interrupted by combat, and for that opportunities were conveniently on the increase. [13] Bessus had assumed royal robes and given orders that he be addressed as 'Artaxerxes', and he was now in the process of mustering the Scythians and other people living by the Tanais. This news was brought by Satibarzanes, who was guaranteed safe-conduct by Alexander and given command of the region he had previously governed. [14] The column could scarcely get moving under the weight of its spoils and extravagant impedimenta, so Alexander gave orders first for his own and then the whole army's baggage to be hauled into their midst, absolute necessities alone excepted. [15] The men had brought the loaded wagons to a large piece of flat ground, and all were waiting to see what his next command would be. He ordered the animals to be led off, put a torch to his own baggage first and then gave instructions for the rest to be burnt. [16] As their owners set light to them, there now went up in smoke objects that the men had often quenched flames to take intact from enemy cities, yet no one dared lament the loss of what he had paid for in blood, since the same fire was consuming the king's valuables. [17] Presently common sense eased their chagrin. Fit for service and ready for anything, they were pleased that they had sacrificed their baggage and not their discipline.

[18] They therefore proceeded towards Bactriana, but the sudden death of Parmenion's son Nicanor[35] had brought bitter grief to the entire army, [19] and Alexander, saddened more than anyone, wanted to call a halt to attend the funeral. However, a shortage of supplies made haste imperative, so he left Philotas with 2,600 men to perform the last rites for his brother while he himself hastened on to Bessus. [20] While he was *en route*, letters were delivered to him from the neighbouring satraps. From these he discovered that Bessus was actually on the offensive and coming to meet him with his army, while Satibarzanes, whom Alexander had personally installed as satrap of the Arii, had also defected from him.[36] [21] Accordingly, although he was intent

on facing Bessus, he thought it best to turn his attention to crushing Sati-barzanes. Taking the light-armed troops and the cavalry, he made a speedy march through the night and came upon the enemy unawares. [22] When Saltibarzanes heard of his arrival, he fled to Bactra with 2,000 cavalry – the most that could be mustered at short notice – and the remainder of his forces occupied the nearby hills.

[23] There is here a rocky outcrop, sheer on the west side but with a gentler gradient towards the east. It has dense tree-cover and a year-round spring with a generous flow of water. Its circumference is thirty-two stades [24] and on its summit is a grassy plateau. The Arii told their men who were unfit to fight to take up a position on the plateau and then piled up tree-trunks and rocks as a barricade where the precipice gave out. The Arii numbered 13,000 armed men. [25] Leaving Craterus to blockade them, Alexander went off in swift pursuit of Satibarzanes; then, realizing he was too far off, he returned to storm those who had taken over the mountain heights.

[26] At first he ordered the clearing of any ground they could reach but, when they came up against impassable crags and sheer precipices, the effort seemed useless against the natural barrier. [27] Alexander, however, had a mind that constantly wrestled with problems. Since going forward was difficult and going back dangerous, he entertained all manner of ideas as his mind produced plan after plan, as usually happens when we reject the initial ones. In a quandary as he was, chance provided him with a scheme when his reasoning could not. [28] The wind was blowing strong from the west and, in their efforts to make a way over the rocks, the soldiers had cut large quantities of wood, which had dried out in the torrid heat. [29] So Alexander ordered more trees to be piled on to fuel a fire and the heap of logs swiftly rose to equal the height of the mountain. [30] Then it was lit on every side, and the whole mass took fire. The wind began to carry the flames into the faces of the enemy and thick smoke veiled the sky as if in a cloud. [31] The woods crackled as they burned, and the parts that the soldiers had not fired ignited as well and started to consume everything near them. The barbarians tried to escape their agonizing torture if the flames died down anywhere, but wherever the fire had left a passage stood their enemy. [32] So they perished in various ways. Some threw themselves into the midst of the fire; some hurled themselves from rocks; others resigned themselves to the attacks of the enemy while a few came half-burnt into their hands.

[33] From here Alexander returned to Craterus, who was engaged in the siege of Artacana[37] and who, after making the necessary preparations, was awaiting the king's arrival in order to cede to him the honour of taking the city, as was right and proper. [34] Alexander therefore ordered siege towers to be advanced. The mere sight of them so terrified the barbarians that they held their hands out from the walls, palms upwards, and began to beg him to save his wrath for Satibarzanes, the instigator of the rebellion, and to spare them since they were suppliants offering to surrender. The king pardoned

them and not only raised the siege but also restored all their property to the inhabitants.

[35] On leaving this city, Alexander was met by fresh reinforcements. Zoilus had brought 500 cavalry from Greece; Antipater had dispatched 3,000 from Illyricum; Philip had 130 Thessalian cavalry with him; from Lydia had come 2,600 foreign infantry and with them came 300 cavalry of the same race. [36] Thus reinforced, Alexander advanced to the Drangae, a warlike people whose satrap, Barzaentes, had been Bessus' accomplice in his crime against the king. Fearing the punishment he deserved, Barzaentes fled into India.[38]

7

[1] Alexander was not merely undefeated by foreign assailants but secure from attack, when after eight days back in camp he became the object of an internal conspiracy.[39] [2] Dymnus,[40] a man of slight influence or favour with the king, had a passionate infatuation for a catamite called Nicomachus; he was totally devoted to the boy, whose favours he alone enjoyed. [3] Practically beside himself, as one could see from his face, Dymnus went with the young man into a temple, with no one else present, saying to him first that what he had to tell him were secrets that were not to be divulged. [4] Nicomachus was now on tenterhooks, and Dymnus begged him in the name of their mutual affection and the pledges each had made of their feelings to swear on oath to remain silent about his disclosures. [5] Nicomachus did not think that Dymnus would tell him anything he would be obliged to divulge even if it meant perjury on his part, so he took the oath by the gods of the place. [6] Then Dymnus revealed that a plot had been hatched against the king which was to be executed in two days' time, and that he was involved in the plan along with some courageous and distinguished men.

[7] On hearing this, the youth resolutely denied that he had sworn to be party to treason and asserted that he could not be constrained by any religious consideration to cover up a crime. [8] Demented with both passion and fear, Dymnus grasped the catamite's right hand. In tears, he first begged him to take part in planning and executing the plot [9] and then, if he could not bring himself to concur with that, at least not to give him away. He said that he had given Nicomachus ample proof of his devotion by his behaviour towards him in general, but now especially by entrusting his life to one of untested loyalty. [10] Finally, when Nicomachus persisted in expressing abhorrence of the crime, he resorted to threats of death to deter him, telling him that the conspirators' noble enterprise would start with Nicomachus' assassination. [11] Then, alternately calling him an effeminate coward and a traitor to his lover, and making him lavish promises (sometimes adding one of royal power), he kept working on a character that utterly recoiled from so heinous a crime. [12] Next, drawing his sword, he put it first to Nicomachus'

throat, then to his own, both entreating him and threatening him, and finally he extracted from him a promise not just of silence but even of cooperation. [13] In fact, Nicomachus possessed the steadfast resolve appropriate to a clean-living man; he had not wavered from his earlier decision but pretended that out of love for Dymnus he could deny him nothing. [14] He now proceeded to inquire about the identity of the accomplices in this important enterprise, saying that the quality of the people involved in so significant an undertaking made all the difference. [15] Crazed as much by love as by guilt, Dymnus offered him both thanks and congratulations on unhesitatingly joining a brave group of young men, comprising the bodyguard Demetrius,[41] Peucolaus and Nicanor. To these Dymnus added the names of Aphobetus, Iolaus, Dioxenus, Archepolis and Amyntas.

[16] Following this conversation Nicomachus relayed what he had heard to his brother, whose name was Cebalinus. They decided Nicomachus should remain in the tent in case, by entering the royal quarters, he made the conspirators aware that they had been betrayed, for he was not an intimate of the king's. [17] Cebalinus himself stood before the entrance to the royal tent, not being permitted to proceed further, and waited for someone of the first order of Alexander's friends who would take him in to the king. [18] As it happened, only Parmenion's son Philotas had remained in the royal quarters after the others had been dismissed; why he did so is not known. To him Cebalinus, noticeably in great agitation, disclosed in confused speech what he had learned from his brother, and insisted that it be reported to the king without delay. [19] Philotas commended him and straightway went in to Alexander but, after engaging him in lengthy conversation on other matters, he reported none of the information he had received from Cebalinus. [20] Towards evening the young man caught Philotas at the entrance to the royal tent as he was on his way out, and asked if he had carried out his request. [21] Philotas claimed Alexander had had no time to talk to him and then went on his way. The next day Cebalinus was there when Philotas came to the royal quarters and, as he went in, he reminded him of the matter he had communicated to him the day before. Philotas replied that he was seeing to it – but even then he failed to disclose to the king what he had heard.

[22] Cebalinus had begun to suspect him. Thinking it inadvisable to accost him again, he gave the information of the villainous plot to a young nobleman called Metron[42] who had charge of the armoury. [23] Metron hid Cebalinus in the armoury and immediately revealed the informer's allegations to the king, who happened to be taking a bath. [24] Alexander dispatched guards to arrest Dymnus and went into the armoury. Cebalinus was transported with joy. 'You are safe!' he said, 'I see you delivered from the hands of criminals!' [25] Alexander then inquired into the pertinent details and, after he was given a coherent account, made a point of asking how many days it had been since Nicomachus brought him his information. [26] When Cebalinus admitted it had been two days, Alexander ordered him to be clapped in irons

because he thought that the fact that he had taken so long to report what he had heard meant that his loyalty was questionable. [27] Cebalinus, however, began to cry out that he had run to Philotas the very moment he had heard of the plot, and that Philotas had learned the details from him. [28] The king asked again if he had approached Philotas, if he had insisted that they come to Alexander. When Cebalinus persistently reaffirmed his story, Alexander held his hands up to the sky and, bursting into tears, bemoaned the fact that he had been so repaid by one who had formerly been the dearest of his friends.

[29] Dymnus, meanwhile, well aware of the reason for his summons by the king, dealt himself a mortal wound with the sword he happened to be wearing, but guards rushed up to restrain him and he was carried into the royal quarters. [30] Alexander looked at him. 'Dymnus,' he said, 'what is the vicious crime I have plotted against you to justify your decision that Philotas deserves royal power more than I myself?' But Dymnus had already lost the power of speech. He groaned, turned his face away from the king's eyes, and immediately collapsed and died.

[31] The king ordered Philotas to the royal quarters. 'Cebalinus deserved the supreme penalty,' he said, 'if for two days he covered up a plot that had been hatched against my life. But he shifts the guilt for his crime to Philotas by his claim that he passed the information on to him immediately. [32] Because of your closer ties of friendship with me, such suppression of information on your part is all the more reprehensible, and it is my opinion that conduct such as this suits Cebalinus more than it does Philotas. You now have a judge who is on your side – if there is any way of clearing yourself of what should not have happened.'

[33] Philotas was not in the slightest alarmed, if his emotions could be judged by his expression. In reply he said that, yes, Cebalinus had indeed reported to him his conversation with the catamite, but Philotas had set no store by it since the source was so unreliable – he feared that reporting a quarrel between a male prostitute and his lover would make him a laughing stock. [34] However, Dymnus' suicide now revealed that the facts, whatever they were, should not have been suppressed. Philotas put his arms around the king and proceeded to entreat him to consider his past record rather than his present error – which, anyway, involved merely keeping silent, not committing an act. [35] It would be difficult to say whether the king believed him or kept his anger concealed deep in his heart. He offered Philotas his right hand as a sign of reconciliation, and said that in his opinion it was a case of information not being taken seriously rather than being deliberately suppressed.

8

[1] Even so, Alexander called a meeting of his friends, without inviting Philotas, and ordered Nicomachus to be brought before it. [2] The latter

repeated the whole story which he had brought to the king. Now Craterus, being an especially close friend of the king's, was consequently hostile to Philotas because of their competing for position,[43] [3] and he was not unaware that Philotas' excessively boastful talk about his courage and his services had often grated on the ears of Alexander, who therefore entertained the notion that while he was no criminal he was certainly self-willed. [4] Believing there would be no better opportunity for crushing his opponent, Craterus masked his personal animosity with feigned loyalty to Alexander and declared: 'I wish you had also discussed this matter with us in the beginning! [5] If you were set on pardoning Philotas, we would have urged you to keep him ignorant of how much he owed you. Rather that than that he now have cause to think more about his own danger – since he has been taken to the brink of death – than about your generosity. You see, *he* will always be able to plot against you, but you will not always be able to pardon Philotas. [6] And you have no reason to suppose that a man whose daring has been so great can be changed by a pardon: he knows that those who have exhausted someone's clemency can expect no more in future. [7] But even supposing penitence or your generosity induced him to take no further action, I for my part am sure that his father Parmenion will not be happy at being indebted to you for his son's life – he is the leader of a mighty army and because of his long-standing influence with your men holds a position of great authority not much inferior to yours. [8] Some acts of kindness we resent. A man is ashamed to admit that he has deserved execution; the alternative is to foster the impression that he has been dealt an injury rather than granted a reprieve. So you can be sure that you must fight for your life against the men in question. [9] The enemies we are about to pursue are still numerous enough. Protect yourself against enemies within our ranks. Eliminate those and I fear nothing from the foreigner.'

Such were Craterus' words, [10] and the others were also in no doubt that Philotas would not have suppressed evidence of the conspiracy if he had not been the ringleader or an accomplice.[44] For, they reasoned, any loyal and well-intentioned person, even if he were of the lowest order and not a friend of Alexander, would have run immediately to the king on hearing the charges that had been brought to Philotas. [11] But the son of Parmenion did not do that, commander of the cavalry and confidant of all the king's secrets though he was, not even when he had before him the example of Cebalinus who had reported to Philotas what he had learned from his brother. He had even pretended that the king had had no time to talk to him, intending thereby to prevent the informer from looking for a second go-between. [12] Nicomachus had rushed to unburden his conscience in spite of the sacred obligation of his oath; Philotas, who had spent almost the entire day on frivolous amusements, was reluctant to insert into his lengthy and possibly inconsequential conversation a word or two vital to the king's survival. [13] But, if he had felt no confidence in such a report from mere boys, why then would he have made the affair drag on for two days as if he believed their disclosures? He ought to have sent Cebalinus away if he rejected his charges. [14] Being brave is appropriate when it is a question of one's own risk, but when there is concern for the life of the king one should be credulous and pay attention even to men who bring false information.

[15] So the decision was unanimous that Philotas should be interrogated under torture to force him to name his accomplices in the crime. Then Alexander dismissed them, telling them to remain silent about their decision and, in order not to betray any hint of the course of action they had recently adopted, he had marching orders issued for the following day. [16] Philotas was even invited to a banquet, which was to be his last, and the king was able not merely to dine with the man he had condemned but even to engage him in friendly conversation. [17] Then, at the time of the second watch, when the lights were out, some of the king's friends, namely Hephaestion, Craterus, Coenus and Erigyius, met in the royal quarters with a few men, along with Perdiccas and Leonnatus from the bodyguard.⁴⁵ Orders were issued by these for the men on guard at the king's tent to keep watch under arms. [18] Cavalrymen had already been posted at all the entrances to the camp with orders also to block the roads so that no one could slip off secretly to Parmenion, who at that time was governor of Media and in command of strong forces.

[19] Atarrhias had now entered the royal tent with 300 armed men. He was given ten attendants, each accompanied by ten armour-bearers [20] and, while these were sent in groups to arrest the other conspirators, Atarrhias and his 300 were dispatched to Philotas. With fifty of his best young men around him he set about forcing the door, which was closed, having ordered the others to cordon off the house entirely so that Philotas could not slip away by a secret entrance. [21] Philotas was in a deep slumber, his relaxation the result of an easy conscience or else of exhaustion, and he was still half-asleep when Atarrhias grasped him. [22] Finally he shook off the drowsiness and, as the shackles were placed on him, said: 'Your Majesty, the bitter hatred of my enemies has triumphed over your kindness.'⁴⁶ This was all he said before they covered his head and took him into the royal quarters. [23] The next day the king gave orders for a general assembly in arms.

Some 6,000 soldiers had arrived and a crowd of camp-followers and servants added to the total in the royal tent. [24] Philotas was hidden by a column of men-at-arms so that he could not be seen by the crowd until the king had addressed the men. [25] In capital cases it was a long-established Macedonian practice for the king to conduct the trial while the army (or the commons in peace-time) acted as jury, and the position of the king counted for nothing unless his influence had been substantial prior to the trial. [26] So now, at the start, the corpse of Dymnus was brought in, the majority of the crowd having no idea of his plot or of how he had died.

9

[1] Alexander marched into the assembly. His expression betrayed the anguish he felt, and the gloominess of his friends had charged the affair with considerable anticipation. [2] The king stood for a long while with eyes fixed on the ground, looking dazed and nonplussed. Finally he pulled himself together and said: 'Men! I was almost snatched from you by a criminal conspiracy: it is thanks to the gods' providence and mercy that I still live. And the awe-inspiring sight of your gathering has made me feel even more angry with the traitors because my first pleasure in life – no, my only pleasure – is that I am still able to repay all the brave men who have deserved well of me.'

[3] Groans from the men interrupted him, and tears welled up in every eye. 'I shall stir far deeper emotions in your hearts when I reveal to you the instigators of such villainy,' the king continued. 'I still shudder to mention them and I keep from naming them as though it were possible to save them. [4] But the memory of my former intimacy with them must be expunged; a conspiracy plotted by treacherous citizens of ours must be exposed. How could I remain silent about such an outrage? Parmenion, despite his age and obligations from all the benefits he received from me and from my father; although he is the oldest of all my friends – it was he who offered to head this monstrous crime. [5] His accomplice was Philotas, who suborned Peucolaus, Demetrius and Dymnus, whose body you see before you, and other equally insane individuals to assassinate me.' [6] Roars of pained outrage broke forth throughout the gathering, as typically happens in a crowd, and especially in a crowd of soldiers, when it is fired with enthusiasm or anger. [7] Nicomachus, Metron and Cebalinus were now brought in. They repeated their various accounts, but the evidence of none of them marked Philotas as an accomplice in the crime and so, after the initial outburst of indignation from the crowd, the statements of the witnesses were received in silence.

[8] Then Alexander said: 'So what do you think were the intentions of a man who suppressed the actual information he was given about this affair? That there was some substance to it is shown by Dymnus' death. [9] When the matter was still uncorroborated, Cebalinus reported it, undeterred by fear of torture, and Metron lost no time at all in unburdening himself of his information – going as far as to break into my bathroom! [10] Only Philotas feared nothing and believed nothing. What a courageous fellow! Would a man like that be distressed at the thought of his king's peril? Would he alter his expression or feel anxiety as he listened to the bearer of such momentous news? [11] Obviously some criminal intention lurks in his silence: it was greedy anticipation of the throne that sent his thoughts speeding towards the vilest of crimes. His father governs Media and, because of my support, Philotas himself exercised great influence with many of the officers – so that his aspirations exceed his ability to fulfil them. [12] My childless state, the fact

that I have no offspring, also arouses his contempt. But Philotas is wrong. In you I have children, parents, kinsmen, and while you are safe I cannot be childless.'

[13] He then read out a letter which had been intercepted, written by Parmenion to his sons Nicanor and Philotas.[47] But it did not really contain evidence of some dangerous plot. Its gist was as follows: [14] 'First of all take care of yourselves and then of your people – that is how we shall accomplish our purpose.' [15] The king added that the letter was worded in this way so that if it reached his sons it could be understood by those involved in the plot whereas, intercepted, its meaning would escape those who were ignorant of it.

[16] Alexander continued: 'Dymnus, you will say, did not name Philotas despite designating the others involved in the crime. That is not evidence of Philotas' innocence but of his standing: he is so feared by the people who can betray him that, even when they confess their own guilt, they withhold his name. But Philotas' own record accuses him. [17] When my cousin Amyntas[48] engineered a treacherous plot against me in Macedonia, it was Philotas who made himself his ally and his accomplice. It was Philotas who gave his sister in marriage to Attalus, the worst enemy I have ever had![49] [18] In view of our close association and friendship, I had written to him of the oracular response of Jupiter Ammon. It was Philotas who had the effrontery to reply that, while he congratulated me on being received among the gods, he nevertheless felt pity for people who would have to live under a man who was more than human. [19] These are all indications that he has long been alienated from me and become envious of my fame. I have kept them locked in my heart for as long as I could, men, thinking that to bring down in my own estimation men to whose careers I had made such great contributions was like ripping away part of myself. [20] But it is no longer mere words that call for punishment. Unbridled speech has led to the sword – which, if you believe me, Philotas has sharpened against me or which, if you believe him, he has permitted to be sharpened against me. [21] Where am I going to turn, men? To whom am I to entrust my life? I made Philotas sole commander of the cavalry, the pick of my troops, the best of our young noblemen. To his loyalty and his protection I have entrusted my life, my hopes, and my victory. [22] I have promoted his father to the same eminence in which you have placed me; I have set under his command and authority the richest of all countries, Media, along with many thousands of our citizens and allies. Where I looked for help I found only danger. [23] How happy should I have been to die in battle, a prey to my enemy rather than a victim of a fellow-citizen! As it is, I have been saved from the only perils I feared, only to face others which I should not have had to fear. [24] Men, you keep on asking me to look after myself, and now it is within your power to help me follow your advice. I take refuge in your hands and your weapons. To survive against your will I do not wish; but even in accordance with your will, survival is impossible unless you avenge me.'

[25] Alexander then ordered Philotas to be brought in with his hands tied behind his back and his head covered with an old cloak. There was clearly an emotional reaction to the pitiful condition of a man who shortly before had been regarded with envy. [26] The men had seen him as cavalry commander on the previous day, and they knew he had attended the king's banquet. Suddenly they saw him not merely on trial but condemned – even in fetters! [27] They also began to reflect on the misfortunes of Parmenion: a great general and an illustrious citizen, he had recently lost two sons, Hector and Nicanor,[30] and now in his absence he would be on trial with the only son his calamitous fate had left him. [28] Consequently, since the assembly was inclining towards pity, Amyntas, one of the king's generals, stirred it up again with a speech attacking Philotas. They had been betrayed to the barbarians, he said. None of them would have returned to his wife and his parents, but they would have been like a decapitated body devoid of life, without a name, an object of ridicule to the enemy in a foreign land. [29] Amyntas' words were not at all as pleasing to the king as he had hoped – reminding the men of their wives and country merely decreased their enthusiasm for tackling the jobs that remained.

[30] Coenus spoke next and, although he had married a sister of Philotas, he attacked him more fiercely than anyone,[31] loudly proclaiming him a traitor to his king, country and army. [31] He then picked up a stone which happened to be lying before his feet to throw at Philotas – from a wish to save him from torture, many thought – but the king stayed his hand, declaring that the defendant must first be given an opportunity to make his defence and that he would not permit the case to proceed otherwise. [32] Philotas was then instructed to make his defence. Distracted and nonplussed, either from a guilty conscience or because of the magnitude of his peril, he did not dare to lift his eyes or open his mouth. [33] Then he burst into tears and fainted into the arms of the man holding him. He gradually recovered both his breath and his voice and, using his cloak to wipe his eyes, seemed to be about to speak. [34] Alexander fixed his gaze on him. 'The Macedonians are going to judge your case,' he said. 'Please state whether you will use your native language before them.'

[35] 'Besides the Macedonians,' replied Philotas, 'there are many present who, I think, will find what I am going to say easier to understand if I use the language you yourself have been using, your purpose, I believe, being only to enable more people to understand you.'[32]

[36] Then the king said: 'Do you see how offensive Philotas finds even his native language? He alone feels an aversion to learning it. But let him speak as he pleases – only remember that he is as contemptuous of our way of life as he is of our language.' So saying, Alexander left the meeting.

10

[1] Then Philotas spoke. 'When a man is innocent, finding words is easy,' he said, 'but when he is in trouble, limiting them is difficult. [2] I am caught between a clear conscience and calamitous misfortune, not knowing how to find terms to match both my feelings and my circumstances. [3] The man who can best judge my case is not present, though why he should refuse to hear me himself I simply cannot understand. After hearing both sides, he is as much at liberty to condemn as to acquit me whereas, if he does not hear both, I cannot be absolved by him in his absence – not after being declared guilty by him when he was present.

[4] 'The defence of a man in fetters is not merely useless; it also engenders ill-feeling, because the defendant appears not to be giving his judge information but to be finding fault with him. Even so I shall not forfeit my case, however I am allowed to conduct my defence, nor shall I foster the impression that I have added my own vote to the conviction.

[5] 'I do not understand, quite frankly, of what crime I stand accused. None of the conspirators names me; Nicomachus said nothing about me; and Cebalinus could have known no more than what he had been told. [6] And yet Alexander believes I headed the conspiracy. Then could Dymnus have omitted to mention the man whose lead he followed? Especially when my name *should* have been included, even falsely, at the time when Nicomachus was asking Dymnus about his confederates – should have been included to persuade Nicomachus when overtures were being made to him. [7] Now Dymnus' motive for omitting my name when the conspiracy was uncovered was not that he might be seen to be protecting a confederate. When he confessed to Nicomachus who, he believed, would keep secret his part in the affair, he identified all the others but still omitted my name and mine alone. [8] I ask you, my comrades: if Cebalinus had not come to me, if he had wanted me to know nothing about the conspirators, would I be on trial today – when no one names me? [9] Let us suppose that Dymnus were alive and also that he wished to protect me. What about the others? Of course they are going to confess their own guilt but omit me! Misfortune is spiteful. Generally speaking, a guilty person finds comfort in another's punishment when he feels the pain of his own. [10] Will so many conspirators fail to admit the truth, even when put on the rack? No, just as no one protects the condemned man so, I believe, the condemned man protects no one.

[11] 'I must turn to the one real charge against me, which goes: "Why did you remain silent about the matter that was reported to you? Why so little concern when you heard?" Alexander, wherever you are, I confessed to this misdemeanour, such as it is, and you pardoned me. I clasped your right hand, a gesture of our reconciliation, and I attended your banquet. [12] If you believed me, I was declared innocent; if you forgave me, I was given a reprieve. Just abide by your decision. What was it that I did last night after

leaving your table? What new crime has been reported to you to make you change your mind? [13] I was in a deep sleep when, as I rested unperturbed by misfortune, my enemies put the fetters on me and woke me. How does a murderer and a traitor achieve such deep, relaxed sleep? [14] Criminals cannot get to sleep because their consciences will not let them: they are hounded by the Furies not just after committing a crime but even after planning one. But I had gained a feeling of security, first from my innocence and then from your right hand, and I felt no apprehension that the cruelty of others would influence you more than your own merciful inclinations.

[15] 'But (not to have you regret that you believed me) the matter was reported to me by a mere boy. He was unable to produce any witness or any corroboration for his charges and, if he had begun to be heard, he would have filled everybody with alarm. [16] Unfortunately for me, I thought that what was coming to my ears was a quarrel between lover and boyfriend, and my doubts about Nicomachus' reliability arose from the consideration that he did not bring the information in person but induced his brother to bring it. [17] I was afraid he would deny having given instructions to Cebalinus and I myself would then appear responsible for having put many of the king's friends in jeopardy. [18] Even as things are, when I have done nobody any harm, I have found someone who prefers to see me dead than safe – so what kind of hostility do you think I would have incurred by attacking innocent people?

[19] 'But Dymnus committed suicide, you will say. Surely you do not think I could have foreseen that he would? Of course not. So the one thing supporting this charge – that thing could not possibly have had any effect on me when I was accosted by Cebalinus. [20] My god! Suppose I *had* been Dymnus' accomplice in such a horrible crime. I ought not to have hidden for those two days the fact that we had been betrayed – and Cebalinus himself could have been eliminated without difficulty. [21] Then, after the information which I was going to suppress had been brought, I went into the king's bedroom alone, actually wearing a sword. Why did I postpone the deed? Was it that without Dymnus I didn't dare do it? [22] Then it was Dymnus who was the leader of the conspiracy! I was merely lurking in his shadow – I, Philotas, who have eyes on the throne of Macedon! Was any one of you suborned with bribes? To what general or what officer did I pay undue attention?

[23] 'One charge made against me is that I disdain to communicate in my native language, that I have no respect for Macedonian customs (which means I have designs on an empire I despise!). That native language of ours has long been rendered obsolete through our dealings with other nations, and conquerors and conquered alike must learn a foreign tongue.

[24] 'Indeed, that kind of charge is as little damaging to me as the charge that Perdiccas' son, Amyntas, plotted against the king. As for my friendship with him, I am not reluctant to defend myself on that score – unless it was wrong for us to feel affection for a brother of the king.[53] [25] If, however,

someone of such elevated status also demanded respect, then tell me, please, am I on trial because I did not see into the future or is death also mandatory for the innocent friends of traitors? And if *that* is justice, why have I been left alive so long? If it is injustice, why then am I facing death at this very moment?

[26] 'Another charge: I wrote that I felt sorry for people who had to live under anyone who believed himself to be Jupiter's son. Ah, loyalty in friendship! Ah, perilous candour in giving honest advice! It was you who let me down! It was you who urged me not to conceal what I felt! [27] I admit I wrote this *to* the king – but not *about* the king. I was not trying to generate animosity against him – I was afraid for him. It seemed to me more befitting Alexander's dignity that he acknowledge in silence his descent from Jupiter than bandy it about in public declarations. [28] But since the trustworthiness of the oracle is beyond question, let the god bear witness in my case: keep me in shackles while Ammon is consulted as to whether I embarked on some dark, sinister crime. After acknowledging our king as his son, he will not suffer any of those who have plotted against his progeny to escape detection. [29] If you think torture to be more reliable than oracles, I do not refuse even this method of exposing the truth.

[30] 'Men on capital charges usually bring their relatives before you. In my case I have recently lost my two brothers while I cannot produce my father, nor dare I name him since he is also accused of this terrible crime. [31] Until recently the father of many children, he must now be content with one, and it is not enough for him to be deprived of that one, too – no, he is being placed upon my funeral pyre himself. [32] So, dearest father, you are going to die along with me as well as because of me. It is I who take away your life, I who terminate your advanced years. Why did you give me my wretched life when the gods were against it? Was it to reap from me the harvest that now awaits you? [33] I do not know which is more pitiful, my youth or your old age, for I die in the prime of my years while the executioner will take from you a life that nature was already calling in – were fortune only prepared to be patient.

[34] 'The reference to my father reminds me of how necessary my timidity and hesitation really were in disclosing the information that Cebalinus had brought to me. After Parmenion heard of a plot to poison the king by the physician Philip, he wrote a letter because he wished to deter Alexander from drinking the potion which the doctor intended to give to him.[54] My father wasn't believed, was he? His letter had no influence, did it? [35] In my own case, how often have I reported things I have heard only to be snubbed and laughed at for being over-credulous! If we face unpopularity when we report things and suspicion when we remain silent, what must we do?' [36] And when one of the crowd of onlookers exclaimed, 'Don't hatch plots against your benefactors,' Philotas said: 'You're right, whoever you are. [37] So if I have hatched a plot, I do not ask to be excused punishment, and I conclude my speech since my last words were apparently offensive to your ears.' Then he was led away by the men acting as his guards.

11

[1] Among the officers was a certain Bolon, a good fighter but a man of no refinement or cultivation, an older soldier who had risen from the ranks to his present position. [2] The rest now fell silent but Bolon, with boorish impudence and in a brazen manner, began to remind them all of the time they had each been ejected from quarters they had taken over so that the scum of Philotas' slaves might have the places from which they had thrown out his colleagues. [3] Philotas' wagons, piled high with gold and silver, had been parked all through the streets, he said, while not one of their comrades had even been allowed close to his quarters; no, the servants he had guarding him while he slept moved them all far away so that fop would not be disturbed by the noise – no, *silence* is a better word – of hushed conversation. [4] Philotas had ridiculed men from the country, he continued, calling them Phrygians and Paphlagonians – this from a man who, Macedonian born, was not ashamed to use an interpreter to listen to men who spoke his own language. [5] Why did he now want Ammon consulted? It was Philotas who had accused Jupiter of lying when he acknowledged Alexander as his son; he was, of course, afraid that this gift of the gods would excite envy! [6] When he plotted against the life of his king and friend, he did not consult Jupiter; now he wanted to send to the oracle so as to give his father time to win over his subjects in Media and use the money placed in his care to hire desperate men to abet their crime. [7] Yes, he said, they *would* send a deputation to the oracle, not to ask Jupiter about what they had heard from Alexander but to give him thanks and to repay their vows for his protection of their fine king.[55]

[8] At this the whole assembly really became aroused. It started with the bodyguards crying out that they should tear the traitor to pieces, a suggestion which Philotas in fact heard without undue anxiety, since he feared more dire punishment. [9] The king returned to the assembly and adjourned the hearing to the following day, either to subject Philotas to further torture in prison or to conduct a more thorough investigation of the entire episode and, though the day was drawing on towards evening, he nevertheless called a meeting of his friends. [10] The general feeling was that Philotas should be stoned to death according to Macedonian custom, but Hephaestion, Craterus and Coenus declared that torture should be employed to force the truth out of him, and those who had advocated other punishment went over to their view. [11] So, when the council was adjourned, Hephaestion, Craterus and Coenus got up together to conduct the interrogation of Philotas. [12] The king summoned Craterus and, after some conversation with him, the contents of which were not made public, withdrew to the inner section of his quarters. There, dismissing all who were present, he awaited the outcome of the investigation till late in the night.

[13] The torturers laid out before Philotas' eyes all the instruments used

to inflict pain. [14] Philotas, on an impulse, asked: 'Why hesitate to execute your king's enemy, a confessed assassin? What need is there for interrogation under torture? I planned the crime; I wanted it to succeed.' Craterus insisted that he also make his confession under torture. [15] Philotas was seized, blindfolded and his clothes stripped from him, while all the time he invoked the gods of his country and the laws of humanity – to no avail, for their ears were deaf. He was racked with the most cruel tortures: not only was he a condemned man but his torturers were personal enemies trying to please the king. [16] Though subjected both to fire and beatings – no longer to make him talk but as punishment – he managed at first to keep not only from screaming but even groaning. [17] But his body began to swell with weals and he could not bear the blows that cut to the bone. He promised to tell them what they wished to know if they put an end to the torture, [18] but he wanted them to swear on Alexander's life that the interrogation would be terminated and the torturers removed. On being granted both those terms Philotas said: 'Craterus, say what you want me to say.' [19] Craterus was annoyed that Philotas was mocking him and he recalled the torturers. But Philotas began to beg for time to get his breath back, after which he was prepared to tell all he knew.

[20] In the meantime word of the torture of Philotas had got around, and this spread panic among the cavalry, the men from the best families and especially those closely related to Parmenion. What they feared was the Macedonian law which provided the death penalty also for relatives of people who had plotted against the king. Some, therefore, committed suicide and others fled into remote mountains and desert wastes as sheer terror spread throughout the camp. Finally, the king learned of the consternation and proclaimed that he was suspending the law relating to the punishment of relatives of the guilty.

[21] Whether Philotas told the truth or whether he lied from a wish to deliver himself from torture is debatable, for the end in view of both those who confess the truth and those who lie is termination of the pain. [22] 'You are aware of the close friendship my father had with Hegelochus,' said Philotas. 'I mean that Hegelochus who died in combat[56] – he was the cause of all our problems. [23] When the king first commanded that he be addressed as the son of Jupiter, Hegelochus was indignant and said: "Well, do we recognize this man as our king? He disclaims Philip as his father. If we can stand that, we're done for. [24] A man who demands to be believed a god shows contempt not only for men but for the gods as well. We have lost Alexander, we have lost our king! We have come up against an arrogance that can be tolerated neither by the gods, to whom he considers himself an equal, nor by men, from whom he excludes himself. [25] Have we spilt our blood to make a god who despises us, who balks at attending a meeting of mere mortals? Listen to me: if we are true men, we also will be adopted by

143

the gods! [26] Who avenged the murder of this man's ancestor Archelaus, of Alexander after that, and of Perdiccas?[57] But this man granted a pardon to his father's murderers."[58]

[27] 'Such were Hegelochus' words over dinner. The next day at dawn I was sent for by my father. He was in low spirits and could see that I was also dejected; for what we had heard was enough to strike anxiety into our hearts. [28] So, to see whether Hegelochus had poured out those ideas under the influence of drink or whether they were spawned of some deep conviction, we decided he should be summoned. He came and without prompting spoke again in the same terms, adding that if we dared take the lead he would stand right behind us, but if we lacked the heart for it he would keep silent about the plan. [29] With Darius still alive, Parmenion thought the plan premature, since killing Alexander would benefit the enemy, not themselves, whereas with Darius removed the reward of killing the king that would fall to his assassins would be Asia and all of the East. The plan was approved and pledges given and accepted on it. [30] As for Dymnus, I know nothing. I realize, though, that after this confession it does me no good that I am entirely unconnected with his crime.'

[31] Once again they applied the instruments of torture, now themselves also using their spears to strike him in the face and eyes, and they extracted from him a confession to this crime as well. [32] Then they demanded the full programme of the crime they had contrived. Philotas replied that it appeared as though Alexander would be detained in Bactra for a long time and he had feared that his father might die in the meantime, since he was seventy years old. Parmenion was then leader of a great army and in charge of a large quantity of money; if he, Philotas, were deprived of such great resources, killing the king would serve no purpose. [33] Accordingly he had made haste to execute the plan while he still had the prize in his hands. If they did not believe his father took no part in it, he did not refuse further torture, even though he could no longer endure it.

[34] After conferring, his tormentors concluded that the interrogation had gone far enough. They went back to the king, who gave orders for Philotas' confession to be read out the next day and for Philotas himself to be carried to the assembly because he was unable to walk. [35] Since Philotas admitted everything, they brought in Demetrius, who was accused of complicity in the most recent conspiracy. With vigorous protestations and with the confidence which he felt showing in his expression, he denied any plot against the king, going so far as to demand torture for himself. [36] Then Philotas' eyes shifted round, falling eventually on one Calis who stood close by. Philotas told him to come closer and, when Calis showed agitation and refused to come over to him, he said, 'Are you going to permit Demetrius to lie and me to be tortured again?' [37] Calis was left speechless and pale. The Macedonians began to suspect that Philotas wished to incriminate the innocent, for the young man had been named neither by Nicomachus nor by Philotas himself

under torture but, when he saw the king's officers around him, Calis confessed that he and Demetrius had planned the crime. [38] Thereupon all those named by Nicomachus, when the signal was given, were stoned to death in the traditional Macedonian manner.[59]

[39] Alexander had been saved from great danger, danger to his popularity as much as to his life. Parmenion and Philotas had been his principal friends and their condemnation would have been impossible without causing personal indignation among the troops, unless they were demonstrably guilty. [40] So attitudes to the interrogation shifted. While Philotas denied the crime his torture was thought cruel, but after his confession he no longer won pity even from his friends.[60]

BOOK SEVEN

[1] While the traces of Philotas' crime were still fresh, the troops had judged that his punishment had been warranted but, when the man they had hated was no longer among them, their loathing turned to pity. [2] They were moved by the young man's reputation and also by his father's advanced age and bereavement. [3] It was Parmenion who had first opened up Asia for the king,[1] sharing all of Alexander's dangers and invariably taking charge of one of the wings in battle. He had been Philip's foremost friend, and his loyalty to Alexander himself had been such that the latter was not willing to use anyone else's services to kill Attalus.[2] [4] Such were the thoughts that presented themselves to the troops, whose mutinous remarks began to filter back to the king. He was not particularly disturbed by them, being well aware that the ill-effects of idleness are dispelled by work. So he issued orders for a general assembly of the men at the entrance to the royal tent. [5] When he learned that the men were present in large numbers, he marched into the meeting. Then Atarrhias began to make what was no doubt a pre-arranged demand that Alexander Lyncestes be brought before them (the man who, long before Philotas, had planned to assassinate the king). [6] This Alexander had been denounced by two informers, as I stated above, and was now in the third year of imprisonment.[3] It was thought certain that he had also conspired with Pausanias to murder Philip, but the fact that he had been the first to salute Alexander as king had gained him a reprieve, though not an acquittal. [7] Moreover, the pleas of Lyncestes' father-in-law, Antipater, also served to reduce the king's warranted anger. But the festering resentment against him broke out afresh, for anxiety over the current crisis began to revive memories of the former one. [8] Alexander was therefore brought from confinement and told to plead his case. Although he had had all of three years to rehearse his defence, he was faltering and nervous, deploying few of the arguments which he had stored up in his mind, until finally his very thought processes, not just his memory, failed him. [9] No one doubted that his discomposure betokened a guilty conscience rather than a defective memory. Accordingly some of the men standing next to him ran him through with their lances while he still grappled with his loss of memory.

[10] After Lyncestes' body was removed, the king had Amyntas and

Simmias brought in. (The youngest of the brothers, Polemon, had fled on hearing of the torture of Philotas.)⁴ [11] Of all Philotas' friends these had been his closest, and their promotion to positions of importance and prestige was mostly due to Philotas' support. The king also remembered the great enthusiasm with which they had been recommended to him by Philotas, and he was convinced that they, too, had been involved in his final intrigue. [12] He had long suspected them, he said to himself, because of a letter from his mother which warned him to be on his guard against them and, despite his unwillingness to believe pejorative reports, he had now been compelled by incontrovertible evidence to order their imprisonment. [13] There could be no doubt that they had met Philotas secretly on the day before his crime had been uncovered, and their brother had clearly revealed the reason for his flight by taking to his heels when Philotas was being interrogated. [14] In recent days, ostensibly out of concern for him, they had taken the unusual step of removing all others and planting themselves at his side, though they had no plausible reason for doing so. Alexander had been surprised at their performing this service out of turn, he remembered, and he was frightened by their nervousness, so he had swiftly retreated to his bodyguards who were following close behind. [15] There was a further consideration, too. The day before Philotas' crime was exposed, Antiphanes, the clerk to the cavalry, had instructed Amyntas to follow the normal practice and give some of his horses to men who had lost theirs, but Amyntas had arrogantly replied that if Antiphanes did not drop that plan he would soon know with whom he was dealing. [16] And, besides, the blustering and reckless language which these men directed against Alexander himself was nothing less than clear evidence of a criminal intent. If the charges against them were true, Alexander thought, then they deserved the same as Philotas; if they were false, then he demanded that they refute them.

[17] Antiphanes was brought forward. He gave evidence about Amyntas' refusal to transfer the horses and the haughty threats that accompanied this. Then, granted the opportunity to speak, Amyntas said: [18] 'If it is all the same to His Majesty, I request to be relieved of my fetters while I speak.' The king ordered both men to be freed and, when Amyntas asked that his guard's uniform also be restored to him, further ordered that he be given a lance. [19] Amyntas took it in his left hand and, avoiding the spot where Alexander Lyncestes' body had lain moments before, he said: 'Your Majesty, whatever remains in store for us, we admit that we shall owe a successful outcome to you while a less happy result we shall attribute to fortune. [20] We state our case without having been prejudged and we are free in body and mind – you have even restored to us the customary uniform we wear to attend you. We cannot feel fear about our cause, and we shall cease to fear fortune.

[21] 'Please allow me to answer the last of your charges first. We are not aware, Sire, of any talk on our part directed against your royal person. I would say that you long ago dispelled any feelings of ill-will towards you – I would,

if there were no risk of your believing that I am using flattery to make amends for malicious remarks on other occasions. [22] But even supposing that some criticisms had been heard from a soldier of yours when faint and exhausted on the march, or when facing danger in battle, or when injured and tending his wounds in his tent – even so we had by our gallant record earned the right to have you attribute such remarks to our circumstances rather than to genuine feelings. [23] When anything unfortunate occurs, everybody incurs our blame. We lay violent hands on our own bodies (which we certainly do not hate), and parents are exposed to their children's displeasure and odium if they come into their presence just then. When, on the other hand, we are given gifts of honour and we return home laden with prizes – who can bear us then? Who can subdue our elation? [24] When men are on active service, neither their indignation nor their joy knows any bounds. We are swept violently into every emotion: we blame, we praise, we feel pity or anger, just as the mood takes us. At one point we wish to go to India and the Ocean; at another our thoughts return to wives, children and homeland. [25] But these reflections, these topics of our conversation are terminated by the trumpet-call. We run to our respective ranks and whatever resentment has been generated in the tent is discharged upon the heads of the enemy. I wish that Philotas' wrongdoing had also been confined to words!

[26] 'So I turn now to the substance of the charge against us. That we were on friendly terms with Philotas I do not deny – indeed I admit that from this we sought and gained substantial benefits. [27] Are you really surprised at our cultivating the friendship of the son of Parmenion – the man whom you decided should rank second to you – when he surpassed almost all your friends in authority? [28] Indeed, Your Majesty, if you wish to hear the truth, it is you who are responsible for this predicament of ours. Who else was it who ensured that people wishing to win your approval would turn to Philotas? It was through his recommendation that we have risen to our present degree of friendship with you, and his standing with you was such that we could only seek his favour and fear his anger. [29] We have all sworn, almost coerced by threats of violence from you and in formulae dictated by you, to regard as enemies or friends the same people as you so regard. Bound by this sacred oath of allegiance, could we be expected to turn our backs on a man you used to set above all others? [30] So, if this is a crime, you have few blameless subjects – no, indeed, not one. Everyone wanted Philotas' friendship, but not all who wanted it could have it. So if you make no distinction between Philotas' friends and those involved in the conspiracy, you will also make no distinction between his friends and those who wanted to be his friends.

[31] 'So what is the evidence for our complicity? It is, I suppose, that on the day before he had engaged in friendly conversation with us without others present. As a matter of fact, I would find proving my innocence impossible if I had made any change in my previous day-to-day habits on that

"day before". As it is, if on that particular day which incriminates us we behaved just as on every other day, then our consistency of habit will rebut the charge against us.

[32] 'But we did not give horses to Antiphanes! And that was the day before Philotas was found out! Shall I argue this point with Antiphanes? If he wants to put us under suspicion because we did not surrender the horses on that particular day, he will be unable to justify his own action in asking for them. [33] Indeed, it is not clear who is guilty, the man keeping back the horses or the man asking for them – except that the man refusing to surrender his own property has a stronger case than the man demanding someone else's. [34] As a matter of fact, Your Majesty, I had ten horses. Eight of these Antiphanes had already distributed to men who had lost theirs and two were all that I had left. When this man insolently, or at least unfairly, attempted to commandeer them, I was obliged to hold on to them unless I was prepared to fight on foot. [35] I do not deny that my language was that of a gentleman to an arrant coward whose military experience goes no further than distributing other people's horses to men who are going to fight. This is how bad matters have become: I am simultaneously apologizing for my words to Alexander and to Antiphanes!

[36] 'But indeed your mother wrote to you about us saying we were your enemies! I wish her concern for her son had been more prudent and that her worry had not made her prey to idle delusions. Why does she not add the grounds for her fears? Why, finally, does she not divulge her source? What actions or words of ours prompted her to write you such an anxious letter? [37] What a terrible situation for me to be in – being silent is perhaps no more perilous than speaking out! But whatever the result, I prefer that you should be disappointed with my defence rather than with my cause. You will concede the point I am going to make. You remember saying, when you sent me to bring recruits from Macedonia, that a large number of able-bodied young men were in hiding at your mother's residence. [38] You instructed me accordingly to pay attention to no one but you and to deliver to you the men trying to avoid military service. Which is just what I did, following your instructions with less caution than was good for me. I brought from there Gorgias, Hecataeus and Gorgatas, who have been serving you well. [39] What can be more unfair than that I should now perish for obeying you, when in fact I would have deserved punishment if I had *not* obeyed you? For the only reason your mother has for victimizing us is that we set your welfare above a woman's favour. [40] I brought here 6,000 Macedonian infantry and 600 cavalry,[5] some of whom would not have come with me had I been willing to connive at those refusing to serve. It follows, therefore, since this is the reason for her anger with us, that *you* should placate your mother, being the one who exposed us to her displeasure.'

2

[1] While Amyntas was making this speech, there chanced to arrive men bringing back in chains his fugitive brother Polemon (referred to above) whom they had overtaken.⁶ The assembly was in an ugly mood and could barely be restrained from stoning Polemon immediately, after their usual custom. Polemon, however, was not in the least frightened. [2] 'I make no plea for myself,' he declared, 'only do not let my running away prejudice the case of my innocent brothers. If this action is indefensible, then let the charge be against *me*. The very fact that I ran away and thereby incurred suspicion actually improves *their* case.'

[3] With these words he won the support of the whole gathering. Presently they all began to shed tears, and their feelings were suddenly so radically transformed that the one thing now in his favour was what had most harmed his case before. [4] He was a young man in the early bloom of youth, and when the cavalry had been alarmed at Philotas' torture, he had been carried away by the spreading panic. Then, deserted by his companions and undecided whether to return or run, he was overtaken by his pursuers.

[5] Polemon started to weep and to rain blows on his own face, distressed not for himself but for his brothers, whose peril was of his making. [6] By now he had touched the heart of the king and not only the assembly. Only his brother remained implacable. 'Idiot!' he exclaimed, looking at him grimly. 'The time for your tears was when you were putting the spurs to your horse, deserting your brothers and accompanying deserters. Wretch! Where were you running to? From what? I am on trial for my life and you have made me talk like your prosecutor.'

[7] Polemon confessed he had done wrong, more to his brothers than to himself, at which the men now showed no restraint in their tears and the acclamations with which crowds demonstrate approval. A single cry went up as they unanimously urged the king to pardon these innocent and gallant men. His friends also rose to their feet when given an opportunity to express compassion, and they tearfully appealed to Alexander. [8] When silence fell, the latter said: 'I, too, cast my vote for acquitting Amyntas and his brothers. As for you, young men, I prefer you to forget my kindness to you rather than remember your danger. Resume your friendship with me with as much loyalty as I return to your friendship. [9] Had I not subjected the reports brought to me to close scrutiny, the resentment I would have concealed might have festered sorely. Better to be cleared than remain under suspicion. Bear in mind that no one can be acquitted without standing trial first. [10] You, Amyntas, must forgive your brother, a gesture which will also signify that you are sincerely reconciled to me.'⁷

[11] Then, dismissing the assembly, Alexander ordered Polydamas to be summoned. He was Parmenion's closest friend by far and had generally stood at his side in battle.⁸ [12] He had come to the royal quarters with a confidence

based on a clear conscience, but when he was told to produce his brothers, who were very young and, because of their age, not known to Alexander, his self-assurance turned to anxiety. He began to panic, and his thoughts turned more often to charges that could damage them than to ways of countering these.

[13] The guards instructed to bring the brothers in had now done so. Alexander told Polydamas, whose fright had drained him of colour, to come closer, and dismissed all the others present. 'We are all victims of Parmenion's crime,' said the king, 'but you and I more than anyone, since he deceived us by pretending to be our friend. [14] To hunt him down and punish him I have decided to use your services – observe the confidence I have in your loyalty. While you are engaged in this, your brothers will serve as hostages for you. [15] Go to Media and take my governors there a letter written in my own hand. You need speed to outrun the fast pace of rumour. I want you to arrive there at night and execute your written orders the next day. [16] You will also deliver letters to Parmenion, one written by me and a second ostensibly by Philotas, whose seal I have in my possession. If the father believes the letter was sealed by his son, he will have no fear when he sees you.'

[17] Relieved of his abject terror, Polydamas promised his support even more enthusiastically than was required of him. After being showered with compliments and promises, he took off the clothes he was wearing and put on Arab dress. [18] He was given two Arabs as companions, their wives and children remaining with the king as hostages to guarantee their loyalty. Using camels to cross stretches of arid desert, they reached their destination ten days later. [19] Before news of his arrival could be brought, Polydamas resumed Macedonian dress and came to the tent of Cleander,[9] the king's general, at the fourth watch. [20] He delivered the letter and they agreed to meet at dawn at Parmenion's quarters, since Polydamas had brought letters from the king for the others as well.

They were on the point of coming to Parmenion when he was himself given the news of Polydamas' arrival. [21] Parmenion was delighted that his friend had come and he was also eager to learn of the king's exploits, having received no letter from him over a long period, so he issued orders for Polydamas to be found. [22] Now country houses in that part of the world possess ample grounds attractively planted with trees, a special source of pleasure for kings and satraps. [23] Parmenion was strolling in a grove, surrounded by the officers who had been instructed by the king's letter to kill him. The time they had determined for executing the deed, however, was when Parmenion started to read the letters handed to him by Polydamas. [24] As Polydamas came and was sighted in the distance by Parmenion, his face assumed an expression of joy and he ran to embrace him. After an exchange of greetings Polydamas handed him the letter written by the king. [25] While he broke the seal of the letter, Parmenion asked how the king fared, to which

Polydamas replied that he would find out from the letter. [26] Parmenion read it and remarked: 'The king is preparing an expedition against the Arachosii. What an energetic man – he never rests! But after winning so much glory it is time he considered his own well-being.'

[27] Then he began to read (with pleasure, as could be observed from his expression) the second letter, the one ostensibly written by Philotas. It was at that point that Cleander drove his sword into his side, and then stabbed him in the throat. The others ran him through even as he lay dead. [28] When the guards on duty at the entrance to the grove learned of the assassination, not knowing the motive for it they came to the camp and aroused the men with their alarming report. [29] The soldiers armed themselves and converged on the grove where the murder had taken place, threatening to demolish the wall surrounding it if Polydamas and the others involved in the crime were not surrendered, and to make all of them pay with their blood for their general's life. [30] Cleander ordered their leaders to be admitted, and read out a letter written by the king to the men which contained news of Parmenion's plots against Alexander and pleas that they avenge him. [31] When they learned of the king's wishes, their mutiny was suppressed, though not their indignation. Most of them dispersed, but a few stayed behind, begging at least to be granted permission to bury Parmenion's body. [32] This request was for a long time denied because of Cleander's fear of displeasing the king but, when their entreaties became more insistent, he thought it advisable to remove anything that could fuel a riot, and so he cut off Parmenion's head and allowed them to bury the body. The head was sent to Alexander.

[33] Such was the end of Parmenion, an eminent man in war and peace. He had gained many successes without Alexander, while Alexander had achieved nothing of significance without him.[10] He was able to give satisfaction to a king who was one of fortune's favourites and expected everything to reach the level of his own good luck. At the age of seventy he performed the duties of a young commander, often even those of a common soldier. He was a shrewd tactician and a good fighter, well-liked by his officers and more popular still with the rank and file. [34] Whether such qualities made him covet royal power or only brought him under suspicion of doing so is debatable, for even when the affair lay in the recent past and a verdict was more attainable, it was uncertain whether Philotas, broken by the cruellest tortures, actually told the truth about matters which could not be verified or simply resorted to lies to end his torment.

[35] Alexander thought that the men who, he had learned, had openly expressed regret over Parmenion's death should be isolated from the rest of the force. He formed them into a single unit and gave command of it to Leonidas,[11] who had himself in the past been on intimate terms with Parmenion. [36] This group more or less comprised those against whom the king bore a grudge on other grounds. Wishing to test the sentiments of the

troops, he had urged anyone who had written letters to relatives in Macedonia to hand them over to men whom he was personally sending back and who could be trusted to deliver them. They had all frankly expressed their feelings in writing to their kinsfolk: some were sick of military service, though most did not object to it. [37] So it was that Alexander intercepted the correspondence both of those expressing satisfaction and of the malcontents, and those who had chanced to complain in writing about being tired of the hardships of the campaign he formed into a separate unit which he ordered to encamp away from the other men as a mark of disgrace. Thus he would have their bravery at his disposal in battle while at the same time removing their outspokenness from ears too ready to listen. This idea, which was perhaps foolhardy in that the bravest of the younger soldiers were angered by the affront, fell like everything else within the compass of the king's good fortune. [38] The eagerness of those men for battle was second to none. They were inspired to courageous action both by a desire to eradicate their disgrace and by the fact that their small numbers made it impossible for feats of bravery to go unnoticed.

3

[1] These adjustments made, Alexander appointed a satrap over the Arii[12] and then had orders issued for a march into the land of the Arimaspi. (Even at that time they were still called the Euergetae,[13] a name-change dating from the time when they had given assistance to Cyrus' army in the form of shelter and supplies when it was ravaged by cold and shortages of food.) [2] Four days after entering that region Alexander learned that Satibarzanes, who had defected to Bessus, had made a second incursion against the Arii with a force of cavalry. He therefore dispatched Caranus and Erigyius together with Artabazus and Andronicus, and along with them went 6,000 Greek infantry and 600 horse.

[3] As for Alexander himself, within sixty days he drew up ordinances relating to the Euergetae, including a large financial reward for their outstanding loyalty to Cyrus. [4] He then left the former secretary of Darius, Amedines,[14] to govern them and proceeded to subdue the Arachosii, whose territory extends to the Pontic sea. There he was met by the army which had been under Parmenion's command: 6,000 Macedonians, 200 noblemen and 5,000 Greeks (with 600 cavalry), undoubtedly the pick of all the king's forces. [5] Menon[15] was appointed governor of the Arachosii and was left a garrison of 4,000 infantry and 600 cavalry.

Alexander advanced with his army into the territory of a tribe scarcely known even to its neighbours since it had no trading connections. [6] They are called the Parapamisadae and are a backward tribe, extremely uncivilized even for barbarians, the harshness of the environment having hardened the character of the people. [7] Most of their territory faces the cold northern pole,[16] but it touches Bactria to the west and extends as far as the Indian Ocean in the south. [8] Their huts they build of brick from the foundations up and, because the country is devoid of timber (even the mountain range is bare), they employ the same brickwork right to the top of their buildings. [9] Their structure is fairly broad at the base but gradually narrows as the work rises until it finally converges to form what looks most like a ship's keel. [10] At this point an aperture is left to admit light from above. Such vines and trees as have been able to survive in the frozen soil the inhabitants set deep in the ground. They remain hidden beneath the surface in winter and return to the air and sunlight only when winter ends and exposes the earth. [11] In fact, the snow cover is so thick on the ground and so hardened with ice and almost permanent frost that no trace is to be found even of birds or any other animal of the wild. The overcast daylight, which would be more accurately called a shadow of the sky, resembles night and hangs so close to the earth that near-by objects are barely visible. [12] Cut off in this area, which was so devoid of any trace of human presence, the army faced every hardship it is possible to bear: lack of provisions, cold, fatigue, despair. [13] The numbing cold of the snow, of which they had no experience, claimed many lives; for many others it brought frost-bite to the feet and for a very large number snow-blindness. It was especially deadly for men suffering from exhaustion. They stretched their fatigued bodies on the surface of the ice and, once they stopped moving, the intensity of the cold made them so stiff that all their efforts to get up again were to no avail. [14] Their comrades would try to shake the languor from them, and the only remedy was to make them go on – only then, with the vital heat set in motion, would some energy return to their limbs.

[15] Anyone who managed to reach the huts of the barbarians quickly recovered, but the gloom was so dense that the location of these buildings was only revealed by the smoke from them. [16] The inhabitants had never before seen a foreigner in their lands, and the sudden sight of armed intruders almost frightened them to death. They began to bring out whatever they had in their huts, begging the Macedonians to spare their lives. [17] The king made the round of his troops on foot, raising up some who were on the ground and using his body to lend support to others when they had difficulty keeping up. At one moment he was at the front, at another at the centre or rear of the column, multiplying for himself the hardships of the march. [18] Finally they reached a more cultivated area where the troops were revived by a plentiful supply of provisions, while the men who had been unable to keep up also came into the camp they established there.

[19] The force advanced from here to the Caucasus mountains,[17] a range forming a continuous chain that splits Asia in two. In one direction it faces the sea that washes Cilicia, in another the Caspian, the river Araxes and also the desert areas of Scythia. [20] The Taurus range, which is of lesser height, joins the Caucasus, rising in Cappadocia, skirting Cilicia and merging into the

mountains of Armenia. [21] Thus interconnected in a series, these ranges form an unbroken chain, which is the source for practically all the rivers of Asia, some flowing into the Red, some into the Caspian, and others into the Hyrcanian[18] and Pontic seas. The army crossed the Caucasus in seventeen days. [22] According to ancient tradition, it was on a rocky crag in this chain – one with a perimeter of ten stades and a height of four – that Prometheus was bound.[19] [23] The foot of this mountain was selected as a site for building a city, and permission to settle in the new town was granted to 7,000 of the older Macedonians as well as to other soldiers retired by Alexander. This, too, was called Alexandria by its inhabitants.[20]

4

[1] Bessus was terrified by Alexander's speed. He had made due sacrifice to the local gods and, after the practice of those races, was holding a council of war with his friends and officers over a banquet. [2] Sodden with drink, they began to flatter themselves on their strength and to make disparaging remarks about both the over-confidence and the numerical weakness of the enemy. [3] Bessus was especially boastful in his language; his arrogance after treacherously usurping his throne bordered on madness. He began to claim that it was Darius' negligence that had increased the enemy's reputation, [4] that he had faced them in the narrowest defiles of Cilicia when retreat would have enabled him to lead them on into naturally protected areas without their realizing it. There were so many rivers to serve as obstacles and so many hiding-places in the mountains, he said; caught among these, the enemy would have had no chance to escape, much less offer resistance. [5] His decision now, he declared, was to draw back into the territory of the Sogdians and to use the river Oxus as a barrier against the enemy until strong reinforcements could amalgamate from the neighbouring tribes. [6] The Chorasmii would come, and so would the Dahae, the Sacae, the Indians and the Scythians living beyond the river Tanais – and not a man among these was so short that his shoulders could not stand level with a Macedonian soldier's head! [7] His drunken friends all shouted out that this was the only sound idea, and Bessus ordered more generous helpings of neat wine to be carried around as he planned his defeat of Alexander at the dinner table.

[8] Attending this banquet was Cobares[21] who, though a Mede by birth, had a reputation in the magical arts (if arts they really are, and not simply the foolish imaginings of the superstitious mind), more as one who practised them than as a genuine savant. Generally, though, he was a reasonable and honest man. [9] He began by saying that he realized it was more to a slave's advantage to obey orders than to give advice, since those following orders face the same treatment as anyone else while those giving advice run a risk all of their own. Bessus actually handed Cobares the cup which he held in his hand[22] ... [10] and taking it, Cobares continued: 'Human nature can be

called misguided and perverse for this reason, too, that a person is less perceptive in handling his own business than he is handling another's. [11] Those who are their own advisers produce disordered plans. Fear obstructs them; or on other occasions it is greed, or sometimes a natural affection for one's own ideas (for in your case arrogance can be discounted). Experience has taught you, of course, that a person considers the plan he has himself devised as the only one, or the best. [12] That is a great burden which you carry on your head, the royal diadem. You must bear it with moderation or (something I pray will not happen) it will come crashing down upon you. You need careful planning, not impulsive action.' [13] Cobares then added some aphorisms popular among the barbarians, that a frightened dog barks more fiercely than it bites and that it is the deepest rivers that flow with least noise. I have included this to put on record the practical wisdom (whatever its quality) that was to be found among barbarians.

[14] With these words Cobares had caught his audience's attention. He then revealed a plan that was more profitable than welcome to Bessus. 'A king who travels with great speed,' said Cobares, 'stands at the doorway of your kingdom. He will move his forces before you can move that table. [15] Now you are going to send for troops from the Tanais and use rivers as barriers to his arms! Of course your enemy cannot follow you wherever you flee! The road is the same for the two of you, but it is safer for the victor. You may think fear gives one speed – yet hope is faster. [16] Why do you not gain in advance the goodwill of your enemy, who is stronger than you, by surrendering? Whatever happens, you will be better placed after surrender than by remaining his enemy. [17] The kingdom you hold is another's, which makes it easier for you to part with it – you will perhaps begin to be a legitimate king when you are made one by the man with the power both to give a throne and take it away. [18] You have honest advice – further details are unnecessary. A pedigree horse is controlled just by the shadow of a whip; even the spur cannot arouse a hack.'

[19] Bessus' tendency to violence was aggravated by heavy drinking. He was so furious he could hardly be restrained by his friends from murdering Cobares – he had, in fact, drawn his scimitar. As it was, he charged from the banquet completely out of control of himself, and Cobares, slipping away in the uproar, deserted to Alexander.

[20] Bessus had an army of 8,000 Bactrians who faithfully carried out his orders as long as they thought their intemperate climate would make the Macedonians head for India but, when it was discovered that Alexander was approaching, they all slipped off to their villages and abandoned him. [21] With a group of dependants who had not changed their allegiance, he crossed the river Oxus, burned the boats used for crossing to stop the enemy using them, and started levying fresh troops among the Sogdians.

[22] Alexander had already crossed the Caucasus, as was related above, but grain shortages had brought the troops to the verge of starvation. [23]

The men rubbed their bodies with juice from pressed sesame in lieu of oil, though the cost of this juice was 240 denarii per jar, and honey and wine respectively cost 390 and 300 denarii. As for wheat, there was none, or very little, to be found. [24] (Their crops were hidden by the barbarians in what they called *siri*, so cunningly concealed that only the men who dug them could find them.) Lacking such provisions, the men survived on fresh-water fish and herbs [25] and, when even those means of sustenance had run out, they were given orders to slaughter the pack-animals. They managed to stay alive on the meat from these until they reached the Bactrians.

[26] The geographical features of Bactria are diverse and heterogeneous. In one area plentiful trees and vines produce abundant crops of succulent fruits. The rich soil here is irrigated by numerous springs and the more fertile parts are sown with wheat, while the rest the inhabitants leave as grazing land for their animals. [27] After that a large area of the country is engulfed by desert sands, and this desolate and arid region supports no human or vegetable life. When the winds blow from the direction of the Pontic sea,[23] they sweep together the sand lying on the plains. When this is piled up, it has the appearance at a distance of large hills, and all traces of roads that existed before are obliterated. [28] Consequently, people crossing the plains follow the practice of sailors, watching the stars at night and plotting their course by their movement (and the darkness of night is almost brighter than the daylight!). [29] The area is impossible to traverse by day, because one finds no tracks to follow and the light of the celestial bodies is hidden in a misty darkness (and anyone overtaken by the wind that rises from the sea is buried in sand). [30] Where the soil is more fertile, it supports large populations of humans and horses; and thus the Bactrian cavalry totalled 30,000. [31] Bactra[24] itself, the area capital, lies at the foot of Mt Parapanisus. The Bactrus river, which runs past its walls, gave the city and the region its name.

[32] While Alexander was in stationary camp here, reports arrived from Greece of the insurrection of the Peloponnesians and the Laconians.[25] These had not been crushed by the time the messengers were setting off to bring word of the early stages of the revolt. News also came in of a threat close at hand: the Scythians who lived beyond the Tanais[26] were coming with help for Bessus. A report also arrived at this time of Caranus' and Erigyius' progress in the territory of the Arii. An engagement had been fought between the Macedonians and the Arii. [33] The deserter, Satibarzanes, commanded the barbarians. When he saw the battle flagging, with both sides equally matched in strength, he rode up to the front ranks, removed his helmet, ordered the men who were hurling missiles to halt, and challenged to a duel anyone willing to fight him in single combat, adding that he would remain bare-headed in the fight. [34] Erigyius[27] found the barbarian general's display of bravado intolerable. Though well advanced in age, Erigyius was not to be ranked second to any of the younger men in courage or agility. He took off his helmet and revealed his white hair. 'The day has arrived,' he said, 'on

which I shall show by victory or by an honourable death the quality of Alexander's friends and fighting men.' [35] Saying no more, he rode towards his foe. One might have thought an order to cease fighting had been given on both sides. At all events they immediately fell back, leaving an open space, eager to see how matters would turn out not just for the two men but for themselves for, though others fought, the decision would encompass them all. [36] The barbarian threw his spear first. Moving his head slightly to the side, Erigyius avoided it. Then, spurring on his horse, he brought up his lance and ran it straight through the barbarian's gullet, so that it projected through the back of his neck. [37] The barbarian was flung from his mount, but still fought on. Erigyius drew the spear from the wound and drove it again into his face. Satibarzanes grabbed it with his hand, aiding his enemy's stroke to hasten his own death. [38] The barbarians had lost a leader whom they had followed under duress rather than out of choice and, remembering Alexander's past kindness to them, they surrendered to Erigyius.

[39] Though this pleased the king, he was by no means free from anxiety about the Spartans. However, he took the revolt with fortitude, declaring that the Spartans had not dared to reveal their intentions until they had heard of his arrival at the borders of India. [40] Alexander set his troops on the move in pursuit of Bessus and was met on the road by Erigyius, who carried before him the barbarian's head, his trophy of the war![28]

5

[1] Entrusting Bactria to Artabazus, Alexander left his baggage and equipment there under guard while he entered the desert areas of Sogdiana with a light-armed force, leading the troops by night. [2] The lack of water, mentioned above, is such that desperation produces a parching thirst even before a natural craving to drink appears. For 400 stades[29] no trace of water is to be found. [3] The heat of the summer sun scorches the sands and, when these start to heat up, everything on them is baked as if by perpetual fire. [4] Then a misty vapour thrown up by the burning heat of the earth obscures the daylight, giving the plains the appearance of one vast, deep ocean. [5] Travel by night seemed bearable because dew and the early morning freshness would bring relief to their bodies; but with the dawn comes the heat, draining with its aridity all natural moisture and deeply burning the mouth and the stomach. [6] So it was their resolution that failed first, and then their bodies. They were unwilling to stop and unwilling to go on. [7] A few had followed the advice of people who knew the country and stored up some water. This slaked their thirst for a short time, but then the increasing heat rekindled their craving for water. Consequently, all the wine and oil in anyone's possession was consumed, too, and such was the pleasure they gained from drinking it that they had no fear of thirst in the future. [8] Subsequently, the liquid they had greedily drained put such a weight on their

stomachs that they could neither hold up their weapons nor continue their journey, and the men who had been without water now seemed to be more fortunate than they themselves, since they were forced to spew up the water they had immoderately consumed.

[9] These urgent problems distressed Alexander. His friends stood around him and begged him to remember that his intrepid spirit was all that could restore the fortunes of his languishing army. [10] At this point he was met by two of the men who had gone ahead to select a camp-site. They were carrying skins of water to bring relief to their sons who, they knew, were suffering from severe thirst in Alexander's column. [11] On meeting the king one of them opened a skin, filled a cup he was carrying, and offered it to him. Alexander took it. Then he asked for whom they were carrying the water and learned it was for their sons. [12] He returned the cup, as full as when it was offered to him, saying: 'I cannot bear to drink alone and it is not possible for me to share so little with everybody. Go quickly and give your sons what you have brought on their account.'[30]

[13] Finally, around early evening, Alexander reached the river Oxus,[31] but most of the troops had been unable to keep pace with him. He had beacons lit on a mountain-peak so that men having difficulty keeping up could see they were not far from camp. [14] Those at the front of the column, quickly revived by something to eat and drink, were ordered by Alexander to fill skins, or any vessels that could serve for carrying water, and to bring relief to their comrades. [15] But some men gulped the water down too greedily and died from blockage of the windpipe – and the number of these exceeded the numbers Alexander had lost in any battle. [16] As for the king, he stood at the point where the troops were arriving, still wearing his cuirass and without having taken any food or drink, and he did not leave to take refreshment until the entire column had passed him. All night through after that he remained sleepless, his mind deeply troubled. [17] The next day he was no happier. He had no boats, and constructing a bridge was ruled out by the barrenness of the land around the river and specifically by the absence of wood. Accordingly he embarked on the only plan suggested to him by the exigencies of this situation, and distributed to the men, in numbers as great as was possible, skins stuffed with straw. [18] Lying on these the men swam the river, and those first over stood on guard for the others to cross.[32] In this way Alexander deposited the entire army on the far bank in five days.

[19] After deciding to proceed in pursuit of Bessus, he learned of the situation in Sogdiana. Among all Bessus' friends Spitamenes enjoyed a special position of honour – but no benefactions can serve to palliate treachery [20] (though in this case it might have earned less disapproval because no one would regard as abominable any act against Bessus, who had murdered his own king). Spitamenes' coup even had a specious pretext, namely vengeance for Darius, but it was Bessus' success, not his crime, that had aroused his hatred. [21] On learning that Alexander had crossed the river Oxus,

Spitamenes enlisted as associates in his plot Dataphernes and Catanes, who enjoyed Bessus' highest confidence. They were no sooner asked than they gave their support. Taking with them eight sturdy young men, they set the following trap. [22] Spitamenes went to Bessus and in strict privacy told him that he had discovered a plot against him by Dataphernes and Catanes, that these planned to deliver him alive into Alexander's hands. He, however, had anticipated their move and was holding them in custody.

[23] Bessus, believing himself under obligation for this great favour, thanked Spitamenes and at the same time, impatient to punish the culprits, had them brought to him. [24] These had agreed to have their hands tied up and were now dragged in by their fellow-conspirators. Bessus gave them a savage look and rose to his feet, unable to keep his hands off them. But the conspirators dropped their pretence, encircled him and, while he vainly tried to resist, tied him up, pulling from his head the royal diadem and ripping off the clothes he had assumed from the spoils of his dead king. [25] The gods, Bessus admitted, had come to exact vengeance for his crime; but they had not been unfavourable to Darius whom they avenged, but propitious to Alexander, who had always enjoyed even his enemy's help to win a victory. [26] Whether the barbarian masses would have freed Bessus is debatable, but the man who had tied him up frightened those still wavering by falsely claiming that they had acted on Alexander's orders. They put Bessus on a horse and led him away to surrender him to Alexander.

[27] Meanwhile the king selected some 900 men due for discharge and made them gifts of two talents per cavalryman and 3,000 denarii per infantryman. These he sent home with instructions to produce children. The other troops were thanked for their promise of support for the remainder of the campaign.

[28] In pursuit of Bessus the Macedonians had arrived at a small town inhabited by the Branchidae who, on the orders of Xerxes, when he was returning from Greece, had emigrated from Miletus and settled in this spot. This was necessary because, to please Xerxes, they had violated the temple called the Didymeon. [29] The culture of their forebears had not yet disappeared, though they were by now bilingual and the foreign tongue was gradually eroding their own. So it was with great joy that they welcomed Alexander, to whom they surrendered themselves and their city. Alexander called a meeting of the Milesians in his force, [30] for the Milesians bore a long-standing grudge against the Branchidae as a clan. Since they were the people betrayed by the Branchidae, Alexander let them decide freely on their case, asking if they preferred to remember their injury or their common origin. [31] But when there was a difference of opinion over this, he declared that he would himself consider the best course of action.

When the Branchidae met him the next day, he told them to accompany him. On reaching the city, he himself entered through the gate with a unit of light-armed troops. [32] The phalanx had been ordered to surround the city walls and, when the signal was given, to sack this city which provided refuge for traitors, killing the inhabitants to a man. [33] The Branchidae, who were unarmed, were butchered throughout the city, and neither community of language nor the olive-branches and entreaties of the suppliants could curb the savagery. Finally the Macedonians dug down to the foundations of the walls in order to demolish them and leave not a single trace of the city. [34] Woods, too, and sacred groves, they not only cut down but actually uprooted, so that nothing would remain after the removal of the roots but empty wasteland and barren soil. [35] Had this punishment been devised against the people responsible for the treachery, it might have appeared to be fair revenge rather than brutality but, as it was, the guilt of their ancestors was being atoned for by descendants who had not even seen Miletus and accordingly could not possibly have betrayed it to Xerxes.[33]

[36] Alexander advanced from there to the river Tanais, where Bessus was brought to him, not only in irons but entirely stripped of his clothes. Spitamenes held him with a chain around his neck, a sight that afforded as much pleasure to the barbarians as to the Macedonians. [37] 'I have avenged both you and Darius, my two sovereigns,' said Spitamenes. 'I have brought you the man who killed his master, after capturing him in a manner for which he himself set the precedent. I wish Darius could open his eyes to see this spectacle! I wish he could rise from the dead – he ill deserved such an end and well deserves this consolation!'

[38] Alexander bestowed enthusiastic praise on Spitamenes and then turned to Bessus. 'What bestial madness possessed you,' he said, 'that you should dare to imprison and then murder a king from whom you had received exemplary treatment? Yes, and you rewarded yourself for this treachery with the title of king which was not yours.' [39] Bessus dared not make excuses for his crime. He claimed that he adopted the title of king so that he could surrender his country to Alexander, and failure to do so would have resulted in another seizing the throne.[34]

[40] Alexander told Darius' brother Oxathres (who was one of his bodyguards) to approach him, and had Bessus put in his charge. Bessus was to be hung on a cross, his ears and nose cut off, and the barbarians were to shoot arrows into him and also protect his body from the carrion birds.[35] [41] Oxathres promised to take care of everything but added that the birds could be kept off only by Catanes, whose superb marksmanship Oxathres wished to put on display. Catanes, in fact, was so accurate in hitting what he aimed at that he could even pick off birds. [42] These days, when archery is a widespread practice, this expertise of his might seem less remarkable; but at that time spectators found it an absolutely amazing phenomenon and Catanes won great respect. [43] Gifts were then awarded by Alexander to all responsible for bringing in Bessus, but his execution he postponed so that he could be killed in the very spot where he had himself murdered Darius.[36]

6

[1] Meanwhile a group of Macedonians had gone off to forage out of formation and were surprised by some barbarians who came rushing down on them from the neighbouring mountains. More were taken prisoner than were killed, [2] and the barbarians retired once more to the high ground, driving their captives before them. These bandits numbered 20,000, and the weapons they used in combat were slings and arrows. [3] Alexander laid siege to them and, while he fought in the forefront of the battle, he was hit by an arrow, the head of which was left firmly lodged in his leg. [4] Dismayed and alarmed, the Macedonians carried him back to camp.

The barbarians were also aware that he had been removed from the fight, since they had a full view of the conflict from their high position on the mountain. [5] So the next day they dispatched an embassy to the king, which Alexander ordered be given an immediate audience. Then, unwinding his bandages but concealing the extent of his wound, he showed the barbarians his leg. [6] After they were told to be seated, the envoys declared that the Macedonians were no more saddened at the news of the king's wound than they were themselves and, if they had found the culprit, they would already have surrendered him, since it was only the sacrilegious who fought against gods. [7] Furthermore, they continued, they had now because of his wound been constrained to surrender to him. Alexander gave them assurances, took back the Macedonian prisoners, and accepted their surrender.[37]

After this he moved camp, and was carried on a military litter, [8] but who should carry this was disputed by the cavalry and the infantry. The cavalry, with whom the king usually went into battle, thought it was their prerogative, while the infantry, since it had been usual for them to carry their wounded comrades, kept complaining that a job that was rightfully theirs was being filched from them just at the time when it was the king who needed carrying. [9] Since the quarrel between the two sides was so acrimonious, and the choice both difficult for him to make and sure to cause offence to the losers, the king ordered them to take turns in carrying him.

[10] Three days later they arrived at Maracanda[38] (a city with a wall seventy stades in circuit and a citadel surrounded by a second wall), and after leaving a garrison in the city Alexander pillaged and burnt the neighbouring villages. [11] Then a deputation arrived from the Scythian Abii, who had been free since Cyrus' death but who were now prepared to submit to Alexander.[39] The Abii were generally regarded as the barbarians with the best sense of justice. They refrained from warfare except under provocation and they exercised their liberty with restraint and impartiality, setting those of humble birth on an equal footing with their leading citizens. [12] After addressing the deputation courteously, Alexander sent a man called Derdas, who was one of his friends, to the Scythians living on European soil, to warn them not to cross the river Tanais without the king's order. Derdas was

further instructed to explore the terrain and make an expedition also to those Scythians who live beyond the Bosphorus.[40] [13] On the banks of the Tanais, Alexander had selected a site for establishing a city[41] which was to serve as a barrier between those peoples already subjugated and all whom he had determined to invade at a later date. However, his plan was postponed when news arrived of a rebellion of the Sogdians which also spread to the Bactrians. [14] It began with 7,000 cavalrymen whose influence induced the rest to fall in with them.

Alexander issued a summons for Spitamenes and Catanes, the men who had delivered Bessus to him, for he was sure that with their assistance the rebels could be reduced. [15] In fact these two were the leaders of the insurrection they were being called upon to suppress, and they had circulated the story that the entire Bactrian cavalry was being summoned by Alexander to be executed,[42] that they personally had been given these orders, but had found themselves unable to carry them out for fear of committing a crime against their own countrymen for which atonement would be impossible. Alexander's brutality they had found just as intolerable as Bessus' treason, they said. In this way they had no difficulty in inciting the Bactrians to armed insurrection, for the latter were already so inclined through fear of such disciplinary measures.

[16] When Alexander learned of the defection of these deserters, he ordered Craterus to blockade Cyropolis. He himself threw a cordon of troops around another city in the area, took it, and gave the signal for the execution of all adult males, the other inhabitants becoming the booty of the victor. The city was demolished so that its destruction could serve as an example to keep the others in line. [17] The Memaceni, who were a powerful tribe, had decided on withstanding a siege, not just as the more honourable but also as the safer course of action; so, to soften their obstinacy, Alexander sent fifty horsemen ahead to inform them of his mercy towards those who surrendered and also of his inexorability towards those he conquered. [18] Replying that they harboured no doubts either about Alexander's honour or his strength, the Memaceni instructed the horsemen to pitch camp outside the city fortifications. They then offered them hospitality and, late at night, when they were heavy with sleep and food, they fell on them and murdered them.

[19] Alexander was duly angered. He threw a cordon of troops around the city, its defences being too strong for it to be captured on the first assault, and he brought in Meleager and Perdiccas to help with the siege ... besieging Cyropolis as was noted above.[43] [20] He had determined to spare this city which Cyrus had founded, for he admired no members of those races more than this king and Semiramis whose magnanimity and illustrious achievements far surpassed those of others. [21] But the stubborn resistance of its people so inflamed his rage that after its capture he ordered it to be sacked. When it had been destroyed, he returned to Meleager and Perdiccas with feelings of justified hostility towards the Memaceni. [22] However, no other

city mounted stronger resistance to a siege. Alexander's best soldiers fell here, and he himself also faced extreme danger when he was struck so severely on the neck by a stone that everything went dark and he collapsed unconscious. The army wept for him as if he were dead; [23] but what intimidates others could not crush his spirit. Before his wound was properly healed, he intensified the siege, his anger spurring on his instinctive speed of action. He tunnelled beneath the walls and opened up a massive breach through which he burst into the city. When victory was his, he ordered its destruction.[44]

[24] From here Alexander sent Menedemus[45] with 3,000 infantry and 800 cavalry to the city of Maracanda, within whose walls the turncoat Spitamenes had taken cover, after expelling the Macedonian garrison. The townspeople did not support his defection, but they nevertheless seemed to accept it since they had not the power to stop it. [25] Meanwhile, Alexander returned to the river Tanais and built a wall around the entire area of his camp. The wall thus formed, sixty stades long, constituted the wall of a city, which the king also ordered should be called Alexandria. [26] The work was so swiftly completed that the city buildings were finished on the seventeenth day after the fortifications were erected; fierce competition had arisen among the soldiers over who would be the first to display his completed project (for there had been a division of labour). [27] Inhabitants for this new city were provided in the form of captives whom Alexander liberated by paying their value to their masters. Even today, after such a lengthy lapse of time, the descendants of these people have still retained their identity among the population because of the memory of Alexander.

7

[1] The kingdom of Scythia at that time stretched beyond the Tanais, and its king believed that the city founded by the Macedonians on the bank of the river was a yoke placed upon his neck.[46] So he sent his brother, whose name was Carthasis, and a large cavalry detachment to destroy it and push the Macedonian forces back some distance from the river. [2] The Tanais is what separates the Bactrians from the so-called European Scythians, and its course also constitutes the boundary between Asia and Europe. [3] The Scythian people located close to Thrace extend in a north-easterly direction, and are a member-tribe of the Sarmatians and not, as some have believed, neighbours of them. [4] The Scythians also inhabit another area directly beyond the Ister and they touch the furthest reaches of Asia at Bactra. Their settlements extend quite far north, beyond which the land is covered with deep forests and endless wilderness. Conversely, the areas looking towards the Tanais and Bactria are not dissimilar to others in terms of human cultivation.

[5] With this race Alexander was, for the first time, about to fight a war he had not anticipated – when his enemy rode up before his eyes. He still had not recuperated from his wound, and in particular he had difficulty in

speaking, a condition arising from a sparse diet and the pain in his neck. Nevertheless he called a meeting of his friends. [6] What alarmed him was not his enemy but the inopportune timing. The Bactrians had rebelled and the Scythians posed a further threat, while Alexander himself could not stand in the ranks, ride a horse, or give his men instructions or encouragement. [7] Under the pressure of this double threat, he railed at the gods, complaining that he, a man in earlier days so swift that none had been able to escape him, was now lying idle and that his own men could scarcely believe that his illness was not a pretence. [8] Accordingly, although he had stopped consulting soothsayers and prophets after the defeat of Darius, he now relapsed into superstition, which deludes the minds of men. He told Aristander, in whom he had placed his uncritical trust, to divine the outcome through sacrifice.

It was customary for seers to inspect the entrails with the king absent and to report to him the portents. [9] In the interval, while animal entrails were being inspected to discover the secrets of destiny, Alexander had his friends sit closer to him than usual so that he would not reopen his scar, as yet unhealed, by straining his voice. Hephaestion, Craterus and Erigyius had been admitted to his tent along with the bodyguards.

[10] 'This crisis has overtaken me at a time which favours the enemy more than me,' he said to them. 'But necessity takes precedence over calculation, especially in warfare where one is rarely given the opportunity to choose the timing. [11] There is an insurrection among the Bactrians, whom we have in subjection; they are testing our mettle with a war which others are fighting. What lies ahead is clear. If we ignore the Scythians, who are actually on the offensive, we shall have no respect from the rebels when we return to them. [12] But suppose we cross the Tanais and with a bloody slaughter of the Scythians demonstrate that we are universally invincible – who then will hesitate to submit to us when we are also the conquerors of Europe? [13] It is a mistake to measure our glory by the distance we shall cover. One river is in our way; crossing it means armed invasion of Europe. [14] And what a prize that must be judged – while we subjugate Asia, to establish trophies practically in a new world and, by a single victory, to unite in a moment areas that nature appears to have kept so far apart. [15] Mind you, the slightest hesitation on our part and the Scythians will be on our backs. Are we alone in being able to swim rivers? Many things that until now have given us victory will recoil upon us. [16] Fortune teaches the arts of war to the defeated as well as the victors. Recently we demonstrated how to cross a river on skins and, even supposing the Scythians could not now copy that, they will learn from the Bactrians. [17] Besides, only a single army of this people has arrived so far – the rest can be expected. So by avoiding war we shall strengthen them, and instead of launching an attack we shall have to be on the defensive. [18] The logic of my strategy is clear. But because I have not ridden a horse or done any marching since receiving this wound, I doubt if the Macedonians will let me execute my plan. [19] Yet if you are ready to follow me, my friends, I am

165

well. I have strength enough to meet the demands of the operation. Alternatively, if my life's end is already at hand, in what exploit could I achieve a finer death?'

[20] Such were Alexander's words, which were spoken in a quavering voice that became increasingly feeble, so that it was difficult even for those next to him to hear. They all began to discourage the king from such a headstrong scheme, [21] especially Erigyius who, when his personal influence had no effect on Alexander's determination, tried to inspire in the king superstitious fears against which he had no resistance: he told him that the gods were opposed to his plan and that dire peril was predicted for him if he crossed the river. [22] While he was entering Alexander's tent, Erigyius had met Aristander who had informed him of the unfavourable portents in the entrails, and he was now in fact reporting what he had heard from the seer.

[23] Alexander was disconcerted, feeling as much embarrassment as anger at the exposure of the superstition which he had been concealing. He silenced Erigyius and had Aristander summoned. [24] When he arrived, Alexander stared at him and said: 'When I instructed you to offer sacrifice, I did so not as your king but as a private citizen. Why did you divulge the portents to someone other than myself? From your disclosures Erigyius knows of my confidential and private affairs, and I am convinced he interprets the entrails according to his own fear. [25] But I am instructing you[47]†††† to tell me what you learned from the entrails, so you cannot later deny having told me what you say now.'

[26] Aristander stood there looking pale and bemused. He was speechless with fear, and this fear finally prompted him not to keep the king waiting. 'I predicted a perilous situation ahead of us that would involve hard, but not fruitless effort,' he said, [27] 'and my concern is prompted less by my professional knowledge than by my devotion to you. I see that you are in poor health and I know how much depends on you alone. I fear that you may not be equal to the situation you face.' [28] Alexander told him to trust in his own good luck – it was for further exploits that the gods granted him glory, he said.[48] [29] Then, as he was discussing with the same group some means of crossing the river, Aristander reappeared, declaring that he had never seen more favourable entrails; they were certainly very different from the previous set. What had appeared on the earlier occasion gave cause for alarm, he said, but the omens now were very favourable indeed.

[30] However, news brought to the king immediately after this marred his record of unbroken success. [31] As stated above,[49] he had dispatched Menedemus to blockade Spitamenes, the ringleader of the Bactrian revolt. Hearing of his enemy's approach, Spitamenes lay in ambush on the path he knew Menedemus would take. He wanted to avoid being boxed in within the city walls, and he was also confident that Menedemus could be taken by surprise. [32] The road, which ran through a wood, was well-suited for an

ambush. Here Spitamenes concealed the Dahae. The Dahae ride two armed men to a horse, each of them suddenly jumping in turns from it and throwing the cavalry lines into confusion. [33] The agility of the men matches the speed of their horses.

Spitamenes ordered the Dahae to encircle the wood, and then he revealed their presence to his enemy simultaneously on the flanks, in front and in the rear. [34] Completely penned in and no match for them even in numbers, Menedemus put up prolonged resistance, shouting to his men that after being surprised by an ambush nothing now remained for them but to seek the consolation of an honourable death by cutting down their enemies. [35] Menedemus himself, riding an extremely powerful horse, had repeatedly charged at full gallop into the barbarians' wedge-shaped contingents, scattering them with great carnage. [36] But when the entire enemy force turned their attack on him alone, he lost a lot of blood from his many wounds and encouraged one of his friends, Hypsides, to take his horse and save himself by flight.[50] With these words he expired, and his body slumped from his horse to the ground. [37] Escape was certainly possible for Hypsides, but with his friend gone he decided on death. His one concern was that his death should count for something. Putting the spurs to his horse he charged straight into the enemy, and only after an extraordinary fight was he brought down by their weapons. [38] When they saw this, the survivors of the slaughter occupied a hillock slightly higher than the others, and Spitamenes besieged them, intending to starve them into surrender.

[39] In that engagement 2,000 infantry and 300 cavalry fell. Alexander made the prudent decision to conceal this disaster, and threatened those who had come from the battle with death if they divulged what had happened.

8

[1] When he could no longer maintain an expression at variance with his feelings, Alexander withdrew into his tent, which he had deliberately set on the river bank. [2] There, in complete seclusion, he spent a sleepless night weighing up one by one the plans he had formulated, often lifting the skins of his tent to get a view of the enemy fires, from which he could estimate their numbers. [3] As dawn was approaching, he put on his cuirass and walked to the men, the first time he had done so since receiving the most recent wound. [4] The men idolized their king so much that his presence easily dispelled thoughts of the impending danger which had been filling them with dread. [5] They greeted him joyfully, with tears of happiness streaming from their eyes, and they insistently called for action, which they had balked at earlier. [6] Alexander proclaimed that he would use rafts to transport the cavalry and the phalanx; the lighter-armed troops he ordered to swim over on skins. [7] The situation required no further talk, nor was Alexander's health up to it.

The boats were put together with such zest by the men that some 12,000 were completed within three days. [8] When they had completed all the preparations for the crossing, twenty Scythian ambassadors came riding through the camp (a practice of their race) and ordered that the king be informed that they wished to deliver a message to him personally. [9] The ambassadors were admitted to his tent and told to take a seat. They kept their eyes fixed on the king's face, presumably because they judged a man's courage according to his physique and they thought Alexander's slight build entirely at odds with his reputation. [10] The Scythians differ from other barbarians, however, in not being intellectually backward and unrefined – some of them are even said to have a capacity for philosophy (as far as is possible for a race perpetually under arms). [11] What they are reported to have said before the king is perhaps foreign to our way of thinking and our character, since we have enjoyed more cultivated times and intellects but, though their oratory could be criticized, my accurate reporting should not. I shall relate without alteration the account as it has been passed down to us. [12] According to my sources, one of the Scythians, the eldest, spoke as follows:

'Had the gods willed that your stature should match your greed the world could not hold you. You would touch the east with one hand and the west with the other, and reaching the west you would want to know where the mighty god's light lay hidden. Even as it is, you covet things beyond your reach. [13] From Europe you head for Asia; from Asia you cross to Europe. Then, if you defeat the whole human race, you will be ready to make war on woods, on snow, on rivers, on wild animals. [14] Don't you know that, though big trees take a long time to grow, it takes only an hour to uproot them? It is a stupid man who looks at their fruit and does not measure their height. See to it that, in striving to reach the top, you do not fall down along with the branches which you have grasped. [15] The lion, too, is sometimes the food of tiny birds, and iron is devoured by rust. Nothing is so strong that it is not threatened, even by the weak. [16] What do we have to do with you? We have never set foot in your country. May we not live in our endless forests ignorant of who you are and where you come from? We cannot be slaves to anyone and do not wish to be anyone's masters. [17] To give you some idea of the Scythian race, we have been provided with the gifts of a yoke of oxen, a plough, an arrow, a spear and a cup. These we use with our friends and against our enemies. [18] We give to our friends crops produced by the toil of our oxen; and with them we use the cup to make libations to the gods. Our enemies we attack at long range with the arrow, and at short range with the spear. This was how we defeated the king of Syria,[51] and the king of the Medes and Persians after him, and the road lay open for us right into Egypt.

[19] 'As for you, you proudly claim that you come in pursuit of bandits, but to all the people you have visited *you* are the bandit. You took Lydia; you over-ran Syria; you are in control of Persia; you have the Bactrians in your power;

you have set your course for India. Now you are stretching out your greedy, insatiable hands towards our flocks. [20] Why do *you* need riches? They merely stimulate your craving for more. You are the first man ever to have created hunger by having too much – so that the more you have the keener your desire for what you do not have. [21] Do you not realize how long you have been delayed around Bactra? While you have been subjugating the Bactrians, the Sogdians have commenced hostilities. In your case victory spawns further war. No matter how far you surpass others in power and strength, the fact remains that nobody wants a foreign master.

[22] 'Just cross the Tanais and you will discover the extent of Scythian territory – but you'll never catch the Scythians. With our meagre belongings we shall outrun your army with its cargo of booty from so many nations. Then, when you think we are far away, you will see us inside your camp. We pursue and retreat with equal speed. [23] I am told that the Scythian deserts are ridiculed in Greek proverbs. But we seek the desert and unin-habited lands in preference to cities and rich farmland. [24] So keep a firm grip on your fortune; she is slippery and cannot be held against her will. The future is a better indicator of sound advice than the present. Put some constraints on your prosperity – you will more easily control it. [25] Our people have a saying that Fortune has no feet, only hands and wings. When she stretches out her hands, grab her wings, too.

[26] 'Finally, if you are a god, it is your duty to confer benefits on mortal men, not filch their possessions from them. But if you are a man, always remember that that is what you are. It is folly to have your mind on things that make you forget your condition. [27] You will be able to rely on the firm friendship of those you do not attack. For friendship is strongest between equals, and men who have not put each other's strength to the test appear to be equals. [28] See that you don't regard those whom you have conquered as friends: there is no friendship between master and slave – even in peacetime these observe a state of war. [29] Don't think Scythians take an oath to ratify a friendship: their oath consists in keeping their word. That kind of caution – sealing pacts and invoking the gods – is typically Greek. We consider keeping one's word to be the true religion and those who disrespect men cheat the gods. And you have no need of a friend whose goodwill you doubt. [30] But in us you will have men to guard both Asia and Europe. We border on Bactra (except that the Tanais separates us). We inhabit territory beyond the Tanais and all the way to Thrace, and they say Macedonia stands next to Thrace. We are neighbours to both your empires. Consider whether you want us to be your enemies or your friends.' So spoke the barbarian.

9

[1] The king replied that he would rely on his own fortune and heed their advice; that he would be guided by his fortune because he had confidence in

it and by the advice they proffered in order to avoid reckless or foolhardy action. [2] He then dismissed the deputation and put his army aboard rafts which he had prepared in advance. He set in the prows men equipped with bucklers, having ordered them to kneel to gain better protection against arrows. [3] Behind them stood men to work the slings, covered by armed soldiers on both flanks and in front. The rest stood behind the slings, armed and making a tortoise-formation with their shields to give cover to the oarsmen who wore no protective corselets. This disposition was also preserved on the rafts carrying the cavalry, [4] most of whom drew their horses along by the reins, letting them swim at the stern. The men who made the crossing on skins stuffed with straw were shielded by the rafts before them.

[5] The king, accompanied by a hand-picked group, was the first to cast off. He gave instructions for the raft to be steered to the bank opposite. To block him the Scythians brought up lines of cavalry and stationed them right on the water's edge so that the rafts could not even be landed. [6] Apart from this sight of troops defending the banks, another factor also brought terrible panic to the men in the rafts: the steersmen could not maintain a straight course because of the current's side-on thrust, while the soldiers, losing their balance and scared of being thrown overboard, disrupted the proper functioning of the crews. [7] Even throwing their javelins with any force proved impossible, since they were more concerned with getting a secure balance than with attacking the enemy. What saved them was the slings, which effectively discharged their missiles against an enemy massed together and exposing itself to danger in a foolhardy manner. [8] The barbarians in their turn rained huge quantities of arrows on the rafts, and there was barely a shield not penetrated by a number of arrowheads.

[9] As the rafts began to touch shore, the troops equipped with bucklers rose to their feet and hurled their spears from the rafts, with accuracy now because their throw was unimpeded. As soon as they saw that the Scythians were alarmed and pulling back their horses, they leaped ashore, mutual encouragement firing their spirit, and began to press their disordered foe vigorously. [10] Then the cavalry squadrons, who had their horses bridled, burst through the barbarian line. In the meantime the other Macedonians, who were covered by the fighting line, prepared themselves for the battle. [11] The king himself compensated for his deficient strength (he was still not recovered) by his resolute courage. Although his words of exhortation could not be heard because of his neck-wound,[52] which was not as yet properly healed, all the men could see how he fought. [12] So they all acted as their own commanders. They urged each other on and began a charge at the enemy with no thought for their own lives, [13] at which the barbarians were unable to withstand their adversaries – not their faces, not their weapons, not their shouts. They all took to flight at full gallop and, though his infirmity made the jolting unbearable, Alexander maintained pursuit for eighty stades. [14] As he began to lose consciousness, he ordered his men to stay on the

heels of the fleeing Scythians as long as some daylight remained, and then his strength of mind gave out, he returned to camp and remained there for the duration of the engagement.[53]

[15] By now the pursuers had crossed the bounds of Father Liber,[54] marked by stones set out at frequent intervals and by tall trees with ivy-covered trunks. [16] But fury drove the Macedonians on. They returned to camp around the middle of the night after killing many of the Scythians, capturing more, and driving off 1,800 horses. Of the Macedonians sixty horsemen fell and about 100 infantrymen. A thousand were wounded.[55]

[17] It was this expedition, with the news of the timely victory, that brought Asia into subjection, though most of it had been in revolt. People had believed the Scythians invincible, but after this crushing defeat they had to admit that no race was a match for Macedonian arms. So the Sacae[56] sent a delegation to promise submission, [18] prompted to do so less by the king's valour than by his clemency towards the defeated Scythians. (He had returned all their prisoners without ransom in order to make people believe that his struggle with the fiercest tribe in the world had been a test of courage rather than motivated by anger.) [19] So he received the Sacae delegation courteously and gave them Euxenippus as their companion for the return journey. Euxenippus was still very young and a favourite of Alexander's because he was in the prime of his youth, but though he rivalled Hephaestion in good looks he could not match him in charm, since he was rather effeminate.

[20] Alexander now came to the city of Maracanda,[57] having ordered Craterus to follow by relatively easy marches with the main part of the army. Spitamenes had fled from there to Bactra when he heard Alexander was approaching. [21] After covering a considerable distance within four days, the king had reached the spot at which he had lost the 2,000 infantry and 300 cavalry under Menedemus.[58] He had their bones buried in a mound and performed the traditional funeral rights for them. [22] Craterus, who had been ordered to follow with the phalanx, had by now reached the king and, so that all who had rebelled should equally share the calamity of defeat, Alexander divided his forces and ordered the burning of the countryside and the execution of men of military age.

10

[1] Sogdiana is mainly desert: barren wastes cover an area some 800 stades wide. [2] The country is of enormous length, and through it flows a river, called by the inhabitants the Polytimetus.[59] As a torrent it is compressed into a narrow channel by its banks; then it enters a cave which takes it underground. [3] The only indication of its invisible course is the sound of running water, for the actual soil under which this considerable river flows betrays not the slightest trace of bogginess.

[4] The king had been brought thirty of the most noble Sogdian prisoners

who were possessed of remarkable strength. When these learned through an interpreter that they were facing execution on Alexander's orders, they behaved as if they were happy: they started to sing and express some inner exuberance with dance steps and suggestive body movements. [5] Alexander was amazed that they should face death with such a noble spirit. He ordered that they be brought back and he asked them the reason for such an outpouring of joy when they had the spectre of their execution before their eyes. [6] They answered that they would have been dismayed at facing death at someone else's hands but, as it was, they were being restored to their forefathers by a great king who had conquered the world, and so they were joyfully singing their traditional songs to celebrate an honourable death such as brave men would actually pray for. [7] Admiring their noble spirit, Alexander said: 'I ask you this. Would you be prepared to go on living, but not as my enemies, since it will be to me that you will owe your lives?' [8] They replied that they had never been his personal enemies; they had been attacked and had been on terms of enmity with their aggressor. If someone had chosen to test their character with kindness rather than provocation, they would have made every effort not to be outdone in fulfilling the obligations of friendship. [9] Alexander asked what security they could offer that they would keep their word, to which they replied that the life they were being given would be their security – this they would return whenever he asked for it. And they kept their promise. Those sent home saw to it that their compatriots remained loyal, while the four retained as bodyguards by Alexander fell short of none of the Macedonians in their devotion to the king.

[10] Alexander left Peucolaus in Sogdiana with 3,000 infantry, which was as large a garrison as he needed, and then came to Bactra. He gave orders for Bessus to be transferred from there to Ecbatana, where he would pay for the murder of Darius with his life.[60] [11] At about the same time, Ptolemaeus and Maenidas brought 4,000 infantry and 1,000 cavalry, all mercenary fighters. [12] Asander also came from Lycia with as many infantry and 500 cavalry. The same number came with Asclepiodorus from Syria, and Antipater had sent 8,000 Greeks, including 600 cavalry. [13] His forces thus augmented, Alexander advanced to establish order in the areas disturbed by the insurrection.[61] He executed the ringleaders of the revolt, and three days later reached the river Oxus. This is invariably dirty because of its silt content, and it is unhealthy as drinking water, [14] so the men had proceeded to dig wells. However, no water was forthcoming, although they dug down deep in the earth. At last, a spring was discovered right inside the king's tent, and as the men had taken a long time to notice this they pretended it had appeared all of a sudden; Alexander himself was happy to have it believed that the spring was a gift from the gods.

[15] After this he crossed the Ochus and Oxus rivers and came to the city of Margiana, in the vicinity of which sites for six towns were chosen, two to the south and four to the east. They were spaced only a short distance apart

so that mutual aid could be sought by them without travelling great distances, and all the towns were founded on high hills. [16] At that time they served to check the conquered nations, but now, their origins forgotten, they are subordinate to the people they formerly ruled.

11

[1] After Alexander had restored order elsewhere, there remained only a rocky outcrop which the Sogdian Arimazes was occupying with a force of 30,000.[62] Arimazes had stored provisions in sufficient quantities to maintain a force of this size for as long as two years. [2] The rock reaches a height of thirty stades, has a circumference of 150, and is precipitously steep on every side, with access only by a very narrow path. [3] Half-way up is a cave, its mouth narrow and dark. Little by little it widens inside until it finally terminates in deep recesses. There are springs virtually throughout the cave, their waters eventually combining to send a river down the mountain slopes.

[4] After examining the difficulties of the terrain, Alexander had decided to leave, but then he was overcome by a desire to bring even nature to her knees. [5] However, before gambling on a siege he sent Cophes, who was the son of Artabazus, to urge the barbarians to surrender the rock. Arimazes felt confident in his position and replied with a number of arrogant remarks, finally asking whether Alexander could fly as well. [6] When this was reported to Alexander, it so incensed him that he brought in the group he normally consulted and told them of the insolence of this barbarian who ridiculed them for not having wings.[63] The following night, he said, he would see to it that the barbarians believed that Macedonians could fly too.

[7] 'Each of you bring me 300 men from your command,' he said. 'The most agile you have, men used to driving sheep over mountain pasture and almost trackless rocks at home.' [8] They promptly brought him men of exceptional agility and spirit. The king looked at them. 'Young men!' he said, 'My comrades! With you I have stormed the fortifications of cities that had remained undefeated. With you I have crossed mountain chains snow-covered throughout the year, entered the defiles of Cilicia and endured without exhaustion the fierce cold of India.[64] I have given you proof of my character and I have proof of yours. [9] The rock which you see is accessible by one path only and that is occupied by the barbarians, who are ignoring everything else – no guards are posted apart from those facing towards our camp. [10] You will find a way up if you use your skill in searching for tracks that lead to the top. Nature has set nothing so high that it cannot be surmounted by courage. It is by using methods of which others have despaired that we have Asia in our power. [11] Get to the top. When you have reached it, give me a signal with pieces of white cloth and I shall advance troops to divert the enemy's attention from you to us. [12] The first to reach the summit shall have a reward of ten talents; the man behind him will

receive one less and so on up to ten men. But I am sure that my wishes are of more concern to you than my generosity.'

[13] They reacted so enthusiastically to the king's words that one might have thought they had already taken the peak. After they were dismissed they made ready iron pins (to wedge between the rocks) and sturdy ropes.[65] [14] Alexander rode around the outcrop and at the second watch, with a prayer for the mission's success, he ordered the men to begin their ascent at a point where the way up seemed least rough and precipitous. Taking two days' provisions and armed only with swords and spears, the men began the climb. [15] They started out on foot, but then they reached the sheer parts. Here some pulled themselves up by grasping protruding rocks with their hands; others climbed by means of ropes with sliding knots which they threw ahead of themselves; others again used the pins, wedging them between rocks to serve as steps on which they could get a footing from time to time. They spent the day in fear and toil. [16] After struggling past the difficult spots, worse awaited them, and the rock seemed to increase in height. It was truly pitiful to see men who had been deceived by an unsure footing plunge headlong, and such a calamity overtaking another served to warn the rest that the same fate would soon be theirs. [17] Despite the difficulties, however, they reached the summit of the mountain, though all were exhausted by the unremitting effort and some were partially maimed. Night and sleep came upon them simultaneously. [18] Their bodies stretched here and there over rough, trackless rocks, they slept till dawn, oblivious to the danger of the situation.

They awoke at last as if from a deep sleep. They surveyed the sequestered valleys that now lay below them, not knowing where on the rock an enemy force of such magnitude could be concealed. Then they observed smoke billowing from a cave below them, [19] and from this they surmised it to be the enemy's hide-out. So they placed the agreed signal upon their spears, and now discovered that from the entire group thirty-two had perished making the ascent. [20] Alexander stood the whole day gazing at the mountain peaks, as much preoccupied with the fate of the men he had sent into such evident peril as with his desire to take the position. Finally night came and, when the darkness made it impossible for him to see, he withdrew to take refreshment.

[21] The next day, before it was full daylight, Alexander was the first to catch sight of the cloths which signalled that the top had been gained. But the varying condition of the sky, with sunlight breaking through the clouds at one time and hidden by them at another, made him wonder if his eyes were deceiving him: but as the day brightened all doubt was removed. [22] He called for Cophes, the man he had used to try to bring the barbarians round, and sent him to them to warn them that the time had come to adopt sounder strategy. If they remained obdurate through confidence in their position, however, Alexander ordered that they be shown behind them the men who had reached the peak.

[23] Cophes was given an audience, and set about urging Arimazes to

surrender the outcrop and thereby win Alexander's favour through not forcing him to waste time blockading a single rock when he had such important projects under way. Arimazes' reply was more defiant and insolent than before, and he ordered Cophes to depart. [24] Cophes took the barbarian's hand and asked him to accompany him outside the cave. When Arimazes agreed, Cophes showed him the young men on the peak and, with a well-deserved gibe at his arrogant conduct, declared that Alexander's soldiers did have wings. [25] By this time one could hear the blast of trumpets from the Macedonian camp and the entire army in an uproar. It was this which (like many other events in war of no significance or import) prompted the barbarians to surrender, for in their terror they could not get an impression of how few the men to their rear actually were. [26] Accordingly they hastily recalled Cophes, who had left them to their panic, and sent thirty of their chieftains with him to surrender the rock and negotiate terms that would allow them to leave unharmed.

[27] Alexander was afraid that the barbarians would dislodge his young men when they saw their small numbers. However, he relied on his good fortune and he was also furious at Arimazes' arrogance, so he answered that he would accept no conditions for the surrender. [28] Arimazes despaired of his situation, though it was not in fact hopeless, and came down to the Macedonian camp with his relatives and the foremost noblemen of his people. All of these Alexander ordered to be whipped and crucified right at the foot of the rock.[66] [29] A large number of those surrendering were presented as a gift, together with a sum of captured money, to inhabitants of the newly-founded cities. Artabazus was left in charge of the rock and the area surrounding it.

BOOK EIGHT

[1] Alexander gained more notoriety than credit from reducing the rock. Afterwards the dispersal of the enemy made it necessary for him to fragment his forces, so he divided the army into three sections, giving Hephaestion command of one, Coenus another and retaining command of the third himself.[1] [2] But the barbarians were not all similarly inclined: some had been beaten into submission, though the majority had accepted Alexander's authority without military confrontation. Alexander ordered that the latter should receive the cities and land belonging to those who had persisted in their insurrection. [3] Now some Bactrian exiles, joined by 800 cavalry of the Massagetae, destroyed the neighbouring villages, and to check these the regional commander, Attinas, took to the field with 300 cavalry, unaware of the ambush that was being laid for him. [4] The enemy hid an armed detachment in some woods which happened to adjoin the plain, and a few men drove herds of animals ahead – booty to lure the unsuspecting Attinas into the trap. [5] Attinas followed, pillaging as he went, his troops out of regular formation and not preserving the ranks. He had passed the wood when the men posted in it took him by surprise and killed him along with all his men.[2]

[6] News of the disaster was swiftly brought to Craterus, who arrived on the scene with his entire cavalry force only to find that the Massagetae had already fled. A thousand Dahae were cut down, and their defeat terminated the insurrection throughout the area. [7] As for Alexander, he once more subdued the Sogdians and returned to Maracanda. Here he was met by Derdas, the emissary he had sent to the Scythians beyond the Bosphorus, with a deputation of that people.[3] [8] The ruler of the Chorasmii, Phrataphernes,[4] whose territory shared a border with the Massagetae and the Dahae, had also sent messengers to promise his allegiance. [9] The Scythians requested that Alexander marry a daughter of their king or, if he thought this marriage alliance beneath him, that he permit the leading Macedonians to intermarry with the nobility of their race.[5] They also assured him that their king would visit him in person. [10] He gave both deputations a courteous hearing and remained in stationary camp waiting for Hephaestion and Artabazus. When they joined him, he came into the area called Bazaira.[6]

[11] In that part of the world there are no better indicators of the wealth of the barbarians than their herds of fine animals enclosed in spacious tracts of wooded grazing-land. [12] They select for this purpose large areas of forest, attractively watered by numerous year-round springs. The woods are encircled by walls and contain lodges which serve as shelters for the hunters. [13] Alexander and his whole army entered one such forest, known to have been left undisturbed for four consecutive generations, and he issued orders for the animals to be beaten from their coverts throughout its length. [14] Among these animals was a lion of unusual size which came charging forward to pounce on the king himself. Lysimachus (who subsequently gained royal power) happened to be standing next to Alexander, and had started to aim his hunting spear at the beast when the king pushed him aside, told him to get out of the way, and added that he was as capable as Lysimachus of killing a lion single-handed. [15] In fact, once when they were hunting in Syria, Lysimachus had on his own killed a lion of extraordinary size, though his left shoulder had been lacerated right down to the bone and he had been within an inch of his life. [16] This was the point of Alexander's taunt to Lysimachus but his actions were, in fact, more courageous than his talk – he not only took on the animal but he dispatched it with a single stroke. [17] (I am inclined to think that it was the event I have described above that gave rise to the widespread but unsubstantiated story that Lysimachus was deliberately exposed to a lion by the king.[7]) [18] Although Alexander brought the episode to a successful conclusion, the Macedonians still decreed – as was their right, by the established procedure of their race – that he should not hunt on foot or unaccompanied by a select group of officers and friends. [19] As for Alexander, after 4,000 animals had been brought down, he feasted with the entire army in that same wood.

From here they returned to Maracanda. Alexander now accepted Artabazus' plea of advanced age and assigned his province to Clitus.[8] [20] It was Clitus who had used his shield to protect the king when he was fighting bareheaded at the river Granicus, and who had lopped off Rhosaces' hand with his sword when he threatened Alexander's life.[9] He was an old soldier of Philip's with a distinguished record in numerous campaigns, [21] and his sister Hellanice,[10] who had brought Alexander up, was loved like a mother by the king. These were the reasons why he now committed to Clitus' loyal protection the strongest section of his empire.

[22] Clitus was ordered to prepare for a march the following day, and he was then invited to one of the usual early-starting banquets. At this, being tipsy with wine and no impartial judge of his own worth, the king began to eulogize his exploits to the point of annoying even those of his audience who accepted the truth of his statements.[11] [23] However, the elder guests remained silent, until Alexander proceeded to disparage Philip's record and to boast that it was he himself who was responsible for Philip's famous victory at Chaeronea.[12] The credit for that great achievement, he said, had been

filched from him by his father's ill-will and jealousy. [24] A quarrel had arisen between the Macedonian forces and the Greek mercenaries, he explained, and Philip had been put out of action by a wound he had received in the mêlée. He lay on the ground, finding that to play dead was his safest course of action, and Alexander had protected him with his shield and killed with his own hand the men attacking his father. [25] His father, he said, could never bring himself to admit this: he resented the fact that he owed his life to his son. Then there was the campaign which he had conducted against the Illyrians without Philip.[13] After his victory he had written to his father that the enemy were defeated and routed – and Philip had taken no part in the war. [26] The men who deserved credit, Alexander continued, were not those who attended the mystery ceremonies of Samothrace[14] at the time when Asia should have been burned and pillaged; rather it was those whose magnificent achievements had surpassed belief.

[27] The younger men were elated to hear these and similar remarks, but the older ones found them offensive, mostly because of Philip, under whom they had lived most of their lives. [28] Then Clitus, who was himself not very sober, turned to the men reclining below him and recited a passage from Euripides[15] so that the king could catch the tone without fully hearing the words. [29] The gist of the passage was that the Greeks had established a bad practice in inscribing their trophies with only their kings' names, for the kings were thus appropriating to themselves glory that was won by the blood of others. Alexander suspected Clitus' words were in a caustic vein and he proceeded to ask those next to him what they had heard him say. [30] These men maintained a resolute silence, and Clitus, gradually raising his voice, now recounted Philip's exploits and the wars he had fought in Greece, ranking them all above their current campaigns, [31] and this led to an argument between the younger and older soldiers. As for Alexander, while he appeared unruffled as he heard Clitus' disparaging remarks on his achievements, he had in fact become furiously angry. [32] It looked as if he would control his temper if Clitus discontinued the insolent line of talk he had taken, but when he showed no restraint whatever, Alexander's irritation increased.

[33] By this time Clitus had the nerve to defend even Parmenion, and he favourably compared Philip's victory over the Athenians with the destruction of Thebes[16] – for he was carried away not only by the drink but also by a perverse desire to pick a quarrel. [34] Finally he said: 'If someone has to die for you, then Clitus comes first. But when you come to judge the spoils of victory, the major share goes to those who pour the most insolent insults on your father's memory. [35] You assign to me the province of Sogdiana,[17] which has often rebelled and, so far from being pacified, cannot even be reduced to subjection. I am being sent against wild animals with bloodthirsty natures. But my own circumstances I pass over. [36] You express contempt for Philip's men, but you are forgetting that, if old Atarrhias here had not

brought the younger fellows back into line when they refused to fight, we should still be delayed around Halicarnassus.[18] [37] How is it then that you have still conquered Asia with young men like that? The truth, I think, lies in what your uncle is generally believed to have said in Italy, that he had faced men in battle and you had faced women.'[19]

[38] Of all these ill-considered, impulsive comments none had provoked the king more than the reference to Parmenion, but he suppressed his resentment and was satisfied to order Clitus from the banquet. [39] His only other comment was that, if he had gone on talking, Clitus might possibly have cast in his teeth the claim that he had saved the king's life, an arrogant boast which, he said, he had often made. [40] Clitus hesitated to get up, so those reclining next to him grabbed him, scolding and warning him as they tried to lead him off. [41] As he was dragged away, Clitus' anger rose, augmenting his characteristic impetuosity. In the past, he exclaimed, his breast had given protection to Alexander's back, but time had passed since he performed that valuable service and even the memory of it annoyed the king. [42] He also taunted Alexander with the murder of Attalus,[20] and finally ridiculed the oracle of Jupiter whom Alexander claimed as his father, saying that he, Clitus, had been more truthful in his declarations to Alexander then his 'father' had been.

[43] By now Alexander's temper was such that even sober he could hardly have controlled it; and since his senses had long since succumbed to the wine, he suddenly leapt from the couch. [44] His friends were startled. They rose in a body, throwing aside rather than setting down their cups, all agog to see how the affair he was starting so impulsively would resolve itself. [45] Alexander snatched a lance from the hands of a guard and, while Clitus persisted with his frenzied outpouring of wild abuse, tried to run him through. He was stopped by Ptolemy and Perdiccas, [46] who grabbed him around the waist and held him back as he continued to struggle. Lysimachus and Leonnatus relieved him of the lance. [47] Alexander then appealed to the loyalty of the rank and file, crying out that he was being set upon by his closest friends as had recently happened to Darius, and he ordered a trumpet-signal to be sounded for the men to come in armour to the royal quarters.

[48] At this, Ptolemy and Perdiccas fell to their knees and begged him not to persist with such hasty anger but to allow himself time to consider – he would settle the matter more equitably the next day. [49] But, deaf with anger, his ears took in nothing. He stormed into the vestibule of the royal quarters in uncontrollable fury. There he grabbed a spear from the guard on watch and stood at the doorway by which his dinner-guests had to exit. [50] The others had left, and Clitus was the last to come out, without a lamp. The king challenged him, and the tone of his voice testified to the appalling nature of his criminal intent. [51] Clitus thought now not of his own anger, but only of the king's. He replied that he was Clitus and that he was leaving the

179

banquet. [52] As he said this Alexander plunged the spear into his side and, bespattered with the dying man's blood, said to him: 'Now go and join Philip, Parmenion and Attalus!'

2

[1] The human character has been ill-served by nature: we tend to consider matters carefully after the fact, not before. When his anger had subsided and he had shaken off his intoxication, the king clearly perceived the enormity of his crime as he reflected upon it, but all too late. [2] He could see that he had murdered a fine soldier, even if he had taken liberties on that particular occasion, and a man who, if Alexander were not ashamed to admit it, had saved his life. Although he was king, he had assumed the abominable role of executioner: with a foul murder he had punished intemperate language that was attributable to wine. [3] The vestibule was completely soaked in the gore of a man who shortly before had been his guest. Shocked and looking dazed, the guards kept their distance from Alexander, and his isolation gave him even more opportunity for remorse. [4] He pulled the spear from the dead man's body and turned it on himself. He had already put it to his chest when the guards rushed up and, despite his resistance, wrested it from his hands, picked him up and carried him into his tent. [5] Alexander flung himself on the ground, and his entire quarters rang with the sound of his pitiful weeping and wailing. Then he tore at his face with his nails and begged the men standing around him not to let him survive such dishonour.

[6] His entire night was spent in entreaties such as this. He wondered whether it was divine anger that had driven him to this heinous crime, and it occurred to him that he had failed to offer the annual sacrifice to Father Liber at the appointed time. So it was that the god's anger had displayed itself against him – for the crime was committed amid drinking and feasting.[21] [7] But what was more distressing was that he could see the alarm of all his friends. He felt that nobody would now hold a conversation with him; that he would be obliged to live a solitary existence like a wild beast which terrifies other animals and is in turn terrified by them.

[8] At dawn he ordered the corpse, still covered with gore, to be taken into his tent, and when it lay before him he said, with tears in his eyes: 'This is how I have repaid my nurse, whose two sons fell at Miletus to win renown for me.[22] This is her brother, her only source of comfort after her loss, and he has been murdered by me at the dinner-table! [9] Where will the poor woman turn now? Of all her relatives only I survive – the one person she will be unable to look at without pain. I am the destroyer of my saviours. Shall I return home unable to hold out my right hand to my nurse without reminding her of her personal tragedy?' [10] And since his tearful lamentations continued without end, the corpse was removed on his friends' instructions.

The king shut himself away for three days. [11] When his attendants and bodyguards realized that he was determined to die, they burst into his tent in a body and, though he long resisted their entreaties, finally prevailed on him to take nourishment. [12] To ease his feeling of shame over the killing, the Macedonians formally declared that Clitus' death was justified, and they would have refused him burial had not the king ordered it.

[13] Ten days were spent at Maracanda, mainly devoted to restoring Alexander's self-respect. He then dispatched Hephaestion with a section of the army into the territory of Bactriana to organize supplies for the winter. [14] The province he had previously reserved for Clitus he gave to Amyntas.[23] He then came himself to Xenippa,[24] an area on the borders of Scythia which contains a large number of heavily-populated villages (the fertile soil attracting immigrants as well as retaining its native population). [15] Xenippa had served as a haven for Bactrian exiles who had defected from Alexander but, when news of the king's approach arrived, these were driven out by the inhabitants. Now they were gathered in a body numbering some 2,500, [16] all of them horsemen who had made their living out of looting even in peacetime. On this occasion their naturally wild disposition had been further brutalized not only by the war but also by their despair of receiving a pardon. Accordingly they made a surprise attack on Alexander's general, Amyntas. They managed to keep the fight on even terms for a long time, [17] but finally, with 700 of their men lost (300 of them captured by the enemy), they fled before the victors, though not without inflicting damage, since they killed eighty Macedonians and wounded 350 more. [18] Even after their second defection the Bactrians still gained a pardon.

[19] After accepting their surrender, Alexander came in full force into the area called Nautaca. Its satrap, Sisimithres, had two sons by his own mother, it being acceptable in that society for parents to have sexual relations with their children. [20] Sisimithres had armed his people and had established strong defensive works at the narrowest point of the defile which afforded access to the area. Past these flowed a torrent, and the rear was blocked by a rocky outcrop, through which the inhabitants had bored a pathway.[25] [21] This tunnel lets in light at the entrance, but its interior sections remain dark unless artificial light is brought in. A continuous passageway, known only to the inhabitants, affords access to the plains.

[22] Although the defile was protected by its position and was also defended by a strong barbarian contingent, Alexander moved up battering rams, smashed the man-made fortifications and shot down most of the defenders with heavy artillery and archers. After scattering and routing the enemy, he crossed the shattered fortifications and moved his forces towards the outcrop. [23] However, the river, formed from streams that ran together into the valley from the peak above them, blocked their way. Filling in a chasm of such size seemed a great operation. [24] Even so, Alexander issued orders for trees to be felled and rocks piled together. Unacquainted as they were with works of

this kind, the barbarians were struck with sheer panic when they suddenly beheld the structure that was thrown up. [25] Alexander thought they could be frightened into submission, so he sent Oxartes,[26] a fellow-tribesman of theirs but subject to himself, to urge their leader to surrender the rock. [26] In the meantime, to increase their fear, siege-towers were moved forward and a barrage of missiles flashed from the siege-engines. Losing confidence in all forms of defence, the barbarians headed for the top of the outcrop, [27] while Oxartes set to work on the frightened Sisimithres, who had little faith in his position. Oxartes urged him to test the honour rather than the fighting ability of the Macedonians, and not to impede a conquering army that was heading swiftly to India, since anyone getting in its way would bring upon his own head disasters intended for others.

[28] Sisimithres was actually in agreement over a surrender, but his mother (who was also his wife) declared that she would die rather than submit to anyone's power. Thus she set the barbarian's mind on a course more honourable than safe, making him feel ashamed that liberty was more highly valued by women than men. [29] Therefore, he sent the mediator away, having resolved to face the siege. But when he considered the relative strength of his enemy and himself, he had a change of heart and he began to regret listening to the advice of a woman, advice he considered reckless and ill-befitting the circumstances. [30] He swiftly recalled Oxartes and said he would submit to Alexander. He did, however, have a plea to make, that Oxartes should not divulge his mother's wishes and advice – thus she, too, might more easily gain a pardon. [31] He sent Oxartes ahead and then followed with his mother, his children and all his relatives in a body, not even waiting for the guarantee of safe-conduct from Alexander which Oxartes had promised him.

[32] Alexander sent a rider ahead to tell them to go back and await his coming. Arriving on the scene, he offered sacrifices to Minerva Victoria and then restored Sisimithres' rule to him, giving him reason to expect an even larger province if he loyally cultivated Alexander's friendship. [33] Sisimithres handed over his two sons to the king, who instructed them to accompany him on his campaigns.

After this Alexander left the phalanx behind and advanced with the cavalry to suppress the rebels. [34] At first the men somehow coped with the road, which was steep and obstructed with rocks, but soon their horses suffered exhaustion as well as worn hooves. Most could not keep up, and the line became progressively thinner as the excessive effort crushed their sense of shame, as often happens. [35] But the king, frequently changing horses, pressed the retreating enemy relentlessly. The young noblemen who formed his usual retinue had given up the chase, all except Philip, the brother of Lysimachus, who was in the early stages of manhood and, as was readily apparent, was a person of rare qualities. [36] Incredibly, Philip kept up with the king on foot although Alexander rode for 500 stades. Lysimachus made him frequent offers of his horse, but Philip could not be induced to leave the king, even though he was wearing a cuirass and carrying weapons. [37] On reaching a wood in which the barbarians had hidden, this same young man put up a remarkable fight and gave protection to his king when engaged in hand-to-hand combat with the enemy [38] but, after the barbarians scattered in flight and left the forest, that vital spark which had kept him going in the heat of the fight deserted him. Sweat poured suddenly from all his limbs and he leaned against the nearest tree, [39] but even that failed to hold him up; the king took him in his arms, where he collapsed and died.[27] Further grief, equally painful, awaited the sorrowful king. [40] Shortly before returning to camp, he learned of the death of Erigyius, who had been one of his most distinguished generals.[28] The funerals of both men were conducted with ceremony and honours of every kind.

3

[1] Alexander had determined to march next on the Dahae, after learning that Spitamenes was among them. Fortune, which never tired of indulging him, also brought this expedition, like many other exploits, to a successful conclusion for him even in his absence. Spitamenes' ardent love for his wife exceeded the bounds of moderation, but she tired of their flight and repeated changes of place of exile as he dragged her with him into all his dangers. [2] Exhausted by the hardships, time and again she employed her female charms in trying to induce him to stop running and to appease a man whose mercy in victory he had already tasted and whom he could not escape anyway. [3] She had had three children by Spitamenes who were now grown up, and these she brought into their father's arms, begging that he pity them at least – and to add weight to her entreaties, Alexander was not far off. [4] Spitamenes thought this was treachery on her part, not advice, and that her desire to surrender to Alexander at the first opportunity arose from her confidence in her beauty. He drew his scimitar and would have run his wife through if her brothers had not rushed up to stop him. [5] He ordered her from his sight, threatening her with death if she met his eyes again, and to ease his passion for her he began to spend his nights with concubines. [6] But his deep-seated love was actually inflamed by dissatisfaction with his bed-fellows of the moment. So, devoting himself exclusively to his wife once more, he incessantly begged her to eschew such advice as she had given and to acquiesce in whatever it was that fortune had in store for them, since he would find death less painful than surrender. [7] She excused herself by saying that she had given him what she thought was profitable advice, and that her recommendations, though characteristically feminine, nonetheless arose from loyal intentions. In future, she said, she would abide by her husband's will.

[8] Spitamenes was taken in by this show of devotion. He ordered a banquet arranged while it was still day, after which he was carried to his room, languid from excessive drinking and eating, and half-asleep. [9] As soon as

his wife saw him in a deep, heavy sleep, she drew a sword which she had hidden under her clothes and cut off his head which, spattered with blood, she handed to a slave who had acted as her accomplice. [10] With the slave in attendance she came to the Macedonian camp, her clothes still drenched with blood, and had the message taken to Alexander that there was a matter of which he should hear from her own lips. [11] Alexander immediately had the barbarian shown in. Seeing her bespattered with blood, he assumed she had come to complain of an assault, and he told her to state what she wanted. [12] She asked that the slave, whom she had told to stand at the doorway, now be brought in. This slave had aroused suspicion because he had the head of Spitamenes concealed under his clothes; and when the guards searched him he showed them what he was hiding. [13] Pallor had disfigured the features of the bloodless face so that a firm identification was impossible. The king was now informed that the slave was bringing him a human head, so he went out of the tent, asked what was going on and learned the details from the statement made by the slave.

[14] Alexander was now prey to conflicting thoughts as he considered the various aspects of the matter. He believed it a great benefit to himself that a treacherous deserter had been assassinated, a man whose continued existence would have proved an obstacle to his great designs, but he was also repelled by the enormity of the crime – a woman treacherously murdering a man who had treated her well and who was the father of their children. [15] The savagery of the deed carried more weight with him than gratitude for the favour, however, and he had her ordered from the camp. He did not want her tainting the character and civilized temperament of the Greeks with this example of barbarian lawlessness.[29]

[16] On learning of Spitamenes' murder the Dahae imprisoned Dataphernes, his partner in the rebellion, and surrendered him along with themselves to Alexander.[30] The latter, thus freed from most of his urgent problems, now concentrated on righting the wrongs done to those suffering under the rapacious and tyrannical rule of his governors. [17] Accordingly, he assigned Phrataphernes control of Hyrcania, the Mardians and the Tapuri, instructing him to send to him his predecessor, Phradates,[31] for imprisonment. Stasanor replaced Arsames as governor of the Drangae, and Arsaces [32] was dispatched to Media to enable Oxydates to leave. Since Mazaeus had died, Babylonia was put in Ditamenes' charge.[33]

4

[1] After completing this reorganization and spending two months in winter quarters, Alexander advanced his forces for an attack on the region called Gazaba.[34] [2] On the first day they had an untroubled march. The second was still not stormy or bleak, but it was more overcast than the first and did not end without warnings of some trouble in the making. [3] On the third day

lightning started to flash in every quarter of the heavens and, as the light alternately flashed and faded, brought terror to the hearts as well as the eyes of the marching troops. [4] There was an almost incessant peal of thunder from the sky, and bolts of lightning were to be seen falling on every side. The column was deafened and stunned, daring neither to advance nor yet to halt. [5] Suddenly a torrential cloudburst poured down on them, showering them with hail.

At first they withstood this bombardment by using their shields for protection, but then their frozen hands proved unable to grip their slippery weapons, and they could not decide which way to turn, for the storm would meet them everywhere with a violence greater than that which they were running from. [6] So the column broke ranks and wandered aimlessly thoughout the woods. Many were exhausted by fear before fatigue; and these flung themselves on the ground even though the intense cold had turned the rain to hard ice. [7] Others leaned against tree-trunks, which served both as a means of support and a place of shelter for most of them, [8] though they well knew that they were choosing a spot to die, for the vital warmth would desert them when they stopped moving. But in their exhausted state they welcomed such immobility, accepting death in return for a chance to rest. For this grievous torment was persistent as well as violent, and the light, nature's comfort, was eliminated by the woodland shade and also by the storm which was itself black as night.

[9] Only the king could endure this great calamity. He went around the men, rallied the stragglers, helped up those who had fallen, pointed to smoke spiralling from huts in the distance, and encouraged them to seize on anything in the vicinity that would provide shelter. [10] What contributed most to their survival was the fact that they were ashamed to let down the king who, redoubling his efforts, was coping with difficulties which had vanquished them. [11] But it was the urgency of the situation – more efficacious in adversity than any calculations – that devised a remedy for the cold. They proceeded to chop down the forest with axes, and they set light to the wood which they stacked in piles at various points. [12] One might have thought the wood was one uninterrupted blaze and that among the flames there could hardly be room for the troops. The heat thus produced revived their numbed limbs, and by degrees their breath, which the cold had constricted, began to flow freely. [13] Some found shelter in the barbarians' huts (which, in their predicament, they had tracked down although they were hidden in the depths of the forest), others in a camp which they pitched on wet ground, but at a time when the storm was abating. That particular catastrophe claimed the lives of 2,000 soldiers, camp-followers and servants. [14] It is recorded that some men could be seen frozen to tree-trunks. They not only looked alive but appeared to be in conversation with each other, retaining the posture in which death had overtaken them.

[15] It happened that a Macedonian private had reached the camp

although he was hardly able to carry himself or his weapons. When Alexander saw him, he sprang from his chair even though he was at that moment warming himself at the fire. He relieved the benumbed and barely conscious soldier of his arms and told him to take his seat. [16] For some time the man was unaware of where he was resting or by whom he had been received but, when he finally recovered his vital heat and saw the throne and the king, he got up in terror. [17] Alexander looked at him: 'Soldier,' he said, 'do you realize how much better a lot you Macedonians enjoy under a king than the Persians do? For them sitting on a king's throne would have meant death; for you it meant life.'[35]

[18] At a meeting of his friends and commanders the following day, he ordered a proclamation to be made that he would personally make good all losses; and he kept his word. [19] Sisimithres had brought a large number of pack-animals and 2,000 camels, plus flocks of sheep and herds of cattle, so Alexander divided these evenly among the men, simultaneously relieving them of loss and of hunger. [20] He gave Sisimithres a public commendation for thus displaying his gratitude towards him and then, telling the men to take a six-days' supply of cooked food, he headed for the Sacae. He ravaged their entire land and from the spoils made a gift of 30,000 head of cattle to Sisimithres.

[21] After this Alexander entered the country governed by the illustrious satrap, Oxyartes. Oxyartes placed himself under the king's authority and protection, whereupon Alexander restored his position to him and demanded only that two of Oxyartes' three sons join him on his campaigns. [22] In fact, the satrap also committed to him the son who was being left behind with himself.

Oxyartes had arranged a banquet of typical barbaric extravagance, at which he entertained the king. [23] While he conducted the festivities with warm geniality, Oxyartes had thirty young noblewomen brought in, one of whom was his own daughter Roxane, a woman of remarkable physical beauty with a dignified bearing rarely found in barbarians. [24] Though she was one of a number chosen for their beauty, she nonetheless attracted everybody's attention, especially that of the king, whose control over his appetites was weakening amid the indulgences of Fortune, against whom mankind is insufficiently armed. [25] So it was that the man who had looked with what were merely paternal feelings on the wife and two unmarried daughters of Darius – and with these none but Roxane could be compared in looks – now fell in love with a young girl, of humble pedigree in comparison with royalty, and did so with such abandon as to make a statement that intermarriage of Persians and Macedonians would serve to consolidate his empire, that only thus could the conquered lose their shame and the conquerors their pride. [26] Achilles, he said, from whom he traced his descent, had also shared his bed with a captive.[36] Her people should not think they were being done any wrong – he was willing to enter into a lawful marriage with Roxane.[37]

[27] Roxane's father was transported with unexpected delight when he heard Alexander's words, and the king, in the heat of passion, ordered bread to be brought, in accordance with his ancestral tradition, for this was the most sacred symbol of betrothal among the Macedonians. The bread was cut with a sword and both men tasted it. [28] I presume that those responsible for establishing the conventions of their society used this modest and readily available food because they wanted to demonstrate to people uniting their resources how little should be enough to content them.[38] [29] Thus the ruler of Asia and Europe married a woman who had been introduced to him as part of the entertainment at dinner – to produce from a captive a son to rule over her conquerors! [30] His friends were ashamed that he had chosen his father-in-law at a dinner-party and from subject peoples but, with the suspension of free speech following Clitus' murder,[39] they signified their approval with their facial expressions, the feature of a man most prone to servility.

5

[1] It was now Alexander's intention to head for India, then the Ocean. To obviate any difficulties behind him that could interfere with his plans, he gave orders for 30,000 men of military age to be selected from all the provinces and brought to him in arms, to serve simultaneously as hostages and as soldiers. [2] Craterus[40] he dispatched to hunt down the defectors, Haustanes and Catanes, and of these Haustanes was taken prisoner while Catanes fell in battle. Polyperchon also reduced the land called Bubacene.[41]

Thus, with everything settled, Alexander directed his thoughts towards the Indian campaign. [3] India was thought to be a land rich in gems and pearls as well as in gold, inclined towards ostentatious luxury rather than true grandeur. [4] Those who knew the country claimed that its warriors gleamed in gold and ivory; so, not to be bettered in any respect (since in all others he was unsurpassed), Alexander added silver-plating to his soldiers' shields,[42] gave their horses golden bits and ornamented their cuirasses with either gold or silver. The total number of men following the king on this campaign was 120,000.

[5] With all the preparations made, Alexander now believed that the time was ripe for the depraved idea he had conceived some time before, and he began to consider how he could appropriate divine honours to himself. He wished to be believed, not just called, the son of Jupiter, as if it were possible for him to have as much control over men's minds as their tongues, [6] and he gave orders for the Macedonians to follow the Persian custom in doing homage to him by prostrating themselves on the ground.[43] To feed this desire of his there was no lack of pernicious flattery – ever the curse of royalty, whose power is more often subverted by adulation than by an enemy. [7] Nor were

the Macedonians to blame for this, for none of them could bear the slightest deviation from tradition; rather it was the Greeks, whose corrupt ways had also debased the profession of the liberal arts. [8] There was the Argive Agis who, after Choerilus, composed the most execrable poems;[44] Cleon of Sicily, whose penchant for flattery was a national as much as a personal defect; and the other dregs of their various cities. These were given preferential treatment by the king even over his relatives and the generals of his greatest armies, and these were the men who were then opening up the road to heaven for him, publicly declaring that Hercules, Father Liber and Castor and Pollux would make way before the new divinity!

[9] Accordingly, one festive day, Alexander had a sumptuous banquet organized so that he could invite not only his principal friends among the Macedonians and Greeks but also the enemy nobility. The king took his place with them but, after dining for only a short time, he withdrew from the banquet. [10] Following a prearranged plan, Cleon now launched into a speech of admiration for Alexander's fine achievements, and then listed all that the king had done for them. They only way to thank him for this, said Cleon, was to acknowledge openly his divinity – of which fact they were well aware – and to be prepared to pay for such great benefactions with incense that cost but little. [11] The Persian practice of worshipping their kings as gods was as much a matter of prudence as piety, he said, for it was the majesty of the empire that guaranteed their protection. Even Hercules and Father Liber were deified only after triumphing over the envy of their contemporaries, he continued, and what posterity believes about a man depends on the assurances they have of him from the present generation. [12] If the rest of them felt any hesitation, he would prostrate himself on the ground when the king entered the banquet, and the rest should do the same, especially those possessed of good sense, for it was they who should set the example of worshipping the king.

[13] These remarks were quite obviously aimed at Callisthenes, whose serious disposition and outspokenness had earned the king's displeasure, as if he were the only obstacle to the Macedonians' readiness to adopt such obsequious behaviour. [14] Silence fell and all eyes were on Callisthenes.

'Had the king been present when you spoke,' he said, 'then certainly no words of reply would be required, since he would himself be asking you not to force him to lapse into the ways of foreigners and strangers, and not to stir up envy of his highly successful exploits by such adulation. [15] But in Alexander's absence I answer you for him in this way: a fruit cannot be both long-lived and early to ripen. You are not giving the king divine honours but depriving him of them. For a man to be believed a god takes time, and it is always posterity that gives thanks to great men in this fashion. [16] My own prayer for the king is that he achieve immortality late – so that his life be long and his majesty eternal. Divinity sometimes comes to a man after his life, but never attends him in it.

[17] 'Just now you cited Hercules and Father Liber as instances of the granting of divine status. Do you believe they were deified after a decision made at a single banquet? No; the course of nature removed them from the eyes of men before fame took them up to heaven. [18] Of course, Cleon, you and I can create gods, and from us the king will gain complete assurance of his divinity! I should like to put your power to the test. If you can make a god, make someone a king. Is it easier to grant someone heaven than it is an empire? [19] I pray that in their mercy the gods have not taken offence at what they heard from Cleon, and that they allow matters to proceed as they have done until now. Let them grant that we be content with our own customs. I am not ashamed of my country, nor have I any wish to be told by peoples we have conquered how to pay my respects to my king. [20] In fact, I am prepared to recognize them as the victors if we accept from them rules by which to live.'

Callisthenes was heard with approval as the champion of public freedom.⁴⁵ He had extracted not only silent agreement from his audience but vocal support as well, especially from the older men who were offended by the substitution of foreign customs for their established traditions. [21] Nor was Alexander unaware of any of the comments made on either side, for he was standing behind a curtain which he had drawn as a screen around the couches. So he sent a message to Agis and Cleon instructing them to terminate the conversation and be content to have only the barbarians prostrate themselves in their usual manner when he entered the room. Shortly afterwards he returned to the banquet, as though he had been dealing with some particularly important business.

[22] The Persians now did homage before him and, when one of them touched the ground with his chin, Polyperchon, who was reclining above the king, began to ridicule him by telling him to beat it harder on the ground. This provoked an angry response from Alexander, who for some time now had been unable to keep his temper. [23] 'Are *you* not going to do homage before me?' he said. 'Is it only you who think we deserve ridicule?' Polyperchon answered that the king did not deserve ridicule, but no more did he himself deserve contempt. [24] Dragging him off the couch, Alexander threw him on the floor, and Polyperchon fell forward on his face. 'You see,' said Alexander, 'you are doing just what you laughed at in another a moment ago.' Then he ordered Polyperchon to be put under guard and terminated the banquet.⁴⁶

6

[1] Although he punished him for a long time after this, Alexander did eventually pardon Polyperchon, but in the case of Callisthenes, whom he had long suspected because of his outspokenness, his resentment was more persistent. An opportunity to indulge this soon came his way. [2] As was

observed above, it was customary for the Macedonian nobility to deliver their grown-up sons to their kings for the performance of duties which differed little from the tasks of slaves. [3] They would take turns spending the night on guard at the door of the king's bedchamber, and it was they who brought in his women by an entrance other than that watched by the armed guards. [4] They would also take his horses from the grooms and bring them for him to mount; they were his attendants both on the hunt and in battle, and were highly educated in all the liberal arts. [5] It was thought a special honour that they were allowed to sit and eat with the king. No one had the authority to flog them apart from the king himself. [6] This company served the Macedonians as a kind of seminary for their officers and generals,[47] and from it subsequently came the kings whose descendants were many generations later stripped of power by the Romans.[48]

[7] Now Hermolaus was a young nobleman who belonged to the group of royal attendants. He was flogged on Alexander's orders for having speared a boar before the king when the latter had ear-marked it for himself. Stung by this humiliation, Hermolaus began to complain to Sostratus, [8] who also belonged to the group and was passionately in love with him. Sostratus now saw the lacerations on the body he desperately loved, and it is possible that he bore the king some other grudge from the past. So, after the two had exchanged oaths of loyalty, Sostratus prevailed on the boy, who was already so inclined on his own account, to enter into a plot with him to assassinate the king. [9] Nor was it with the impulsiveness of youth that they put their plan into action, for they were discreet in selecting the people they would invite to join the conspiracy. They decided that Nicostratus, Antipater, Asclepiodorus and Philotas should be enlisted, and through these Anticles, Elaptonius and Epimenes were also brought in.[49] [10] However, no easy method of executing the plan presented itself. It was imperative that all the conspirators be on guard-duty the same night, so that there should be no problem with people not party to the plot, but it turned out that they were all on duty on different nights. [11] As a result, thirty-two days were taken up with altering the rota for guard-duty and other preparations for bringing off the coup.

[12] It was now the night on which the conspirators were to be on duty. They were cheered by their unanimous commitment to the cause, demonstrated by the number of days that had gone by during which none had wavered through fear or hope – so strong was their common resentment towards Alexander or their loyalty to each other. [13] They now stood at the door of the room in which the king was dining, intending to escort him to his bedroom when he left the banquet. [14] But Alexander's good fortune, plus the conviviality of the banqueters, led the company to drink more than usual, and the dinner-party games also drew out the time, which made the conspirators alternately happy at the prospect of falling on a drowsy victim and anxious that he might prolong the party till daylight. [15] The problem was that others were due to relieve them at dawn, their turn of duty would

not recur for seven days and they could not expect the discretion of all of them to last till that time.

[16] At the approach of dawn, however, the banquet broke up and the conspirators received the king, pleased that an opportunity for executing the crime had arrived. Then a woman appeared who, it was thought, was out of her senses[50] and who used to frequent the royal quarters (for she appeared inspired and able to foretell the future). She not only met the king as he took his leave but actually threw herself in his path. Her facial expression and her eyes indicating some inner agitation, she warned him to return to the banquet. [17] By way of a joke Alexander answered that the gods gave good advice. He once more summoned his friends and prolonged the banquet until almost the second hour of the day.

[18] By now other members of the group of attendants had succeeded to their positions and were ready to stand guard before Alexander's bedroom door, but the conspirators kept standing around even though their turn on duty was completed; so long-lived is hope once the human mind has seized upon it. [19] Addressing them more warmly than usual, the king told them to go and rest since they had been on their feet all night. They were each given fifty sesterces and commended for remaining on duty even when the turn of others had come. [20] Their great hope frustrated, they went home. They now began to wait for their next night on duty, all except Epimenes who experienced a sudden change of heart, either because of the friendly manner in which the king had greeted him and the other conspirators or because he believed that the gods opposed their scheme. So he revealed what was afoot to his brother Eurylochus, whom he had previously wished to remain ignorant of the plot.

[21] The spectre of Philotas' punishment was hanging before everyone's eyes, and so Eurylochus immediately seized his brother and came with him into the royal quarters. He alerted the bodyguards and declared that the information he brought related to the king's security. [22] The time of their coming and the expressions on their faces, revealing obviously troubled minds, plus the dejection of one of them – all this alarmed Ptolemy and Leonnatus,[51] who were standing guard at the bedroom door. They opened the door, took in a lamp and woke Alexander, who now lay in a deep, drunken sleep. Gradually coming to his senses, he asked what news they brought. [23] Without a moment's hesitation Eurylochus asserted that the gods could not have entirely abandoned his family because his brother, although he had embarked on an impious crime, now regretted his actions and wished no one but himself to bring information about the plot to Alexander. The coup, he said, had been planned for that very night which was now passing, and those responsible for the heinous plot were men the king would least suspect.

[24] Epimenes then gave a detailed and systematic account, including the names of the conspirators. Callisthenes was certainly not named as one involved in the plot, but it did come out that he was in the habit of giving

a ready ear to the talk of the pages when they were criticizing and finding fault with the king.[52] [25] Some people also assert that, when Hermolaus complained before Callisthenes of having been flogged by Alexander, Callisthenes commented that they ought to remember that they were men; but they add that it is unclear whether this remark was meant to comfort Hermolaus after his beating or to provoke resentment in the young men.

[26] Shaking the drowsiness from mind and body, Alexander saw before his eyes the great danger he had escaped. He immediately gave Eurylochus fifty talents, plus the rich property of a certain Tyridates, and he restored his brother to him even before Eurylochus could beg for his life. [27] The culprits – and Callisthenes was included – he ordered to be kept in chains. They were brought to the royal quarters, but Alexander was tired from the drink and lack of sleep, and so he slept throughout the day and the next night. [28] The day after that, however, he convened a general assembly. This was attended by the fathers and relatives of the accused, not free of concern for their own safety in view of the Macedonian custom which required their death, since all blood relations of the guilty party were liable to execution. [29] Alexander had all the conspirators apart from Callisthenes brought in, and without hesitation they confessed their plan. [30] There was a general outcry against them, and the king himself asked what he had done to merit their hatching such a wicked plot against him.

7

[1] They were dumbfounded, all except Hermolaus. 'You ask as if you did not know,' he said. 'We plotted to kill you because you have begun to act not as a king with his free-born subjects but as a master with his slaves.' [2] Of the whole assembly the first to react was Hermolaus' father, Sopolis.[53] He rose to his feet shouting that Hermolaus was also the murderer of his own father and, putting his hand over his son's mouth, stated he should be heard no further because he was crazed by his guilt and his misfortune. [3] Alexander restrained the father and told Hermolaus to state what he had learned from his teacher, Callisthenes.

'I avail myself of your kindness,' replied Hermolaus, 'and state what I have learned from our misfortunes. [4] How few are the Macedonians who have actually survived your ruthlessness! How few, indeed, apart from those of meanest birth! Attalus ... Philotas ... Parmenion ... Alexander Lyncestes ... Clitus.... As far as the enemy is concerned, these are still alive today, are still standing in the battle-line, protecting you with their shields, receiving wounds for your glory and your victory. [5] A fine thanks *you* gave them! One has spilled his blood on your table; another was not even granted a simple death; leaders of your armies have been put on the rack to provide a spectacle for the Persians they had conquered. Parmenion was butchered without trial – the man whose services you had used to kill Attalus. [6] Yes, you first use the hands of unfortunates to effect your assassinations, then you suddenly order others to butcher the men who shortly before served as your assassins.'

[7] At this, cries of protest against Hermolaus came from the entire assembly. His father had drawn his sword to kill him and would certainly have run him through had he not been restrained by the king, who told Hermolaus to continue and asked the men to listen patiently as he added to the reasons for his own punishment. [8] The meeting was brought to order with difficulty and Hermolaus continued: 'How kind of you to give the floor to boys inexperienced in speaking! But Callisthenes' voice is shut away in a prison – because he alone is able to speak. [9] Otherwise why is he not brought out, when even those who have confessed are being heard? Because, of course, you are frightened to hear an innocent man speak freely; you cannot even look him in the face. [10] Yet I say he is not guilty. Here are the men who planned the noble deed with me. No one can say that Callisthenes was in league with us – although he has long been marked out for execution by a very just and tolerant king! [11] Such are the rewards Macedonians can expect from you for the blood which you squander as if it were overabundant and cheap. For you, 30,000 mules are transporting captured gold – yet your soldiers will take home nothing but scars for which they receive no compensation.

'Even so, we could have tolerated all this, until you delivered us to the barbarians and (a novel twist!) sent the victors under the yoke! [12] But you revel in Persian clothes and Persian etiquette; you abhor the customs of your own country. Thus it was a king of the Persians, not of the Macedonians, we wanted to kill and, in accordance with the conventions of war, we pursue you as a deserter. [13] You wanted Macedonians to kneel before you and worship you as a god. You repudiate your father Philip and, if any of the gods were thought superior to Jupiter, you would despise Jupiter, too. [14] We are free men – are you surprised if we cannot bear your vanity? What can we hope for from you if even innocent men must either face death or – a fate worse than death – a life of slavery? [15] Actually, you are much indebted to me, if you can change your ways; for it was from me that you first came to learn what free-born men cannot endure. For the rest, have mercy: do not heap punishments on old men now deprived of their children. Have us taken to our execution that we may win from our own deaths what we had sought from yours.' Such were the words of Hermolaus.

8

[1] The king replied: 'The falseness of these charges (which that fellow has picked up from his teacher) is obvious from my patience. [2] Although he admitted to the most heinous crime, I not only gave him a hearing myself but made you hear him, too; for I was aware that, when I gave this assassin[54] permission to speak, he would exhibit the madness which drove him to decide to kill me – me, whom he should have respected as a father! [3] Recently he

behaved rather impudently on a hunt. I resorted to our traditional custom, followed by kings of Macedon from the earliest times, and ordered him to be flogged. Such discipline is necessary. Pupils accept it from their teachers, wives from their husbands; we even allow our slaves to beat boys of this age. [4] Such is my 'savagery' against him, which he wanted to avenge with a treacherous murder. As for the other pages, they all allow me to follow my inclinations, and you know how mild I am in my treatment of them – reminding you of that is unnecessary.

[5] 'That the execution of traitors does not earn Hermolaus' approval causes me very little surprise, for he has himself earned that penalty. In fact, he praises Parmenion and Philotas to further his own cause. [6] Now as for Alexander Lyncestes, he twice plotted against my life and despite the testimony of two informers I still let him go free.[55] When he was found guilty once again, I nevertheless delayed the matter for three years until *you* demanded that he finally pay the due penalty for his crime. [7] Attalus, you remember, posed a threat to my life before my accession. And Clitus – I wish he had not forced me to lose my temper with him! But I tolerated his scurrilous comments, his insults to you and to me, longer than he would have tolerated the same coming from me. [8] The clemency of kings and leaders depends not just on their own character but on the character of their subjects, too. Authority is rendered less harsh by obedience; but when respect leaves men's minds and we mix the highest and lowest together without distinction – then we need force to repel force.

[9] 'But why should I be surprised at that fellow's accusing me of cruelty when he has had the audacity to charge me with avarice? I do not wish to cite individual cases among you: I might come to resent my own generosity if I offend your self-respect. Look at the army as a whole. The soldier who had nothing but his weapons a short time ago now reclines on silver couches! The men pile their tables with gold, lead along troops of slaves and cannot carry all the spoils taken from the enemy!

[10] 'But, says Hermolaus, the Persians whom we have defeated are held in high regard by me! Now that is actually the clearest proof of my restraint – my rule is not tyrannical even in the case of conquered peoples. I did not come into Asia to wipe out its races entirely or to transform half the world into a desert. Rather it was to make the people I conquered in warfare feel no regret at my victory. [11] As a consequence, you have men fighting along with you and shedding blood for your empire who would have rebelled had they been treated disdainfully. Possession achieved by the sword is not of long duration, but gratitude for kindness shown is everlasting. [12] If we wish to hold Asia and not merely pass through it we must impart our clemency to these people – it is their loyalty which will make our empire stable and enduring. And, to tell the truth, we have more possessions than we can use, and it is insatiable greed to keep on filling up something that is already overflowing. [13] But, he claims, I am foisting Persian habits on the

Macedonians. True, for I see in many races things we should not blush to imitate, and the only way this great empire can be satisfactorily governed is by our transmitting some things to the natives and learning others from them ourselves.

[14] 'Then there was Hermolaus' insistence that I repudiate Jupiter who recognized me as a son by his oracle – that almost called for laughter. [15] Does he think I have power over the gods' oracular responses? Jupiter held out to me the title of son; accepting it has not been disadvantageous to the operations in which we are engaged. I only wish the Indians would also believe me a god! For reputation determines military success, and often even a false belief has accomplished as much as the truth. [16] Do you think I emblazoned your arms with gold and silver to indulge an extravagant taste? No! For the Indians nothing is a more common sight than these metals, and I wished to show them that the Macedonians, unsurpassed in all else, cannot be outclassed even in respect to gold. [17] So I shall bedazzle them from the start: they are expecting a completely humble and sordid force, and I shall show them that we come not lusting after gold and silver but to subjugate the whole world. You, traitor, wished to abort this glorious enterprise and to deliver up the Macedonians to the races they had conquered by eliminating their king.

[18] 'You suggest now that I pardon your relatives! Really, you should be kept ignorant of my decision concerning them, so that your deaths may be the more distressing, that is if you have any thought or concern for your kin. But in fact I long ago suspended that notorious custom of executing innocent kinsmen and relatives along with the guilty, and I publicly declare that they all shall retain their former rank. [19] As for your Callisthenes, the only person to think you a man (because you are an assassin[56]), I know why you want him brought forward. It is so that the insults which you sometimes uttered against me and sometimes heard from him can be repeated by his lips before this gathering. Were he a Macedonian I would have introduced him here along with you – a teacher truly worthy of his pupil. As it is, he is an Olynthian and does not enjoy the same rights.'

[20] With that Alexander closed the meeting and had the condemned men transferred to members of their own unit. The latter tortured them to death so that they would gain the king's approval by their cruelty. [21] Callisthenes also died under torture.[57] He was innocent of any plot to kill the king, but the sycophantic character of court life ill-suited his nature. [22] As a result no other person's execution engendered greater resentment against Alexander among the Greeks. Callisthenes was a man of the finest character and accomplishments who had restored Alexander to life when he was determined to die after the murder of Clitus.[58] Alexander had not merely executed him but had tortured him as well – and without trial. [23] This barbarous act was, all too late, followed by feelings of remorse.

9

[1] In order not to promote inactivity, which naturally spawns gossip, Alexander now moved towards India, for his reputation was always greater in combat than after victory.

[2] Almost the whole of India faces eastward, and it is a country greater in length than width. [3] The areas exposed to the south wind are of higher elevation, but the rest of the country is flat, and the many famous rivers that rise in the Caucasus are afforded a gentle course through its plains. [4] The Indus is colder than the others, and its waters are little different from the sea in colour. [5] The Ganges, greatest of all the rivers of the East, flows in a southerly direction and, taking a direct route, skirts the great mountain ranges, after which it is diverted eastward by some rocky mountains which bar its course. [6] Both these rivers flow into the Red Sea.[59] The Indus tears away its banks and many trees on them along with large tracts of soil. Its channel is also obstructed with boulders from which its waters are violently deflected at many points, [7] but when it reaches softer ground it becomes sluggish and forms islands. [8] Its volume is augmented by the Acesines,[60] which the Ganges meets[61] before it reaches the sea, the two rivers colliding with great violence (for the Ganges makes the entry of its tributary difficult, so that its waters are checked, though not repelled).

[9] The Diardines is less well-known because it runs through the most remote parts of India, but it supports a population not only of crocodiles, like the Nile, but also of dolphins and creatures unknown among other peoples. [10] The Ethymantus, a meandering river with frequent bends, is drained off for irrigation by the natives, which explains why its waters are low when it empties into the sea and why it no longer has a name. [11] The entire country is furrowed with many other rivers besides these, but they are little known because they flow through uncharted territory.

[12] The areas closer to the sea are parched more than others by the North wind. The wind is blocked by the mountain ranges, however, and fails to penetrate to the interior which, as a result, is favourable for fruit-growing. [13] But in that part of the world the earth inverts its regular seasonal changes, so that when other places are baking in the heat of the sun, India is covered with snow; conversely, when everywhere else is frozen, the heat there is intolerable. And there is no explanation for this aberration of nature. [14] The sea skirting the country is certainly no different from other seas, even in its colour. Its name derives from king Erythrus, and for this reason people who know no better think its waters are red.[62] The country produces flax in abundance and this provides the clothing for most of the inhabitants. [15] Tree-bark is soft here and capable of being written on, like papyrus. [16] Birds can be trained to imitate the human voice and the country also supports a population of rhinoceroses, though this is not indigenous. [17] Its elephants possess greater strength than those trained in Africa, and their size matches

that strength. [18] The rivers are gold-bearing, their waters sluggish and flowing at a slow, easy pace. [19] Its sea throws up precious stones and pearls on the beaches, and nothing contributes more to its wealth than these, especially since the spread of the use of such items of depravity to other nations – for the value of this rubbish cast up by the surging tide is determined by the lust for it.

[20] As elsewhere, the environment also shapes the character of the people. [21] They wear linen clothes which cover the body right down to the feet. They have sandals on their feet, linen turbans on their heads, and precious stones hanging from their ears. Gold bracelets are also worn on the forearm and upper arm by those in their society pre-eminent for rank or wealth. [22] Their hair they often comb but rarely cut, and their beards are always left unshaven, though they do shave the rest of the face until the skin appears very smooth. [23] The extravagance of their royalty (which they themselves term 'grandeur') transcends the vices of all other peoples. When the king deigns to be seen in public, his servants carry silver censers along and fill with incense the entire route along which he has decided to be carried. [24] He lounges in a golden litter fringed with pearls, and he is dressed in linen clothes embroidered with gold and purple. The litter is attended by men-at-arms and by his bodyguard [25] amongst whom, perched on branches, are birds which have been trained to sing in order to divert the king's thoughts from serious matters.

[26] The palace has gilded pillars with a vine in gold relief running the whole length of each of them and silver representations of birds (the sight of which affords them greatest pleasure) at various points. [27] The palace stands open to all visitors at the time of the combing and dressing of the king's hair, and this is when he makes his response to foreign embassies and dispenses justice to his countrymen. When his sandals are removed, his feet are smeared with perfume.

[28] On the hunt his hardest exercise is to shoot animals penned in a preserve, his concubines all the time praying and singing for him! His arrows are two cubits long, and shooting them demands an effort disproportionate to the results; for the effectiveness of such a weapon (which depends entirely on lightness) is frustrated by its unwieldy weight. [29] The king makes shorter journeys on horseback, but when he has to cover some distance he uses an elephant-drawn carriage, the bodies of the huge beasts completely covered with gold. To add the finishing touch to his decadent life-style, he is followed by a long retinue of concubines in golden sedan-chairs. This is an entirely separate column from the queen's train, and it rivals it in extravagance. [30] Women prepare the king's meals and they also serve him his wine, which is drunk in copious quantities by all Indians. When a drunken drowsiness comes over him, the concubines carry him to his bedroom, at the same time chanting a traditional hymn to the gods of the night.

[31] Who would believe that an interest in philosophy was to be found

amid such degeneracy? There is an unkempt, squalid class of men called 'wise men'. [32] According to these, it is a noble thing to anticipate the appointed day of one's death and, if they are enfeebled by old age or afflicted with ill-health, they give instructions for themselves to be burned alive. They consider it a disgrace to await a natural death, and no respects are paid to the remains of those who have died of old age – they believe the fire is polluted unless those whom it receives are living.[63] [33] It is said that those who live conventional lives in the cities expertly observe the movements of the stars and foretell the future. These men, however, believe that nobody advances the day of his death if he can await it fearlessly. [34] To anything they have started to cultivate they give divine status, especially to trees, violating which con-stitutes a capital offence. [35] They have fixed their months as fifteen-day periods, though the year retains its full span. [36] For temporal divisions they use the lunar cycle, but the terminal point is not, as with most peoples, the full moon but the time at which it has started to form a crescent, and that is the reason why their months are shorter, because they determine their length by this phase of the moon. [37] Many other pieces of information are transmitted concerning the Indians, but it did not seem worth holding up my narrative to report them.

10

[1] After entering the boundaries of India, Alexander was met by the petty kings of the area, who were prepared to submit to his authority. He was, they said, the third son of Jupiter to have reached them but, whereas they knew of Father Liber and Hercules only by report, Alexander had come in person and was before their eyes. [2] The king gave them a courteous welcome and instructed them to accompany him, for he intended using them as guides for his journeys. When no one else came to meet him, he sent Hephaestion and Perdiccas ahead with a section of his troops to crush any opposition to his power, giving them orders to advance to the river Indus and construct boats to ferry the army to the far banks.[64] [3] Because a number of rivers had to be crossed, they put the boats together in such a way that they could be dismantled, transported by wagon and then reassembled.

[4] Alexander instructed Craterus to follow him with the phalanx, and then led out his cavalry and light-armed infantry. After a slight skirmish with some Indians who confronted him, he drove them into the nearest city. [5] By this time Craterus had arrived and so, to strike terror right at the start into a people which had, as yet, had no experience of Macedonian arms, he told him to show no mercy after the fortifications of the city under siege had been fired. [6] Riding up to the walls, however, Alexander was hit by an arrow, despite which he took the town, butchered its inhabitants to a man, and even unleashed his fury on its buildings.

[7] Next, after subduing some tribe of little account, he came to the city

of Nysa. It so happened that after he had pitched camp in a wooded spot right before the walls, there was an unprecedented drop in temperature during the night which made the men shiver with cold. A fire offered itself as a convenient remedy. [8] Cutting down some trees, they started a blaze, but this, fuelled by the logs, engulfed the sepulchres of the townspeople. The sepulchres had been made of old cedar which, once they had caught fire, spread the flames over a wide area until they were all razed to the ground. [9] From the city came the sound first of dogs barking, then of men in an uproar, and it was at this point that the townspeople realized that their enemy had reached their city and the Macedonians that they had arrived.

[10] After Alexander had led out his troops and was laying siege to the walls, a number of the enemy attempted a sortie, only to fall beneath a barrage of missiles. Accordingly, some of the inhabitants advocated surrender, while others were for risking a battle. When Alexander learned that they were hesitating, he ordered a blockade but no bloodshed. Worn down by the difficulties of the siege, the enemy finally capitulated.

[11] The people of Nysa claimed Father Liber as their founder, and this piece of genealogy is a fact. [12] The city is situated at the foot of a mountain which the local people call Meron, and it was because of this name that the Greeks presumed to invent their story of Father Liber being concealed in the thigh of Jupiter.[65] [13] When the king learned from the local people how to reach the mountain he had supplies sent ahead and went up to its summit with his entire army. Ivy and vines grow in large quantities all over the mountain, and many year-round streams flow down it. [14] There are also various fruits whose juices have health-giving properties, the soil spontaneously producing a harvest from any seeds that happen to fall there. There are laurels and berry-bushes – a thick forest on the mountain's cliffs. [15] Personally I do not believe it was as a result of divine inspiration but simply to amuse themselves that the soldiers began to pick ivy and vine fronds here and there, and wandered the length of the wood wearing leaf-garlands like bacchants. [16] The mountain-tops and hills echoed with the voices of many thousands worshipping the tutelary god of that wood for, as usually happens, though the fooling started with a few it suddenly spread to them all. [17] As if the world were at peace around them, they flung themselves down on the grass and on beds of leaves while the king, who did not object to this chance offer of merriment, provided an abundance of all things needed for a feast and had his army spend ten days in the worship of Father Liber. [18] Who would deny that even an illustrious reputation is a benefit conferred more often by fortune than merit? Not even when they were feasting and were drowsy with drink did the enemy venture to attack them – being just as terrified by their uproarious revelling and yelling as if what they had heard was the Macedonian battle-cry. The same good fortune protected the Macedonians while they were returning from the ocean and held a drunken revel before the eyes of their enemy.[66]

[19] From here they came into the area called Daedala, the inhabitants of which had abandoned their homes and sought refuge in some remote, tree-clad mountains. Accordingly Alexander passed on to Acadira, also burned and deserted by its fleeing inhabitants. [20] He was, therefore, obliged to alter his plan of campaign: splitting his forces, he made a simultaneous show of strength at several points. The Indians, under pressure in places where they had not expected their enemy, were totally overwhelmed and crushed. [21] Ptolemy captured the largest number of cities, but Alexander the greatest ones. Now he reunited the forces which he had divided.

[22] Next he crossed the river Choaspes and, leaving Coenus to besiege a large city which its inhabitants called Beira, pressed on himself to Mazagae.[67] This had been the kingdom of the recently-deceased Assacanus and was now, both the province and its capital, under the rule of his mother, Cleophis. [23] The city had an infantry garrison of 38,000 and was protected by fortifications as well as its position. On the east side it is encompassed by a swift river which, with banks sheer on both sides, prevents any approach to the city. [24] To the west and on the south side nature has, as if intentionally, thrown up a barricade of beetling crags, at the foot of which lie caves and chasms hollowed to a great depth over a long period of time. Where these terminate, a ditch of massive proportions forms a barrier. [25] A wall thirty-five stades long encircled the city, its lower sections made of stone, the upper of unbaked brick. The brickwork was bonded by pebbles sandwiched between the bricks (so that the weaker material could rest on the firmer base) and by earth moistened with water. [26] To prevent the whole structure from settling, firm beams were incorporated into it on which were set planks which served to protect the walls and also afford passage along them.

[27] Alexander surveyed the fortifications, uncertain how to proceed; for the caverns could be filled only with earth, and only by filling them could siege engines be brought up to the walls. At this point, someone on the walls hit him with an arrow, [28] which happened to lodge in his leg. Alexander pulled out the barb, had his horse brought up and, without even bandaging the wound, rode around fulfilling his objectives no less energetically. [29] But as his injured leg hung down and, after the blood dried, the wound stiffened, aggravating the pain, Alexander is reported to have said that, though he was called the son of Jupiter, he could still feel the impairment of physical injury. [30] However, he did not return to camp until he had made a thorough inspection and given orders for what he wanted done. Then, following his instructions, some set about demolishing buildings outside the city, bringing back huge quantities of timber for the land-fill, while others proceeded to throw the trunks of large trees, complete with branches, and massive rocks into the caverns. [31] When the land-fill had reached ground-level, they began erecting towers and, thanks to the tremendous enthusiasm of the men, these operations were all completed within nine days.

Alexander came out to inspect the work before a scab had formed on his wound. He commended the men and ordered the engines moved up. From these, huge quantities of missiles were showered on the defenders. [32] Particularly terrifying for people with no experience of such contrivances were the movable towers and, since the huge structures relied on no observable means of propulsion, the townspeople believed they were driven by divine power. They also claimed that the Macedonian wall-fighting pikes and the heavy spears hurled from the engines were not weapons such as mortals used. [33] So they abandoned all hope of defending the city and retreated to their citadel. Since the besieged townspeople now had no option but to surrender, a deputation came down to the king to seek a pardon, [34] which was granted to them. Then the queen came with a group of ladies of noble birth who made libations from golden bowls. [35] The queen herself placed her little son at Alexander's knees, and from him gained not only a pardon but also the restitution of her former status, for she retained the title of queen. Some have held the belief that it was the queen's beauty rather than Alexander's compassionate nature that won her this, [36] and it is a fact that she subsequently bore a son who was named Alexander, whoever his father was.[68]

II

[1] From here Polyperchon was dispatched with an army to the city of Ora,[69] where he defeated the disorganized inhabitants in battle, drove them within their fortifications and, pressing his advantage, brought the city into subjection. [2] Many cities of little consequence fell to the king after being deserted by their inhabitants. The latter took up arms and occupied a rocky outcrop called Aornis.[70] According to popular tradition this had been unsuccessfully besieged by Hercules, who had been obliged to abandon the siege by an earthquake. [3] Alexander was baffled: the rock was precipitously sheer on every side. Then he was approached by an old man who knew the area. He came to him with his two sons and promised that he would show him a way up, for a price. [4] Alexander contracted to give him eighty talents and, keeping one of the young men behind as a hostage, sent the old man off to fulfil his commitment. [5] The king's secretary, Mullinus, was put at the head of a light-armed unit which, Alexander decided, was to make its way to the summit by a circuitous route to avoid detection by the enemy.

[6] Unlike most rocky prominences, this one does not reach its high elevation by gradual and gentle slopes. It rises very much like a cone, its lower section comparatively broad but the upper part tapering until it terminates in a sharp peak at the top. [7] Its base is lapped by the Indus river, which is extremely deep with steep banks on both sides. On the far side of the rock are sheer chasms and ravines, and the only way to take it by storm was by filling them in. [8] Alexander issued orders for a nearby wood to be felled and the logs thrown into the chasm stripped (since the branches and their foliage

would have hindered the men carrying them). Alexander was himself the first to strip and throw in a tree, and the shout that followed from the troops revealed their enthusiasm, for none refused a job the king had undertaken before him. [9] Within seven days they had filled in the caverns, and the king now ordered the archers and the Agrianes to scale the steep cliffs. From his own unit he selected thirty of the bravest young men, [10] and assigned to them as leaders Charus and Alexander (reminding the latter of the name they both shared). In view of such palpable danger, it was at first decided that the king should not take part in the hazardous undertaking himself; [11] but as soon as the trumpet-signal was given, this resolute man of action turned to his bodyguards, told them to follow him, and was the first to clamber up the rock. After that not one Macedonian held back. They left their posts and followed the king of their own accord. [12] Many were overtaken by a pitiful fate. Slipping from the sheer cliff-face, they were swallowed up by the river flowing past it. This was a painful spectacle even to those not in danger but, when another's death demonstrated to them what they had to fear themselves, their pity turned to terror and their lamentation was no longer for the dead but for themselves.

[13] By now they had reached the stage where returning was impossible without destroying themselves, unless they were victorious. As they climbed, the barbarians rolled huge boulders on to them, and those who were hit fell headlong from their unsure and slippery footholds. [14] Alexander and Charus, however, had scaled the cliff, and had already begun to engage the enemy in hand-to-hand fighting, though, since the barbarians were pouring weapons on them from higher ground, they received more wounds than they inflicted. [15] Alexander, bearing in mind both his name and his promise, fought with more vigour than caution and finally fell, pierced by weapons from every side. [16] Charus saw him on the ground. Everything but revenge left his mind and he began a charge at the enemy, many of whom he dispatched with his lance, some with his sword. But he was alone and his antagonists many. He fell dead on his friend's body.[71] [17] Distressed, as one might expect, by the death of his best young fighters and others of his men, the king signalled a retreat. [18] What saved them was the fact that they withdrew gradually and confidently, while the barbarians were content with having driven back their enemy and refrained from pressing them as they retreated.

[19] Alexander had now decided to abandon the project – there was apparently no hope of gaining the rock – but he nonetheless made a show of persevering with the siege, ordering roads to be blocked, siege-towers moved up, and exhausted troops replaced by others.

[20] The Indians saw his persistence but they spent two days and nights feasting and beating drums in their usual manner, ostentatiously demonstrating not only their confidence but their belief that they had won. [21] On the third night, however, drumbeats were no longer heard. Torches blazed all over the rocky hill, lit by the barbarians to make their flight safer when

they would, in the darkness of night, be running over crags impossible to negotiate. [22] Alexander sent Balacrus ahead to reconnoitre and learned that the barbarians had fled and abandoned the rock. Then, giving the signal for his men to raise a concerted shout, he struck terror into the Indians in their disordered flight. [23] Many thought the enemy were upon them and hurled themselves to their deaths down the slippery crags and impassable rocks. A larger number suffered mutilations to some part of their bodies and were abandoned by their uninjured comrades.

[24] Although his victory was over the terrain rather than the enemy, the king nonetheless fostered the belief that he had won a decisive victory by offering sacrifices and worship to the gods. Altars were set up on the rock in honour of Minerva Victoria. [25] The reward was duly paid to the guides for the path on which Alexander had ordered the light-armed to ascend, although they had accomplished less than they had contracted to do; and the rocky prominence and the adjoining land was put under Sisocostus'[72] authority.

12

[1] From there Alexander advanced to Ecbolima. On learning that a narrow pass on the road was occupied by a certain Erices[73] with an armed force of 20,000, he entrusted his heavier-armed troops to Coenus, who was to take them on at an easy pace. [2] He himself went forward at the head of his slingers and archers, dislodged the force blockading the pass and cleared the road for the troops following him. [3] Out of hatred for their leader, or else hoping to win the goodwill of the conqueror, the Indians fell on the fleeing Erices, killed him, and brought his head and armour to Alexander. The king granted them pardon for their deed but refused to give approval to such a precedent.

[4] Sixteen days later he reached the river Indus, where he found that all the preparations he had ordered for the crossing had been made by Hephaestion. [5] The ruler in that area was Omphis.[74] It was he who had been responsible for his father's surrender of the kingdom to Alexander and, after the death of his father, he had sent the king a deputation to ask whether he wished him to act as interim ruler or await his arrival as a private citizen. [6] Given permission to act as regent, Omphis nevertheless did not presume to exercise the authority and, though he had courteously welcomed Hephaestion and dispensed corn to his forces free of charge, he had not gone out to meet him, reluctant to entrust himself to anyone's protection but the king's. [7] So, as Alexander approached, Omphis came forth from the city to meet him with his forces under arms and with elephants interspersed in his line at brief intervals, looking like castles from a distance.

[8] At first Alexander thought it was an enemy and not an ally that was approaching; anticipating an engagement, he had given orders for the

infantry to take up arms and the cavalry to divide to the wings. The Indian, however, saw that the Macedonians had misread the situation, so he called a general halt and spurred on the horse he was riding. Alexander did the same – whether it was a friend or enemy coming towards him, he felt secure in his own prowess or the other's honour. [9] Their meeting, as could be inferred from the expressions of the two, was friendly. Conversation was impossible without an interpreter, however, so one was brought up. The barbarian explained that the reason for his coming out to Alexander with his army was so that he could at one stroke surrender to him the entire strength of his kingdom, and he had not even waited to be given assurance of safety through intermediaries. [10] He put his own person and his kingdom at Alexander's disposal, he said, for he knew him to be a man who fought to gain glory and who feared nothing more than achieving a reputation for perfidy. The king was delighted with the barbarian's candour. He gave him his right hand as an assurance of his good faith and restored his kingdom to him. [11] Omphis handed over to Alexander fifty-six elephants, large numbers of sheep of exceptional size, and some 3,000 bulls (these animals being very valuable in that part of the world and highly prized by royalty).

[12] Alexander asked Omphis whether he had in his realm more farmers or soldiers, to which Omphis replied that, since he was at war with two kings, he needed a larger force of soldiers than he did farm-workers. [13] The two kings were Abisares and Porus,[75] the latter enjoying the greater authority. Both had kingdoms beyond the Hydaspes river and had resolved to try the fortunes of war against any aggressor who came. [14] With Alexander's permission, Omphis assumed both the royal diadem and, after the tradition of his race, the name that had been his father's. He was now called Taxiles by his people, for the name went along with the authority to whomsoever it passed.

[15] Omphis entertained Alexander hospitably for three days. On the fourth he revealed how much grain he had supplied to the forces under Hephaestion's command, and he also made gifts of golden crowns to Alexander and all his friends, to which he added eighty talents of coined silver. [16] His generosity brought immense pleasure to Alexander. He returned to him his gifts and added to them 1,000 talents from the booty he was carrying, plus large quantities of gold and silver dinnerware, copious amounts of Persian clothing, and thirty horses from his own stables, together with the trappings they wore when he rode them himself.

[17] While it put the barbarian under an obligation to him, this generosity of Alexander's seriously offended his own friends. One such was Meleager who, having drunk too much at dinner, offered Alexander his congratulations on having at least found in India a man worth 1,000 talents.[76] [18] The king did not forget how remorseful he had been over killing Clitus for his hasty tongue and so he repressed his anger, though he did comment that envious men only torment themselves.

[1] The next day ambassadors of Abisares came to the king. As they had been instructed, they made a total submission to Alexander and, after pledges had been exchanged, they were sent back to their king. [2] Believing that Porus could also be pressed into capitulation by the spreading fame of his name, Alexander sent Cleochares to him to instruct him to pay tribute and meet the king at the point of entry into his territory. One of these demands Porus agreed to meet: he would be present when Alexander entered his kingdom – but he would be under arms.

[3] Alexander had now determined to cross the Hydaspes when Barzaentes, the ringleader of the Arachosian revolt, was brought to him in irons, together with thirty elephants which had been captured along with him. The latter were timely reinforcements against the Indians, for they put greater confidence and military strength in these beasts than in regular forces. [4] Samaxus was also brought to him in irons. He was the ruler of a small area of India who had allied himself with Barzaentes.[77] [5] Alexander placed the deserter and the petty king under guard and delivered the elephants up to Taxiles. After this he came to the river Hydaspes, where Porus had taken up a position on the far bank, intending to bar his enemy from crossing.

[6] Against the Macedonians Porus had marshalled eighty-five enormously powerful elephants and, behind them, 300 chariots and some 30,000 infantry, including archers (who, as observed above, were equipped with arrows too heavy to be shot effectively).[78] [7] Porus himself rode an elephant which towered above the other beasts. His armour, with its gold and silver inlay, lent distinction to an unusually large physique.[79] His physical strength was matched by his courage, and he possessed as much acumen as could exist among savages. [8] The Macedonians were alarmed not only by the appearance of their foes but also by the size of the river which had to be crossed: four stades wide and with a deep bed that nowhere revealed any shallow areas, this presented the appearance of a vast sea. [9] Nor was the current's force any the less in view of the wide expanse of water; in fact, it rushed ahead as a torrential cataract just as if it had been narrowly constricted by its banks, and waves rebounding at several points indicated the presence of unseen rocks.

[10] The bank supplied an even more terrifying scene, covered as it was with horses and men and, standing among them, those immense bodies with their huge bulk; deliberately goaded, these deafened the ears with their horrendous trumpeting. [11] The combination of the river and the enemy suddenly struck terror into hearts which were generally given to confidence and had often proved themselves in battle; for the Macedonians believed their unstable boats could neither be steered to the bank nor safely landed there.

[12] In mid-stream lay a thick cluster of islands. Indians and Macedonians both swam over to these, holding their weapons above their heads, and light

skirmishes were in progress on them, with both kings using these small-scale encounters to assess the outcome of the major one. [13] Now in the Macedonian army Hegesimachus and Nicanor had a reputation for daring and recklessness; they were young noblemen, encouraged by the continuing success of their countrymen to disregard any danger. [14] Led by these two and armed only with lances, the most intrepid of the young Macedonians swam to an island which was occupied by a large body of the enemy and, with nothing more than their enterprise for armour, cut down many of the Indians. [15] To retire with glory was possible – if recklessness when it meets with success could ever know moderation! But while they awaited the approaching enemy with disdainful arrogance, they were encircled by men who had swum over unobserved and fell beneath a shower of missiles hurled at long range. [16] Those escaping the enemy were either swept away by the force of the current or sucked down into whirlpools. The engagement did much to bolster the confidence of Porus, who watched the whole thing from the bank.

[17] Perplexed, Alexander finally devised the following scheme to dupe his enemy. There was in the river an island larger than the others; it was, moreover, wooded and well suited for an ambush. There was also a very deep ravine close to the bank which he himself commanded, and this could conceal not only his infantry but even men on horseback.[80] [18] To distract his enemy's attention from this promising spot, Alexander therefore told Ptolemy to make cavalry manoeuvres with all his squadrons at a point far from the island and to strike fear into the Indians at regular intervals by shouting as if he were going to swim across the river. [19] Ptolemy did this for several days, and by this stratagem he also made Porus concentrate his forces in the area he was pretending to attack.[81]

[20] By now the island was out of the enemy's view. Alexander ordered his tent to be pitched elsewhere on the river bank, the unit usually in attendance on him to stand guard before it, and all the sumptuous trappings of royalty to be deliberately flaunted before the enemy's eyes. [21] Attalus,[82] who was Alexander's age and not dissimilar to him in face and build (especially when seen at a distance), he also dressed in royal robes to make it appear that the king himself was protecting that part of the bank and not planning to cross.

[22] The execution of this plan was first delayed, then assisted, by a storm, as fortune directed even disadvantages to a successful outcome. [23] Alexander was preparing to cross the river with the rest of his troops in the direction of the island mentioned above, the enemy's attention having now been diverted to the men occupying the bank downstream with Ptolemy. At this point a storm let loose a downpour scarcely tolerable even under cover and, overwhelmed by the rainstorm, the soldiers fled back to shore, abandoning their boats and rafts. However, the roaring winds rendered the noise of their confusion inaudible to the enemy. [24] Then, in an instant, the rain

stopped, but the cloud-cover was so thick that it blocked out the daylight and even men in conversation could barely make out each other's features. [25] Another man would have been terrified by the darkness that shrouded the sky: they had to sail on a strange river, and the enemy was possibly occupying that very part of the bank to which they were directing their blind and reckless course. [26] But the king derived glory from perilous situations, and he saw as his opportunity the darkness which frightened all the others. He gave the signal for all to board the rafts in silence and ordered the boat in which he himself was sailing to be pushed off first. [27] The bank for which they were making was deserted by the enemy, for Porus' eyes were fixed entirely on Ptolemy. With the exception of one ship, stranded after a wave smashed it on to a rock, they all reached land and Alexander ordered his men to take up their arms and form ranks.

14

[1] Alexander was advancing at the head of his army, now split into two wings, when news reached Porus that the banks were occupied by armed troops and that a decisive moment was imminent. His initial reaction was to indulge in that natural weakness of mankind, wishful thinking: he believed that it was his ally Abisares who was approaching, as the two had arranged. [2] Presently the brightening daylight revealed the enemy battle-line, and so Porus dispatched 100 chariots and 4,000 cavalry against the advancing column.

These forces which he sent ahead were led by his brother Spitaces,[83] and their main strength lay in the chariots, [3] each of which carried six men, two equipped with shields, two archers stationed on each side of the vehicle and finally the two charioteers who were, in fact, well-armed themselves; for when it came to fighting at close quarters they would drop the reins and fire spears upon the enemy. [4] On this particular day, however, the unit's effectiveness was virtually eliminated since, as mentioned above, there had been an unusually violent rainfall which had left the ground slippery and impossible to ride upon; and the heavy and almost immovable chariots became stuck in the mud and quagmires. [5] Alexander, on the other hand, made a brisk charge with his light-armed troops which could be easily manoeuvred. First to attack the Indians were the Scythians and the Dahae, after which Alexander sent Perdiccas and his cavalry against the enemy's right wing.

[6] When the battle was under way at all points, the charioteers began to drive into the thick of the fray at full speed, believing this to be the last resort for their side. [7] This inflicted damage on both sides for, while the Macedonian infantry were crushed under foot at the first charge, the chariots, being driven over slippery ground which it was impossible to negotiate, flung out their drivers. [8] Others found that their startled horses dragged the

chariots not just into the quagmires and pools of water but even into the river, and a few of the animals, driven by the spears of the enemy, penetrated the ranks as far as Porus, who was vigorously urging on the fight.

[9] When Porus saw his chariots scattered and wandering driverless all over the field, he distributed his elephants to the friends closest to him, [10] and behind the elephants he stationed his infantry, his archers and the drummers. (The Indians used this instrument instead of the trumpet-call – the beat did not alarm the elephants, whose ears had long since become accustomed to the familiar noise.) [11] Before the infantry column was carried a statue of Hercules, which was a great stimulus to the warriors, and to desert its bearers was considered a disgrace for a soldier. [12] The Indians had even authorized the death-penalty for failure to bring it back from battle, the fear they had once felt for that particular foe having been actually transformed into religious veneration.

The Macedonians were momentarily checked by the appearance not only of the elephants but also of the Indian king himself. [13] Set at intervals among the troops, the elephants looked like towers from a distance, while Porus himself was of almost superhuman size. The elephant which he was riding seemed to increase that size, for it stood above the other animals by as much as Porus towered over the other Indians.

[14] Alexander surveyed both the king and the army of the Indians. 'At last', he declared, 'I see a danger that is a match for my courage – I must take on beasts and fine warriors together!' Then he looked at Coenus and said: 'Together with Ptolemy, Perdiccas and Hephaestion I am going to attack the enemy left wing. When you see me in the thick of the fight, set our right wing in motion and attack the enemy while they are in confusion. Antigenes, Leonnatus, Tauron! You three will attack the centre and put pressure on their front. [16] Our spears are long and sturdy; they can never serve us better than against these elephants and their drivers. Dislodge the riders and stab the beasts. They are a military force of dubious value, and their ferocity is greater towards their own side; for they are driven by command against the enemy, but by fear against their own men.'

[17] So saying, Alexander was the first to spur on his horse. When he had attacked the enemy ranks according to plan, Coenus made a vigorous attack on the left wing. [18] The phalanx also succeeded in bursting through the Indian centre with a single charge. Porus meanwhile ordered elephants to be driven to the points at which he had observed the enemy cavalry attacking, but, being a ponderous, practically immobile animal, the elephant was no match for the swift Macedonian horses. The barbarians were even unable to use their arrows [19] because of their length and weight: it was awkward and difficult to fit them to the bow without first setting it on the ground, and in the second place the ground was slippery, causing them difficulty when they tried this, so that as they struggled to make a shot they were overtaken by

their swift-moving enemy. [20] Thus they ignored the king's orders – as commonly happens when men are in confusion and fear usurps the leader's authority – and there were as many commanders-in-chief as there were groups of men wandering about. [21] One was giving orders to form a united line, another to split into companies; some called for making a stand, others for encircling the enemy rear. There was no common plan of action. [22] Porus, however, accompanied by a few whose sense of shame surpassed their fear, began to rally his scattered troops and to advance on his enemy, issuing instructions for the elephants to be driven before his line. [23] The beasts caused great panic. Their strange trumpeting unsettled not only the horses – animals always very easily startled – but also the men in the ranks.

[24] Victors moments before, the Macedonians were now casting around for a place to flee. Then Alexander sent the Agrianes and the Thracian light-armed against the elephants, for they were better at skirmishing than at fighting at close quarters. [25] These released a thick barrage of missiles on both elephants and drivers, and the phalanx also proceeded to bring steady pressure to bear on the frightened animals. [26] Some, however, pursued the elephants too energetically, provoking them to turn on them by the wounds they inflicted. Trampled underfoot, they served as a warning to the others to be more cautious in their pursuit. [27] A particularly terrifying sight was when elephants would snatch up men in armour in their trunks and pass them over their heads to the drivers. [28] So the fortunes of the battle kept shifting, with the Macedonians alternately chasing and fleeing from the elephants, and the contest dragged on inconclusively till late in the day. Then the Macedonians began to use axes – they had equipped themselves with such implements in advance – to hack off the elephants' feet, [29] and they also chopped at the trunks of the animals with gently curving, sickle-like swords called *copides*. In their fear not just of dying, but of suffering novel kinds of torment as they died, they left nothing untried.

[30] The elephants were finally exhausted by their wounds. They charged into their own men, mowing them down; their riders were flung to the ground and trampled to death. More terrified than menacing, the beasts were being driven like cattle from the battlefield [31] when, mounted on his elephant, Porus, who had been deserted by most of his men, began to shower on the enemy swarming around him large numbers of javelins which he had set aside in advance. He wounded many Macedonians at long range but he was himself the target of weapons from every direction. [32] He had already received nine wounds both to the back and to the chest, and had suffered severe loss of blood, so that the missiles he was throwing were slipping from his weakened hands rather than being hurled. [33] His elephant, roused to a frenzy and as yet unwounded, attacked the enemy ranks no less aggressively than before, until its driver caught sight of his king in a barely conscious state, arms dangling and weapons fallen. [34] At that he spurred the beast

to flee. Alexander followed, but his horse was weak from taking many wounds and it toppled forwards, setting the king on the ground rather than throwing him. [35] Changing horses thus slowed down his pursuit.

In the meantime the brother of Taxiles, the Indian king, had been sent ahead by Alexander, and he began to advise Porus not to persevere to the end but to surrender to the victor. [36] Although Porus' strength was spent and he had suffered considerable loss of blood, he started at the sound of this voice which he recognized. 'I know you,' he said, 'brother of Taxiles, traitor to his empire and his throne,' and he flung at him the one javelin which by chance had not fallen from his hands. It passed straight through his chest to emerge at the back. [37] After this final courageous act, Porus began to flee with greater urgency, but his elephant had received numerous wounds and it also began to falter, so he stopped running and threw his infantry in the path of the pursuing enemy.

[38] By now Alexander had caught up. He saw Porus' obstinacy and ordered that no mercy be shown to any who resisted. From every direction, missiles were showered on the Indian infantry and on Porus himself who, finally overwhelmed by them, began to slip from his elephant. [39] The Indian driving it thought he was dismounting, and ordered the animal to come to its knees in the usual way. When the elephant crouched down the others also sank to the ground as they had been trained to do, [40] and it was this that delivered Porus and the other Indians into the hands of the victors. Believing Porus dead, Alexander ordered his body to be stripped. Men quickly gathered to remove his cuirass and his clothing but then the elephant began protecting his master, attacking the men stripping him and lifting and setting Porus' body on his back once more.[84] So the beast was subjected to a volley of weapons from every direction and, when he was dispatched, Porus was placed in a chariot.

[41] Then Alexander saw him lift his eyes. Moved by pity, not hatred, he said to him: 'What folly forced you, knowing as you did the fame of my achievements, to try the fortunes of war, when Taxiles served as an example of my clemency towards those who surrender, an example so close to you?' [42] 'Since you ask,' replied Porus, 'I shall answer you with the frankness your inquiry has granted me. I did not think there was anyone stronger than I. Though I knew my own strength, I had not yet tested yours, and now the outcome of the war has shown you to be the stronger. Even so, being second to you brings me no little satisfaction.'[85]

[43] Alexander questioned him further, asking his opinion on what his victor should do with him. 'What this day tells you to do,' said Porus, 'the day on which you have discovered how transitory good fortune is.' [44] Porus' advice did him more good than pleas would have done. His greatness of spirit was not cowed or broken even in adversity, and Alexander felt obliged to treat him not only with mercy but with respect. [45] He tended to his wounds just as if Porus had fought on his side and, when he recovered

contrary to everyone's expectations,[86] Alexander made him one of his friends and, shortly afterwards, bestowed on him an empire larger than he had formerly held. [46] In fact, no trait of Alexander's was more firmly held or enduring than his admiration for genuine excellence and brilliant achievement, though he was fairer in his estimation of an enemy's praiseworthiness than a fellow citizen's, believing as he did that his own greatness could be eclipsed by his countrymen whereas it would be increased proportionately by the greatness of the peoples he defeated.

BOOK NINE

I

[1] Alexander was pleased to have won so memorable a victory which, he believed, opened up to him the limits of the East. He made a sacrifice of animals to the Sun[1] and, to strengthen his men's enthusiasm for undertaking the remainder of the campaign, commended them publicly in a general assembly and declared that any strength the Indians had possessed had been shattered in the recent contest. [2] From now on, he continued, they would have rich plunder: the area for which they were bound was renowned for its wealth. In fact, he said, the spoils from the Persians were cheap and paltry in comparison, and the soldiers would now fill Macedonia and Greece, not just their own homes, with pearls and precious stones, gold and ivory. [3] The men were eager for both riches and glory and, since nothing Alexander had ever told them had proved to be wrong, they promised their support.

They were dismissed full of confidence, and Alexander ordered ships to be constructed so that after completing his expedition across Asia he might visit the sea at the world's end. [4] Wood for ship-building was abundant on the neighbouring mountains. When they began cutting it, they came upon snakes of extraordinary size, [5] and there were also rhinoceroses on the mountains, animals rare elsewhere. (In fact, the name rhinoceros was given to the animal by the Greeks; the natives, who are ignorant of this language, use a different word in their own tongue.)[2]

[6] The king founded two cities here, one on each bank of the river he had crossed.[3] He then gave each of his generals a crown plus 1,000 gold pieces, and the rest of the men were also rewarded according to the degree of their friendship with Alexander or the service they had rendered.

[7] Abisares, who had sent a deputation to Alexander before the battle with Porus, now sent a second promising to follow all the king's commands on the one condition that he should not be forced to surrender himself, for he was prepared neither to live without royal power nor to rule as a prisoner.[4] [8] Alexander had word sent to him that, if he were reluctant to come to him, then Alexander would come to Abisares. After this he crossed the river and marched into the interior of India. [9] Here almost interminable tracts of countryside were covered with forests darkened by tall trees that reached extraordinary heights. [10] Most of the branches were like huge tree-trunks.

They would bend down to the ground where they would turn and rise once more, creating the impression of being not a branch rising up again but a tree generated from an independent root.[5]

[11] The climate is healthy: the sun's intensity is alleviated by the shade and there are plentiful supplies of spring-water. [12] Here too, however, there were large numbers of snakes. They had scales which emitted a golden gleam and a venom of unique virulence – until the Macedonians were supplied with an antidote by the natives, a bite would be followed by instant death.

[13] From here Alexander came through deserts to the river Hiarotis.[6] Bordering the river was a well-shaded wood consisting of trees not found elsewhere and thickly populated by wild peacock. [14] Moving camp from there, he took a near-by town with a military cordon and imposed tribute on it after taking hostages. He then proceeded to what was, for that region, a comparatively large city which was protected by a marsh as well as a wall.[7] [15] The barbarians came forth to fight with chariots lashed together; some of them were equipped with spears, others with lances, and they would jump nimbly from chariot to chariot whenever they wished to aid comrades who were under pressure. [16] At first this strange style of combat terrified the Macedonians who were sustaining wounds at long range, but their fear was soon replaced by contempt for such undisciplined tactics and, surrounding the chariots on both sides, they began to cut down any offering resistance. [17] Alexander ordered the lashings of the chariots to be severed so that the individual vehicles could be more easily surrounded, and the enemy, after losing 8,000 men, ran back into the town. [18] The next day scaling-ladders were put up on every side and the walls were taken. A few were saved by their speed: when they realized that the city was falling they swam across the marsh and struck sheer terror into the neighbouring towns with stories of the arrival of an invincible army, surely composed of gods!

[19] Alexander now dispatched Perdiccas and a light-armed unit to ravage the area. He then transferred some of his troops to Eumenes[8] so that he could help force the barbarians into submission, while Alexander himself led the remainder to a strongly fortified city in which the inhabitants of other cities had also sought refuge. [20] The townspeople sent a delegation to intercede with the king but prepared for war all the same, for an argument had arisen which had split the people into two factions, some thinking any course preferable to surrender and others that they were unable to put up effective resistance. [21] As they unsuccessfully tried to reach agreement, the party in favour of surrender flung open the gates and admitted the enemy. [22] Although the war faction might have deserved his anger, Alexander nevertheless declared a general amnesty, accepted hostages and moved on to the next city. [23] The hostages were taken along ahead of the troops and, when the inhabitants of the town recognized them as belonging to the same race as themselves, they invited them to parley. By emphasizing the king's mercy as well as his might, the hostages induced them to surrender, and the

other cities were similarly subdued and given his assurance of protection.

[24] From here the Macedonians came into the kingdom of Sophites.[9] His nation, so barbarians believe, is pre-eminent in wisdom and governed by high moral principles. [25] When children are born, whether they are acknowledged and how they are reared is decided not by the parents but by a group of people given the responsibility of examining the physical condition of infants. Those found to possess any abnormality or physical disability they order to be put to death. [26] Marriage is based not on considerations of tribe or class but on physical attractiveness, since that is the criterion for judging children.[10]

[27] The town of this tribe to which Alexander had now advanced his troops was actually occupied by Sophites. The gates were closed but there were no armed men in evidence on the walls or parapets, and the Macedonians could not decide whether the inhabitants had abandoned the town or were lying in ambush. [28] Suddenly a gate opened and the Indian king came out with his two adult sons. In handsomeness he far surpassed all other barbarians. [29] His robe, which covered even his legs, was embroidered with gold and purple; his sandals were golden and studded with precious stones; his arms, both upper arm and forearm, were adorned with pearls; [30] from his ears hung jewels of remarkable brilliance and size; his sceptre was of gold and decorated with beryl. The sceptre he now handed to Alexander with a prayer that good fortune should attend his taking it, and he surrendered himself together with his children and his people.

[31] In that region the hunting-dogs are renowned. It is said they will not bark on sighting a wild animal, and lions are especially their quarry. [32] To demonstrate the power of the dogs to Alexander, Sophites had an enormous lion let out in his sight and only four dogs pitted against him. The dogs swiftly fell on the animal. Then one of the men who usually performed such duties began to tug at the leg of a dog which, along with his fellows, was holding fast to the lion. The dog would not come away, so the man proceeded to cut off the leg with a knife. [33] Since even this failed to crush the dog's determination, the man set about cutting another part of his body and, when the dog clung on with no less persistence, he began to slash at him repeatedly with the knife. Even as he died, the dog kept his teeth fastened on the beast – such is the appetite for hunting that instinct has reputedly implanted in those animals! [34] Personally, I report more than I believe, for, while I cannot bear to declare as fact matters of which I am uncertain, I also cannot omit what I have been told. [35] Leaving Sophites in his kingdom, Alexander now advanced to the river Hypasis.[11] By this time he had been joined by Hephaestion, who had brought another area into subjection. [36] Phegeus was the king of the next tribe to which they came. He told his people to continue with their usual farm work and came with gifts to meet Alexander, ready to obey his every order.

2

[1] Alexander spent two days with Phegeus and by the third had made up his mind to cross the river. This presented difficulties not only because of its width but also because its channel was obstructed with rocks.[12] [2] He therefore asked Phegeus for all the pertinent information and was told that beyond the river lay a twelve-day journey through barren wastes, [3] after which came the Ganges, the largest river in all India.[13] On the far bank of the Ganges, he was told, lived two tribes, the Gangaridae and the Prasii, and their ruler was Aggrammes who was now blockading the roads with a force of 20,000 cavalry and 200,000 infantry. [4] In addition to this he had behind him 2,000 chariots and (his most frightening armament) elephants, which according to Phegeus totalled 3,000.[14]

[5] This all seemed incredible to Alexander; he therefore asked Porus, who was with him, whether Phegeus' information was correct. [6] Porus declared that, as far as the strength of the tribe and its kingdom were concerned, there was no exaggeration, but he added that their ruler was not merely a commoner but a man from the lowest class.[15] His father had been a barber whose regular employment barely kept starvation at bay, but by his good looks he won the heart of the queen. [7] By her he had been brought into a comparatively close friendship with the king of the time, whom he then treacherously murdered, seizing the throne ostensibly as protector of the king's children. He then killed the children and sired this present ruler, who had earned the hatred and contempt of the people by behaviour more in keeping with his father's station in life than his own.

[8] Porus' corroboration had generated many worries in the king's mind. For his enemy and the elephants he felt only contempt, but the terrain and the violence of the rivers alarmed him. [9] To track down and ferret out peoples removed almost to the limits of human habitation seemed a difficult undertaking, and yet his craving for renown and his insatiable lust for reputation permitted him to think nothing inaccessible or remote. [10] He also occasionally harboured doubts about the Macedonians. After covering so many huge expanses of land and after growing old in battle and military service, would they now follow him over the rivers that blocked their path, over all the natural obstacles confronting them? He thought that, laden as they were with a wealth of booty, they would prefer to enjoy what they had won rather than exhaust themselves acquiring more. [11] He and his soldiers saw things differently: while his thoughts encompassed world-wide empire and his programme was still in its initial stages, the men were exhausted by the hardships of the campaign and wished only to enjoy what profits from it lay closest to hand, now that the danger was finally past.[16]

[12] Alexander's ambition prevailed over reason. He called the men to an assembly and addressed them as follows:

'Men! I realize that in recent days many rumours which could alarm you have for that very purpose been circulated by the people of India. [13] However, false and lying reports are nothing new to you. That was how the Persians had invested with terror the Cilician passes and the plains of Mesopotamia, then the Tigris and the Euphrates – one of which we forded and the other we bridged! [14] Rumour is never accurate: everything she passes on is exaggerated. Even our distinguished record, solid though its basis be, owes more to report than actual achievement. [15] Who until recently would believe it possible to withstand elephants that look like city walls, or the Hydaspes river and all the other things which are greater in report than in fact? Why, if stories could have defeated us we should have fled from Asia long ago!

[16] 'Do you believe that their elephant-herds are larger than cattle-herds elsewhere – when the elephant is a rare animal, not easy to capture and much more difficult to tame? [17] It is the same kind of misrepresentation that is responsible for their infantry and cavalry numbers. As for the river, the broader it is the gentler its flow. It is when rivers are compressed between narrow banks and crushed into too narrow a channel that the waters they carry become torrents; a broad channel, conversely, slows the current. [18] Besides, the danger all lies on the bank where the enemy are waiting for us to land our boats. So whatever the size of the river between them and us, the danger when we disembark will be just the same.

[19] 'But let us imagine all those reports to be accurate. What is it that frightens us, the size of the elephants or the numbers of the enemy? As far as the elephants are concerned, we have this recent example to consider: they charged their own men more violently than they did us, and for all their bulk their bodies were hacked to pieces with axes and scythes. [20] What difference does it make if their numbers equal those that Porus had or whether there are 3,000 of them, since we see that they all turn to flight after one or two have been wounded? In the second place, the Indians find it difficult to control even a few elephants, [21] and when so many thousands of them are brought together they collide with each other – the cumbersome bulk of their huge bodies makes standing their ground and running away equally impossible! In fact, I had such a low opinion of those animals that I did not employ them against the enemy even when I had some myself, for I well knew that they pose a greater risk to their masters than to the enemy.

[22] 'But, you will reply, the numbers of their cavalry and infantry cause you concern. I suppose, then, you have been used to fighting against small forces and this is the first time you will face a disorderly horde! [23] Evidence for the invincibility of Macedonian strength before superior numbers comes from the river Granicus, from Cilicia swimming in warm Persian blood, from Arbela and its plains strewn with the bones of our defeated foes. [24] It is too late to start counting the legions of your enemy after your conquests have made a desert in Asia! The time for thinking about our numerical inferiority was when we were sailing across the Hellespont. Now we have Scythians following our banner, Bactrian auxiliaries helping us, Dahae and Sogdians

fighting in our ranks. [25] Not that I place my confidence in that motley band – it is to your hands that I look for assistance, on your courage that I count as a guarantee and assurance of the success I shall achieve. As long as I have you standing with me in battle, I shall not make a tally of my own troops or my enemy's. Only offer me hearts full of enthusiasm and confidence. [26] We are not at the start of our efforts and hardships, but at their end. We are coming to where the sun rises, to the Ocean. Unless cowardice stands in our way, we shall return home from there in triumph, after bringing the ends of the earth into subjection!

'Do not do as lazy farmers do and let a ripe harvest escape your grasp through shiftlessness. [27] The rewards are greater than the dangers – this country is both rich and unfitted for warfare. So it is not so much to glory that I lead you as to plunder. You deserve to take home the riches which the sea deposits there on the shores – you owe it to yourselves to leave nothing untried, nothing passed by because of fear. [28] I beg and beseech you for your own sakes and in the name of your glorious record with which you rise above the level of mortals, in the name of your services to me and mine to you (a rivalry in which neither of us can outdo the other): do not abandon your foster-son and your comrade – let me not say your king – as he approaches the limits of the inhabited world. [29] So far I have imposed everything as an order; for this one thing I shall be in your debt. And I who ask you this have never given you a command without first exposing myself to the risks involved, and I have often protected your line with my own shield. Do not break in my hands the palm branch with which I shall rival Hercules and Father Liber, if I do not incur divine envy. [30] Grant this to my entreaties and finally break your obstinate silence. Where is that shout of yours that shows your enthusiasm? Where that characteristic look of my Macedonians? I do not recognize you, men, and it seems that I am not recognized by you. For some time I have been assailing ears that are deaf and trying to rouse spirits that are alienated from me and broken.'

[31] The men maintained their silence, hanging their heads. 'I must have done you some wrong without knowing it,' said Alexander, 'because you do not even want to look at me. I seem to be in utter isolation – nobody answers me, nobody even says no to me. [32] To whom am I talking? For what am I asking? It is *your* glory, *your* greatness that I am trying to uphold. Where are those men I saw a little while ago competing to carry their wounded king? I am abandoned, forsaken, delivered up to the enemy. [33] But even alone, I shall press on with my journey. Expose me to rivers, to wild animals, to those tribes whose names make you shudder. I shall find men to follow me, though deserted by you. The Scythians and Bactrians will be with me: my enemies recently, they are now my soldiers. [34] Better death than to be a general dependent on the whims of others. Go back home! Desert your king and go in triumph! *I* shall find here a way to gain the victory of which you despair, or else death with honour.'

3

[1] Not even this could force a response from any of the men, who were waiting for their generals and officers to report to the king that they were exhausted from their wounds and the relentless hardship of the campaign, that they were not evading their responsibilities but unable to fulfil them. The generals, however, were overwhelmed by fear and kept their eyes fixed on the ground. [2] So at first a spontaneous murmuring broke out among the men, followed by groans. Little by little their feelings of sadness began to gain freer expression and tears started to flow, so much so that the king's anger turned to pity and he was, despite himself, unable to keep the tears from his own eyes. [3] Finally, when the entire assembly was weeping profusely, Coenus ventured to approach the tribunal, while the others all hung back, and he indicated his desire to speak.[17] [4] Seeing him take his helmet from his head (the conventional procedure when addressing the king), the men started urging him to plead the army's case.

[5] 'May the gods keep disloyal thoughts from us!' Coenus declared, 'and indeed they do so! Your men are as willing as ever to go wherever you command, to fight, to face danger, to shed our blood in order to transmit your name to posterity. So, if you are going on, we shall follow or go before you wherever you wish, even though we be unarmed, naked and exhausted. [6] But if you are prepared to hear the sincere words of your soldiers, wrung out of them by dire necessity, then please lend a sympathetic ear to men who have unfailingly followed your orders and your leadership and will continue to do so wherever you go.

[7] 'By your magnificent achievements, Your Majesty, you have triumphed not over your enemies alone but over your own soldiers, too. Whatever mortals were capable of, we have achieved. We have crossed lands and seas, all of them now better known to us than to their inhabitants. [8] We stand almost at the end of the earth; you are preparing to enter another world and you seek an India even the Indians do not know. You wish to flush out from their coverts and lairs men who live among wild animals and serpents, so that you may traverse in victory more land than the sun looks upon! [9] That is a programme appropriate to your spirit, but beyond ours. For your valour will ever be on the increase, but our energy is already running out. [10] Look at our bodies – debilitated, pierced with all those wounds, decaying with all their scars! Our weapons are already blunt; our armour is wearing out. We put on Persian dress because our own cannot be brought out to us – we have stooped to wearing the clothes of foreigners! [11] How many of us have a cuirass? Who owns a horse? Have an inquiry made into how many are attended by their slaves and what anyone has left of his booty. Conquerors of all, we lack everything! And our problems result not from extravagance; no, on *war* have we expended the equipment of war. [12] Will you expose this fine army naked to wild beasts? Although the barbarians deliberately

exaggerate how many they have of these, even from false reports I realize the quantity is large.

[13] 'If you remain determined to push further into India, the area to the south is not so vast. Subdue that and you can proceed quickly to that sea which nature has decided should be the limit of human existence. [14] Why strive for glory by a circuitous route when it sits close at hand? Here, too, you face the Ocean. Unless you prefer aimless wandering, we have reached the point to which your fortune has been leading you. [15] I preferred to say these things to you rather than to the men behind your back not in order to win the approval of the army standing around us but so that you should hear men speaking their minds rather than making disgruntled murmurings.'

[16] When Coenus concluded his speech, shouting and weeping arose all round him, the mingled cries of the men declaring Alexander their 'king', their 'father', their 'lord'. [17] By now, the same entreaties were also coming from other officers, especially those with some seniority, whose age gave them greater authority and made their plea to be excused less discreditable. [18] Alexander could not upbraid them for obstinacy, nor yet could his anger be appeased. At a loss for what to do, he jumped down from the dais and ordered his royal quarters to be closed, granting entrance to no one but his customary attendants. [19] Two days were devoted to his anger and on the third he emerged from his tent to issue instructions[18] for twelve altars of square-cut stone to be erected to commemorate his expedition. He further ordered the camp fortifications to be extended, and couches on a larger scale than their size required to be left behind, his intention being to make everything appear greater than it was, for he was preparing to leave to posterity a fraudulent wonder.[19]

[20] Retracing his steps from here, Alexander pitched camp at the River Acesines where it so happened that Coenus fell ill and died.[20] Alexander grieved for his death but nonetheless added the comment that it was merely for the sake of a few days that Coenus had made his long speech, as if he were the only one who would see Macedonia again.

[21] By this time the fleet which Alexander had ordered to be built was afloat. Meanwhile, to supplement his forces, Memnon[21] had brought 5,000 cavalry from Thrace plus 7,000 infantry from Harpalus.[22] He had also transported armour emblazoned with gold and silver, sufficient for 25,000 soldiers. [22] and, after this was distributed, Alexander ordered the old armour to be burned. The king's plan now was to go to the Ocean with 1,000 ships.[23] The Indian kings, Porus and Taxiles, had been at variance and reviving their old animosity, but Alexander strengthened their friendship by a marriage alliance and left them in their kingdoms, for he had benefited from the unqualified support of the two of them in the construction of the fleet. [23] He also founded two cities, naming one Nicaea and the other Bucephala, thereby dedicating the latter to the memory and name of the horse which he had lost.[24] [24] Then, after giving instructions for the elephants and baggage

to follow by land, he set off downstream, covering some forty stades a day so that troops could occasionally be disembarked at convenient points.

4

[1] They had now reached the area where the Hydaspes joins the Acesines, after which it flows into the country of the Sibi. [2] The Sibi claim that their ancestors were members of Hercules' army, that these had been left behind when they fell ill and had settled where they themselves were now living.[25] [3] Their clothes were animal skins, their weapons clubs; and although Greek customs had died out among them, they still exhibited many traces of their ancestry.

[4] Alexander disembarked and advanced 250 stades. Here he ravaged the countryside and took its capital town by throwing a cordon around it. [5] Another tribe had stationed 40,000 infantry against him on the river bank[26] but, after crossing the water, Alexander forced them to flee and blockaded them within their city walls, which he then took by storm. The adult males were executed and the rest of the population sold into slavery.

[6] Alexander now attempted to take a second city by assault, but he met fierce resistance and was driven back with heavy Macedonian losses. However, when he persisted with the siege, the townspeople lost all hope of saving themselves, and set fire to the buildings, burning themselves in the blaze along with their wives and children. [7] Since the townspeople were trying to spread the conflagration and the enemy to extinguish it, the battle took on an unusual complexion, with the inhabitants destroying their city and the enemy defending it! So does war reverse even the laws of nature.[27] [8] The town citadel was undamaged and Alexander left a garrison in it. He himself sailed around the citadel which is protected by three of the largest rivers in India (the Ganges excepted): it is washed by the Indus on the north side, while the confluence of the Acesines and the Hydaspes lies to the south of it. [9] The meeting of the two rivers produces waves like those at sea, and the navigable parts are confined to a narrow channel by a thick, heavy silt which is constantly being churned up by the collision of the rivers. [10] Since the waves broke upon them in quick succession, striking the ships both on the prow and on the sides, the sailors began to furl the sails; but their work was frustrated both by the swell of the water and the extreme rapidity of the rivers. [11] Two of the larger ships went down in full view of the men while the lighter vessels, though equally impossible to steer, were thrown up on shore without damage. The king himself encountered the most violent eddies, which slewed his ship around and drove it forward heedless of the rudder. [12] Alexander had already removed his clothes in readiness for leaping into the river, and his friends were swimming close by to pick him up. Swimming and remaining on board appeared equally dangerous, [13] so the men set to the oars in a mighty spirit of emulation, and all the effort that was humanly

possible went into lashing the waves that dashed upon them. You might have thought the waves were parted and the raging waters were in retreat! [14] But though the ship was finally released from them, it could not be brought to shore and ran aground on the nearest sandbank. You would have thought they were at war with the river![28] Alexander therefore established altars equal in number to the rivers and, after sacrificing, marched on for thirty stades.

[15] Now they came into the country of the Sudracae[29] and the Malli. At other times these were usually at war with each other, but now the danger they shared had brought them into alliance. They had 90,000 young men under arms as infantrymen as well as 10,000 cavalry and 900 chariots.[30] [16] The Macedonians, who had believed themselves quit of any danger, were suddenly terror-stricken when they realized that a fresh war with India's most belligerent tribes still lay before them, and once more they began to criticize their king with seditious talk. [17] Alexander had been made to forgo the Ganges and what lay beyond it, they said, but he still had not terminated the war, only changed its location. They themselves were thrown before savage tribes so that they could by their blood open up a path to the Ocean for him; [18] they were dragged beyond the stars and the sun and made to visit places that nature had removed from the sight of men. Each successive re-arming met with fresh enemies. And suppose they scattered and routed those enemies – what reward lay in store for them? Gloomy darkness and a never-ending night brooding over the deep ... a sea filled with shoals of savage sea-monsters ... stagnant waters where dying nature had lost her power.

[19] Unperturbed himself, but worried by his men's anxiety, Alexander called a meeting. The enemy which they feared, he said, were no soldiers, and apart from those tribes nothing stood in the way of their covering the intervening stretches of land and coming simultaneously to the end of the earth and of their hardships. [20] He had given in to their fear of the Ganges and the multitude of tribes beyond it; he had changed direction to a place where equal glory was to be found but less danger. [21] Now they had the Ocean in view; now the sea-breezes were blowing on them. They should not, he added, begrudge him the renown he sought – they would pass beyond the boundaries of Hercules and Father Liber to give their king undying fame at little cost to themselves, and they should let him *return* from India, not flee from it.

[22] Every crowd, and especially a crowd of soldiers, is impulsive and easily swayed, so what quells a mutiny may be as trivial as what starts it. [23] Never did such an enthusiastic cheer come from the army as on this occasion: they bade him lead them on with heaven's favour and go on to match the glory of those whom he tried to emulate. Cheered by their expressions of support, Alexander immediately moved against the enemy. [24] These were the most powerful of the Indian tribes and they were making vigorous preparations for war; as commander-in-chief they had chosen a man of proven courage from

the Sudracae. This man pitched camp at the foot of a mountain and made his fires visible over a wide area to increase the impression of his numbers. Also, while the Macedonians were resting, he made repeated, but unsuccessful, attempts to terrify them with shouts and yells in barbarian fashion. [25] When dawn was approaching, a confident and hopeful Alexander ordered his men, who were in good spirits, to take up arms and proceed to their battle-stations. The barbarians, however, had suddenly taken to their heels. Whether they were scared or whether a mutiny had broken out among them is not recorded, [26] but at all events they occupied some remote hills difficult of access and, after an unsuccessful pursuit of their troops, Alexander succeeded in capturing only their baggage.

After this the Macedonians came to the capital town of the Sudracae.[31] Most of the enemy had sought refuge here, though their confidence in its walls was no greater than their confidence in their arms. [27] Alexander was already making his move towards the town when a seer began to issue warnings against the siege which, he said, the king should at least postpone since it was predicted that his life was in danger. [28] Alexander looked at Demophon (that was the seer's name). 'If someone interrupted you like this,' said the king, 'when you were preoccupied with your craft and observing the entrails, I am sure you would consider him an exasperating nuisance.' [29] After Demophon replied that such would certainly be the case, Alexander continued: 'When I have my mind on weighty matters and not on animal intestines, do you think anything could be a greater hindrance to me than a superstitious seer?'

[30] Waiting only to give this reply, he ordered the ladders to be taken forward and, as the others hesitated, scaled the wall. This had a narrow cornice and, on top, in place of the usual crenellated battlements, passage was blocked by a continuous parapet. [31] Thus the king was hanging, rather than standing, on the parapet, using his shield to parry the weapons falling all round him, [32] for he was the target of projectiles hurled at long range from all the towers about him. His men were unable to reach him because they were overpowered by the missiles showered on them from above, but finally shame prevailed over the magnitude of their danger, since they could see that by hanging back they were delivering their king to the enemy. Their haste, however, actually retarded their aid: [33] while they all tried to scale the wall before their comrades, they overloaded the ladders, which then failed to support them so that they fell to the ground and robbed the king of his only hope. Now he stood in total isolation in the face of a huge army.

5

[1] By now his left arm was weary from swinging around his shield to parry enemy missiles. His friends called to him to jump down to them and were standing ready to catch him. At this point Alexander made an incredible and

phenomenal move which added far more to his reputation for recklessness than to his glorious record. [2] With a wild leap, he flung himself into a city full of his enemies – even though he could barely hope to die in combat without uselessly sacrificing his life, since he could have been overpowered and taken alive before he got up. [3] As it happened, his balance was such that he landed on his feet, and so he began to fight from a standing position – and fortune had seen to it that he would not be surrounded. [4] Not far from the wall stood an old tree whose thickly-leaved branches gave the king some cover, as though its purpose had been to provide him with protection. Alexander pressed himself against its thick trunk so that he could not be encircled and then used his shield to parry the weapons being showered on him from in front. [5] For, though he stood alone, being attacked by so many at long range, no one dared move up on him, and more spears hit the branches than his shield.

[6] Supporting the king in the fight was, first of all, the widespread fame of his name; then there was his desperation, providing a keen incentive to gain an honourable death. [7] But the enemy kept pouring on to him and by now he had taken a large number of missiles on his shield, his helmet had been shattered by rocks and his knees had buckled under the severe and relentless pressure. [8] Accordingly, the Indians standing closest to him rushed at him without due regard or caution. Alexander disposed of two of them with his sword so that they fell dead at his feet. After that no one had the courage to come to close quarters with him: they kept their distance and hurled spears and arrows at him. [9] Though exposed to all these enemy weapons, Alexander still had no difficulty in protecting himself, down on his knees as he was, until an Indian fired an arrow two cubits long (for the Indians had arrows of this size, as I explained above) which passed through his cuirass to lodge itself slightly above his right side. [10] When he received the wound, a thick jet of blood shot forth. He dropped his weapons and appeared to be dying. He was so weak that he did not even have the strength to pull out the arrow with his right hand. [11] The man who had inflicted the wound therefore ran up to strip the body, all eager and exultant. Alexander felt him put his hands on his body and I suppose the indignity of this final insult brought him round. Summoning back his failing spirit, he brought his sword beneath his enemy and plunged it into his unprotected side.

[12] Three bodies now lay around the king, and the other Indians kept their distance in bewilderment. Alexander tried to pull himself up on his shield, intending to go down fighting before his last breath left him. [13] He had not the strength left for the effort, so he attempted to stand by grasping the overhanging branches with his right hand. Even thus he could not control his movements. He sank back to his knees, with a gesture of his hand challenging any of the enemy to come and fight him.

[14] Finally, after dislodging the defenders in another sector of the city, Peucestes appeared,[32] following in the king's steps. [15] When he saw him,

Alexander thought Peucestes' arrival meant consolation in death rather than hope of life, and he allowed his exhausted frame to drop on his shield. Immediately afterwards Timaeus[33] came up, and shortly after him Leonnatus, then Aristonus.[34] [16] The Indians, neglecting everything else when they learned the king was within their walls, also converged swiftly on that spot and proceeded to attack Alexander's defenders. Of these Timaeus went down with many frontal wounds after a heroic fight. [17] Peucestes, too, had received three javelin-wounds, but even so he was using his shield to protect his king, not himself. Leonnatus received a serious neck-wound while trying to check a fierce barbarian charge, and fell half-dead at the king's feet. [18] By now Peucestes was also exhausted from his wounds and had let his shield drop. Alexander's last hope lay in Aristonus – but he, too, was seriously wounded and unable to withstand further the violent pressure of the enemy.

[19] Meanwhile a report reached the Macedonian main body that the king had fallen. What would have dismayed others stirred them to action. Regardless of risk, they smashed through the wall with pick-axes and, bursting into the city where they had made the breach, they cut down the Indians, more of whom took to flight than dared engage the enemy. [20] Old men, women, children – none was spared. Anyone the Macedonians encountered they believed responsible for their king's wounds. Mass slaughter of the enemy finally appeased their just rage. [21] According to Clitarchus and Timagenes, Ptolemy (who was subsequently a king) took part in this battle. Ptolemy himself, however, certainly from no desire to detract from his own reputation, records that he was not there, since he had been sent on an expedition.[35] Such was the carelessness of the compilers of the older histories or, an equally reprehensible shortcoming, their gullibility.

[22] Alexander was brought back to his tent, where the doctors cut off the shaft of the arrow embedded in his body without moving the arrow-head. [23] They then stripped him naked and observed that the arrow was barbed and could only be removed without serious damage to Alexander if the wound were surgically enlarged. [24] They feared, however, that the operation would be impeded by profuse bleeding, since the arrow buried in his flesh was huge and had apparently penetrated his vital organs. [25] Critobulus[36] was a doctor possessed of extraordinary skill, but in such a critical situation he was terrified, fearing to undertake the operation in case an unsuccessful outcome resulted in serious repercussions for himself. [26] Alexander caught sight of him weeping and fearful, the anxiety almost draining him of colour. 'Why are you waiting?' he said to the doctor. 'What is the moment you are waiting for? If I have to die, why do you not at least free me from this agony as soon as possible? Or are you afraid of being held responsible for my having received an incurable wound?'

[27] Eventually, his fear passing or else hidden, Critobulus started urging Alexander to let himself be held down until he extracted the arrow-head, since even a slight movement of the body would have grave consequences.

[28] The king declared that he had no need of people to hold him and, following instructions, he submitted his body to the knife without flinching.

So the wound was enlarged and the barbed head extracted. A stream of blood now began to gush forth. Alexander started to lose consciousness and, as darkness covered his eyes, he lay stretched out as though on the point of death. [29] In vain they tried to check the bleeding with medications, and shouting and wailing broke out simultaneously from his friends who believed their king was dead. Finally the bleeding stopped; Alexander gradually regained consciousness and began to recognize those at his bedside. [30] All through that day and the night that followed, the troops remained in arms crowded around the royal quarters, admitting that the lives of them all depended on his alone. They refused to leave until they were told that he was taking a short sleep, after which they returned to camp with more sanguine hopes for his recovery.

6

[1] After seven days of treatment Alexander's wound had still not closed. Nevertheless, when he heard that rumours of his death had been gaining strength among the barbarians, he had two ships lashed together and a tent erected in the centre of them (and thus easily seen from all sides) so that he could display himself to those who thought he had died. Once seen by the local people, he dashed the hopes the enemy had conceived on the basis of the false report. [2] He then proceeded downstream, keeping some distance from the rest of the fleet so that the stroke of the oars would not disrupt his sleep (which his very fragile condition still required).

[3] Three days after the start of the voyage he reached an area which, though abandoned by its inhabitants, was rich in grain and cattle, so he thought it a good place for his men and himself to get some rest. [4] Now it was customary for his principal friends and his bodyguards to keep watch before the king's quarters whenever he had fallen ill. This custom was observed on this occasion too, and they now all entered Alexander's chamber in a body. [5] Alexander was worried that, since they had all come together, they might be bringing some news, so he asked if there were reports of an unexpected enemy advance. [6] Craterus, who had been charged with the task of conveying to him the entreaties of his friends, replied: 'Do you think that an enemy advance – even supposing they were now standing on our rampart – would cause us more anxiety than does our concern for your health, on which, as matters now stand, you set little value? [7] No matter how powerful an army unite against us from the world over; no matter though it fill the entire earth with arms and men or pave the seas over with ships or bring strange monsters against us – *you* will make us invincible. [8] But which of the gods can guarantee that this mainstay, this star of Macedon will long continue when you are so ready to expose yourself to obvious

225

danger, unaware that you draw the lives of so many of your fellow-citizens into disaster? [9] Who wants to survive you? Who is able to? Following your authority and your command we have reached a place from which returning home without your leadership is impossible for any of us.

[10] 'Now if you were still contesting the rule of Persia with Darius, no one could be surprised at your incautious bravado in every dangerous situation, even though he might wish it were otherwise. When the danger and the reward are equally great, there is more substantial profit from success and likewise more comfort in failure. [11] But who could bear that your life should pay for a village of no consequence – not just who among your soldiers, but what member of any barbarian race who knows of your greatness? [12] I shudder to think of what we saw a short time ago! I fear to put it into words – how those vile hands would have sullied spoils taken from your invincible body had not fortune pitied us and intervened to save you.

[13] 'We who were unable to keep up with you are all traitors and deserters. You may brand the mark of disgrace on your soldiers one and all – none will refuse to atone for the offence, even though he could not avoid committing it. Please, let your contempt for us show itself in some other way. We shall go wherever you order. [14] We demand for ourselves the dangers that bring no fame, the battles that confer no glory; but *you* save yourself for those which are appropriate to your greatness. A reputation swiftly fades when one's foes are undistinguished, and nothing is more unworthy than squandering it on operations where it cannot be displayed to advantage.' [15] Ptolemy's comments were much the same, and those of the others in a similar vein. By now they were weeping and begging with mingled voices that he should finally terminate his quest for glory, of which he had had more than enough, and consider his own safety – in other words, the public safety.

[16] The king was pleased at his friends' devotion to him.[37] He embraced them individually with more than usual warmth, and told them to be seated. [17] Then, adopting a more elevated style of expression, he said: 'Oh my faithful and devoted fellow-citizens and friends! To you I express my heartfelt thanks, not just because today you set my well-being above your own but because from the campaign's early days you have overlooked nothing which might serve as an assurance or proof of your goodwill towards me; so much so that I must admit that I have never valued my life as much as I have now begun to do, through my desire to have long enjoyment of your friendship.

[18] 'But my thoughts differ from those of the men who wish to die in my place and I, in fact, believe that it was by my courage that I earned this support of yours. You may wish to enjoy long-lived, perhaps even never-ending profit from me, but my own assessment of myself is based on the extent not of my life but of my glory. [19] I could have been content with my father's inheritance, and within Macedonia's bounds have enjoyed a life of ease as I awaited an old age without renown or distinction (though even inactive men cannot control their destiny, and those who believe that a long life is

the only good are often overtaken by a premature death). But no – *I* count my victories, not my years and, if I accurately compute fortune's favours to me, my life has been long.

[20] 'Starting with Macedonia, I now have power over Greece; I have brought Thrace and the Illyrians under my control; and I rule the Triballi and the Maedi. I have Asia in my possession from the Hellespont to the Red Sea. Now I am not far distant from the ends of the earth; I have decided to go beyond these to open up a second natural sphere, a second world for myself. [21] From Asia I crossed to the frontiers of Europe in the space of a single hour. I am now conqueror of both continents after the ninth year of my rule and the twenty-eighth of my life.[38] Do you think I can relinquish this quest for glory, the one thing to which I have dedicated my entire life? No, I shall not fail in my duty and wherever I fight I shall believe myself to be playing to the theatre of the world. [22] I shall give distinction to places that have none; I shall open up to all the people of the world lands set far away by nature. To die in such exploits, if fortune so will it, is a noble fate. Such is the stock from which I am descended that I must wish for a full life rather than a long one.

[23] 'Remember, I beg you, that we have arrived in territory where a woman's name is celebrated because of her courage. What cities did Semiramis found![39] What nations did she reduce! What great feats did she accomplish! We have not yet matched a woman in reputation, and already feelings of being glutted with fame have overtaken us. [24] If the gods be kind, greater things still await us. But the way to achieve what yet lies before us is to consider nothing of little importance that provides an opportunity for great glory. All you must do is keep me safe from treachery within and from domestic treason – then shall I fearlessly face the perils of war and its presiding god.

[25] 'Philip was safer in combat than in the theatre: often avoiding the hands of his enemies, he could not escape those of his own people.[40] If you also reflect on the deaths of other kings, you will find that a greater number were killed by their own subjects than by the enemy. [26] Anyway (since I have now been given the opportunity to express an idea I have long been considering), the greatest reward for my efforts and my labours will be if my mother Olympias be granted immortality on her departure from life. I shall see to this personally, if I am allowed to do so but, if destiny forestalls me, remember that I have entrusted it to you.' With that he dismissed his friends, but he maintained camp in that spot for a number of days.

7

[1] While this was taking place in India, unrest had arisen among the soldiers recently settled by the king in colonies around Bactra, and they had revolted against Alexander, less out of hostility towards him than from fear of

punishment.⁴¹ [2] After murdering some of their compatriots, the stronger party began to contemplate armed insurrection. Occupying the citadel of Bactra, which had been rather carelessly guarded, they had also compelled the barbarians to join the uprising. [3] Their leader was Athenodorus, who had even assumed the title of king, though his desire was not so much for power as for returning home with men who acknowledged his authority. [4] A certain Biton, who was his countryman but hated Athenodorus because of personal rivalry, hatched a plot against him, and through the agency of a Bactrian called Boxus invited him to a banquet and had him murdered at the table. [5] Calling a meeting the next day, Biton persuaded most of the people that Athenodorus had actually been plotting against his life, but there were others who suspected Biton of treachery and this suspicion gradually began to spread. [6] Accordingly, the Greek soldiers took up their arms and would have killed Biton, if they had been given the chance, but their leaders appeased the anger of the mob.

[7] Unexpectedly rescued from imminent danger, Biton shortly afterwards conspired against those responsible for saving him. His treachery was discovered, however, and the Greeks arrested both him and Boxus. [8] They decided that Boxus should be executed immediately, but that Biton should be tortured to death. As the torture-irons were already being applied to his body, the Greeks for some unknown reason rushed to arms like madmen [9] and, when those who had been ordered to torture Biton heard the uproar, they abandoned their task, fearing that the cries of the rioters were intended to stop them. [10] Stripped as he was, Biton came to the Greeks and the pitiful sight of the man under sentence of death brought about a sudden transformation of their feelings. So they ordered his release. [11] Twice reprieved in this manner, Biton returned home with the others who had deserted the colonies allotted them by the king.⁴² Such were the events in the area of Bactra and the Scythian borders.

[12] In the meantime, Alexander was approached by 100 ambassadors from the two tribes mentioned above.⁴³ They all rode in chariots and were men of extraordinarily large physique and dignified bearing, with clothes of linen embroidered with gold and purple. [13] They stated that they were surrendering to Alexander their cities and lands along with their persons; that they were entrusting to his protection and authority an independence that they had preserved intact for many generations. It was the gods, not fear, that were responsible for their surrender, they said, for they were accepting Alexander's yoke when their power was still unimpaired. [14] After holding a council-meeting, the king accepted their surrender and imposed on them the tribute which both tribes were then paying to the Arachosii. He also requisitioned from them 2,500 horsemen, and all his instructions were dutifully followed by the barbarians.

[15] Alexander then invited the ambassadors and petty kings of the two tribes to a banquet and had a sumptuous feast prepared for them. A hundred

golden couches were set out a short distance from each other, around which he had set tapestries glittering with purple and gold. In that banquet he put on show all the decadence that had long existed among the soft-living Persians or had been recently acquired by the Macedonians, thus combining the vices of the two peoples.

[16] One person present at the banquet was the Athenian Dioxippus, a former boxer whose superlative strength had rendered him well known to and well liked by Alexander.[44] Jealous and spiteful men would make cutting remarks about him, partly in jest, partly in earnest, saying that they had along with them a useless, bloated animal and that, while they went into battle, he was dripping with oil and preparing his belly for a banquet. [17] Now at this feast the Macedonian Horratas,[45] who was already drunk, began to make the same type of insulting comment to Dioxippus and to challenge him, if he were a man, to fight a duel with him with swords the next day. Only then, said Horratas, would Alexander be able to decide whether he was reckless or Dioxippus a coward. [18] Dioxippus accepted the challenge, contemptuously scoffing at the soldier's bravado. The next day the two men were even more insistent in their demands for the contest and, since Alexander could not deter them, he allowed them to carry out their plan. [19] A huge crowd of soldiers, including the Greeks, supported Dioxippus. The Macedonian had equipped himself with regular weapons: he held a bronze shield and a spear, which they call a *sarisa*, in his left hand and a lance in his right, while he also had a sword at his side – as if he were going to fight a number of men simultaneously. [20] Glistening with oil and wearing a garland, Dioxippus grasped a purple cloak in his left hand and a stout, knotty club in his right. The equipment itself had generated tense expectation in the whole crowd, for it appeared sheer lunacy rather than recklessness for a naked man to take on one in armour.[46]

[21] The Macedonian hurled his lance, certain his adversary could be killed at a distance. Dioxippus avoided it by leaning slightly to the side and, before Horratas could transfer the spear to his right hand, he sprang at him and broke the weapon in two with his club. [22] With both missiles gone, the Macedonian had now started to draw his sword, but Dioxippus caught him in a bear-hug, quickly kicked his feet from beneath him and smashed him to the ground. Then, grabbing the sword, he set his foot on the neck of the prone Macedonian and, lifting his club, would have battered his defeated foe to death had he not been stopped by the king.

[23] The outcome of the show dismayed Alexander, as well as the Macedonian soldiers, especially since the barbarians had been present, for he feared that a mockery had been made of the celebrated Macedonian valour. [24] So it was that the king's ears were opened to accusations made by envious men. A few days later a golden cup was deliberately set aside during a banquet and the servants came to the king pretending to have lost what they had, in fact, themselves removed. [25] Often one shows less presence of

mind in an embarrassing situation than when really guilty. Dioxippus could not bear the eyes that all turned on him and marked him out as the thief. On leaving the banquet he wrote a letter which was to be delivered to the king and then fell on his sword. [26] Alexander was pained by his death, which he thought indicated resentment rather than remorse on Dioxippus' part, especially when the excessive jubilation of the men jealous of him revealed the falseness of the accusation against him.

8

[1] The Indian ambassadors were sent home, and returned a few days later with the following gifts: 300 horsemen; 1,030 chariots drawn by teams of horses yoked four abreast; a quantity of linen; 1,000 Indian shields; 100 talents of white iron; lions of extraordinary size and tigers, [2] both species thoroughly tamed; and, in addition, skins from huge lizards and the shells of turtles.

[3] Alexander now instructed Craterus to lead the troops on a course not far distant from the river down which he himself intended to sail. Then he embarked his customary escort on the ships and sailed downstream into the teritory of the Malli. [4] After this he came to the powerful Indian tribe, the Sabarcae,[47] whose government was run by the people, not by royalty. The Sabarcae possessed 60,000 infantry and 6,000 cavalry, with 500 chariots attending this force, and they had selected three generals of proven valour in combat. [5] The people who were in the fields in the neighbourhood of the river (the Sabarcae had many villages, especially on the river-bank) perceived that the water was entirely covered with boats as far as the eye could see, and they observed the flashing arms of all those soldiers. Terrified by this strange sight, they believed an army of gods was approaching with a second Father Liber (a name famous among those peoples). [6] From one side came the shouts of the soldiers, from the other the stroke of the oars and assorted cries of mutual encouragement from the sailors, all of which filled and terrified the natives' ears. [7] They ran in a body to their soldiers who were under arms, shouting to them that they were insane, that they were going to fight with gods, that the ships carrying these invincible warriors were beyond number. So great was the terror they instilled in their own troops that the latter sent a deputation to surrender their people.

[8] Accepting their surrender, Alexander arrived three days later in the land of other tribes[48] who possessed no more spirit than the rest. He founded a city there which he ordered to be named Alexandria, and then entered the territory of the so-called Musicani.[49] [9] Here he put on trial Terioltes,[50] the man he had appointed satrap of the Parapanisadae, the charges being brought against him by the Parapanisadae themselves. Alexander found him guilty of many rapacious and tyrannical acts and ordered his execution. [10]

The governor of the Bactriani, Oxyartes, was not only acquitted but, because of Alexander's affection for him, was also given more extensive territory to govern.[51]

Alexander then reduced the Musicani and established a garrison in their city, [11] after which he proceeded to the Praesti who were also an Indian tribe. Their king, Porticanus,[52] had barricaded himself within a well-fortified city with a large contingent of his countrymen, but Alexander stormed it two days after beginning a siege. [12] Porticanus fled to the citadel and sent spokesmen to the king to negotiate terms of surrender but, before they could reach Alexander, two towers collapsed with a thunderous crash and the Macedonians made their way into the citadel through the ruins. After the citadel was taken, Porticanus was killed as he tried to resist with a few of his men.

[13] Once the citadel was demolished and all captives sold into slavery, Alexander entered the territory of King Sambus.[53] He accepted the surrender of numerous towns and captured the tribe's strongest city by undermining it. [14] To the barbarians, who had no experience of military operations, it seemed like a miracle – armed men emerging from the earth almost in the centre of the city, though there was no prior indication of a passage having been dug. [15] According to Clitarchus, 80,000 Indians were slaughtered in this area and many captives auctioned off as slaves.[54] [16] The Musicani rebelled again, and Pithon was sent to crush them. He captured the tribe's chieftain, who was also the ringleader of the insurrection, and brought him to the king. Alexander crucified him and then returned to the river where he had instructed the fleet to wait for him.

[17] Three days later he came downstream to a town which lay within the kingdom of Sambus.[55] He had recently surrendered, but the townspeople refused to accept his authority and had shut their gates. [18] Deriding their small numbers, Alexander ordered 500 Agrianes to move up to the walls and by a gradual retreat to entice the enemy from their fortifications: they would certainly follow, the king said, if they believed the Agrianes to be fleeing. [19] Following their instructions, the Agrianes provoked the enemy and then suddenly turned tail. The barbarians made a disordered pursuit, only to meet more Macedonians, including the king himself. The battle was renewed, and of the 3,000 barbarians 600 were killed, 1,000 captured and the remainder pinned down within the city walls. [20] However, in its final result the victory was less happy than had at first appeared. The barbarians had smeared poison on their swords, and so the Macedonian wounded died in rapid succession. No diagnosis could be reached by the doctors for such a swift death, as even superficial wounds defied treatment.

[21] The barbarians had hoped that the king's recklessness and lack of caution might be his undoing, but it so happened that he emerged without a scratch despite being in the thick of the fight. [22] Ptolemy had given the king special cause for concern, for he had received a wound in the left

shoulder which, slight though it was, posed a danger disproportionate to its size. He was a blood-relative of Alexander and some believed he was Philip's son (it was known for certain that he was the child of a concubine of Philip's).[56] [23] A member of Alexander's bodyguard and a first-rate soldier, Ptolemy was even more talented at, and better known for, the civilian rather than military skills. His manner was modest and unassuming, and he was superlatively generous and approachable, having assumed none of the pride of royalty. [24] One could not tell whether these traits endeared him more to the king or to his fellow-citizens. At all events, on that occasion he was first made aware of his countrymen's feelings for him which were such that, in his hour of peril, the Macedonians seemed to have had some presentiment of the position in life which he was later to obtain. [25] Indeed, their concern for Ptolemy was no less than the king's. Exhausted though he was from battle and anxiety, Alexander kept watch at Ptolemy's side and ordered a bed brought in on which he himself might sleep. [26] As soon as he lay upon it, a deep sleep immediately came over him. On waking, he declared that he had had a dream about a snake carrying a plant in its mouth which it had indicated was an antidote to the poison. [27] Alexander also described the colour of the plant, claiming that he would recognize it if anyone found it. It was subsequently located – for it was the object of a large-scale search – and Alexander applied it to the wound. Ptolemy's pain immediately ceased and within a short time a scab formed.[57] [28] Frustrated in their initial hopes, the barbarians surrendered the city and themselves.

From here the Macedonians came to Patalia,[58] the city of the neighbouring tribe. Their king, Moeris, had abandoned the town and fled into the hills, [29] so Alexander occupied it and ravaged the countryside. Large quantities of booty were taken from here in the form of sheep and cows, and a great amount of grain was found. [30] After this Alexander took guides who knew the river, and sailed downstream to an island approximately in mid-stream.

9

[1] Alexander's stay here had to be prolonged because the guides had been too slackly guarded and had run off. He sent men to look for others but, when none were found, his obsessive desire to see the Ocean and reach the ends of the earth impelled him to entrust his own life and the safety of so many brave warriors to an unknown river, unaccompanied by guides who knew the area. [2] So they sailed on, in complete ignorance of the terrain through which they were passing: their distance from the sea, what tribes inhabited the region, how free of turbulence the river-mouth was and how far it was navigable by warships – all this could be divined only on the basis of hazardous and blind guesswork. The one comfort they had in their foolhardy enterprise was their invariable good fortune.[59]

[3] They had gone 400 stades when the helmsmen informed Alexander

that they could smell sea air and that in their opinion the Ocean was not far off. [4] Delighted, Alexander began to urge the sailors to ply the oars, telling them that the end of their toil, to which they had devoted all their prayers, was imminent. Now their glorious record was brought to perfection, he said: nothing stood in the way of their courage and they were conquering the world without a military engagement and without bloodshed. Not even nature could extend beyond their destination, and they would shortly behold what was known only to the immortals. [5] Nevertheless, he dispatched a few men to the bank in a boat to capture some peasants who were roaming about; from these he hoped to gather more accurate intelligence. After searching all the huts, the men eventually found some of them in hiding [6] and these, when asked how far they were from the sea, replied that they had not even heard of the sea but that after two days one could reach bitter-tasting water which spoiled the fresh water. The Macedonians understood that it was the sea that was being referred to, by people ignorant of what it was, [7] so the sailors put tremendous vigour into their rowing and, with each passing day, as their hoped-for destination drew nearer, their enthusiasm increased. Two days later they came into mixed sea- and river-water, the still gentle tide blending the two. [8] Then, approaching another mid-stream island at a slightly slower pace (since their progress was retarded by the current), they landed the fleet and split up to look for provisions, not expecting the calamity which now took them by surprise.

[9] At about the third hour the Ocean tide, in its regular alternation, began its flow, pushing back the river-waters. At first the river-current was arrested; then, driven with increased violence, it ran backwards with greater force than that of torrents rushing on a down-hill course. [10] The rank and file were ignorant of the behaviour of the sea, and they thought they were witnessing prodigies and signs of heaven's displeasure. Time after time the sea would swell and come pouring over fields that had been dry shortly before. [11] By now the ships had been lifted by the tide and the entire fleet scattered. The men who had been set ashore came running back to their vessels from every direction, alarmed and panic-stricken by this unforeseen disaster. [12] But in moments of consternation even haste is a hindrance. Some were pushing off the vessels with poles; some had taken their seats and in doing so obstructed the fitting of the oars; [13] some rushed to get under way, without waiting for their full complement, and were feebly attempting to move their disabled and unmanageable vessels; other ships had been unable to hold all the men who thoughtlessly rushed on to them. Thus, in their haste, they were impeded by numbers both too great and too small. [14] Cries on one side urging them to wait, on the other to go ahead, and the conflicting shouts of men who were in no quarter striving after a common goal – all rendered ears as well as eyes ineffective. [15] Even the helmsmen were of no help: in the confusion their calls were inaudible to the men, whose panic and consternation anyway rendered them unable to carry out the orders.

[16] So ships began to collide and to sheer off oars one from the other as the sailors ran afoul of each other's vessels. One might have thought that it was not a single fleet that was on the water, but the ships of two navies starting a sea-battle. [17] Prows smashed into sterns, and ships which had fouled those in front of them were themselves being struck from behind. Their frustration as they quarrelled even brought the sailors to blows. [18] By now the tide had flooded all the flat land around the river, though a few hillocks remained above the surface like small islands, and to these most of the men quickly swam in panic, abandoning the ships. [19] The scattered vessels were either riding on extremely deep water where there had formerly been low-lying valleys or were stuck in shallows where the waves had covered ground higher than the rest. Then, suddenly, they were struck with fresh terror, greater than before. [20] The sea began to ebb and the waters ran back to their former position with a strong undertow, restoring land that had been submerged in deep sea-water a little while before. Ships were left high and dry, some pitched forward on their prows, others lying on their sides. The fields were littered with baggage, armour and bits of planks and oars torn from the ships. [21] The soldiers dared not disembark, but they did not dare stay on board either: each moment they expected their present afflictions to be followed by even worse. They could scarcely believe their eyes as they looked at what was happening – shipwreck on dry land and the sea in a river! [22] Nor was this all they suffered: not knowing that the tide would shortly return to float their vessels, they foresaw starvation and utter catastrophe for themselves. There were also frightful sea monsters wandering around, left by the tide.

[23] By now night was approaching and the king himself felt anguish and despair of ever reaching safety. But his spirit was indomitable, and even his overwhelming cares could not prevent him from remaining on watch all night and sending riders ahead to the river mouth so that they could run back before the tide when they saw it rise again. [24] He also gave orders for the damaged vessels to be repaired and those overturned to be set upright, while the men were to be ready and alert for the time when the sea should once more flood the land. [25] All that night he spent keeping watch and giving the men encouragement. Then the riders came charging back at a tremendous gallop, just as swiftly followed by the tide. At first this began to raise the ships, the waters pushing gently under them and soon, when all the flat land was flooded, it even set the fleet in motion. [26] The shore and banks rang with cheers from the soldiers and sailors as they welcomed their unexpected rescue with exuberant joy. In amazement they kept asking where this great sea had suddenly returned from, where it had vanished to the previous day, and what was the nature of an element which variously disobeyed and complied with the laws of time. [27] Alexander had worked out from what had taken place that the due time for the tidal flow was after sunrise; thus, to anticipate the rising water, he sailed down river with a few vessels in the

middle of the night. Passing beyond the river-mouth he sailed 400 stades out to sea, finally bringing to fruition his heart's desire. Then, after sacrificing to the tutelary gods of the sea and the locality, he returned to the fleet.

10

[1] The fleet now moved upstream, and came to anchor the next day close to a salt lake. Ignorant of its properties, some of the men were beguiled into foolishly entering the water: they were attacked by a skin disease and the infection also spread to others. [2] The remedy for it was oil. Then, since the area was arid, Leonnatus was sent ahead to dig wells along the land-route on which it seemed likely that Alexander would take the army. Alexander himself halted with the troops, awaiting the arrival of spring. [3] In the meantime he founded several cities. He also ordered Nearchus and Onesicritus, who were expert seamen, to take the strongest ships downstream to the Ocean and advance into it as far as they could with safety, to examine the sea's characteristics. Alexander told them that, when they wished to return to him, they could sail back up the same river or up the Euphrates.[60]

[4] By now winter had lost its severity. Alexander burned the ships which seemed unserviceable and proceeded to lead the army on by land. [5] After nine days' march they reached the territory of the Arabites and after a further nine that of the Cedrosii. The latter, an independent nation, surrendered after holding a council meeting and, on their surrender, only provisions were levied from them. [6] Four days later Alexander came to the river which the local people call the Arabus. Then he found himself in a tract of waterless desert, crossing which he came to the Horitae.[61] There he entrusted the major part of his force to Hephaestion, splitting the light-armed among himself, Ptolemy and Leonnatus. [7] Three armies were thus simultaneously looting the Indians, and rich spoils were carried off. Ptolemy put the maritime areas to the torch while Alexander himself and, in another region, Leonnatus burned the rest. In this quarter, too, Alexander founded a city, peopling it with Arachosii.

[8] From here he came to the coastal Indians. These inhabit a broad tract of barren desert and engage in no trade whatsoever, not even with the peoples closest to them. [9] Their naturally fierce temperament has been made even more savage by such isolation. They have protruding nails (which they never trim) and shaggy, uncut hair. [10] They decorate their huts with shells and other objects left by the tide. They dress in animal skins and their diet consists of fish dried in the sun plus the flesh of larger creatures beached by the waves.[62] [11] Their provisions exhausted, the Macedonians began to experience first shortage of food and eventually starvation. They rummaged about for palm roots (that being the only tree growing there) [12] but, when even this means of sustenance ran out, they began to slaughter their pack-animals, sparing not even their horses. Then, having nothing to carry their

baggage, they proceeded to burn the spoils they had taken from the enemy, spoils for which they had penetrated the furthest reaches of the East.

[13] In the wake of famine came plague. The strange juices in their unhealthy diet combined with the hardships of the journey and their mental depression to spread diseases among them. Staying behind and advancing both spelled disaster for, if they stayed, they were assailed by hunger and, if they advanced, by even more virulent disease. [14] As a result, the plains were strewn with almost as many half-alive bodies as dead ones, and even men only slightly ill were unable to keep pace with the column, which was moving along at a rapid pace, each man believing that the more ground they hastily covered the closer they came to realizing their hopes for safety. [15] Those who had collapsed would beg others to help them up, whether they knew them or not. But there were no pack-animals they could be put on and the soldiers had difficulty carrying even their weapons – and the spectre of the catastrophe threatening themselves, too, was ever before their eyes. So, though often called back by their comrades, they could not even bear to look at them, for their pity had now turned to panic. [16] Those left behind called on the gods to witness their plight, appealed to the religion they all shared and begged the king for help; but finding that they vainly importuned unheeding ears, their despair would turn to rage and they would wish on their fellows a fate such as theirs, finding similar friends and comrades.

[17] Alexander was simultaneously beset by grief and shame at being responsible for such a calamity. He sent orders to Phrataphernes, satrap of the Parthyaei, for cooked food to be brought on camels, and he also informed the governors of the neighbouring districts of his difficulties.[63] [18] There was no delay on their part. So, rescued from starvation at least, the army was finally brought into the territory of Cedrosia, the only district in those parts producing all commodities in abundance, and Alexander established a stationary camp in order to rest and strengthen his beleaguered troops. [19] Here he received a letter from Leonnatus with the news that he had fought a successful engagement against 8,000 infantry and 400 cavalry of the Horitae.[64] A message also came from Craterus that two Persian nobles, Ozines and Zariaspes, had been fomenting rebellion, but that they had been apprehended by him and were now in irons.[65]

[20] Alexander gave Sibyrtius charge of this district (its governor, Menon, having recently died after an illness) while he himself advanced into Carmania. [21] The satrap of this people was Astaspes, who was suspected of having advocated rebellion while Alexander was in India.[66] Astaspes came to meet Alexander who, concealing his anger, addressed him affably and let him retain his position until he could examine the reports about him.

[22] Following orders, the district governors now sent from the entire area under their jurisdiction large numbers of horses and pack-animals, and Alexander thereupon redistributed baggage to men who lacked it. [23] Their arms were also restored to their original magnificence, for they were not far

distant from Persia, which was rich as well as pacified. [24] So it was that Alexander, his pride soaring above the human plane, now proceeded, as mentioned above, to emulate not only the glory won from those peoples by Father Liber, but the Bacchic tradition as well: he decided to imitate the god's procession (whether that was, in fact, the original triumphal march that the god instituted or merely sport on the part of his bacchants). [25] He gave orders for villages along his route to be strewn with flowers and garlands, and for bowls full of wine and other vessels of extraordinary size to be set out on the thresholds of houses. Then he had wagons covered with planks (so that they would hold a greater number of soldiers) and rigged out like tents, some with white curtains, others with costly material.

[26] The friends and the royal company went in front, heads wreathed with various kinds of flowers woven into garlands, with the notes of the flute heard at one point, the tones of the lyre at another. The army joined the revels in wagons decorated as far as individual means allowed, and with their finest arms hung around them. The king and his drinking companions rode in a cart weighed down with golden bowls and huge goblets of the same metal. [27] In this way the army spent seven days on a drunken march, an easy prey if the vanquished races had only had the courage to challenge riotous drinkers – why, a mere 1,000 men, if sober, could have captured this group on its triumphal march, weighed down as it was from seven days of drinking.[67] [28] But it is fortune that allots fame and a price to things, and she turned even this piece of disgraceful soldiering into a glorious achievement! People of those and later times marvelled that drunken men had made their way through countries as yet unsubdued, the barbarians mistaking for self-confidence what was in fact sheer recklessness. [29] This pageant was followed by the executioner, for orders were issued for the aforementioned Astaspes to be put to death. It is true indeed: luxurious living and base cruelty are not mutually exclusive.

BOOK TEN

[1] There arrived at about this time Cleander, Sitalces, Heracon and Agathon, the men who had assassinated Parmenion on the king's orders.[1] Five thousand infantry and 1,000 cavalry came with them, [2] but there also came from the province which they had governed men who brought charges against them. Grateful as Alexander was for their services in the matter of the assassination, this could not compensate for all the crimes they had committed. [3] After plundering everything in the secular sphere, they had not even refrained from what was sacred: virgins and women of the highest breeding had been sexually assaulted and were bemoaning the physical abuse they had suffered.[2] [4] The greed and lust of these men had made the barbarians abhor the Macedonian name. [5] Worst of all was the lust-crazed Cleander, who had raped a virgin of noble birth and then given her to his slave as a concubine.

[6] What preoccupied the majority of Alexander's friends was not so much the atrocities of which these men were openly accused as the recollection that they had been responsible for Parmenion's murder, a fact which could secretly help their defence before the king. They were delighted now that Alexander's wrath had recoiled upon those who had been the instruments of that wrath and that no power which someone gains by crime is of long duration.

[7] After examining the case, Alexander announced that one charge had been overlooked by the prosecutors, and the most important one at that, namely the defendants' assumption that he would not survive. For, he said, men wishing or believing that he would safely return from India would never have ventured upon such crimes. [8] So he clapped them in irons and ordered the execution of 600 common soldiers responsible for putting their barbarous decisions into effect. [9] On the same day the men brought in by Craterus as ringleaders of the Persian insurrection were also put to death.[3]

[10] Shortly afterwards Nearchus and Onesicritus arrived,[4] the men whom Alexander had instructed to proceed some way into the Ocean. They brought reports based partly on hearsay and partly on their own observation. [11] There was an island lying close to the river-mouth, they said, which was rich in gold but without horses. (These, they had discovered, the inhabitants would buy for a talent each from men who ventured to transport them from

the mainland.) The sea was full of monsters, they claimed, [12] brought in on the incoming tide, their bodies the size of large ships. Deterred from following the ships by a strident shout, these would submerge themselves, producing a mighty roar from the water, as when ships have been sunk.

[13] Their other information they had taken on trust from the natives, including the assertion that the Red Sea derived its name not, as was generally believed, from the colour of its waters but from King Erythrus.[5] [14] There was an island not far from the mainland thickly planted with palm trees and with a high column standing approximately in the middle of the wood; this was a monument to king Erythrus and it bore writing in the script of that race. [15] They added that vessels carrying food-traders and merchants had crossed to the island, their pilots following up reports of gold, and had never been seen again. [16] Eager to know more, Alexander told them to resume a course close to land until they put in at the mouth of the Euphrates, after which they were to go up river to Babylon.

[17] His ambitions knowing no bounds, Alexander had decided that, after the subjugation of the entire eastern seaboard, he would head from Syria towards Africa, because of his enmity to the Carthaginians. Then, crossing the Numidian deserts, he would set his course for Gades, where the pillars of Hercules were rumoured to be; [18] afterwards he would go to Spain (which the Greeks called 'Hiberia', after the river Hiberus). Then he would skirt past the Alps and the Italian coastline, from which it was a short passage to Epirus.

[19] Accordingly, Alexander instructed his governors in Mesopotamia to cut timber on Mt Libanus, transport it down to the Syrian city of Thapsacus, and there lay down keels for 700 ships. These were to be all septemremes, which were to be transported to Babylon. The kings of Cyprus were instructed to furnish bronze, hemp and sails.[6]

[20] While he was thus engaged, Alexander was brought letters from the kings, Porus and Taxiles, informing him that Abisares had died after an illness and Alexander's governor, Philip, of a wound (but those who had inflicted it had been punished). [21] Alexander therefore replaced Philip with the Thracian general, Eudaemon,[7] and assigned Abisares' kingdom to Abisares' son.

[22] They next came to Parsagada, city of a Persian tribe whose satrap was Orsines, a man pre-eminent among all the barbarians for his nobility and wealth. [23] He traced his lineage from Cyrus,[8] the former Persian king, and his wealth was partly inherited from his ancestors and partly amassed by himself during his long tenure of the satrapy. [24] Orsines met Alexander with all manner of gifts, which he intended to give not only to the king but to his friends as well. With him were herds of horses, already broken in, chariots trimmed with silver and gold, expensive furniture, fine jewels, heavy gold vessels, purple garments and 3,000 talents of silver coin. [25] However, it was his great generosity that occasioned the barbarian's death. Although

he had honoured all the king's friends with gifts greater than they could have wished for, he paid no court to the eunuch Bagoas, who by now had gained Alexander's affection through putting his body at his service.[9] [26] He was advised by certain people of Alexander's strong attachment to Bagoas, but he replied that he paid his respects to the king's friends, not his whores, and that it was not the Persian custom to regard as men those who allowed themselves to be sexually used as women.

[27] When he heard this, the eunuch directed the power gained from his shameful self-degradation against the life of an innocent man of supreme distinction. He furnished the most worthless of Orsines' people with false accusations, telling them to divulge these only when he gave the order. [28] Meanwhile, whenever no one else was in earshot, he filled the king's credulous ears, but concealed the reason for his rancour so that his charges would carry more weight. [29] Though not yet under suspicion, Orsines was already losing Alexander's favour. In fact, he was being tried in secret, ignorant of the unseen danger, and the unconscionable male whore did not forget his scheming even when he was submitting to the shame of the sexual act for, whenever he had roused the king's passion for him, he would accuse Orsines on one occasion of greed, on another even of treason.

[30] The time had now come for the lies to destroy the innocent man, and fate, whose decrees are inevitable, was approaching fulfilment. It chanced that Alexander ordered the opening of Cyrus' tomb, wishing to pay funeral honours to the corpse of Cyrus buried in it. [31] He had believed the tomb to be full of buried gold and silver, as had been commonly rumoured among the Persians, but he found nothing more than Cyrus' decomposing shield, two Scythian bows and a scimitar. [32] Alexander set a golden crown on the sarcophagus in which the body lay and draped it with his own cloak, expressing surprise that so famous a king who possessed such great wealth should have received no more expensive a burial than if he had been one of the common people. The eunuch was at Alexander's side. [33] 'What's surprising about kings' sepulchres being empty,' he said, looking at the king, 'when satraps' houses cannot hold all the gold taken from them? [34] Speaking for myself, I had never set eyes on the tomb before, but I was told by Darius that 3,000 talents were buried with Cyrus. [35] That explains Orsines' generosity towards you: unable to keep his loot with impunity, he wanted to curry favour with you by giving it away.'

[36] Bagoas had already roused Alexander to anger when the men he had charged to assist his undertaking came up. Bagoas on one side, and those he had suborned on the other, filled the king's ears with false accusations [37] and, before he could even suspect that charges were being laid against him, Orsines was arrested. Not satisfied with seeing an innocent man executed, the eunuch seized him as he went to his death. Looking at him, Orsines said: 'I had heard that women once were rulers in Asia but this really is something new – a *eunuch* as king!' [38] Such was the end of the most noble of Persians,

a man who was not only innocent but who had also shown the king exemplary kindness.[10]

[39] Phradates was also executed at this time on suspicion of having had designs on the throne.[11] Alexander had begun to be quick to order summary execution and also to believe the worst of people. [40] Of course, success can alter one's natural inclinations, and rarely is a person sufficiently circumspect with regard to his good fortune. For, shortly before, this same man had been unable to condemn Alexander Lyncestes despite the evidence of two witnesses;[12] [41] he had also, against his own inclinations, acquiesced in the acquittal of prisoners of lesser consequence, simply because the others thought them innocent; he had given back kingdoms to defeated enemies. [42] At the end of his life, his degeneration from his former self was so complete that, though earlier possessed of unassailable self-control, he followed a male whore's judgement to give some men kingdoms and deprive others of their lives.

[43] At about this same time, Alexander received a letter from Coenus[13] concerning events in Europe and Asia while he was himself engaged in the conquest of India. [44] Zopyrion, who governed Thrace, had been lost with his entire army with the sudden onset of stormy weather and squalls while he was on an expedition against the Getae. [45] On learning of this set-back, Seuthes had driven his subjects, the Odrysians, to rebellion. Thrace had almost been lost and not even Greece ...[14]

2

[1] So, with thirty ships, they crossed to the Attic promontory of Sunium, having decided to make for the port of Athens[15] from there. [2] On learning this, the king was equally incensed with Harpalus and the Athenians. He ordered a fleet to be mustered for an immediate journey to Athens[16] [3] but, while he was privately considering this plan, a letter arrived. Harpalus, it said, had entered Athens and had won the support of leading citizens by bribery,[17] but soon an assembly of the people was held which ordered him to leave the city. He had come to the Greek troops who arrested him and, at the instigation of a friend of his, treacherously murdered him.[18]

[4] Pleased with the news, Alexander dropped his plan of crossing to Europe. However, he ordered the restoration of exiles (except those with the blood of citizens on their hands) by all the cities which had expelled them.[19] [5] The Greeks dared not disobey his order, despite their belief that it constituted the first step towards the collapse of their laws, and they even restored what remained of their property to the condemned men. [6] Only the Athenians, champions of everybody's cause and not just their own, were reluctant to tolerate such a hotchpotch of classes and individuals, for they were used to government based on law and tradition, not a king's command. [7] Accordingly, they barred the exiles from their territory and were prepared to

suffer anything rather than admit what was once the scum of their city and subsequently the scum of their places of exile.

[8] Sending his older soldiers home,[20] Alexander ordered a force of 13,000 infantry and 2,000 cavalry to be selected for him to keep back in Asia. He believed he could hold Asia with an army of modest proportions because he had deployed garrisons in a number of places and populated the recently established cities with colonists who wanted only to make a fresh start. [9] However, before choosing the men he would keep back, he ordered all the troops to declare their debts; for he had discovered that many were deeply in debt, and he had decided to discharge their obligations himself even though these derived from their own extravagance.[21] [10] The men thought they were being put to a test to make it easier for Alexander to tell the extravagant from the thrifty, and so they let time slip by without doing anything. Alexander was well aware that it was embarrassment rather than insubordination that stopped them acknowledging their debts, so he had tables set at points throughout the camp and 10,000 talents put out on them. [11] With that an honest disclosure was finally made by the men and, from all that money, what remained was a mere 130 talents! Yes, that army which had defeated so many rich nations took from Asia more prestige than booty.

[12] Now when it was discovered that some were being sent home and others detained, the men assumed that Alexander was going to fix the royal seat permanently in Asia. Beside themselves and oblivious of military discipline, they filled the camp with mutinous comments and attacked the king with more abuse than ever before.[22] Then they all proceeded to demand demobilization, at the same time displaying their scarred faces and grey heads. [13] Neither reprimands from their officers nor their own respect for the king restrained them. Alexander wished to address them, but they prevented him with their mutinous shouting and soldierly truculence, as they publicly declared their refusal to take a step in any direction save homewards. [14] At last silence fell, more because they thought Alexander had experienced a change of heart than because they could do so themselves, and they awaited his reaction.

[15] 'What does this uproar mean,' asked Alexander, 'and such violent and wild disorder? I am afraid to speak. You have publicly flouted my authority and my kingship depends on your whim. You have not left me the privilege of addressing you, acquainting myself with your feelings, advising you or even looking you in the eye. [16] I decided to send some men home and take others with me shortly afterwards – and I see as much opposition from those who are going to leave as from those with whom I have decided to follow the advance party. [17] What is going on? You all join the uproar, but for different reasons. I should dearly like to know whether the complaints about me are coming from those leaving or those being kept back.'

[18] You would have thought the shout they all raised together came from

a single mouth, so concerted was the answer 'We all complain' from the whole gathering.

[19] 'No,' said Alexander, 'you cannot make me believe that you all have these grounds for complaint which you indicate; most of the army is not involved since I have discharged more than I am going to retain. [20] There must be some deeper problem which is turning all of you against me. For when has a king been abandoned by his entire army? Not even slaves run away from their masters in a single body – even they feel some shame at leaving those whom the rest have deserted. [21] But I am forgetting your wild uproar, and I am trying to cure incurables! Yes, I abandon all the hope I had conceived in you, and I have decided to treat you not as my soldiers – for that you have now ceased to be – but as thoroughly ungrateful hirelings. [22] The prosperity all around you has begun to unbalance you. You have forgotten the circumstances which, through my kindness to you, you were able to leave behind – though heaven knows you deserve to grow old in them, since you find adversity easier to cope with than prosperity. [23] Look! Men who a short while ago were tribute-paying subjects of Illyria and Persia are now turning up their noses at Asia and at the spoils from all its nations! For men who recently went half-naked under Philip, purple robes are not good enough! They cannot stand the sight of silver and gold, and long instead for their old wooden bowls, their wickerwork shields, their rusty swords! [24] This was the smart equipment you had when I took you on, together with a debt of 500 talents, when the entire royal assets were no more than sixty talents[23] – such was the basis for the great achievements to come, the basis on which I nonetheless established, if I may be forgiven for saying so, an empire comprising most of the world! [25] Are you sick of Asia, where your glorious achievements have made you the equals of the gods? You hasten to desert your king and go into Europe, though most of you would not have had the money for the trip if I had not discharged your debts – with plunder from Asia, of course! [26] And you feel no shame at carrying around the spoils of conquered nations in your deep bellies and nevertheless wishing to return to your wives and children, though few of you can display to them the prizes of victory! The rest of you have pawned even your weapons on your way to fulfilling your hopes!

[27] 'Yes, fine soldiers I shall lose – soldiers who are concubines to their own bed-wenches (that is all you have left of your great riches, and on them you spend money!). So those who are leaving me – let the roads be open for them! Get away from here quickly. Along with the Persians I shall cover your rear as you go. I keep no one back. Let me take my eyes off you, my ungrateful citizens. [28] Happily will your parents and children welcome you when you return without your king: out they shall come to meet the deserters and runaways! [29] Yes, I shall triumph over your desertion of me and make you pay for it wherever I am, bestowing honour and preference upon those whom

243

you leave behind with me. Apart from that, you will soon know how strong an army is without its king, and also what assistance I can provide by myself.'

[30] Furious, he leaped down from the dais and plunged into the midst of the armed men. He had taken note of those who had been most outspoken, and these he seized one by one. They dared not offer resistance, and Alexander handed thirteen of them over to his bodyguard to be kept in custody.

3

[1] Who would have believed that a gathering fiercely hostile moments before could be paralysed with sudden panic [2] at the sight of men being dragged off for punishment whose actions had been no worse than the others'? [3] They were terror-stricken, whether from respect for the title of king, for which people living in a monarchy have a divine reverence, or from respect for Alexander personally; or perhaps it was because of the confidence with which he so forcefully exerted his authority. [4] At all events they were the very model of submissiveness: when, towards evening, they learned of their comrades' execution, so far from being infuriated at the punishment, they did everything to express individually their increased loyalty and devotion. [5] The next day they were denied an audience with Alexander, who admitted only his Asiatic soldiers; whereupon they filled the entire camp with lugubrious cries, claiming they would die on the spot if the king persisted in his anger. [6] Alexander, however, who was always determined to carry his plans through to the end, ordered the foreign troops to be mustered, with the Macedonians confined to their camp. When the foreign soldiers had assembled in large numbers, he had an interpreter called and gave the following address.

[7] 'When I was crossing from Europe to Asia, I hoped to annex to my empire many famous peoples and large numbers of men. I was not wrong in believing the reports I had heard of these men. [8] But there is more than that: I am looking upon brave soldiers of unfailing loyalty to their kings. [9] I had believed everything here to be swamped in luxury and, through excessive prosperity, submerged in self-indulgence. But, in fact, your moral and physical strength makes you just as energetic as anyone in the performance of your military duties; and yet, brave men though you are, your dedication to loyalty is no less than your dedication to courage. [10] I make this statement now for the first time, but I have long known it to be true. For that reason I have selected younger soldiers from among you and integrated them in the main body of my troops. You have the same uniform and the same weapons. Your obedience, however, and your readiness to follow orders far surpass everybody else's.

[11] 'That is why I married the daughter of the Persian Oxyartes,[24] feeling no hesitation about producing children from a captive. [12] Later on, when I wished to extend my bloodline further, I took Darius' daughter as a wife[25]

and saw to it that my closest friends had children by our captives, my intention
being that by this sacred union I might erase all distinction between conquered and conqueror.²⁶ [13] So you can believe that you are my soldiers by
family, not conscription. Asia and Europe are now one and the same kingdom. I give you Macedonian arms. Foreign newcomers though you are, I
have made you established members of my force: you are both my fellow-
citizens and my soldiers. [14] Everything is taking on the same hue: it is no
disgrace for the Persians to copy Macedonian customs nor for the Macedonians to imitate the Persians. Those who are to live under the same king
should enjoy the same rights' ...²⁷

4

[1] 'How long are you going to indulge in this self-gratification,' he asked,
'with such executions, and executions of a foreign kind at that? Your own
men, your own citizens, are being dragged off to punishment without trial
– led away, alas, by their own captives! If you decide that they have deserved
death, at least change the executioners.'

[2] The advice he was given was well-intentioned, had Alexander only
been able to take the truth! Instead his anger had risen to frenzy. He repeated
the command, since those previously ordered had momentarily hesitated: the
prisoners were to be hurled into the river, still in their bonds. [3] Not even
this punishment could goad the men to mutiny. Instead, they came in
companies to the officers and Alexander's friends with the request that he
order the execution of any he decided were tainted by association with the
former crime. They offered up their persons to his anger, urging him to
slaughter them ...²⁸

5

[1] Tears welled up as they looked at him, and they appeared not as an army
visiting its king but one attending his funeral. [2] The grief was especially
intense among those at his bedside. Alexander looked at them and said: 'After
my death will you find a king who deserves such men?'

[3] Incredibly, he maintained the same posture which he had adopted
before admitting the men until he had received the last salute from the whole
army. He then dismissed the rank and file and, as though released from all
life's obligations, collapsed in exhaustion. [4] He bade his friends draw near
since, by now, even his voice had started to fail, and then took his ring from
his finger and handed it to Perdiccas. He also gave instructions that they
should have his body transported to Hammon.²⁹ [5] When they asked him
to whom he bequeathed his kingdom, he answered, 'To the best man,'³⁰ but
added that he could already foresee great funeral games for himself provided
by that issue. [6] When Perdiccas further asked when he wished divine

honours paid to him, he said he wanted them when they themselves were happy. These were Alexander's last words; he died moments later.

[7] At first the sounds of lamentation, weeping and the beating of breasts echoed throughout the royal quarters. Then a sad hush fell, enveloping all in a still silence like that of desert wastes, as from grief they turned to considering what would happen now. [8] The young noblemen who formed his customary bodyguard could neither suppress their bitter anguish nor confine themselves to the vestibule of the royal tent. They wandered around like madmen, filling the whole city with the sound of their mournful grieving, forgoing no kind of lament that sorrow suggests in such circumstances. [9] Accordingly, those who had been standing outside the royal quarters rushed to the spot, barbarians and Macedonians alike, and in the general grief conqueror and conquered were indistinguishable. The Persians recalled a master of great justice and clemency, the Macedonians a peerless king of outstanding valour; together they indulged in a kind of contest in mourning.

[10] Expressions of indignation as well as grief could be heard – indignation that, through the envy of the gods, a man of such vigour had been removed from the world when he was at the peak of his life and career. They pictured for themselves his energy and his expression as he led the men into battle, laid siege to cities, scaled walls or made presentations for gallantry before the assembled army. [11] The Macedonians then regretted having refused him divine honours, and admitted they had been disloyal and ungrateful in robbing him of a title his ears should have heard. And then, after long declaring their veneration for their king and bemoaning his loss, their pity focused on themselves. [12] They had passed from Macedonia beyond the Euphrates, and they could see that they were cut off among enemies who balked at the new régime. Lacking a definite heir to Alexander and to his throne, they saw that individuals would try to appropriate to themselves their collective power. [13] Then they had premonitions of the civil wars which actually followed: once more they would be obliged to shed their blood not to win dominion over Asia but to have a king. Their old scars must burst under fresh wounds. [14] Ageing and weak, having recently requested a discharge from their legitimate king, they would now face death to win power for someone who might be an obscure underling!

[15] While such considerations occupied their minds, night came on to increase their terror. The soldiers kept watch under arms, and the Babylonians maintained a lookout from their walls or from the roofs of their own houses, in the expectation of gaining clearer information. [16] No one dared to light lamps and, since they were unable to use their eyes, their ears strained after noises and voices. Often they would be gripped by irrational fear and go rushing along dark alleyways, suspected and worried in turn as they ran into each other.

[17] The Persians had their hair shorn in traditional fashion and wore garments of mourning. Together with their wives and children they grieved

with genuine feelings of regret, not for a man who had recently been their conqueror and enemy, but for one who had been a superlatively just king over their nation. They were people accustomed to living under monarchy, and they admitted they had never had a worthier ruler. [18] Nor was grief confined to the area within the city walls; tidings of the great tragedy had spread to the neighbouring countryside and then to most of Asia this side of the Euphrates. [19] They quickly reached Darius' mother, too. She ripped off the clothes she wore and assumed the dress of mourning; she tore her hair and flung herself to the ground. [20] Next to her sat one of her two granddaughters who was in mourning after the recent loss of her husband, Hephaestion, and the general anguish reminded her of her personal grief.[31] [21] But Sisigambis alone felt the woes that engulfed her entire family: she wept for her own plight and that of her granddaughters. The fresh pain had also reminded her of the past. One might have thought that Darius was recently lost and that at the same time the poor woman had to bury two sons. [22] She wept simultaneously for the living and the dead. Who would look after her girls, she wondered? Who would be another Alexander? This meant a second captivity, a second loss of royal status. On the death of Darius they had found a protector, but after Alexander they would certainly not find someone to guard their interests.

[23] Amid such reflections, Sisigambis was reminded of how her eighty brothers had all been butchered on the one day by the most barbarous of kings, Ochus, and how the slaughter of so many sons was augmented by that of their father; of how only one child remained of the seven she had borne[32] and how even Darius' prosperity had been short-lived and served only to make his death more cruel. [24] Finally, she surrendered to her sorrow. She covered her head, turned away from her granddaughter and grandson, who fell at her knees to plead with her, and withdrew simultaneously from nourishment and the daylight. Five days after deciding on death, she expired. [25] Her end provides firm evidence for Alexander's gentle treatment of her and his fairness towards all the captives: though she could bear to live on after Darius, she was ashamed to survive Alexander.[33]

[26] To be sure, it is obvious to anyone who makes a fair assessment of the king that his strengths were attributable to his nature and his weaknesses to fortune or his youth. His natural qualities were as follows: [27] incredible mental energy and an almost excessive tolerance of fatigue; courage exemplary not just in comparison with kings but even with men possessing this virtue and no other; [28] generosity such that he often granted greater gifts than even the gods are asked for; clemency towards the defeated; returning kingdoms to men from whom he had taken them, or giving them as gifts; [29] continuous disregard for death, which frightens others out of their minds; a lust for glory and fame reaching a degree which exceeded due proportion but was yet pardonable in view of his youth and great achievements. [30] Then there was his devotion to his parents (he had taken the

decision to deify Olympias and he had avenged Philip); [31] then, too, his kindness towards almost all his friends, goodwill towards the men, powers of discernment equalling his magnanimity and an ingenuity barely possible at his age; [32] control over immoderate urges; a sex-life limited to the fulfilment of natural desire; and indulgence only in pleasures which were socially sanctioned.

[33] The following are attributable to fortune: putting himself on a par with the gods and assuming divine honours; giving credence to oracles which recommended such conduct and reacting with excessive anger to any who refused to worship him; assuming foreign dress and aping the customs of defeated races for whom he had had only contempt before his victory. [34] But as far as his irascibility and fondness for drink were concerned, these had been quickened by youth and could as easily have been tempered by increasing age. [35] However, it must be admitted that, much though he owed to his own virtues, he owed more to Fortune, which he alone in the entire world had under his control. How often she rescued him from death! How often did she shield him with unbroken good fortune when he had recklessly ridden into danger! [36] She also decided that his life and his glory should have the same end. The fates waited for him to complete the subjection of the East and reach the Ocean, achieving everything of which a mortal was capable.

[37] Such was the king and leader for whom a successor was now sought, but the burden was too great to be shouldered by one man. So it was that his reputation and the fame of his achievements distributed kings and kingdoms almost throughout the world, with those who clung on even to the tiniest fraction of his enormous estate being regarded as men of great distinction.

6

[1] Now at Babylon,[34] which is where I began my digression, Alexander's bodyguards summoned his principal friends and the army officers to the royal tent. These were followed by a crowd of the rank and file, all anxious to know to whom Alexander's estate would pass. [2] Many officers were unable to enter the royal tent because they were prevented by the milling crowds of soldiers, and this despite a herald's announcement forbidding access to all but those called by name – having no authority, this order was ignored. [3] At first loud weeping and wailing broke out afresh, but then their tears stopped and silence fell as they wondered what was going to happen now.

[4] At this point Perdiccas exposed the royal throne to public view. On this lay Alexander's crown, robe and arms, and Perdiccas placed upon it the ring the king had given him the previous day. The sight of these objects once more brought tears to the eyes of all and rekindled their grief. [5] 'For my part,' said Perdiccas, 'I return to you the ring handed to me by Alexander, the seal of which he would use on documents as symbol of his royal and imperial

authority. [6] The anger of the gods can devise no tragedy to equal this with which we have been afflicted; and yet, considering the greatness of Alexander's achievements, one could believe that such a great man was merely on loan from the gods to the world so that, when his duty to it was complete, they might swiftly reclaim him for their family. [7] Accordingly, since nothing remains of him apart from the material which is excluded from immortality, let us perform the due ceremonies to his corpse and his name, bearing in mind the city we are in, the people we are among and the qualities of the leader and king of whom we have been deprived.

[8] 'Comrades, we must discuss and consider how we can maintain the victory we have won among the people over whom we have won it. We need a leader; whether it should be one man or more is up to you. But you must realize this: a military unit without a chief is a body without a soul. [9] This is the sixth month of Roxane's pregnancy.[35] We pray that she produces a male who, with the gods' approval, will assume the throne when he comes of age. Meanwhile, designate those you want as your leaders.' So spoke Perdiccas.

[10] Nearchus then said that, while nobody could express surprise that only Alexander's blood-line was truly appropriate for the dignity of the throne, [11] to wait for a king not yet born and pass over one already alive suited neither the inclinations of the Macedonians nor their critical situation. The king already had a son by Barsine, he said, and he should be given the crown.[36] [12] Nobody liked Nearchus' suggestion. They repeatedly signalled their opposition in traditional fashion by beating their shields with their spears and, as Nearchus pressed his idea with greater insistence, they came close to rioting. [13] Then Ptolemy spoke.

'Yes, a son of Roxane or Barsine really is a fitting ruler for the Macedonian people! Even to utter his name will be offensive for Europe, since he will be mostly captive. [14] Is that what defeating the Persians will have meant for us – being slaves to their descendants? Their legitimate kings, Darius and Xerxes, failed to achieve that with all their thousands of troops and their huge fleets! [15] This is what I think. Alexander's throne should be set in the royal quarters and those who used to be consulted by him should meet there whenever a decision affecting the common good has to be made. A majority decision should stand, and these men should be obeyed by the generals and officers.' [16] Some agreed with Ptolemy, fewer with Perdiccas.

Then Aristonus rose to speak. When Alexander was asked to whom he was leaving his kingdom, said Aristonus, he had expressed the wish that the best man be chosen, and yet he had himself adjudged Perdiccas to be the best by handing him the ring. [17] For Perdiccas was not the only person who had been sitting at the king's deathbed, he continued – Alexander had looked around and selected the man to give the ring to from the crowd of his friends. It followed that he wished supreme power to pass to Perdiccas. [18] The assembly had no doubt that Aristonus' opinion was correct; everyone called for Perdiccas to step forward and pick up the king's ring.

Perdiccas wavered, wishing to do it but bashful, and he thought that the more diffident he was in seeking what he expected to be his the more insistently they would press it upon him.[37] [19] So he hesitated, and for a long time was uncertain how to act, until finally he went back and stood behind those who had been sitting next to him.

[20] Encouraged and reassured by Perdiccas' hesitation, Meleager, one of the generals, now said: 'God forbid that Alexander's fortune and the dignity of so great a throne come upon such shoulders! Men certainly will not tolerate it. I am not talking about those of better birth than this fellow, merely about men who do not have to suffer anything against their will. [21] In fact, it makes no difference whether your king be Roxane's son (whenever he is born) or Perdiccas, since that fellow is going to seize the throne anyway by pretending to act as regent. That is why the only king he favours is one not yet born, and in the general haste to resolve matters – a haste which is as necessary as it is understandable – he alone is waiting for the months to elapse, already predicting that a male has been conceived! Could you doubt that he is ready to find a substitute? [22] God in Heaven, if Alexander had left us this fellow as king in his stead, my opinion would be that this is the one order of his that should not be obeyed. [23] Well, why not run off and loot the treasure chests? For surely it is the people who are heirs to these riches of the king.' [24] So saying he burst through the soldiers, and the men who had made way for him as he left proceeded to follow him to the plunder they had been promised.

7

[1] By now there was a dense crowd of soldiers around Meleager and the meeting had degenerated into a mutinous uproar. Then a man of the lowest class, who was unknown to most of the Macedonians, spoke as follows:[38] [2] 'What's the point of fighting and starting a civil war when you have the king you seek? You are forgetting Philip's son, Arrhidaeus, brother of our late king Alexander;[39] recently he accompanied the king in performing our religious ceremonies and now he is his sole heir. How has he deserved this? What act of his justifies that he be stripped even of this universally recognized right? If you are looking for someone just like Alexander, you'll never find him; if you want his next of kin, there *is* only this man.'

[3] On hearing this, the gathering fell silent, as if at an order. They shouted in unison that Arrhidaeus should be summoned and that the men who had held the meeting without him deserved to die.

[4] Then Pithon[40] began to speak through his tears. This was when Alexander was most to be pitied, he said, for he had been cheated out of the enjoyment and support of such good citizens and soldiers, men who in thinking only of their king's glorious memory were blind to all other considerations. [5] He was obviously opposed to the young man who was being

assigned the throne, but his derogatory remarks generated more animosity against himself than disdain for Arrhidaeus, because as the men commiserated with the latter they also began to favour him. [6] Accordingly, with persistent cheers, they declared that the only man they would entertain as king was the one born to the expectation of that position, and they ordered that Arrhidaeus be summoned. [7] Out of antagonism and hatred for Perdiccas, Meleager promptly brought him to the royal tent, and the men saluted him as king under the name 'Philip'.

[8] Such were the exclamations of the rank and file, but the prominent men felt differently. Pithon began to follow Perdiccas' strategy, designating Perdiccas and Leonnatus, both of royal birth, as guardians for Roxane's future son. [9] He subjoined that Craterus and Antipater should direct affairs in Europe.[41] Then an oath of allegiance to the king born of Alexander was exacted from each of them.

[10] Meleager, who, with good cause, was frightened of being punished, had withdrawn with his men. Now he once more came storming into the royal quarters, dragging Philip with him and shouting that Philip's robust youth justified the hopes they had recently conceived in their new king. They should give Philip's offspring a chance, he declared, for he was son and brother in respect of two kings, and their own judgement should count for more than anything.

[11] No deep sea, no vast and stormy body of water produces waves as violent as the emotions of a mob, particularly in the first flush of a freedom that is to be short-lived. [12] A few wished to confer supreme command on Perdiccas, whom they had recently chosen, but more were for Philip whom they had overlooked. But neither their support nor their opposition in respect of anything could last long and, regretting their decision one moment, they regretted their regret the next. Finally, however, their favour inclined towards royal stock. [13] Arrhidaeus had left the meeting, cowed by the authority wielded by the generals and, with his departure, his support among the common soldiers was hushed rather than weakened. So he was called back and he donned his brother's robe, the one which had been set on the throne. [14] Meleager put on a cuirass and took up his arms to act as the new king's escort. He was followed by the phalanx, the men beating on their shields with their spears and ready to glut themselves with the blood of those who had aspired to a throne to which they had no claim. [15] They were pleased that the strength of the empire would remain in the same home with the same family, and they thought a ruler of royal blood would defend the power he inherited. They were used to showing respect and veneration for the royal name, they reasoned, and this was assumed only by a man born into royal power.

[16] In terror, Perdiccas ordered the chamber in which Alexander's body lay to be locked. With him were 600 men of proven valour, and he had also been joined by Ptolemy and the company of the royal pages. [17] But for

soldiers numbering many thousands it was not difficult to break the locks. The king had also burst in, a crowd of attendants led by Meleager packed around him. [18] In a rage, Perdiccas called aside any who wished to protect Alexander's corpse, but the men who had broken into the room proceeded to hurl javelins at him, keeping their distance. Eventually, after many had been wounded, the older soldiers removed their helmets so that they could be more easily recognized and began to beg the men with Perdiccas to stop fighting and to surrender to the king and his superior numbers. [19] Perdiccas was the first to lay down his arms, and the others followed. Meleager then urged them not to leave Alexander's body, but they thought he was looking for a way to trap them, so they slipped away through another part of the royal quarters and fled towards the Euphrates. [20] The cavalry, composed of young men from the best families, went with Perdiccas and Leonnatus in large numbers, and these were in favour of leaving the city and pitching camp in the plains. [21] Perdiccas, however, had no hope that the infantry would also follow him, and so he remained in the city in order not to seem to have broken away from the main body of the army by pulling out the cavalry.

8

[1] Meleager kept on warning the king that his claim to the throne should be strengthened by Perdiccas' death and that, if the latter's undisciplined spirit was not crushed, he would bring off a coup. Perdiccas well remembered how he had treated the king, he said, and no one could give true allegiance to someone he feared. [2] There was acquiescence rather than positive approval on the king's part, so Meleager interpreted his silence as an order and sent men to summon Perdiccas in the king's name, instructing them to kill him if he hesitated to come. [3] When Perdiccas was informed that the attendants had come, he stood at the threshold of his quarters, a total of sixteen pages from the royal retinue with him. He berated the messengers, time and again calling them 'Meleager's lackeys', and the determination which showed in his expression so terrified them that they fled in panic. [4] Perdiccas told the pages to mount their horses and came with a few friends to Leonnatus so that he could resist any violence offered him with a stronger force.

[5] The next day the Macedonians thought it deplorable that Perdiccas' life had been endangered, and they decided that Meleager's reckless behaviour was to be punished by force of arms[42] ... [6] Meleager, however, saw a revolt coming, so he went to the king and proceeded to ask him if he had himself given the order for Perdiccas' arrest. The king answered that, yes, he had given the order, at Meleager's prompting – but the uproar among the men was uncalled for since Perdiccas was still alive. [7] When the meeting had been dispersed, Meleager was terrified, especially in view of the secession of the cavalry, and he was at a loss what to do, having fallen into the very

danger he had shortly before been planning for his enemy. He spent some three days brooding over plans which he kept changing.

[8] In fact, the royal quarters still looked as they had before: national ambassadors had audiences with the king, generals presented themselves and the vestibule was crowded with attendants and soldiers. [9] But a deep, spontaneous melancholy betokened their sheer desperation. Mutually suspicious, they did not dare to approach or converse with each other; they kept their thoughts to themselves and the comparisons they made of their new king with the old aroused their longing for the one they had lost. [10] Where, they would ask, was the man whose orders and whose lead they had followed? They had been left behind, they would say, among hostile and fierce tribes who would seize the earliest opportunity to avenge all their past defeats.

[11] While such reflections were preying on their minds, news arrived that the cavalry led by Perdiccas had taken control of the plains around Babylon and had blocked the transport of grain to the city. [12] As a result, there were food shortages at first, then outright famine, and the troops in the city began to think they should either reach an accord with Perdiccas or decide the issue in battle.

[13] It transpired that the people in the countryside were seeking refuge in the city, fearing that their farms and villages would be plundered, while the townspeople, running out of provisions, were fleeing to the countryside – each group believing the other's situation safer than their own. [14] Fearing a riot among these, the Macedonians met in the royal quarters and expressed their various opinions. They decided that a deputation should be dispatched to the cavalry to discuss ending the disagreement and laying down their arms. [15] The Thessalian Pasas, Amissus[43] the Megalopolitan and Perilaus were accordingly sent by the king. They delivered the messages given to them by him and returned with the reply that the cavalry would lay down their arms only if the king put in their hands those responsible for the rift.

[16] When this message was brought back, the soldiers took up arms on their own initiative, and the uproar brought Philip from the royal tent. 'This disturbance is unnecessary,' he said. 'Those who stay calm will take the prizes from those who fight each other. [17] Remember, too, that you are dealing with your fellow-citizens and that hastily to deprive them of any hope of reconciliation is to rush into civil war. [18] Let us see if they can be appeased by a second deputation. In fact, since the king's body is still unburied, I think everyone will come together for his funeral. [19] Personally, I should prefer to relinquish this power than shed the blood of citizens while exercising it and, if there is no other hope of achieving an agreement, I beg and entreat you to choose a better man than me.'

[20] Tears welling up in his eyes, he removed the crown from his head, holding it out in his right hand for anyone claiming to deserve it more to take. [21] Such a restrained address excited high hopes for his character, which until that day had been eclipsed by his brother's fame. So all began to insist

that he act on his plan. [22] Arrhidaeus sent the same men back to ask now that they accept Meleager as a third general,[44] a request which was readily granted since Perdiccas wished to isolate Meleager from the king and felt that, on his own, Meleager would be no match for the two of them. [23] So, when Meleager and the phalanx came out to the rendezvous, Perdiccas went forward to meet him at the head of his cavalry squadrons. The two forces greeted each other and united, with harmony and peace now strengthened between them for ever, so they thought.

9

[1] But destiny was already bringing civil war upon the Macedonian nation; for a throne is not to be shared and several men were aspiring to it. [2] Their forces first came into conflict, then split up and, when they had put more of a burden on the body than it could stand, the limbs started to weaken, and an empire that might have stood firm under a single man collapsed while it rested on the shoulders of a number. [3] So it is with justification that the people of Rome acknowledge that they owe their salvation to their emperor, who shone out as a new star in the night that was almost our last. [4] It was his rising, I declare, and not the sun's, that brought light back to a darkened world at a time when its limbs lacked a head and were in chaotic disarray. [5] How many were the torches he then extinguished! How many the swords he sheathed! How violent the storm he scattered, suddenly clearing the skies! So our empire is not merely recovering, but even flourishes. [6] If I may be forgiven for saying it, the line of this same house will prolong the conditions of these times – for ever, I pray, but at least for a long duration.[45]

[7] But let me return to the narrative from which my reflections on our national prosperity diverted me. Perdiccas rested his only hope of survival on Meleager's death, believing that the latter's vanity and unreliability, his readiness to attempt a coup and his bitter enmity to himself, all called for a pre-emptive strike against him. [8] But he well concealed his plan so as to catch Meleager off his guard. He covertly induced individuals among the troops under his command to complain publicly (while he gave the impression of knowing nothing of it himself) that Meleager had been made Perdiccas' equal. [9] When their comments were reported to him, Meleager was furious, and told Perdiccas what he had learned. Perdiccas, appearing alarmed at this unexpected turn, began to express astonishment and displeasure and to put on a show of distress. Finally, they agreed that the men responsible for such mutinous talk should be arrested. [10] Meleager thanked Perdiccas and embraced him, commending him for his loyalty to him and his goodwill. [11] They then discussed the matter and devised a way to punish the guilty. They decided there should be a traditional purification ceremony for the army, and their former dissension provided a plausible reason for this. [12] The customary purification of the soldiers by the Macedonian kings

involved cutting a bitch in two and throwing down her entrails on the left and right at the far end of the plain into which the army was to be led. Then all the soldiers would stand within that area, cavalry in one spot, phalanx in another.

[13] On the day they had set aside for this ceremony the king had positioned himself, along with his cavalry and elephants, opposite the infantry commanded by Meleager. [14] When the cavalry column was already on the move, the infantry suddenly panicked in the expectation of some offensive tactic, in view of the recent discord, and for a while they were in two minds about withdrawing into the city, the flat ground being favourable to the cavalry. [15] Fearing that they might be prematurely impugning their comrades' loyalty, however, they held back, ready to fight if put under attack.

By now the columns were coming together and only a small space separated the two lines. [16] The king began to ride towards the infantry with a single squadron and, at Perdiccas' urging, he demanded for execution the instigators of the discord, although he had a personal obligation to protect them, threatening to attack with all his squadrons plus his elephants if they refused. [17] The infantry were stunned by this unforeseen blow, and Meleager lacked ideas and initiative as much as they did. The safest course in the circumstances seemed to be to await their fate rather than provoke it. [18] Perdiccas saw that they were paralysed and at his mercy. He withdrew from the main body some 300 men who had followed Meleager at the time when he burst from the first meeting held after Alexander's death, and before the eyes of the entire army he threw them to the elephants. All were trampled to death beneath the feet of the beasts, and Philip neither stopped it nor sanctioned it. [19] It seemed that he would claim as his own only those designs of which the outcome demonstrated their soundness.

This proved to be both a forewarning and the commencement of civil war for the Macedonians. [20] Meleager, who all too late saw the treachery of Perdiccas, remained passive in the column on that occasion because he was not himself the target of violence. [21] Presently, however, he abandoned all hope of safety when he perceived that it was the name of the man he had himself made king that his enemies were using to engineer his destruction. He sought refuge in a temple where, failing to gain protection even from the sanctity of the place, he was murdered.[46]

10

[1] Perdiccas led the army into the city and convened a meeting of the leading Macedonians. It was there decided that the empire should be apportioned as follows. The king would hold supreme power, with Ptolemy becoming satrap of Egypt and of the African peoples subject to Macedon. [2] Leomedon was given Syria and Phoenicia;[47] Philotas was assigned Cilicia; Antigonus was instructed to take charge of Lycia, Pamphylia and greater Phrygia;[48]

Cassander[49] was sent to Caria and Menander to Lydia. Lesser Phrygia, which is adjacent to the Hellespont, they designated as the province of Leonnatus. [3] Cappadocia and Paphlagonia fell to Eumenes, who was charged with defending that region as far as Trapezus and with conducting hostilities against Ariarathes,[50] the only chieftain refusing allegiance to Macedon. [4] Pithon was ordered to take command of Media, Lysimachus of Thrace and the Pontic tribes adjoining it. It was decided that the governors of India, Bactra, the Sogdians and the other peoples living by the Ocean or the Red Sea should all retain command of their respective territories. Perdiccas was to remain with the king and command the troops following him.

[5] Some have believed that the distribution of the provinces was prescribed by Alexander's will, but I have ascertained that this report, though transmitted by our sources, is without foundation. [6] In fact, after the division of the empire, it seems they would have all individually established their own dominions – if a boundary could ever stand in the way of unbridled ambition. [7] For men who recently had been subjects of the king had individually seized control of huge kingdoms, ostensibly as administrators of an empire belonging to another, and any pretext for conflict was removed since they all belonged to the same race and were geographically separated from each other by the boundaries of their several jurisdictions. [8] But it was difficult to remain satisfied with what the opportunity of the moment had brought them: initial possessions are disdained when there is hope of greater things. So they all thought that expanding their kingdoms was an easier matter than taking possession of them that had been in the first place.

[9] The king's body had been lying in the coffin for six days while everybody's attention had been diverted from the obsequies to forming a government. [10] Nowhere are more searing temperatures to be found than in the area of Mesopotamia, where they are such as to cause the deaths of many animals caught on open ground – so intense is the heat of the sun and the atmosphere, which bakes everything like a fire. [11] Springs are infrequent and are craftily concealed by the natives who keep them for their own use, while strangers are kept ignorant of them. What I report now is the traditional account rather than what I believe myself: [12] when Alexander's friends eventually found time to attend to his corpse, the men who had entered the tent saw that no decay had set into it and that there was not even the slightest discoloration. The vital look that comes from the breath of life had not yet vanished from his face. [13] So it was that, after being instructed to see to the body in their traditional fashion, the Egyptians and Chaldeans did not dare touch him at first since he seemed to be alive. Then, praying that it be lawful in the eyes of god and man for humans to touch a god, they cleaned out the body. A golden sarcophagus was filled with perfumes, and on Alexander's head was placed the insignia of his rank.

[14] Many believed his death was due to poison, administered to him by a son of Antipater called Iollas, one of Alexander's attendants.[51] It is true that

Alexander had often been heard to remark that Antipater had regal aspirations, that his powers exceeded those of a general, that he was conceited after his famous Spartan victory and that he claimed as his due all the things that Alexander had granted him. [15] There was also a belief current that Craterus had been sent with a group of veterans to murder Antipater.[52] [16] Now it is well known that the poison produced in Macedonia has the power to consume even iron, and that only an ass's hoof is resistant to the fluid. [17] (They give the name 'Styx' to the source from which this deadly venom comes.[53]) This, it was believed, was brought by Cassander, passed on to his brother Iollas, and by him slipped into the king's final drink. [18] Whatever credence such stories gained, they were soon scotched by the power of the people defamed by the gossip. For Antipater usurped the throne of Macedon and of Greece as well, [19] and he was succeeded by his son, after the murder of all who were even distantly related to Alexander.[54]

[20] Alexander's body was taken to Memphis by Ptolemy, into whose power Egypt had fallen, and transferred from there a few years later to Alexandria, where every mark of respect continues to be paid to his memory and his name.

BIBLIOGRAPHY

Extensive bibliographies can be found in P. Green, *Alexander of Macedon* (Harmondsworth, 1974), 569–85, and R. Lane Fox, *The Search for Alexander* (Boston and Toronto, 1980), 443–8. More comprehensive collections include:

N. J. Burich, *Alexander the Great: a Bibliography* (Kent State University Press, 1970).

E. Badian, 'Alexander the Great, 1948–67', *Classical World*, 65 (1971), 37–56, 77–83.

J. Seibert, *Alexander der Grosse* (Darmstadt, 1972).

For other useful discussions of modern literature see:

R. Andreotti, 'Il problema di Alessandro Magno nella storigrafia dell' ultimo decennio', *Historia*, 1 (1950), 583–600.

G. Walser, 'Zur neueren Forschung über Alexander den Grossen', *Schweizer Beiträge zur allgemein Geschichte*, 14 (1956), 156–89.

E. Badian, 'Some Recent Interpretations of Alexander the Great', *Alexandre le Grand: Image et Réalité* (*Entretiens de la Fondation Hardt*, 22, Geneva, 1976).

THE SOURCES

A. PRIMARY SOURCES

The fragments of the lost histories have been collected in F. Jacoby, *Die Fragmente der griechischen Historiker*, IIB, with a commentary in IID (Berlin, 1927, 1930). An English translation of these fragments can be found in C. A. Robinson Jr, *History of Alexander the Great*, vol. 1 (Providence, R. I., 1953), and a full discussion in L. Pearson, *The Lost Histories of Alexander the Great* (New York, 1960).

More specific studies include:

E. Badian, 'The Date of Clitarchus', *Proceedings of the African Classical Association*, 8 (1965), 5–11.

E. Badian, 'The Eunuch Bagoas', *Classical Quarterly*, n.s. 8 (1958), 144–57.

E. Badian, 'Nearchus the Cretan', *Yale Classical Studies*, 24 (1975), 147–70.

T. S. Brown, *Onesicritus: A Study in Hellenistic Historiography* (Berkeley and Los Angeles, 1949).

T. S. Brown, 'Callisthenes and Alexander', *American Journal of Philology*, 70 (1949), 225–48.

T. S. Brown, 'Clitarchus', *American Journal of Philology*, 71 (1950), 134–55.

P. A. Brunt, 'Notes on Aristobulus', *Classical Quarterly*, n.s. 24 (1974), 65ff.

R. M. Errington, 'Bias in Ptolemy's History of Alexander', *Classical Quarterly*, n.s. 19 (1969), 233–42.

J. R. Hamilton, 'Cleitarchus and Aristobulus', *Historia*, 10 (1961), 448–59.

J. R. Hamilton, 'The Letters in Plutarch's Alexander', *Proceedings of the African Classical Association*, 4 (1961), 9–20.

E. Kornemann, *Die Alexandergeschichte des Königs Ptolemaios I. von Aegypten* (Leipzig, 1935).

L. Pearson, 'The Diary and Letters of Alexander the Great', *Historia*, 4 (1954/5), 429–55.

C. A. Robinson, Jr, *The Ephemerides of Alexander's Expedition* (Providence, R.I., 1932).

J. Roisman, 'Ptolemy and his rivals in his History of Alexander the Great', *Classical Quarterly* 34 (1984), 373–85.

A. E. Samuel, 'Alexander's Royal Journals', *Historia*, 14 (1965), 1–12.

F. Schachermeyr, *Alexander in Babylon und die Reichsordnung nach seinem Tode* (Vienna, 1970).

H. Strasburger, *Ptolemaios und Alexander* (Leipzig, 1934).

B. EXTANT SOURCES

CURTIUS

(i) Texts (and translations)

J. E. Atkinson, *Q. Curzio Rufo, Storie di Alessandro Magno*, vol. 1, trans. by Virginio Antelami, Fondazione Lorenzo Valla (1998) vol. 2, trans. by Tristano Gargiulo (2000), Latin and Italian.

H. Bardon, *Quinte-Curce: Histoires*, 2 vols (Budé, Paris, 1961, 1965), Latin and French.

A. Giacone, *Storie di Alessandro magno di Quinto Curzio Rufo* (Torino, 1977), Latin and Italian.

E. Hedicke, *Q. Curti Rufi Historiarum Alexandri Magni Macedonis libri qui supersunt* (Teubner ed., Leipzig, 1908).

K. Müller and H. Schönfeld, *Geschichte Alexanders des Grossen* (Tusculum ed., Munich, 1954), Latin and German.

J. Mützell, *Q. Curtii Rufi de Gestis Alexandri Magni regis Macedonis libri qui supersunt octo*, 2 vols (Berlin, 1841; repr. Hildesheim, 1976).

J. C. Rolfe, *Quintus Curtius: History of Alexander*, 2 vols (Loeb Classical Library, Cambridge, Mass., 1956), Latin and English.

(ii) General

J. E. Atkinson, *A Commentary on Q. Curtius Rufus' Historiae Alexandri Magni Books 3 and 4* (Amsterdam, 1980).

J. E. Atkinson, *A Commentary on Q. Curtius Rufus' Historiae Alexandri Magni, Books 5 to 7.2* (Amsterdam, 1994).

E. Baynham, *Alexander the Great, The Unique History of Quintus Curtius Rufus* (Ann Arbor, 1998).

S. Dosson, *Étude sur Quinte Curce* (Paris, 1886).

E. I. McQueen, 'Quintus Curtius Rufus', in *Latin Biography*, ed. T. A. Dorey (London, 1967).

W. W. Tarn, *Alexander the Great*, vol. 2 (Cambridge, 1948), 91–122.

(iii) The Date

More has been written on the identity of the author and the date of the work than on any other aspect of Curtius' work. The most thorough recent studies (both of which build on G. V. Sumner, 'Curtius Rufus and the *Historiae Alexandri*', *Australasian Universities Modern Languages Association*, 15 [1961], 30–39), are Atkinson, op. cit., 19–73, and A. M. Devine, 'The *Parthi*, the Tyranny of Tiberius and the Date of Q. Curtius Rufus', *Phoenix*, 33 (1979), 142–59. References to earlier literature can be found in these works. cf. also A. B. Bosworth, 'History and Rhetoric in Curtius Rufus', *Classical Philology* 78 (1983), 150–61 and J. R. Hamilton, 'The Date of Q. Curtius Rufus', *Historia* 37 (1988), 445–56.

(iv) Other aspects of Curtius

H. Bardon, 'Quinte-Curce', *Les Études Classiques*, 15 (1947), 3–14, 120–37, 193–220.

J. Blänsdorf, 'Herodot bei Curtius Rufus', *Hermes*, 99 (1971), 11–24.

W. Heckel, 'Notes on Q. Curtius Rufus' *History of Alexander*', *Acta Classica* 37 (1994), 67–78.

F. Helmreich, *Die Reden bei Curtius* (Paderborn, 1927).

A. Rüegg, 'Beiträge zur Erforschung der Quellenverhältnisse in der Alexandergeschichte des Curtius' (Diss. Basel, 1906).

W. Rutz, 'Zur Erzählungskunst des Q. Curtius Rufus: Die Belagerung von Tyrus', *Hermes*, 93 (1965), 370ff.

R. B. Steele, 'Quintus Curtius Rufus', *American Journal of Philology*, 36 (1905), 402–23.

J. Therasse, 'Le jugement de Quinte-Curce sur Alexandre; une appréciation morale indépendante', *Les Études Classiques*, 41 (1973), 23–42.

J. Therasse, *Quintus Curtius Rufus: index verborum* (Hildesheim, 1976).

ARRIAN

E. I. Robson's Loeb edition of Arrian's *Anabasis* and *Indica* has been re-edited by P. A. Brunt (using A. G. Roos' Teubner text) with an improved translation: *Arrian: History of Alexander and Indica* (Cambridge, Mass., 1976, 1988). The most readable translation is still Aubrey de Sélincourt's Penguin, *Arrian: The Campaigns of Alexander*, with an introduction and notes by J. R. Hamilton (Harmondsworth, 1971). A. B. Breebaart's *Enige historiografische Aspecten van Arrianus' Anabasis Alexandri* (Leiden, 1960) is now complemented by A. B. Bosworth, *A Historical Commentary on Arrian's History of Alexander*, vols. 1–2 (Oxford, 1980, 1995), and P. A. Stadter, *Arrian of Nicomedia* (Chapel Hill, 1980).

See also:

A. B. Bosworth, 'Errors in Arrian', *Classical Quarterly*, n.s. 26 (1976), 117–39.

A. B. Bosworth, 'Arrian and the Alexander Vulgate', *Entretiens de la Fondation Hardt*, 22 (Geneva, 1976).

A. B. Bosworth, *From Arrian to Alexander*, (Oxford, 1988).

G. W. Bowersock, 'A New Inscription of Arrian', *Greek, Roman and Byzantine Studies*, 8 (1967), 279–80.

P. A. Stadter, 'Flavius Arrianus: The New Xenophon', *Greek, Roman and Byzantine Studies*, 8 (1967), 155–61.

G. Wirth, 'Anmerkungen zur Arrianbiographie', *Historia*, 13 (1964), 209–45.

DIODORUS

C. B. Welles's edition of *Diodorus of Sicily*, vol. VIII (Loeb Classical Library, Cambridge, Mass., 1963), includes the text and English translation of Books XVI. 66 – XVII. Also useful is P. Goukowsky's Budé edition of *Diodore XVII* (Paris, 1976).

E. N. Borza, 'Cleitarchus and Diodorus' Account of Alexander', *Proceedings of the African Classical Association*, 11 (1968), 25–45.

J. R. Hamilton, 'Cleitarchus and Diodorus 17', in *Greece and the Eastern Mediterranean in Ancient History and Prehistory (Studies Presented to F. Schachermeyr)*, ed. K. Kinzl (Berlin and New York, 1977), 126–46.

PLUTARCH

The notes to this translation of Curtius employ the more precise numbering of K. Ziegler's Teubner edition (II. 2 *Parallelae Vitae*, Leipzig, 1968). See also J. R. Hamilton, *Plutarch, Alexander: A Commentary* (Oxford, 1968).

R. H. Barrow, *Plutarch and His Times* (London, 1968).

A. E. Wardman, 'Plutarch and Alexander', *Classical Quarterly*, n.s. 5 (1955), 96–107.

JUSTIN

O. Seel (ed.), *M. Iuniani Iustini, Epitoma Historiarum Philippicarum Pompei Trogi* (Teubner, Stuttgart, 1972).

J. C. Yardley and R. Develin, *Justin: Epitome of the Philippic History of Pompeius Trogus* (Atlanta, 1994).

J. C. Yardley and W. Heckel, *Justin: Epitome of the Philippic History of Pompeius Trogus, vol. 1: Books 11–12, Alexander the Great* (Oxford, 1997). Translation by John Yardley, commentary by Waldemar Heckel.

J. C. Yardley, 'The Literary Background to Justin/Trogus', *Ancient History Bulletin*, 8 (1994), 60–70.

J. C. Yardley, 'Justin on Tribunates and Generalships, Caesares and Augusti', *Classical Quarterly*, n.s. 50 (2000), 632–4.

J. C. Yardley, *Justin and Pompeius Trogus: A Study of the Language of Justin's Epitome of Trogus* (Toronto, 2003).

OTHER EXTANT SOURCES

E. Baynham, 'An Introduction to the *Metz Epitome*: its Traditions and Value', *Antichthon* 29 (1995), 60–77.

P. H. Thomas (ed.), *Epitoma Rerum Gestarum Alexandri Magni et Liber de Morte Eius* (Teubner, Leipzig, 1960). The Metz Epitome.

GENERAL WORKS ON ALEXANDER

A. B. Bosworth, *Conquest and Empire. The Reign of Alexander the Great* (Cambridge, 1988).

A. B. Bosworth, *Alexander and the East. The Tragedy of Triumph* (Oxford, 1996).

P. Cloché, *Alexandre le Grand et les essais de fusion entre l'Occident gréco-macédonien et l'Orient* (Neuchâtel, 1953).

R. Lane Fox, *Alexander the Great* (London, 1973).

P. Green, *Alexander of Macedon* (Harmondsworth, 1974).

J. R. Hamilton, *Alexander the Great* (London, 1973).

N. G. L. Hammond, *Alexander the Great: King, Commander and Statesman* (London, 1981).

G. Radet, *Alexandre le Grand* (6th ed., Paris, 1950).

J. Roisman (ed.), *Alexander the Great: Ancient and Modern Perspectives* (Lexington, MA, 1995).

F. Schachermeyr, *Aleksander der Grosse: Das Problem seiner Persönlichkeit und seines Wirkens* (Vienna, 1973).

A. Stewart, *Faces of Power: Alexander's Image and Hellenistic Politics* (Berkeley and Los Angeles, 1993).

R. Stoneman, *Alexander the Great*, Lancaster Pamphlets (London, 1998).

W. W. Tarn, *Alexander the Great*, 2 vols (Cambridge, 1948).

C. B. Welles, *Alexander and the Hellenistic World* (Toronto, 1970).

U. Wilcken, *Alexander the Great*, trans. by G. C. Richards, with notes and introduction by E. N. Borza (New York, 1967).

Also, the reader is directed to:

H. Berve, *Das Alexanderreich auf prosopographischer Grundlage*, 2 vols (Munich, 1926).

G. T. Griffith (ed.), *Alexander the Great: The Main Problems* (Cambridge, 1966).

W. Heckel, *The Marshals of Alexander's Empire* (London, 1992).

O. Hoffmann, *Die Makedonen: ihre Sprache und ihr Volkstum* (Göttingen, 1906).

A. B. Tataki, *Macedonians Abroad. A Contribution to the Prosopography of Ancient Macedonia* (Athens, 1998).

BACKGROUND

G. L. Cawkwell, *Philip of Macedon* (London, 1978).

J. R. Ellis, *Philip II and Macedonian Imperialism* (London, 1976).

G. T. Griffith and N. G. L. Hammond, *A History of Macedonia*, vol. 2 (Oxford, 1979).

See also:

E. Badian, 'The Death of Philip II', *Phoenix*, 17 (1963), 244–50.

A. B. Bosworth, 'Philip II and Upper Macedonia', *Classical Quarterly*, n.s. 21 (1971), 93–105.

J. Rufus Fears, 'Pausanias, the Assassin of Philip II', *Athenaeum*, 53 (1975), 111–35.

G. T. Griffith, 'The Macedonian Background', *Greece and Rome*, 12 (1965), 125–39.

J. R. Hamilton, 'Alexander's Early Life', *Greece and Rome*, 12 (1965), 117–24.

MILITARY CAMPAIGNS AND THE ARMY

F. E. Adcock, *The Greek and Macedonian Art of War* (Berkeley, 1957).

E. Badian, 'Orientals in Alexander's Army, *Journal of Hellenic Studies*, 85 (1965), 160–61.

A. R. Burn, 'Notes on Alexander's Campaigns', *Journal of Hellenic Studies*, 72 (1952), 84–91.

A. R. Burn, 'The Generalship of Alexander', *Greece and Rome*, 12 (1965), 140–54.

A. M. Devine, 'Grand Tactics at Gaugamela', *Phoenix*, 29 (1975), 374–85.

A. M. Devine, 'The Strategies of Alexander the Great and Darius III in the Issus Campaign (333 BC), *AncW* 12 (1985), 25–38.

A. M. Devine, 'The Battle of the Hydaspes: A Tactical and Source–Critical Study', *AncW* 16 (1987), 91–113.

A. M. Devine, 'The Macedonian Army at Gaugamela: Its Strength and the Length of Its Battle-Line', *AncW* 19 (1989), 77–80.

Major-General J. F. C. Fuller, *The Generalship of Alexander the Great* (London, 1957).

P. Green, 'Propaganda at the Granicus', in *Alexander of Macedon*, 489–512.

G. T. Griffith, 'Alexander's Generalship at Gaugamela', *Journal of Hellenic Studies*, 67 (1947), 77–89.

J. R. Hamilton, 'The Cavalry Battle at the Hydaspes', *Journal of Hellenic Studies*, 76 (1956), 26–31.

W. Heckel, 'Alexander at the Persian Gates', *Athenaeum*, 58 (1980), 168–74.

R. D. Milns, 'Alexander's Seventh Phalanx Battalion', *Greek, Roman and Byzantine Studies*, 7 (1966), 159–66.

R. D. Milns, 'The Hypaspists of Alexander III', *Historia*, 20 (1971), 186–96.

C. L. Murison, 'Darius III and the Battle of Issus', *Historia*, 21 (1972), 399–423.

THE MACEDONIANS AND THE COURT

E. Badian, 'The Death of Parmenio', *Transactions of the American Philological Association*, 91 (1960), 324–38.

E. Badian, 'Harpalus', *Journal of Hellenic Studies*, 81 (1961), 16–43.

A. B. Bosworth, 'The Death of Alexander the Great: Rumour and Propaganda', *Classical Quarterly*, n.s. 21 (1971), 112–36.

T. S. Brown, 'Callisthenes and Alexander', *American Journal of Philology*, 70 (1949), 225–48.

G. T. Griffith, 'Alexander and Antipater in 323 B.C.', *Proceedings of the African Classical Association*, 8 (1965), 12–17.

N. G. L. Hammond, *The Macedonian State: The Origins, Institutions and History* (Oxford, 1989).

W. Heckel, 'The Conspiracy against Philotas', *Phoenix*, 31 (1977), 9–21.

W. Heckel, 'The *Somatophylakes* of Alexander the Great: Some Thoughts', *Historia*, 27 (1978), 224–8.

W. Heckel, 'Who was Hegelochos?', *Rheinisches Museum*, 125 (1982), 78–87.

W. E. Higgins, 'Alexander's Imperial Administration: Some Modern Methods and Views Reviewed', *Athenaeum* 58 (1980) 129–52.

PERSIA AND INDIA

E. Badian, 'Alexander at Peucelaotis', *Classical Quarterly* 37 (1987), 117–28.

H. Bengston, *Persia and the Greeks* (Minerva Press, 1969).

P. H. L. Eggermont, *Alexander's Campaigns in Sind and Baluchistan and the Siege of the Brahmin Town of Harmatelia* (Leuven, 1975).

F. Holt, *Alexander the Great and Bactria* (Leiden, 1988).

J. W. McCrindle, *The Invasion of India by Alexander the Great* (London, 1896).

A. K. Narain, 'Alexander and India', *Greece and Rome*, 12 (1965), 155–65.

A. T. Olmstead, *History of the Persian Empire* (Chicago, 1948).

Sir Aurel Stein, *On Alexander's Track to the Indus* (London, 1929).

M. Wheeler, *Flames over Persepolis* (London, 1968).

ADMINISTRATION OF THE EMPIRE

E. Badian, 'The Administration of the Empire', *Greece and Rome*, 12 (1965), 166–82.

E. Badian, 'Alexander the Great and the Greeks of Asia', *Ancient Society and Institutions*.

Studies Presented to Victor Ehrenberg (Oxford, 1966), 37–69.

E. Badian, 'Alexander the Great and the Unity of Mankind', *Historia*, 7 (1958), 425–44.

H. Berve, *Das Alexanderreich auf prosopographischer Grundlage*, vol. I (Munich, 1926).

A. B. Bosworth, 'The Government of Syria under Alexander the Great', *Classical Quarterly*, n.s. 24 (1974), 46–64.

A. B. Bosworth, 'Alexander and the Iranians', *Journal of Hellenic Studies*, 100 (1980), 1–21.

G. T. Griffith, 'Alexander the Great and an experiment in government', *Proceedings of the Cambridge Philological Society* (1964), 23–39.

A. J. Heisserer, *Alexander the Great and the Greeks* (Norman, Oklahoma, 1980).

P. Julien, *Zur Verwaltung der Satrapien unter Alexander dem Grossen* (Weida, 1914).

PROSKYNESIS AND RELIGION

E. Badian, *The Deification of Alexander the Great* (Center for Hermeneutical Studies, Colloquy 21, Berkeley, 1976).

E. Badian, 'The Deification of Alexander the Great', *Ancient Macedonian Studies in Honor of Charles F. Edson* (Thessaloniki, 1981), 27–71.

J. P. V. D. Balsdon, 'The "Divinity" of Alexander', *Historia*, 1 (1950), 363–88.

L. Edmunds, 'The Religiosity of Alexander', *Greek, Roman and Byzantine Studies*, 12 (1971), 386ff.

E. A. Fredricksmeyer, 'Alexander, Midas and the Oracle of Gordium', *Classical Philology*, 56 (1961), 160–68.

J. R. Hamilton, 'Alexander and his "so-called" Father', *Classical Quarterly*, n.s. 3 (1953), 151–7.

W. Heckel, 'Leonnatos, Polyperchon and the Introduction of Proskynesis', *American Journal of Philology*, 99 (1978), 459–61.

THE HELLENISTIC WORLD

M. M. Austin, *The Hellenistic World from Alexander to the Roman Conquest* (Cambridge, 1981).

R. A. Billows, *Antigonos the One-Eyed and the Creation of the Hellenistic State* (Berkeley and Los Angeles, 1990).

J. D. Grainger, *A Seleukid Prosopography and Gazetteer* (Leiden, 1997).

M. Grant, *From Alexander to Cleopatra. The Hellenistic World* (New York, 1982).

P. Green, *Alexander to Actium* (Berkeley and Los Angeles, 1991).

G. Hölbl, *A History of the Ptolemaic Empire*, trans. from the German by Tina Saavedra (London, 2001).

F. Holt, *Thundering Zeus: The Making of Hellenistic Bactria* (Berkeley and Los Angeles, 1999).

H. S. Lund, *Lysimachus: A Study in Early Hellenistic Kingship* (London, 1992).

M. I. Rostovtzeff, *Social and Economic History of the Hellenistic World*, 3 vols (Oxford, 1941).

G. Shipley, *The Greek World after Alexander: 323–30 B.C.* (London, 2000).

W. W. Tarn, *The Greeks in Bactria and India* (Cambridge, 1951).

F. W. Walbank, *The Hellenistic World* (Glasgow, 1981).

C. B. Welles, *Alexander and the Hellenistic World* (Toronto, 1970).

LIST OF ABBREVIATIONS

The following abbreviations are used for references which appear frequently in the Introduction, Notes and Appendices.

A.J.P.	*American Journal of Philology*
AncW	*The Ancient World*
Arr.	Arrian, *Alexandri Anabasis*
A.U.M.L.A.	*Australasian Universities Modern Languages Association*
Curt.	Quintus Curtius Rufus
C.Q.	*Classical Quarterly*
Diod.	Diodorus Siculus
F.Gr.Hist.	Jacoby, *Die Fragmente der griechischen Historiker* (see Bibliography)
G.R.B.S.	*Greek, Roman and Byzantine Studies*
J.H.S.	*Journal of Hellenic Studies*
J.N.E.S.	*Journal of Near Eastern Studies*
J.Ö.A.I.	*Jahreshefte des österreichischen archäologischen Instituts in Wien*
Justin	M. Junianus Justinus
P.A.C.A.	*Proceedings of the African Classical Association*
Pliny, N.H.	Pliny, *Natural History*
Plut. Alex.	Plutarch, *Alexander*
Rev.Phil.	*Revue de Philologie*
R.F.I.C.	*Rivista di Filologia e di Istruzione Classica*
Rh.M.	*Rheinisches Museum für Philologie*
T.A.P.A.	*Transactions of the American Philological Association*
Val.Max.	Valerius Maximus
Y.C.S.	*Yale Classical Studies*

NOTES

INTRODUCTION

1. See S. Dosson, *Étude sur Quinte Curce* (Paris, 1887), 315ff., for an inventory.
2. See H. Bardon, 'Quinte-Curce', *Les Études Classiques*, 15 (1947), 1ff.
3. J. E. Atkinson, *A Commentary on Q. Curtius Rufus' Historiae Alexandri Magni, Books 3 and 4* (Amsterdam, 1980).
4. D. Korzeniewski, *Die Zeit des Quintus Curtius Rufus* (Diss. Cologne, 1959) (Augustus); R. Zimmermann, *Rh.M.*, 79 (1930), 381–90 (Gaius); I. Lana, *R.F.I.C.*, n.s. 27 (1949), 48–70; G. V. Sumner, *A.U.M.L.A.*, 15 (1961), 30–39; J. E. Atkinson, *Acta Classica*, 16 (1973), 129–33; A. M. Devine, *Phoenix*, 33 (1979), 142–59 (Claudius); E. I. McQueen, 'Quintus Curtius Rufus', in T. A. Dorey (ed.), *Latin Biography* (London, 1967), 17–43 (Claudius or Vespasian); R. Verdière, *Wiener Studien*, 79 (1966), 490–509 (Nero); R. D. Milns, *Latomus*, 25 (1966), 490–507 (Galba); J. Stroux, *Philologus*, 84 (1928), 233–51; H. U. Instinksy, *Hermes*, 90 (1962), 379–83 (Vespasian); A. Rüegg, *Beiträge zur Erforschung der Quellenverhältnisse in der Alexandergeschichte des Curtius* (Diss. Basel, 1906) (Trajan); A. von Domaszewski, *Sitzungsberichte der Heidelberger Akademie der Wissenschaften*, 16 (1925/6), 3–5 (Hadrian); C. A. Robinson Jr, *A.J.P.*, 82 (1961), 316–19 (Septimius Severus); R. B. Steele, *A.J.P.*, 36 (1915), 402–23 (Severus Alexander); E. Gibbon, *The Decline and Fall of the Roman Empire* (London, 1896), 1.204, n.59 (Gordian III); and R. Pichon, *Rev.Phil.*, 32 (1908), 210–14 (Constantine).
5. Or possibly in 226/7.
6. R. Pichon, 'L' époque probable de Quinte Curce', *Rev.Phil.*, 32 (1908), 210–14; J. Rufus Fears, 'Parthi in Q. Curtius Rufus', *Hermes*, 102 (1974), 623–5.
7. G. V. Sumner, 'Curtius Rufus and the *Historiae Alexandri*', *A.U.M.L.A.*, 15 (1961), 30. I have followed very closely Sumner's interpretation of the evidence for Curtius' date.
8. For Arrhidaeus' mental condition see Appian, *Syriaca* 52; Justin 13.2.11; 14.5.2; Diod. 18.2.2; Plut. *Alex.* 10.2; 77.7–8; *Heidelberg Epitome*, 1. M. J. Fontana, *Le Lotte per la Successione di Alessandro Magno dal 323 al 315* (Palmero, 1960), 128ff., disbelieves the stories of Arrhidaeus' mental incapacity; but cf. E. Badian, *Studies in Greek and Roman History* (Oxford, 1964) 263–4, and R. M. Errington, *J.H.S.*, 90 (1970), 51, n. 23.
9. Sumner, 34; A. M. Devine, 15off.
10. So E. Badian, loc. cit., n.8 above.
11. G. Barbieri, 'I consoli dell'anno 43 d.c.', *Atti della Accademia nazionale dei Lincei*, ser. 8.30 (1975), 153–7; cf. also P. A. Gallivan, 'The *Fasti* for the reign of Claudius', *C.Q.*, n.s. 28 (1978), 419ff.
12. Sumner, 35–6.
13. Of Sumner and Devine, 148ff.; cf. Atkinson, *Curtius*, 57.

14. These are collected in vol. IIB of F. Jacoby, *Die Fragmente der griechischen Historiker* (Berlin, 1927; repr. Leiden, 1962), nos 117–53, and translated by C. A. Robinson Jr, *The History of Alexander the Great*, vol. 2 (Providence, R. I., 1953). See also L. Pearson, *The Lost Histories of Alexander the Great* (New York, 1960).

15. See *Arrian: The Campaigns of Alexander*, translated by A. de Sélincourt, with notes and introduction by J. R. Hamilton (Penguin Classics, 1971).

16. A. B. Bosworth, 'Errors in Arrian', *C.Q.*, n.s. 26 (1976), 117–39; 'Arrian and the Alexander Vulgate', *Entretiens de la Fondation Hardt*, 22 (Geneva, 1976), 1–33.

17. This is the last appearance of the seer Aristander. See C. A. Robinson Jr, *A.J.P.*, 50 (1929), 195ff.

18. R. M. Errington, 'Bias in Ptolemy's History of Alexander', *C.Q.*, n.s. 19 (1969), 241.

19. See also T. S. Brown, 'Clitarchus', *A.J.P.*, 71 (1950), 134–55.

20. F. Schachermeyr, *Alexander der Grosse: Das Problem seiner Persönlichkeit und seines Wirkens* (Vienna, 1973), 155, n.149, assumes that Cleitarchus did not know of Cassander's murder of Roxane and Alexander IV. This may be inferred from Diod. 17.118.2 but appears to be contradicted by Curt. 10.10.19 (if this too comes directly from Cleitarchus).

21. W. W. Tarn, *Alexander the Great*, 2.71–4, 105–6, postulated the mercenaries' source. This has been refuted by P. A. Brunt, 'Persian Accounts of Alexander's Campaigns', *C.Q.*, n.s. 12 (1962), 141–55.

22. See C. Müller, *Fragmenta Historicorum Graecorum* (Paris, 1853–70), II, pp. 88–95.

23. Cicero, *De Legibus* 1.7; *Brutus* 42; *Ad Familiares* 2.10.3; Quintilian, *Institutio Oratoria* 10.1.74; Pliny, *N.H.* 1.6; 1.7; 1.12–13; 10.136; Strabo 11.5.4.

24. See particularly E. Schwartz, *Realencyclopädie der classischen Altertumswissenschaft*, ed. Pauly, Wissowa, Kroll *et al.*, IV (1897), 1880ff.

25. See Schachermeyr (n.20 above), 'Anhang nr. 2: Der Weg zu Kleitarch', 658–62.

26. Suggested by Tarn, *Alexander the Great*, 2.116–22, and refuted by H. Strasburger, *Bibliotheca Orientalis*, 9 (1952), 202–11.

27. Atkinson, *Curtius*, 60, following C. F. Edson, *Classical Philology*, 56 (1961), 198–203.

28. R. B. Steele, 'Quintus Curtius Rufus', *A.J.P.*, 36 (1915), 409.

29. E. Badian, 'The Death of Parmenio', *T.A.P.A.*, 91 (1960), 324–38, argues that Philotas was 'set up' by Alexander.

30. See W. Heckel, 'One More Herodotean Reminiscence in Curtius Rufus', *Hermes*, 107 (1979), 122f.

31. Cf. J. Rehork, 'Homer, Herodot und Alexander', *Festschrift für Franz Altheim* (Berlin, 1969), 251–60; J. Blänsdorf, 'Herodot by Curtius Rufus', *Hermes*, 99 (1971), 11–24.

32. E. I. McQueen, 'Quintus Curtius Rufus', in *Latin Biography*, ed. T. A. Dorey (London, 1967), 17–43.

33. McQueen, op. cit., 38.

34. A. B. Bosworth, 'Arrian and the Alexander Vulgate', *Entretiens de la Fondation Hardt*, 22 (Geneva, 1976), 2.

35. Tarn, *Alexander the Great*, 2.92.

36. Although F. Schachermeyr, *Entretiens de la Fondation Hardt*, 22, p. 34, rightly observes that Cleitarchus' 'Offiziers – und Beamtennachrichten' are very good.

SUMMARY OF THE LOST BOOKS 1 AND 2

1. J. Freinsheim, in his editions of 1648 and 1670 (Strasbourg), began his summaries of the lost books with an 'author's preface' and a full discussion of Alexander's early life. That the latter formed a part of Curtius' first book, or that it was discussed at all by Cleitarchus, is doubtful. I have reconstructed the lost books on the basis of Diodorus (17.2.1–29.4) and Justin (10.1.1–11.7.2), drawing on Plutarch's *Life of Alexander* when it seemed to me to reflect the Cleitarchean tradition. [W.H.]

2. Diodorus mistakenly calls him Antigonus' son-in-law.

3. Diodorus refers to Heracles (Hercules) as the common ancestor.

4. Arses ruled from 338 until 336 B.C.

5. Curtius probably did not identify his source at this point but Cleitarchus, like Curtius, discussed Thebes in his first book.

6. This is probably an error for Ariston (see Berve, 2.201) but if Diodorus took the name Cassander from his source, it may also have appeared in Curtius.

7. 388–361 B.C.

8. Arr. 1.11.7–8 gives a different version.

9. According to Arr. 1.15.7, Mithridates was the name of Darius' son-in-law. Diodorus may have conflated Mithridates and Spithridates (whom he calls Spithrobates); Curtius, on the other hand, might have distinguished between the two.

10. According to Arr. 1.15.8 and Plut. *Alex.* 16.11, Clitus strikes Spithridates not Rhosaces; but Curt. 8.1.20 shows that Curtius follows Diodorus. Both call him 'Rhosaces'.

BOOK 3

1. Cleander, son of Polemocrates and brother of Coenus (who commanded a battalion of the Macedonian infantry, cf. 3.9.7), led the mercenaries. He returned with 4,000 Greek mercenaries (Arr. 2.20.5), rejoining Alexander at Tyre in late Spring 332 (Curt. 4.3.11). It is usually thought that Curtius places Cleander's departure in the spring of 333. But the word-order seems to suggest that Cleander's departure preceded the settlement of Lycia and Pamphylia (winter 334/333). Curtius may have concluded the second book with lengthy discussions of the arrest of Alexander Lyncestes and the death of Memnon. The beginning of Book 3 may recapitulate briefly events of the end of 334 B.C. (cf. Arr. 1.24.2). Similarly the beginning of Book 4 picks up the events of 3.11, after the digressions on Alexander's visit to the Persian queens and Parmenion's capture of Damascus (3.12–13).

2. Celaenae, the chief city of Phrygia, was subject to earthquakes and a centre of Poseidon's worship. Strabo 12.8.18 derives the name from Celaenus, a son of Poseidon and Celaeno, or from the Greek word for black, 'on account of the black stone from the burn-outs'.

3. This myth is otherwise unknown. For the source of the river, and the famous myth of the flaying of Marsyas, see Xenophon, *Anabasis* 1.2.7–8, Livy 38.13.6 and Pliny *N.H.* 5. 106; cf. also Pausanias 10.30.2 for a later legend.

4. By all other accounts the Marsyas flows directly into the Maeander. According to Strabo 12.8.16, the Caprus flows into the Lycus, which joins the Maeander near Laodiceia.

5. In fact, Alexander remained in Celaenae for only ten days (Arr. 1.29.3), and the citadel, garrisoned by 1,000 Carians and 100 Greek mercenaries, surrendered to

Antigonus the One-Eyed, whom Alexander had left behind with 1,500 troops. Antigonus was made satrap of Phrygia, not Lydia, as Curt. 4.1.35 says. Celaenae remained Antigonus' headquarters well after Alexander's death (cf. Diod. 18.52.1).

6. Cf. Arr. 1.16.6; 1.29.5–6. Officially, at this stage, Alexander was fighting a Panhellenic war of vengeance against Persia, and he had sent in chains to Macedonia Greek mercenaries captured while serving the Great King. Apparently, the Athenian legates were asking only for their own countrymen, and these were returned in 331, when Alexander departed from Egypt (Arr. 3.6.2.; Curt. 4.8.12–13).

7. Parmenion, who had come to Phrygia via Sardis (Arr. 1.24.3; cf. Diod. 17.27.6), rejoined him at Gordium, as did the 'newly-weds', who had spent the winter with their wives in Macedonia and had returned with reinforcements (Arr. 1.29.3–4).

8. Cf. Strabo 12.5.3.

9. This may be based on Herodotus (2.34), who thought that from Cilicia to Sinope on the Black Sea was a march of five days. But Cleitarchus too seems to have had a curious interest in the idea of the isthmus, Strabo 12.1.3 (534) and 14.5.22 (677).

10. See also Justin 11.7.3–16; Arr. 2.3.1–8 places the carriage in the palace of Gordius and Midas; Aristobulus (*F.Gr.Hist.*, 139 F7 = Arr. 2.3.7; cf. Plut. *Alex.* 18.4) said that Alexander merely removed a pin that held the intricate knot together.

11. Amphoterus was the brother of Craterus, one of Alexander's most trusted commanders (cf. 3.9.8); according to Arr. 1.25.9 he was involved in the arrest of Alexander Lyncestes (see further 7.1.5). For Hegelochus, see also 6.11.22. A full account of their activities is given by Arr. 2.2.3 and 3.2.3ff. See also H. Hauben, 'The Command Structure in Alexander's Mediterranean Fleet', *Ancient Society*, 3 (1972), 56–8.

12. Alexander had disbanded his fleet the preceding year: cf. Arr. 1.20.1; Diod. 17.22.5.

13. Cf. Arr. 1.17.1; 2.4.2. Calas was probably a cousin of the famous treasurer Harpalus (cf. 10.2.1ff.). In fact, Alexander was adding Paphlagonia to the territory already under Calas' control – he was satrap of Hellespontine Phrygia.

14. For Memnon's illness and death in late spring 333, see the summary of Book 2. Cf. also P. A. Brunt, *Arrian*, vol. 1, 454–5. His importance was doubtless exaggerated by the vulgate tradition (cf. W. W. Tarn, *Alexander the Great*, 2. 72–3). Darius had hoped that Memnon would transfer the war to Europe and force Alexander to abandon his campaign (Diod. 17.30.1).

15. Xerxes was the king of Persia (485–465 B.C.) who invaded Greece in 480 B.C. The enumeration of his troops took place at Doriscus in Thrace in that year; cf. Herodotus 7.59ff. See also the Introduction, p. 9.

16. A small Spanish shield.

17. The text is corrupt at this point, and the Tapurians and Derbices appear courtesy of Foss's emendation (Leipzig, 1879), based in part on Arr. 3.8.4 and 3.11.4 where the Tapurians are placed next to the Hyrcanians at Gaugamela.

18. In all, 312,200 troops (250,000 infantry and 62,200 cavalry). Diod. 17.31.2 and Justin 11.9.1 give Darius 400,000 infantry and 100,000 cavalry; Arr. 2.8.8, Plut. *Alex.* 18.6 and the anonymous Alexander-history (*F.Gr.Hist.*, 148 F44) estimate Darius' military strength at 600,000. The 30,000 Greek mercenaries, by Curtius' own version (3.3.1), were not at Babylon, but brought from the Aegean coast to Cilicia by Thimodes (3.8.1).

19. Charidemus' surrender was demanded by Alexander in 335, along with that of Demosthenes, Lycurgus, Hyperides, Polyeuctas, Chares, Diotimus, Ephialtes and Moerocles (Arr. 1.10.4–6; Plutarch, *Demosthenes* 23.4). These were regarded as the

chief adversaries of Philip and Alexander, but only Charidemus was ordered exiled (Arr. 1.10.6); Ephialtes, however, reappears with a certain Thrasybulus fighting for the Persians at Halicarnassus (Diod. 17.25.6). Diod. 17.30.2 wrongly says that Charidemus had once campaigned 'with King Philip'.

20. Cf. Diod. 17.30.4–7 for the outspokenness and death of Charidemus. Here Charidemus expresses the sentiments which Curtius (3.8.1–2) puts in the mouth of Thimodes. Charidemus' speech, as given by Curtius, is closely modelled on Demaratus' advice to Xerxes at Doriscus (Herodotus 7.101–5). Cf. C. Bradford Welles, *Diodorus*, vol. 8, 200–201, n.1; J. Blänsdorf, 'Herodot bei Curtius Rufus', *Hermes*, 99 (1971), 11–24.

21. Contrast Darius' own comments at 3.8.5–6.

22. Cf. Diod. 17.30.6.

23. Thimodes (Thymondas) was Memnon's nephew, as was Pharnabazus, the latter being a son of Artabazus and Memnon's (and Mentor's) sister. For this shift in command see Arr. 2.2.1. For a good discussion of the family see P. A. Brunt, 'Alexander, Barsine and Heracles', *R.F.I.C.*, 103 (1975), 22–34.

24. Cf. Herodotus 7.12ff.

25. Possibly these are the Persian counterpart of – or, as some suggest, prototype for – the Macedonian royal pages (cf. Xenophon, *Anabasis* 1.9.3; Arr. 4.13.1).

26. That is, to Ahuramazda.

27. Herodotus 7.83. They were called 'Immortals' because their number was never allowed to drop below 10,000.

28. Literally 'Spear-bearers', these were the king's bodyguards. But see W. Heckel, *Rh.M.* 135 (1992) 191–2.

29. Belus was believed by some to be an Assyrian king and the founder of Babylon (cf. 5.1.24); he is the god Baal (Bel-Marduk of Babylon). Ninus was the legendary founder of the Assyrian dynasty.

30. Enclosed wagons used especially for carrying women and children (cf. Xenophon, *Anabasis* 1.2.16; Arr. 3.19.2).

31. Sabictas, Arr. 2.4.2.

32. This was probably the camp of Cyrus the Younger, who campaigned against his brother Artaxerxes; cf. Xenophon, *Anabasis* 1.2.21, Arr. 2.4.3. Curtius' reference to Cyrus the Great and Croesus may well be another Herodotean element. Dosson, 186, simply regards it as an error on Curtius' part.

33. For Memnon's strategy see the summary of Book 2 and Diod. 17.18.2–3; Arr. 1.12.9. For Arsames cf. Arr. 2.4.5–6.

34. Cf. Xenophon, *Anabasis* 1.2.22.

35. For similar descriptions see Arr. 2.4.7; Val. Max. 3.8 ext. 6; Strabo 14.5.12 (673).

36. Cf. 5.3.22.

37. Curtius here ascribes to Parmenion an achievement denied by Arrian (2.4.6), who says Alexander himself captured Tarsus, leaving Parmenion behind in Cappadocia. This is apparently corroborated by Justin 11.8.5, who says that when Alexander fell ill at the Cydnus river, Parmenion sent him a letter from Cappadocia.

38. Probably about July, 333 B.C.

39. The same story is told by Justin 11.8.3–9 and Val. Max. 3.8. ext. 6; Diod. 17.31.4–6 gives no reasons for Alexander's illness, not mentioning the Cydnus river; Arrian 2.4.7–11 and Plut. *Alex.* 19.2ff. give the alternative version of Aristobulus (*F.Gr.Hist.*, 139 F8), who ascribed Alexander's illness to fatigue.

40. See 3.6.4.

41. Philip of Acarnania treats Alexander again at Gaza (4.6.17), but, aside from this famous episode, nothing else is known of him except that he attended Medius' dinner-party in 323, at which Alexander became fatally ill (Ps. Callisthenes 3.31.8; perhaps also *Metz Epitome* 97). See Berve, no. 788.

42. Parmenion's letter was apparently sent from Cappadocia, where Parmenion was following with the less mobile forces (Arr. 2.4.3, 9; Justin 11.8.5). Val. Max. 3.8. ext. 6 says that Alexander was taken into town; hence Parmenion's letter may have come from the camp (as Plut. *Alex.* 19.5. records). But Curtius has Alexander in his own tent (3.5.4), in which case it is odd that Parmenion did not come in person. The claim that Darius offered Philip 1,000 talents and his sister (Ps. Callisthenes 2.8.5 calls her Dadipharta; cf. Plut. *Alex.* 19.5; Justin 11.8.6. mentions only the money) is probably a doublet for the alleged bribery of Alexander Lyncestes, (Arr. 1.25.3).

43. Plut. *Alex.* 19.1 says that Darius believed Alexander's delay in Cilicia was due to cowardice (an idea developed somewhat differently by Curtius 3.8.10–11), suggesting that he was ignorant of his illness. Presumably Darius crossed the Euphrates at Thapsacus (cf. Arr. 2.13.1), where in 401 B.C. Cyrus the Younger had miraculously forded the river without boats or a bridge (Xenophon, *Anabasis* 1.4.18).

44. Aesculapius (Asclepius) was the healing-god, to whom Alexander now gave thanks for his regained health. According to Arrian (2.5.8), the celebrations included a review of the troops, torch races and athletic and musical competitions; but the sacrifice to Minerva (Roman name for Athena) was held not at Soli but at Magarsus.

45. Ptolemaeus and Asander, satrap of Lydia, had conquered Orontobates, the Persian satrap of Caria (Arr. 2.5.7). He had been replaced by Ada but continued to resist Alexander (see Arr. 1.23.7–8).

46. As far as we know no reinforcements ever came. They are not mentioned by other sources, and Curtius may have fabricated them.

47. A rare occasion when Parmenion's advice is accepted by Alexander.

48. The early career of Sisines is otherwise unknown. Arr. 1.25.3 says that he was at the court of Darius III, and not with Alexander the Great. Perhaps, since Darius, or his chiliarch Nabarzanes, sent him to Alexander Lyncestes (Arr. ibid.), Curtius confused the two Alexanders. Possibly, however, Curtius has merely misunderstood Sisines' role in the whole affair and fabricated a new episode.

49. There may be some truth in the suggestion that Sisines was murdered on the king's orders – but not for the reasons given by Curtius. The episode is highly reminiscent of the Philotas affair (see 6.7.17ff.; cf. Atkinson, *Curtius*, 186).

50. This advice is ascribed by Arrian (2.6.3, 6) and Plutarch (*Alex.* 20.1–3) to Amyntas, son of Antiochus.

51. Perhaps an accurate reflection of the rivalry at the Persian court: cf. the rejection of Memnon's advice (Diod. 17.18.3; Arr. 1.12.10), the suspicion of Charidemus (Diod. 17.30.4).

52. Curtius is anxious to dissociate Darius, 'a man of justice and clemency', from his suspicious and barbaric advisers (cf. 3.8.15), and, although his earlier treatment of Charidemus was contrary to the advice given here, he did at least repent his actions on that occasion (3.2.19). Cf. also Arr. 2.6.4.

53. Cf. Diod. 17.32.3; Arr. 2.11.9–10.

54. Arr. 2.7.1. says these prisoners were tortured and killed, but Curtius may again be borrowing from Herodotus. The episode recalls Xerxes' treatment of the Greek spies

(Herodotus 7.146–7), who were led around the army and told to report what they had seen. See W. Heckel, *Hermes*, 107 (1979), 122–3.

55. Alexander had in fact sacrificed to the river Danube (when he crossed it), to Protesilaus at Elaeus, to Poseidon and the Nereids at the Hellespont, to Priam and Athena at Troy, and to Artemis at Ephesus.

56. For discussion of the battle and of tactics see J. F. C. Fuller, *Generalship*, 154–62, and N. G. L. Hammond, *Alexander*, 94–110.

57. Nabarzanes (543) was Darius' chiliarch, the most important official at his court. For his role in the king's assassination see 5.9.2ff.

58. Aristomedes of Pherae (128). After the battle of Issus, he fled with Amyntas, son of Antiochus, Bianor and Thimodes to Egypt (Arr. 2.13.2–3), where, it appears, he perished. Cf. 4.1.27–33; Diod. 17.48.

59. The king also occupied the middle, which was regarded both as the safest place and the best suited for sending commands to either wing. See Arr. 2.8.11 and Xenophon, *Anabasis* 1.8.22.

60. Nicanor (554) commanded the hypaspists (Arr. 2.8.3, and cf. Curt. 4.13.27 with note 85).

61. Ptolemaeus, son of Seleucus (670). Although Curtius does not mention it, Ptolemaeus died in this battle (Arr. 2.10.7). The famous Ptolemaeus (henceforth 'Ptolemy'), son of Lagus and later king of Egypt, does not appear in Curtius' narrative until 8.1.45 (the Clitus episode).

62. The manuscripts of Curtius read *Graecia* ('Greece') at this point. The Agrianes were Thracians and had been with Alexander from the start. But perhaps the contingent had received some reinforcements just before the battle of Issus (see H. Berve, *Alexanderreich*, 1.138; E. Marsden, *Gaugamela*, 30).

63. Hercules and Dionysus were considered to have approached the western and eastern edges of the earth. For Alexander's emulation of these 'heroes' who became gods see L. Edmunds, 'The Religiosity of Alexander', *G.R.B.S.*, 12 (1971), 363–91. Cf. also 8.5.8ff. Here and elsewhere Curtius uses the word *Bactra*, properly the city (Balkh), for the province Bactria or Bactriana.

64. Alexander refers to the battle of Chaeronea in 338 B.C. in which he himself played no small part (Plut. *Alex.* 9.2–4), and the destruction of Thebes.

65. Arr. 1.12.6ff.; Diod. 17.18.4ff; Plut. *Alex.* 16; Justin 11.6.10–13.

66. Darius (king of Persia 521–486 B.C.) had suppressed the Ionian revolt (499–493) and sent a force to Marathon in 490. His son Xerxes invaded Greece in 480–479 and destroyed, among other things, the temples of the Athenians. Alexander was, at this point, ostensibly the leader of a Panhellenic expedition to punish the Persians for their past sins.

67. Cf. 3.3.14, 18; Diod. 17.30.4; 17.35.4.

68. The Latin *opimum decus* is a variation on the well-known formula *opima spolia*, the arms wrested in battle from the enemy general (cf. 7.4.40). Despite its dramatic touches, this may in fact have been Alexander's strategy (Diod. 17.33.5). Cyrus the Younger made a similar attempt on his brother Artaxerxes at Cunaxa in 401 B.C. (Xenophon, *Anabasis* 1.8.26–7). For the battle in general see Fuller, *Generalship*, 154–62; Hammond, *Alexander*, 94–110; and for the preliminaries to the battle see C. L. Murison, 'Darius III and the Battle of Issus', *Historia*, 21 (1972), 399–423.

69. For Oxathres see Diod. 17.34.2. Elsewhere Oxyathres (Berve, no. 586; Strabo 12.3.10 = C 544). Alexander later assigned him to the company of his 'Companions'

(6.2.11; cf. Plut. *Alex.* 43.7, who calls him Exathres). His daughter Amastris became the wife of Craterus in 324 B.C. (Arr. 7.4.5).

70. Cf. Arr. 2.11.8; Diod. 17.21.3 incorrectly says he fell at the Granicus River, but the Antixyes of Diod. 17.34.5 is probably a corruption of Atizyes. He was Darius' satrap of Phrygia, but Alexander had already replaced him with Antigonus.

71. Cf. 4.1.28.

72. Arr. 2.12.1; Diod. 17.34.5; Plut. *Alex.* 20.8; Justin 11.9.9; cf. Marsden, *Gaugamela*, 4.

73. Aelian (*De natura Animalium* 6.48) says that the horse was a mare that had just recently given birth; cf. Herodotus' camels, 3.102.3.

74. This is apparently the Persian right, since Curtius has already told us that Parmenion was on the Macedonian left (3.9.8; cf. 3.11.3).

75. Cf. Xenophon, *Anabasis* 1.8.7. But see Atkinson, *Curtius*, 477–9.

76. Amyntas, son of Antiochus. See 4.1.27 with note 11.

77. Hedicke amended the text to read '4,500 wounded; 302 infantry, 150 cavalry dead'. Cf. Diod. 17.36.6., who gave the Macedonian dead as 300 infantry and 150 cavalry. Justin 11.9.10 gives 130 and 150; Arr. 2.10.7 says that at one point in the battle already 120 Macedonians of note had fallen. There is general agreement about the 110,000 Persian casualties, though Justin 11.9.10 reports 61,000 infantry and 10,000 cavalry dead, and another 40,000 captured.

78. Curtius, after making the point that Mithrenes knew the Persian language, says that Alexander sent Leonnatus, who almost certainly did not. Laomedon, one of his Companions, was bilingual and according to Arrian (3.6.6) was placed in charge of the Persian captives. It is tempting to think that Ptolemy, who may have been the original source for this story, substituted the name of Leonnatus for Laomedon, who was his personal enemy in the years after Alexander's death. For Ptolemy's bias see R. M. Errington, 'Bias in Ptolemy's History of Alexander', *C.Q.*, n.s. 19 (1969), 233–42.

79. This story was not given by Ptolemy or Aristobulus, and it is probably fictitious. Cleitarchus may have invented the story, cf. E. Kornemann, *Die Alexandergeschichte*, 114.

80. The use of the rhetorical plural (cf. Justin 9.8.16). Curtius has Clitus in mind, 8.1.20ff.

81. Philotas (6.7.1–11.40) and Parmenion (7.2.11–33).

82. Cf. 3.8.12.

83. Although it is not clear from Curtius' account, it appears that the above-mentioned satrap and the governor of Damascus are one and the same.

84. Artaxerxes III Ochus ruled Persia from 358 to 338. For his death see Diod. 17.5.3–6; Justin 10.3. Alexander married the youngest of these daughters of Ochus, Parysatis, at Susa in 324 B.C. The names of the other two are unknown.

85. Nothing else is known of Ilioneus. His name apparently reflects the family's interest in the Troad, and there is no need to follow Hedicke in amending it to Hystanes.

86. Memnon's widow was Barsine (206), the first woman to be intimate with Alexander (Plut. *Alex.* 21.7–9; Justin 11.10.2). Their child was Heracles, to whom Curtius later alludes (10.6.11); see P. A. Brunt, *R.F.I.C.*, 103 (1975), 22–34.

87. See Atkinson, *Curtius*, 464–5.

BOOK 4

1. To Thapsacus, Arr. 2.13.1.
2. 'Hollow Syria', the valley between Mt Lebanon and Anti-Lebanon.
3. Arvad.
4. Amrit.
5. The Ionian revolt, 499–493 B.C.
6. After the naval disaster at Salamis in 480, Xerxes returned to Asia, leaving behind Mardonius, who was defeated at Plataea in the following year.
7. Cf. Arr. 2.14.5. Not a plausible charge, although it made good propaganda. But see K. Kraft, *Der 'rationale' Alexander*, 40–41.
8. Gebal.
9. Not Strato, king of Aradus (4.1.6). See Berve, *Alexanderreich*, 2. nos 727, 728.
10. Diod. 17.47 incorrectly places this episode in Tyre. For the story of an individual rising from the rank of gardener to king there is ample Near Eastern precedent: see Robert Drews, 'Sargon, Cyrus and Mesopotamian Folk History', *JNES* 33 (1974), 387–93.
11. Cf. 3.11.18. Amyntas, son of Antiochus, fled from Macedonia very soon after Alexander's accession. Arr. 1.17.9 says that he had not suffered harm at Alexander's hands, but it is clear that his connections with Amyntas, son of Perdiccas, whom Alexander executed in late 336 or early 335, gave him good reason to fear the king. See J. R. Ellis, *J.H.S.*, 91 (1971), 15–24. For his ill-fated campaign in Egypt cf. Arr. 2.13.2–3; Diod. 17.48.2–5.
12. 3.11.10.
13. Antigonus was satrap of Greater Phrygia; Lydia at that time was governed by Asander.
14. Perhaps an error for Autophradates or else a lieutenant of Pharnabazus (see Berve, no. 126). He is not mentioned by other sources.
15. Agis III was king of Sparta, 338–331. His death is described at 6.1.1ff. See E. Badian, 'Agis III', *Hermes*, 95 (1967), 170–92, for his significance to the history of Alexander.
16. January, 332 B.C. For the siege of Tyre see Arr. 2.16.1–24; Plut. *Alex.* 24–5; Diod. 17.40.2–46.6; Justin 11.10.10–14. Cf. Polyaenus 4.3.3–4; 4.13.1. Curtius' narrative is treated by W. Rutz, 'Zur Erzählungskunst des Q. Curtius Rufus: die Belagerung von Tyrus', *Hermes*, 93 (1965), 370–82. Cf. also Fuller, *Generalship*, 206–16.
17. The Argead house claimed to be descended from Hercules (who had been elevated from hero to god) through Temenus. For the legends see N. G. L. Hammond and G. T. Griffith, *Macedonia II* (Oxford, 1979), 3ff. The Tyrians called Hercules 'Melcarth'.
18. 'Old Tyre'; it stood on the mainland. Cf. 4.2.18 below.
19. Less than half a mile.
20. Arr. 2.18.3 says it is about three fathoms deep at this point.
21. Traditionally founded in 814–813 B.C.; but see the discussion in B. H. Warmington, *Carthage* (Harmondsworth, 1964), 13–38.
22. The *corvus* (Greek *korax*) or 'crow', as described by Polybius 1.22.4ff., is a more complex grappling-hook with boarding-platform; Curtius has something much less elaborate in mind (cf. 4.3.26).
23. Polyaenus 4.3.4 implies that Parmenion was left in charge of the forces at Tyre, but this is perhaps another story intended to discredit him (see Polyaenus 4.13 for Craterus' role). Some details of the Arabian campaign are given by Plut. *Alex.* 24.10–14. For the later prominence of Perdiccas see 10.5.4ff.

24. Cf. 3.1.1. above. He returned with 4,000 mercenaries (Arr. 2.20.5).

25. Arr. 2.20.1–3 gives 224 ships in all: 80 Phoenician ships, 10 from Rhodes, 3 from Soli and Mallus, 10 from Lycia and one 50-oared ship from Macedonia; added to these were 120 Cypriot ships. Pnytagoras was king of Salamis.

26. This is not true. The Syracusans did not cross to Africa until the expedition of Agathocles in 310 B.C. (Diod. 20.3.3ff.; Justin 22.4.1ff.).

27. Diod. 17.41.8 says that he narrowly escaped stoning by the Tyrians and took refuge in the temple of Hercules.

28. Cf. Diod. 20.14.4–5, where no fewer than 300 Carthaginians were sacrificed to Cronus (= Saturn) in 310 B.C. Carthage was destroyed by the Romans in 146 B.C.

29. Cf. Diod. 17.41.5–6.

30. Curtius omits to mention the valiant death of Admetus, described by both Arrian (2.23.4–5) and Diodorus (17.45.6).

31. Atkinson, Curtius, 312, makes the attractive suggestion that these 15,000 were actually taken to Sidon to be sold into slavery, and that Curtius misunderstood it to be a 'rescue mission'.

32. Plut. Alex. 24.5 and Diod. 17.46.5 say the siege lasted for seven months, ending in July or August 332 (Arr. 2.24.5, Hecatombaeon). Arr. 2.24.4–5 says 8,000 Tyrians were killed, along with 400 Macedonians; 30,000 were sold into slavery. According to Diod. 17.46.3–4, 7,000 men died in battle, 2,000 were crucified and 13,000 taken prisoner.

33. See the Introduction: 'The Author and the Date', p. 2.

34. For the letter see Arr. 2.25.1, who says that it arrived while Alexander was still besieging Tyre. Statira was also the name of Darius' wife (Plut. Alex. 30.5). Alexander did, in fact, marry the younger Statira in 324 at Susa (Aristobulus ap. Arr. 7.4.4 = F.Gr.Hist., 139 F52 calls her Barsine; but cf. Plut. Alex. 77.6).

35. Balacrus was governor of Cilicia. If this reference to Socrates (apparently the son of Sathon) is correct, he was probably given a purely military command. Curtius 5.7.12 mistakenly calls him Plato. See Berve, Alexanderreich, 2. 429, no. 67. But see (contra Berve) A. B. Bosworth, 'The Government of Syria under Alexander the Great', C.Q., n.s. 24 (1974), 59, n. 1. Philotas here is not the famous son of Parmenion.

36. See 4.8.9–11.

37. Hephaestion was probably charged with bringing the siege-engines from Tyre to Gaza (cf. Arr. 2.27.3).

38. i.e., held at the Isthmus of Corinth every second year.

39. Probably Hydarnes.

40. Arr. 3.2.3–7.

41. Arr. 3.2.4 says five pirate ships, but Curtius often gives higher numbers than other sources (cf. 5.1.45; 5.2.11; 5.3.1–2).

42. The tyrants were returned to their own cities to be punished (4.8.11); Apollonides, Athanagoras and others were sent in chains to Elephantine in Egypt (Arr. 3.2.7).

43. For Bessus' treachery see 5.9.2ff.

44. Batis; Arr. 2.25.4 says he was a eunuch. For the whole episode see Tarn, Alexander the Great, 2. 265–70; Atkinson, Curtius, 334–6.

45. There is evidently a lacuna at this point.

46. Achilles' famous punishment of Hector: Homer, Iliad 22.395ff. See also B. Perrin, T.A.P.A., 26 (1895), 56–68.

47. Arr. 2.27.7 says the entire male population died fighting, and that the women and children were sold into slavery. He gives no Macedonian casualty figures.

48. Amyntas, son of Andromenes. Cf. Diod. 17.49.1. For his return see 5.1.40; cf. Diod. 17.65.1.

49. Amyntas, son of Antiochus. See 4.1.27 above.

50. Mazaces had probably been left as acting governor by Sabaces, who had taken the Egyptian contingent to Issus. Arr. 3.1.2. says the news of Darius' shameful flight from Issus helped to induce his surrender to Alexander.

51. For the visit to the oracle at Siwah, cf. Diod. 17.49–51; Plut. *Alex.* 26–7; Arr. 3.3–4; Justin 11.11.2–13; and Strabo 17.1.43 (814).

52. As a descendant of Hercules, who was a son of Jupiter. But Plut. *Alex.* 3 tells a story, doubtless invented years later, that Philip spied on Olympias, Alexander's mother, in bed with Jupiter Ammon in the form of a snake. See Hamilton, *Plutarch, Alexander*, 6. Alexander may have known that, as the recognized Pharaoh of Egypt, he would be hailed as the son of Ammon.

53. These gifts included 300 war-horses and five four-horse chariots (Diod. 17.49.2).

54. The majority of the primary sources (including Aristobulus, Callisthenes and Cleitarchus) gave this version; Ptolemy (*F.Gr.Hist.*, 138 F8 = Arr. 3.3.5) says the army was led by two 'talking' snakes (Hamilton, *Plutarch, Alexander*, 71) or perhaps 'hissing' snakes (Bosworth, *Arrian*, 273).

55. Diod. 17.50.3. See also H. W. Parke, *The Oracles of Zeus* (Oxford, 1967), 196ff.

56. Diod. 17.50.4–5.

57. Diod. 17.50.6 says there were 80 of them.

58. The chief architect was Deinocrates.

59. Plut. *Alex.* 26.9; Val. Max 1.4 ext. 1.

60. See P. M. Fraser, *Ptolemaic Alexandria*, 3 vols (Oxford, 1972). Arrian (3.1.5–2.2) and Plutarch (*Alex.* 26.4) place the founding of Alexandria before the visit to Siwah.

61. His death is recorded only by Curtius (cf. 6.9.27) of the extant Alexander historians, although other primary sources had apparently dealt with the matter (see Berve, *Alexanderreich*, 2. 149, no. 295).

62. The mss. read Memnon; Arr. 2.13.7 calls him Menon. But see Bosworth, *C.Q.*, n.s. 24 (1974), 47ff.

63. For Aristonicus of Methymna see 4.5.19; Ersilaus is probably an error for Eurysilaus of Eresus.

64. Crete had become the base for the remnants of the Persian fleet, which had been seriously weakened by the loss of Phoenicia, the defection of Cyprus and the Aegean successes of Amphoterus and Hegelochus. The Spartans under Agesilaus, Agis' brother, and then Agis himself, were now cooperating with Persia on and around Crete. See Bosworth, *Phoenix*, 29 (1975), 27–43, especially 30–34.

65. Diod. 17.53.1–2; cf. Xenophon, *Anabasis* 1.8.10.

66. Probably his name was Atropates.

67. The battle was actually fought at Gaugamela (Plut. *Alex.* 31.7) but Arbela, which was more pleasant to the ear, gained a reputation as the scene for the battle (cf. Arrian's comments 6.11.4). Arbela was 600 stades distant from Gaugamela (Arr. 3.8.7).

68. The Khazir.

69. Strabo 11.14.8 (529). For the swiftness of the river cf. Arr. 3.7.5.

70. This eclipse is dated to 20 September 331 B.C. Cf. Arr. 3.7.6; Plut. *Alex.* 31.8; Pliny, N.H. 2. 180. The battle itself was fought on 1 October 331 (26 Boedromion, so Plutarch, *Camillus* 19.5).

71. This is Curtius' dramatic embellishment, but there was clearly already an undercurrent of resentment against Alexander because of his pretensions about Jupiter Ammon. Cf. Plut. *Alex.* 48; Curt. 6.10.26–8, 6.11.21ff., 8.1.42.

72. For Statira's death see Plut. *Alex.* 30 and *Moralia* 338e-f; Arr. 4.20.1–3; Diod. 17.54.7; Justin 11.12.6. Plutarch and Justin say that she died in childbirth, but in 331 she could not have been bearing Darius' child. Her death is therefore dated by Berve, *Alexanderreich*, 2. 363, to 332. All sources place her death in 331; see Bosworth, *Arrian*, 221.

73. His name was probably Teireos (Plut. *Alex.* 30.2; Berve, no. 742).

74. Cf. Plut. *Alex.* 30.11–13; Arr. 4.20.3.

75. The Danube.

76. Plut. *Alex.* 29.7–9; Arr. 2.25.1–3 (at Tyre); Diod. 17.54.4.

77. This is not attested elsewhere and may have been invented by Curtius for dramatic effect.

78. Orxines (Arr. 6.29.2). The seven Persians were the conspirators against Smerdis (a Magus according to Herodotus 3.61ff.; but see Olmstead, 107–18, for the historical background); one of their number was Darius I, who ascended the throne and ruled from 521 to 486 B.C. His queen, Atossa, was the daughter of Cyrus the Great (559–529). For Orxines' later activities see 10.1.22ff.

79. When Datis and Artaphrenes sacked the Euboean city of Eretria in 490 (the campaign against Marathon), the captives were settled near Susa (Herodotus 6.101, 119). Diod. 17.110.4–5 erringly calls them Boeotians, but he says that they retained their Greek language and some of their culture.

80. Persian numbers are greatly exaggerated by the other sources. 1,000,000 infantry and 40,000 cavalry (Arr. 3.8.6); 800,000 infantry, 200,000 cavalry (Diod. 17.53.3); 400,000 infantry, 100,000 horse (Justin 11.12.5). For a discussion of the figures see Brunt, *Arrian*, 510–11; Marsden, *Gaugamela* 31–7, who concludes that Darius had even fewer than the 200,000 infantrymen attested by Curtius, and 34,000 cavalry.

81. Polyperchon, like Parmenion, was a veteran commander (born between 390 and 380). His part in this episode was doubtless invented by Curtius (cf. Berve, *Alexanderreich*, 2. 303); cf. Arr. 3.10.1–2; Plut. *Alex.* 31.10–14; and see note 46, to 8.5.22–4.

82. Cf. Diod. 17.56; Plut. *Alex.* 32.1–4; Justin 11.13.1–3.

83. Clitus commanded the cavalry bodyguard, the *ile basilike*. He saved Alexander's life at the Granicus River (see the Summary of Books 1 and 2; 8.1.20ff.).

84. This was an *ile* of the companion cavalry. Curtius appears to have confused this Meleager with the son of Neoptolemus, whose phalanx-battalion he omits below (cf. Arr. 3.11.8 and 9).

85. This is an anachronism: the unit was called the *hypaspistae*; the argyraspids or 'silver shields' did not come into being until 327 at the earliest (Curt. 8.5.4.) or perhaps as late as 321. For discussions see Tarn, *Alexander the Great*, 2. 151ff.; R. A. Lock, *Historia*, 26 (1977), 374–5; E. M. Anson, *Historia*, 30 (1981), 117–20; W. Heckel, *Symbolae Osloenses*, 57 (1982), 57–67.

86. Perdiccas was their commander, at this point; Curtius omits Meleager's battalion (cf. Diod. 17.57.2; Arr. 3.11.9).

87. The text is corrupt here, and no emendation is entirely satisfactory.

88. The manuscripts read 'Philagrus', which has been emended to Philippus, son of Balacrus (cf. Diod. 17.57.3). But Arr. 3.11.9 says Amyntas' brother, Simmias, commanded his battalion.

89. Curtius has copied his source carelessly. Craterus commanded a phalanx-battalion and, apparently, the infantry on the left wing (Arr. 3.11.10); but Parmenion had supreme command of the left (4.13.35; cf. 3.9.8). Erigyius led the allied cavalry (Diod. 17.57.3; Arr. 3.11.10).

90. *notatumque certo signo locum, ut fraus evitari a suis posset.* The Latin seems to suggest that Darius had marked the spot to enable the Persians to avoid it, but 4.13.37 and 4.15.1 might suggest rather that the spot had been marked by Bion to enable Alexander's men to avoid it.

91. 3.11.24; 3.12.26.

92. Cyrus conquered the Medes in 550 and the Lydians in 547; see Olmstead, 34–41.

93. For a full discussion of the battle see Fuller, *Generalship*, 163–80; Marsden, *Gaugamela*, 40ff.; and A. M. Devine, 'Grand Tactics at Gaugamela', *Phoenix*, 29 (1975), 374–85.

94. For this unfavourable portrait of Parmenion see Arr. 3.15.1; Callisthenes *F.Gr.Hist.*, 124 F37 = Plut. *Alex.* 33.10–11, with Hamilton, *Plutarch, Alexander*, 89; Diod. 17.60.5–8 says that Parmenion sent for help but, when none came, he commanded the Thessalians with great skill.

95. Cf. Diod. 17.59.6–7.

96. Curtius has made a slip: the Agrianes were not mounted but infantrymen armed with the javelin.

97. The Greater Zab; it flows into the Tigris from the north-east between Gaugamela and Arbela.

98. Ninety thousand Persians died, 500 Macedonians and many more wounded (Diod. 17.61.3); 300,000 Persians, 100 Macedonians dead (Arr. 3.15.6); the anonymous Alexander-history (*Oxyrhynchus Papyri*, 1798) is perhaps the most conservative and realistic with 53,000 Persians, 1,200 Macedonians dead.

99. Cf. Diod. 17.61.3; Arr. 3.15.2 significantly omits Perdiccas (see R. M. Errington, *C.Q.*, n.s. 19 (1969), 237).

BOOK 5

1. Curtius deals with European affairs at the beginning of Book 6; cf. Justin 12.1.4–2.17, who postpones his discussion of events in Europe until after Darius' death. But see Diod. 17. 62–3.

2. He went first to Ecbatana and thence to the Upper Satrapies (Diod. 17.64.1–2; cf. Arr. 3.16.1).

3. He also captured Darius' chariot, his shield, bow and arrows, all for the second time (Arr. 3.15.4). Diod. 17.64.3 claims that the treasure amounted to 3,000 talents of silver.

4. A *lacuna* here is suggested by Müller, who supplies *a dextra* before *Arabia*. *Media* is Hedicke's supplement.

5. Used here and elsewhere to mean the Persian Gulf.

6. Otherwise unknown.

7. Cf. Plut. *Alex.* 35.

8. The Chaldeans were astronomer/astrologers and priests of Bel-Marduk (Baal). Arr.

3.16.4 says Alexander ordered the rebuilding of the temple of Bel, which Xerxes had allegedly destroyed in late 482 B.C. (see Olmstead, 236–7; Bosworth, *Arrian*, 314).

9. Sammuramat, an Assyrian queen (perhaps of Babylonian origin), who ruled at the end of the 9th century B.C. until her son Adad-nirari III became of age. Her story was greatly embellished by Greek historiography since Herodotus (see especially Diod. 2.4ff. and Justin 1.1.10ff.).

10. Diodorus does not discuss the site of Babylon in Book 17 because he has already given a full description at 2.7.2–10.6. Curtius' details coincide closely with Diodorus' and their ultimate source is certainly Cleitarchus, who corrected some of Ctesias' information (cf. L. Pearson, *The Lost Histories of Alexander the Great*, 228ff.).

11. Herodotus (1.178) gives 480 stades; Ctesias said they were 360 stades in circumference, which Cleitarchus corrected to 365, or one per day of the year. Neither writer will have measured the circuit of the walls, but Ctesias numbered the days of the year at 360 instead of 365. Cf. the 365 concubines of Darius (3.3.24), which Dinon, Cleitarchus' father, numbered at 360 (Plutarch *Artoxerxes* 27.2). The mss. of Curtius read '368'.

12. A juger (*jugerum*) is really a measure of area (28,000 square feet, or 240 feet × 120), but Curtius perhaps uses it as equivalent to the Greek *plethron* which is both a measure of length (100 feet) and of area (in Greek authors sometimes equivalent to the Roman *jugerum*: e.g. Plutarch, *Camillus* 39). Diodorus (2.7.5) claims that the distance between the buildings and the walls was two *plethra*.

13. The bridge was 5 stades (or more than half a mile) long (Diod. 2.8.2); it was actually built by Nabopolassar, the father of Nebuchadrezzar.

14. Cf. Diod. 2.8.6.

15. For a full description cf. Diod. 2.10.1–6.

16. The translation follows Bardon's punctuation: *quae, desiderio nemorum silvarumque in campestris locis, virum compulit* ... With the commas omitted this could be rendered: 'who missed the woods and forests and made her husband imitate nature's beauty in the flat country ...' Cf. Diod. 2.10.1; the king was Nebuchadrezzar, not a Syrian but a Chaldean.

17. 4.6.30; cf. Diod. 17.65.1.

18. A generalizing plural (*ineuntibus*), following the earlier singular (*regis ministri*). But Vogel's *regibus* is perhaps correct.

19. The royal pages. Cf. Diod. 17.65.1; Arr. 4.13.1.

20. We should perhaps read, with D. R. Shackleton-Bailey (*C.Q.*, n.s. 31 (1981), 176), *regioni Babyloniae ac Cilici ⟨a tenus Mesopotami⟩ ae* in order to retain the sense of Diod. 17.64.5.

21. Diod. 17.64.6: two months' pay.

22. Cf. Diod. 17.65.2–4. The arrival of reinforcements and the casualties at Gaugamela probably made a reform of the army desirable. Arr. 3.16.11, who places the reforms in Susa rather than Sittacene, says that the *ilai* of the Companion cavalry were each subdivided into two companies (*lochoi*). Curtius is here talking about the infantry counterpart of the Companions, the hypaspists, but he appears to have reversed the actual procedure. Eight chiliarchs for the hypaspists are impossible since the unit numbered at most 4,000. Also, a chiliarch of the hypaspists, Adaeus, already existed in 334 B.C. (Arr. 1.22.7) and pentakosiarchs did not cease to exist after 331. If the hypaspists did, in fact, number 4,000, then the eight men named must be pentakosiarchs ('commanders of 500'). See Bosworth, *Arrian*, 148–9.

23. See 8.1.36. For his role at Halicarnassus cf. Diod. 17.27.1.

24. Probably the later commander of the *Argyraspids* (*contra* Berve, no. 84).

25. Perhaps *Aegaeus*, 'from Aegae', the old Macedonian capital, or Augaea in Chalcidice. He may be the Philotas of Arr. 1.21.5.

26. Amyntas, Antigonus, Lyncestes Amyntas and Theodotus are all otherwise unknown.

27. Cf. Arr. 1.21.5.

28. His name was Oxathres (Arr. 3.8.5; 3.19.2).

29. The Kara Su.

30. Cf. Arr. 3.16.7; Plut. *Alex.* 36.1 and Justin 11.14.9 say 40,000 talents. Diod. 17.66.1: 40,000 talents of unminted gold and silver; 9,000 Darics.

31. Diod. 17.66.3–5.

32. This story is not told elsewhere. Diod. 17.67.1 says the Persian captives were given instructors in the Greek language.

33. The Eulaeus River (modern Karun). Diod. 17.67.1 mistakenly calls it the Tigris.

34. The Persian Gulf is normally called by Curtius and the ancients in general the Red Sea (cf. 5.1.16).

35. Madates; he was a cousin of Darius (Diod. 17.67.4 and 5.3.12 below).

36. For the Uxian campaign see Fuller, *Generalship*, 227–8.

37. Apparently a brother of Harpalus, the Treasurer (see Berve, no. 741). He reappears at the Hydaspes in India (8.14.15).

38. The *testudo* (tortoise) is a Roman formation, used anachronistically by Curtius. Cf. Tarn, *Alexander the Great*, 2. 96, with n. 3.

39. Arr. 5.19.6 wrongly says that the Uxians were responsible for stealing Alexander's horse Bucephalas. But see 6.5.18ff.

40. Ariobarzanes was the satrap of Persia. Bosworth, *Arrian*, 325, correctly distinguishes him from the son of Artabazus (*contra* Berve, no. 115). Arr. 3.18.2 exaggerates the Persian numbers, giving 40,000 infantry and 700 horse; Diod. 17.68.1 adds 300 horsemen to Curtius' 25,000 infantry. For this campaign see Fuller, *Generalship*, 228–34; W. Heckel, 'Alexander at the Persian Gates', *Athenaeum*, 58 (1980), 168–74.

41. At Mt Climax the sea had receded to allow Alexander's army to pass.

42. Another allusion to the Roman *testudo* (see n. 38 above).

43. Cf. Polyaenus 4.3.27; Diod. 17.68.4 wrongly 300 stades.

44. Cf. Arr. 3.18.4, who does not mention the bilingual prisoner.

45. The modern Pulvar.

46. Diod. 17.68.5; Plut. *Alex.* 37.1–2; Polyaenus 4.3.27.

47. Polyaenus (4.3.27) says that Philotas and Hephaestion were left in charge of the camp.

48. Apparently Curtius' own invention; Ariobarzanes' position was circumvented in a single night.

49. According to Arrian (3.18.6), Philotas, Coenus and Amyntas were sent in the direction of Persepolis to bridge the Araxes River.

50. The *ile basilike*, the cavalry bodyguard commanded by Black Clitus.

51. Curtius contradicts himself here. By his own description it is now two days since the initial assault on the 'Gates'. Polyaenus and Arrian agree that Alexander dislodged Ariobarzanes on the morning after the first attempt.

52. Arr. 3.18.9 says that Ariobarzanes escaped 'to the hills', and he says nothing further about him. Berve (*Alexanderreich*, 2. 60–61, no. 115) thinks he is the son of Artabazus (cf. Arr. 3.23.7, for his surrender to Alexander) and that he remained alive but received no further office, unusual treatment for the son of a man greatly honoured by Alexander. Bosworth, *Arrian*, 325, accepts Curtius' version that he fled to the plain where he was killed.

53. Diod. 17.69.1. Arrian (3.18.10–12), who gives a very brief account of the fall of Persepolis, does not mention him.

54. Arr. 3.18.10 says that the bridge was already complete when Alexander arrived.

55. Diod. 17.69.3 and Justin 11.14.11 give their number as 800; Plutarch and Arrian do not mention them. The story is probably fictitious and meant to remind the reader of the past atrocities of the Persians. After all, Alexander has come as *ultor Graeciae*, 'the avenger of Greece' (5.5.8).

56. Diod. 17.69.8: 3,000 drachmae; five robes for the men, five for the women; two yoke of oxen; 50 sheep; 50 *medimnoi* of grain; and exemption from taxes.

57. Darius in 490 B.C.; Xerxes in 480–479.

58. Cf. Diod. 17.70.1–3, and Curtius' description of the treasures at Damascus (3.13.10–11).

59. The same figure is given by Diod. 17.71.2.

60. Cf. Arr. 3.18.10.

61. It was Alexander's policy to leave Persian officials in the cities but to surround them with a garrison under Macedonian command (cf. Mazaeus and Agathon at Babylon, 5.1.43–4; Abulites and Archelaus (and Xenophilus) at Susa, 5.2.16–17).

62. This refers to the setting of the Pleiades, about April 330 B.C.

63. In old Macedonia women did not attend drinking parties (Herodotus. 5.18ff.).

64. She was later (and perhaps already in 331/330) the mistress of Ptolemy, to whom she bore three children (Athenaeus 13.576 d-e). Tarn went to some trouble to disprove that she was ever Alexander's lover (*Alexander the Great*, 2. 324). Her story was told by Cleitarchus (F.Gr.Hist., 137 F11), who depicted the burning of Persepolis as part of a drunken *komos*, though she did not (apparently) feature in Ptolemy's own history (cf. Arrian's very brief version, 3.18.11–12).

65. For Persepolis and the Parthians see the Introduction, pp. 2, 11.

66. Alexander's reasons for burning the palace have been the subject of much scholarly debate. Arr. 3.18.11 claims that Parmenion urged Alexander not to destroy his own property and to consider the effect of the burning on the Asiatics, but that Alexander rejected his advice and exacted vengeance for the Persian sack of Athens in 480 B.C. Even if Alexander *did* destroy the palace as an act of policy, he may nevertheless have regretted the action later. He was at that time caught between his roles as avenger of the Greeks and Great King of the Persian empire. As it was, he did not enhance his image in the eyes of the Persians and he encouraged his troops to think that they would soon be turning back (cf. 6.2.15–4.1). See Olmstead, 519ff.; M. Wheeler, *Flames over Persepolis* (London, 1968).

67. Berve (*Alexanderreich*, 2. 429) makes the attractive suggestion that Curtius has confused him with the Socrates who was left behind in Cilicia (4.5.9).

68. Ecbatana is Hamadan; the Parthians wintered at Ctesiphon.

69. Arr. 3.19.5 says that Darius fled with 3,000 cavalry, 6,000 infantry and 7,000 talents of treasure from Media.

70. The women and the baggage had been sent ahead to the Caspian Gates (Arr. 3.19.2).

71. Mazaeus surrendered Babylon (5.1.17); Mithrenes handed Sardis over to Alexander (cf. 3.12.6).

72. Between 513 and 480, Macedonia was a vassal state of Persia under Kings Darius and Xerxes. Persian fleets were far from successful. One fleet was destroyed rounding Mt Athos (492 B.C.); the fleet that sailed to Marathon won only modest victories (490); and the most famous of Persian fleets suffered a major disaster at Salamis in 480 B.C.

73. This was apparently mentioned in one of the lost books (cf. 6.5.2). Artabazus had sought refuge with Philip in 352 B.C. (Diod. 16.52.3).

74. The conspirators included also Barzaentes (Arr. 3.21.1; cf. Diod. 17.74.1, where the names have been somewhat corrupted). For his fate see 8.13.3–4 and Arr. 3.25.8.

75. Patron, a Phocian; he and Glaucus the Aetolian commanded the Greek mercenaries (Arr. 3.16.2).

76. Diod. 17.73.2 gives the same number of Persians; Arr. 3.16.2 says there were only 2,000 Greek mercenaries.

77. Bardon's punctuation; Rolfe and Müller place a strong stop after *agebant*, and a comma only after *posset*. One would then translate: 'To prevent his being pointed out to the more inquisitive soldiers on the march, guards followed at a distance.'

78. Arr. 3.19.4–5 says the news was brought by Bisthanes, son of the former king Ochus.

79. According to Arrian (3.21.1), Bagistanes, accompanied by Mazaeus' son, reported the actual arrest of Darius.

80. Nothing else is known of Melon. But cf. note 85 below.

81. *Dimachae*: they fought both on foot and on horseback (Hesychius 1, p. 997). According to Pollux, *Onomasticon* 1.10, they were more lightly armed than infantrymen, more heavily armed than cavalrymen – and they were Alexander's innovation. Arr. 3.21.7 says there were 500 of them.

82. Orsilos is otherwise unknown. Hedicke emended the text to Orsines (cf. 4.12.8), which may be correct, explaining how he came into Alexander's entourage. But there is no compelling reason to reject the ms. reading. Mithracenes likewise is known only to Curtius.

83. Arr. 3.21.1 calls him Antibelus, but this may be a corruption of Artibolus, who was already with Mazaeus in Babylon. Brochubelus may be the correct form (cf. Bosworth, *Arrian*, 341).

84. According to Arrian (3.21.7), Alexander dismounted some 500 cavalrymen and replaced them with his best infantrymen, but this does not mean he took *only* 500 men (*pace* Hamilton, *Plutarch, Alexander*, 113). Plut. *Alex.* 43.1 says only 60 had kept up with Alexander when Darius' body was found.

85. The text breaks off at this point, and Curtius' account must be reconstructed from other sources. Diodorus (17.73.3–4) reports only that Alexander found Darius already dead and gave him a royal burial, adding that some writers claimed that Alexander found him still breathing and was urged to avenge his death. Curtius' narrative probably resembled closely the versions of Plutarch (*Alex.* 43.3–7) and Justin, which reads as follows: 'Then, after Alexander had covered several miles without finding any trace of Darius, the horses were given a chance to regain their wind. Approaching a nearby spring, one of his men [Polystratus, Plut. *Alex.* 43.3] found Darius in the wagon. The latter had been pierced by many wounds but was still alive. A captive was brought up and Darius recognized from his speech that he was a countryman of his. That at least gave him some consolation in his present misfortune, said Darius, since he would

be speaking to someone who would understand him and not uttering his final words in vain. He told the man to take the message to Alexander that, though he had performed no favours for the king, he now died indebted to him for the greatest services, since in the case of his mother and children he had found Alexander's spirit to be that of a king, not an enemy, and that he, Darius, had been more fortunate in the enemy fate had allotted him than in his relatives and kinsmen. For, he said, his wife and children had been granted their lives by that enemy, whereas he had been deprived of his by his kinsmen – to whom he gave both life and dominion. For this these would now gain the thanks Alexander himself as victor would decide to give them. As for Alexander, Darius as he died gave him the only thanks he could: his prayers to the gods above and below, and to the deities who protect kings, that he achieve rule over all the world, of which he was conqueror. On his own behalf he asked permission for a burial that was appropriate rather than stately. As far as revenge was concerned, the reason for exacting it was not now Darius but the precedent and the common cause of all kings – and to neglect this would be disgraceful as well as dangerous, for both justice and expediency were at stake. To which end he gave him his right hand, as the supreme guarantee of kingly trust which he [i.e. Polystratus] was to take to Alexander. He then stretched out his hand and died. The events were reported to Alexander who, seeing the corpse of Darius, shed tears over a death so unworthy of a man in such a position of eminence. He ordered the body buried in a royal manner and his remains to be taken to the tombs of his ancestors.' Thus Justin 11.15.5–15. Curtius' use of Polystratus makes it clear that he (and Cleitarchus, the source followed also by Justin and Plutarch) did not bring Alexander into contact with Darius while he still lived. Polystratus apparently took the helmet full of water to Darius (Plut. Alex. 43.3), who drank and spoke to him directly. Justin's captive interpreter is not necessary since Curtius has already made Darius sufficiently fluent in Greek (although Melon, the Greek interpreter, is later introduced at 5.13.7) to allow him to converse with Patron in the presence of Bessus (5.11.5ff.). Whether Curtius depicted Alexander as covering Darius' corpse with his own cloak (Plut. Alex. 43.5; Moralia 332f.) is uncertain, but not impossible just because Justin omitted it.

BOOK 6

1. The first pages of Book 6 are lost. Curtius, as promised at the beginning of Book 4, now turns to events in Europe. These are summarized by Justin (12.1.4–2.17), but Curtius probably did not discuss the campaigns of Alexander of Epirus in Italy (Justin 12.2.1–15) or the activities of Zopyrion (Justin 12.2.16–17); for Zopyrion see 10.1.44. While Alexander was occupied with Darius in Asia, the Macedonian governor of Thrace, Memnon, rebelled (Diod. 17.62.4–6). As Antipater moved to deal with the uprising, Agis III of Sparta mustered an army of at least 20,000 infantry and 2,000 cavalry (Diod. 17.62.7). Antipater made peace in Thrace and marched south with some 40,000 troops (Diod. 17.63.1). The first preserved words of Book 6 recount the bravery and death of Agis in the battle of Megalopolis (331 B.C.). For a full discussion of Agis' war see E. Badian, 'Agis III', Hermes, 95 (1967), 170–92.

2. Cf. Diod. 17.63.4.

3. Diod. 17.63.3 gives the same number of Lacedaemonian dead, but says that 3,500 of Antipater's troops fell.

4. According to Plut. Agesilaus 15, Alexander referred to the battle of Megalopolis as 'a war of mice'.

5. Probably in late summer 331.

6. Ochus (Artaxerxes III) reigned from 359 to 338, when he was poisoned by Bagoas; his successor, Arses, ruled from November 338 to June 336. He too fell victim to Bagoas, who then made Darius III king. See Diod. 17.5–6; Justin 10.1–3; Olmstead, 489–90.

7. Arr. 3.20.3 places his appiontment before the death of Darius.

8. For Oxathres see 3.11.8; Diod. 17.34. I and *Metz Epitome* 2. Diod. 17.34.1 says he became one of Alexander's guards (*doryphoros*); cf. 7.5.40. See Berve, *Alexanderreich* 2.292, with n.1.

9. Bardon and other editors have reversed the order of sections 10 and 11.

10. The Borysthenes is the Dnieper; the Tanais is generally the Don, although it is often confused with the Iaxartes.

11. Cf. Diod. 17.75.1.

12. This episode, which took place about mid-July 330 (cf. Brunt, *Arrian*, vol. 1, 497), is significantly omitted by Arrian (3.22–3), who says nothing whatsoever about Alexander at Hecatompylus. With the death of Darius, Alexander's troops felt that the campaign had come to a fitting end.

13. Curtius may be using the plural loosely (cf. 5.2.20). Alexander had only one full sister, Cleopatra, who married Alexander, king of Epirus (he is alluded to at 8.1.37). He had also two living half-sisters, Cynna (or Cynnane) and Thessalonice. A third half-sister, Europa, was killed by Olympias shortly after Philip's death.

14. Cf. 5.13.18.

15. Diod. 17.5.3–6. Bagoas was the chiliarch of Ochus; he killed both Ochus and Arses by poison, but Darius forced him to drink his own medicine (17.5.6).

16. A gross understatement.

17. With Parmenion left behind in Ecbatana, Craterus (who had hitherto been his subordinate, 3.9.8; cf. 4.13.35) now comes to the fore.

18. Stiboites (Diod. 17.75.2). Arrian (4.6.6) describes the Polytimetus River in Sogdiana (cf. Curt. 7.10.2–3) in similar terms, and he names the Epardus, Areius and Etymander as having the same characteristic.

19. 6.3.12 above.

20. Cf. Diod. 17.75.3.

21. The Sea of Azov.

22. According to Diodorus (17.75.4), the villages around here were called the 'Fortunate' or 'Prosperous' villages.

23. Arvae is Ziyavet, south of Asterabad (ancient Zadracarta).

24. Autophrates (Arr. 3.23.7).

25. Arrian (3.22.1) calls him Amminapes, a Parthyaean who surrendered Egypt to Alexander along with Mazaces (cf. 4.7.4). Arrian adds that Tlepolemus was left behind to supervise his activities.

26. Cf. 5.9.1 above.

27. His old age is alluded to again at 8.1.19. Arrian (3.23.7) mentions only three sons who surrendered (Cophen, Ariobarzanes, Arsames); the names of five sons in all are known. Curtius speaks of nine sons; Diod. 16.52.4 says that Artabazus had eleven sons and ten daughters.

28. Democrates is otherwise unknown.

29. Diod. 17.76.2; cf. Arr. 3.23.8–9.

30. Bucephalas, so called because he was branded on the shoulder with the mark of the ox-head (Arr. 5.19.5), was tamed by Alexander when he was still a boy (Plut. *Alex.*

6). His abduction by the Mardi is recorded also by Diod. 17.76.5 and Plut. *Alex*. 44.3; Arr. 5.19.6 carelessly places it in the land of the Uxians. See A. R. Anderson, 'Bucephalas and his Legend', *A.J.P.*, 51 (1930), 1–21.

31. For this Bagoas (Berve, no. 195) see E. Badian, 'The Eunuch Bagoas', *C.Q.*, n.s. 8 (1958), 144–57, against the views of Tarn, *Alexander the Great*, 2. 320–23.

32. Cf. Diod. 17.77.1–3; Justin 12.3.5–7 (Thalestris or Minythyia). Plut. *Alex*. 46. 1–2 lists the primary sources who told the Amazon story, among them Onesicritus and Cleitarchus, who was probably Curtius' source. Justin 12.3.5 says the Amazons travelled for thirty-five days in order to reach Alexander. Onesicritus was reported to have read his account of the Amazon queen to king Lysimachus, who asked him: 'And where was I when all this occurred?'

33. Alexander's reason for adopting Persian dress was political rather than personal, but the practice aroused considerable resentment among the Macedonians. Cf. Diod. 17.77.4–5; Justin 12.3.8ff.; Plut. *Alex*. 45.

34. Diod. 17.77.6 says there were no fewer than the number of days in the year; cf. Plut. *Artaxerxes* 27.2 and Dicaearchus *ap*. Athen. 13. 557b, who say there were 360 of them; the same number was given earlier by Curtius (3.3.24). For Cleitarchus and things equalling the days of the year see L. Pearson, *The Lost Histories of Alexander the Great*, 221–2.

35. Nicanor had commanded the hypaspists (4.13.27, with note 85). For his death see also Arr. 3.25.4. His death left Philotas isolated in the Macedonian army, since their younger brother Hector had died in Egypt (4.8.7–9), and Parmenion had been left behind at Ecbatana.

36. Cf. Arr. 3.25.1; Arr. 3.21.10 wrongly includes Satibarzanes among Darius' murderers. Alexander had sent Anaxippus and 40 javelin-bearing horsemen to accompany Satibarzanes. He put these men to death and planned to support Bessus.

37. Artacoana (Arr. 3.25.6), Chortacana (Diod. 17.78.1); probably Herat.

38. Arr. 3.21.1, 25.8 calls Barzaentes satrap of the Zarangians (apparently Aristobulus' variant for the Drangians). For Barzaentes' capture see 8.13.4–5.

39. The Philotas affair took place at Phrada, the capital of the Drangians, which was named Prophthasia ('Anticipation') because Alexander nipped the conspiracy in the bud. It is probably to be identified with Farah.

40. Plut. *Alex*. 49.3ff. calls him Limnos; he is otherwise unknown, as is the cause of his grievance against Alexander.

41. One of the seven-man élite.

42. Apparently, one of the pages (Diod. 17.79.4).

43. A famous anecdote (Plut. *Alex*. 47.10; Diod. 17.114.2) emphasizes that Craterus was devoted to the person of the king (*philobasileus*), whereas Hephaestion was devoted to Alexander (*philalexandros*). For this rivalry among the junior commanders of Alexander see W. Heckel, 'The Conspiracy *against* Philotas', *Phoenix*, 31 (1977), 9–21.

The naming of Nicomachus in 6.8.1 seems to be confirmed by 6.11.38. Vogel was probably right to insert *frater* in front of *ad regem*, and we should thus read: 'The latter repeated the whole story which his brother had brought to the king.'

44. In fact, no real charge of conspiracy could be brought against Philotas, leading some scholars to believe that Dymnus was used by Alexander to 'frame' Philotas. See E. Badian, 'The Death of Parmenio', *T.A.P.A.*, 91 (1960), 324–38. For a thorough discussion of the affair see Bosworth, *Arrian*, 359ff.

45. This is the first mention of Perdiccas as a member of the seven-man bodyguard (Diod. 16.94.4 seems to refer to the hypaspists); Leonnatus', appointment as bodyguard is recorded by Arr. 3.5.5.

46. Plut. *Alex.* 49.8 describes those who denounced Philotas as 'having hated Philotas for a long time'.

47. A dramatic ploy of either Curtius' or Alexander's making.

48. Amyntas, son of Perdiccas III. Perdiccas fell in battle against the Illyrians in 260/359, and although Amyntas, who was still a boy, perhaps was the rightful heir, Philip II secured the throne for himself. This Amyntas married Alexander's half-sister, Cynnane, and was killed by Alexander in late 336 or early 335. (Arrian, *History of the Successors* 1.22; Arr. 1.5.4.; Justin 12.6.14.)

49. For Attalus see the Summary of Books 1 and 2.

50. 4.8.7–9; 6.6.18–19.

51. Coenus had perhaps married Attalus' widow. His condemnation of Philotas was as much an effort to exculpate himself – to dissociate himself from the party of Philotas – as to bring about his downfall. He was among the newly-weds who rejoined Alexander at Gordium (Arr. 1.24.1, 29.4), and his son, Perdiccas, is named on an inscription (*Sylloge Inscriptionum Graecarum* [3rd edn. Leipzig, 1915–24], I. 332).

52. Plut. *Alex.* 51.6 remarks that Alexander called upon his hypaspists in the Macedonian dialect (*Makedonisti*) during the Clitus episode. The normal tongue on public occasions must have been Greek.

53. Used loosely: he was Alexander's cousin (cf. 6.9.17).

54. 3.6.4.

55. For Philotas' arrogance cf. Plut. *Alex* 48.3; Themistius, *Orationes* 19.229c. Bolon's speech is probably Curtius' creation, but it summarizes charges that were actually brought against Philotas. He had been guilty of speaking out against Alexander in Egypt (Arr. 3.26.1; Plut. *Alex.* 48.4–49.2).

56. He had presumably died at Gaugamela (Arbela); for his identity see W. Heckel, 'Who was Hegelochos?', *Rh. M.*, 125 (1982), 78–87.

57. The manuscripts have the order of Archelaus and Alexander reversed. In that order, Curtius seems to be referring to Alexander I Philhellene, who ruled in the first half of the 5th century B.C. (*c.* 495–450); but we know nothing about his death or of a need to avenge it. Archelaus (413–399) was murdered by a certain Crateuas; Alexander II (369–368) was murdered by Ptolemy of Alorus, and Perdiccas fell in battle against the Illyrians in 359.

58. Alexander Lyncestes was Antipater's son-in-law and spared because he was the first to hail Alexander as king. His brothers Arrhabaeus and Heromenes were executed as accomplices of Pausanias (see 7.1.5–9).

59. Arr. 3.27.5 says that it was later, in the land of the Ariaspians, that Demetrius was deposed as bodyguard for his suspected complicity in the Philotas affair. Although Arrian does not say so, Demetrius was probably executed.

60. Curtius does not describe Philotas' death – his name was not included in Nicomachus' list! Arr. 3.26.3 says that the Macedonians shot down Philotas and his accomplices with javelins.

BOOK 7

1. Parmenion, Attalus and Amyntas (identity uncertain) had commanded the

advance force which crossed into Asia at the beginning of spring 336 (before the death of Philip II): see Justin 9.5.8; Diod. 16.91.2.

2. Diod. 17.2.5-6, 5.2.

3. For the arrest of Alexander Lyncestes (Alexander from Lyncestis in Upper Macedonia) see the Summary of Books 1 and 2.

4. The sons of Andromenes belonged to an important aristocratic family of Tymphaea (Upper Macedonia); they were related to Polyperchon, later regent of Macedon, and a fourth brother, Attalus, was a brother-in-law of Perdiccas (to whom Alexander gave his ring; see 10.5.4).

5. Cf. 5.1.40-42. The 600 horsemen were Thracians; Amyntas also brought 500 Macedonian cavalry.

6. Arrian (3.27.2-3) says that Alexander gave Amyntas himself permission to bring Polemon back to the camp.

7. Although acquitted by Alexander, Amyntas died soon afterwards while attacking a small town (Arr. 3.27.3).

8. Parmenion had sent Polydamas as a messenger to Alexander during the battle of Gaugamela (4.15.6). For his part in Parmenion's death cf. Arr. 3.26.3.

9. Coenus' brother; Sitalces and Menidas are also named by Arr. 3.26.3; cf. Curt. 10.1.1.

10. This statement is untrue, but the same argument has been developed by K. J. Beloch, *Griechische Geschichte* (2nd edn, Berlin/Leipzig, 1912-27), IV, 2, 290-306.

11. The *Ataktoi* or 'Undisciplined Squadron' (Diod. 17.80.4; Justin 12.5.4-8). Curtius alone mentions their leader Leonidas.

12. Arsakes (Berve, no. 146) replaced Satibarzanes officially, although Satibarzanes was still in active revolt against Alexander (Arr. 3.25.7). See also 8.3.17.

13. Arr. 3.27.4; Diod. 17.81.1; *Metz Epitome* 4; Strabo 15.2.10; Justin 12.5.9. The 'Benefactors'.

14. Otherwise unknown.

15. Cf. Arr. 3.28.1; for his death see 9.10.20.

16. i.e., the star Polaris.

17. Used by ancient writers to mean the Hindu Kush. They assumed that the same mountain range stretched from Cilicia to India. Cf. Arr. 3.28.5 (apparently all from Aristobulus, *F.Gr.Hist.*, 139 F23).

18. In Curtius' own terminology (6.4.18) the Caspian and Hyrcanian seas are one and the same. But apparently the names are used mistakenly for different parts of the same sea (cf. Rolfe, *Curtius*, vol. 2, 36-7).

19. The titan Prometheus was chained to the Caucasus because he would not reveal to Zeus an important prophecy, and because he stole fire from Mt Olympus.

20. Alexandria-in-the Caucasus; Arr. 3.28.4; Diod. 17.83.1. For Alexander's cities in general see Tarn, *Alexander the Great*, 2, 232-59.

21. Diod. 17.83.7 calls him Bagodaras, but Gobares may be the correct form.

22. The translator follows Bardon's text but without conviction. Something has surely dropped out of the text between *periculum* and *poculum*, e.g. *Bessus eum dicere iussit intrepidum* (Bessus told him to speak without fear), the supplement of Halm.

23. The Pontic Sea is the Black Sea; Curtius must be thinking of the Caspian.

24. Balkh. It was also called Zariaspa (cf. Arr. 4.1.5).

25. See 6.1 above.

26. The Iaxartes River is meant.

27. He is generally regarded as 'a boyhood friend' of Alexander, but Curtius' description makes it clear that he was probably one of Alexander's older advisers. For his duel with Satibarzanes see Diod. 17.83.4–6; Arr. 3.28.3. Curtius' account is reminiscent of Ariston's victory over Satropates (4.9.25).

28. *opimum decus*: see the note to 3.11.7.

29. Just over 44 miles. One stade equalled 582.5 feet.

30. According to Plutarch (Alex. 42.7), a similar episode took place during the pursuit of Darius; Plutarch's version is also found in Arrian (6.26.1–3), who places it in the Gedrosian desert. See Hamilton, *Plutarch, Alexander*, 113.

31. The Oxus (Amu-darya) formed the boundary between Bactria and Sogdiana.

32. Arr. 3.29.3–4.

33. Herodotus (6.19) says that the Persians sacked the temple at Didyma during the reign of Darius I: Curtius' story is discredited by many scholars (see especially Tarn, *Alexander the Great*, 2. 272–5). See now T. S. Brown, 'Aristodicus of Cyme and the Branchidae', *A.J.P.*, 99 (1978).

34. For the capture of Bessus see also Arr. 3.30.1–5, who gives also the versions of Ptolemy and Aristobulus (*F.Gr.Hist.*, 138 F14; 139 F24). Aristobulus' version is similar to the one given here, but Ptolemy claimed that Spitamenes and Dataphernes fled, leaving him to capture Bessus and bring him to Alexander.

35. This is not recorded elsewhere. The purpose was apparently to maim Bessus without killing him.

36. See 7.10.10, with note 60.

37. See Arr. 3.30.10–11. He says the enemy numbered 30,000, and that Alexander's troops butchered all but 8,000 of them.

38. Samarcand.

39. Arr. 4.1.1; 4.5.1.

40. Derdas was probably a relative of Alexander's treasurer, Harpalus. The Tanais here is the Iaxartes River (Syr-darya).

41. Chojend. Arr. 4.1.3.

42. They were summoned, along with other leaders of the region, to Bactra (Zariaspa), according to Arr. 4.1.5, who agrees that they may have feared treachery.

43. Something is missing from the mss. at this point; Müller accepts the supplement *ipse proficiscitur ad Craterum ... obsidentem* ('While Alexander marched to Craterus who was besieging Cyropolis ...').

44. There were seven cities in all, of which Cyropolis (Ura-Tyube) was the most important. Arrian (4.3.1–4) gives a different version of their capture; the wound to Alexander's neck is said to have come at Cyropolis (4.3.3).

45. Cf. *Metz Epitome* 13. Arr. 4.3.7 adds also Andromachus, Caranus and a Lycian named Pharnuches.

46. Arr. 4.4.2ff. For Alexander's campaign north of Iaxartes see Fuller, *Generalship*, 238–41.

47. Bardon reads *qui scis plus quam potes* ('you who know more than you can'), which makes little sense unless *potes* is regarded as an 'ideal second person' and the remark is sarcastic ('you who [claim to] know more than one can'), and this is very awkward. No emendation carrying real conviction, the translation follows Müller in obelizing the relative clause.

48. So the mss., but Vielhaber's supplement *aliis* after *alia* is attractive: 'The gods indulged different people for different ends, but they indulged *him* so he could win glory.'

49. 7.6.24. See Arr. 4.5.2–6.2
50. Berve, no. 764, s.v. Hypsides. Otherwise unknown.
51. Assyria.
52. 7.6.22 above.
53. Arr. 4.4.8 says Alexander suffered from dysentery from drinking bad water.
54. The god Dionysus or Bacchus.
55. Arr. 4.4.8 gives the Scythian casualties at 1,000 dead, including their commander Satraces, and 150 captured. No Macedonian casualties are given.
56. i.e., the Scythians beyond the Iaxartes (Tanais).
57. Cf. Arr. 4.6.3, who says that only after the Scythian campaign did Alexander learn of Spitamenes' victory.
58. Arrian does not list the Macedonian casualties in this battle, but he says (4.3.7) that Menedemus and his fellow-commanders had 2,360 troops and (4.6.2) that not more than 340 escaped from the ambush at the Polytimetus River.
59. The Zeravshan (Zarafshan); cf. Arr. 4.6.6.
60. Arr. 4.7.3; cf. 7.5.43 above. Plut. Alex. 43.6 says that Bessus was dismembered by recoiling trees (see Hamilton, Plutarch, Alexander, 114–15). It appears that Curtius (or his source) attempted to reconcile two versions, one of which has Bessus executed on the spot (7.5.40), the other sending him to Ecbatana for punishment.
61. A similar catalogue is found in Arrian (4.7.2), where Epocillus accompanies Ptolemaeus (commander of the Thracians) and Melamnidas. Nearchus is said to have come from Lycia with Asander. The insurrection of which Curtius speaks may be the activities of Arsaces of Aria and Brazanes, who opposed Phrataphernes in Parthyaea (Arr. 4.7.1; cf. 4.18.1), but they were brought to Alexander and he did not invade their territory.
62. Curtius places the capture of the Sogdian rock in 328 B.C.; Arrian (4.18.4ff.) dates the event to spring 327, which is probably correct. See also Fuller, Generalship, 243–4.
63. '[They] told Alexander to seek soldiers with wings' (Arr. 4.18.6). Cf. 7.11.24.
64. That part of India just east of the Hindu Kush, Paropanisus.
65. Cf. Arr. 4.19.1.
66. Arr. 4.19.4 says they surrendered but does not say that Alexander put them to death.

BOOK 8

1. 328 B.C. Arr. 4.16.2 mentioned five divisions; Ptolemy, son of Lagus, and Perdiccas commanded the other two. This is Hephaestion's first major independent command, aside from taking the fleet from Tyre to Gaza (4.5.10).
2. Arr. 4.16.5 gives few details and says that the men were captured in a fortress, their commander (presumably Attinas) taken prisoner.
3. 7.6.12.
4. His name was Pharasmanes (Arr. 4.15.4); Phrataphernes had surrendered to Alexander (6.4.23) and was soon to be made satrap of Hyrcania (8.3.17).
5. Cf. Arr. 4.15.2–3.
6. The location of Bazaira is uncertain; it was probably near Maracanda (Samarcand). Diodorus in his summary of Book 17 calls it Basista.
7. Cf. Seneca, de Ira 3.17.2; de Clementia 1.25.1; Pliny N.H. 8.54; Pausanias 1.9.5; Justin 15.3.7–8; Lucian, Dialogi Mortuorum 14.4 (397); Plutarch, Demetrius 27.3. Lysimachus was one of the seven bodyguards; after the king's death he became ruler of Thrace and, for a short time, king of Macedon. He died in 281 B.C.

8. Bactria was Artabazus' province (7.5.1).

9. Plut. *Alex.* 16 and 50.11; Diod. 17.20.6; Arr. 1.15.8. Alexander had not gone into battle bare-headed; his helmet had been split in two by the enemy (see p. 24 above).

10. Arr. 4.9.3 calls her Lanice, possibly an abbreviation of Hellanice.

11. Plut. *Alex.* 50.8ff. says that a certain Pranichus (or Pierio) recited a poem mocking the Macedonian officers who had recently been defeated in battle – perhaps a reference to Spitamenes' attack on Maracanda or the Polytimetus disaster or even the defeat of Attinas. Arr. 4.8.3–4 claims that Clitus was offended by the Greek flatterers who likened Alexander to the Dioscuri and Heracles, and by Alexander's adoption of oriental practices. Justin's version (12.6.1ff.) is closer to that of Curtius.

12. 338 B.C. Plut. *Alex.* 9.2–4.

13. Probably in the spring of 337.

14. It was here that Philip met Alexander's mother, Olympias (Plut. *Alex.* 2.2).

15. Euripides, *Andromache* 693: 'Alas, what evil customs prevail in Greece'. Cf. Plut. *Alex.* 51.8.

16. Philip was content to negotiate with Athens after the battle of Chaeronea, but Alexander razed Thebes in 335 (cf. Arr. 1.8.8; Plut. *Alex.* 11.11–12; Diod. 17.13–14).

17. Bactria and Sogdiana taken together.

18. Cf. 5.2.5.

19. Alexander of Epirus, Olympias' brother, who campaigned in Italy from 334 to his death in 330. Cf. Livy 9.19.10.

20. Cf. 7.1.3.

21. Arr. 4.8.1–2; Diodorus in the summary of Book 17 mentions Alexander's 'sin against Dionysus'.

22. Arr. 4.9.4.

23. Amyntas, son of Nicolaus; he probably ruled until the uprising of the Greeks under Athenodorus in 326/5 (9.7.1ff.).

24. Near Bokhara, west of Samarcand.

25. The rock is located in Pareitacene near the Wakhsh River (a tributary of the Oxus); see Engels, *Logistics*, 106. Arr. 4.21 calls him Chorienes, but this may be his title rather than his name; cf. Brunt, *Arrian*, vol. 1, 407, n.1.

26. According to Arrian (4.21.6), 'Oxyartes', the father of Roxane, who was sent at Chorienes' request.

27. Justin 15.3.12.

28. See particularly 7.4.32–40. His death is not recorded elsewhere.

29. This story is also told in the *Metz Epitome* (20–23), but Arrian (4.17.7) says the Massagetae murdered Spitamenes and brought his head to Alexander.

30. *Metz Epitome* 23 adds Catanes; but he fell in battle against the troops of Craterus (8.5.2; cf. Arr. 4.22.2).

31. Autophradates (Arr. 4.18.2; the mss. also have Phradates, but cf. 3.24.3 for Autophradates).

32. Atropates became satrap of Media (Arr. 4.18.3).

33. Arr. 4.18.3 calls him Stamenes.

34. Gazabes (*Metz Epitome* 28); the location is uncertain.

35. Val. Max. 5.1 ext. 1; Frontinus, *Stratagemata* 4.6.3.

36. Briseis. The example of Achilles and Briseis occurs frequently in ancient poetry and found its way into rhetoric. See R. G. M. Nisbet and Margaret Hubbard, *A Commentary on Horace Odes Book 2* (Oxford, 1978), 67–8.

37. According to Arr. 4.18.4, Oxyartes' wife and daughters were captured at the Sogdian Rock, whereafter Oxyartes himself surrendered (4.20.4). For the marriage see Arr. 4.19.5; Plut. *Alex.* 47.7; *Metz Epitome* 28–31; Strabo 11.11.4 (confused); cf. Hamilton, *Plutarch, Alexander*, 129–30.

38. See M. Renard/J. Servais, 'À propos du mariage d'Alexandre et de Roxane', *L'Antiquité Classique*, 24 (1955), 29–50.

39. This is probably false, though Alexander's comrades will have been less likely to criticize him after the Clitus affair. But cf. Meleager at 8.12.17–18.

40. Arr. 4.22.1–2. He was accompanied by Attalus and Alcetas (cf. Plut. *Alex.* 55.6) and Polyperchon.

41. Polyperchon probably broke away from the main force under Craterus. The exact location of Bubacene is unknown. Cf. Hamilton, *Plutarch, Alexander*, 155.

42. It may be at this time that the hypaspists assumed the name *Argyraspids*; cf. Justin 12.7.5.

43. The ways in which subjects performed *proskynesis* seem to have ranged from prostration to simply blowing a kiss, depending on the subject's status in relation to the king. See Hamilton, *Plutarch, Alexander*, 150–52 for a discussion and earlier literature; cf. also E. Badian (and his commentators), *The Deification of Alexander the Great*, Center for Hermeneutical Studies, Colloquy 21 (Berkeley, 1976).

44. Choerilus of Iasus wrote an epic poem in which Alexander appeared as Achilles. This evoked the remark: 'I would rather be Thersites in Homer's *Iliad* than Achilles in yours.' The translator reads *pessimorum*, despite Bardon's defence of *piisimorum* as found in the mss. Cf. Porphyrio on Horace, *Ars Poetica* 357, who comments *poeta pessimus fuit Choerilus* (= *F.Gr.Hist.*, 153 F10a).

45. According to Arr. 4.12.5 and Plut. 54.4–6 (from Chares of Mytilene, *F.Gr.Hist.*, 125 F14a), Callisthenes refused to do *proskynesis* in Alexander's presence.

46. This is an error for Leonnatus (Arr. 4.12.2); Polyperchon, on Curtius' own testimony, was absent (8.5.2). See W. Heckel, *A.J.P.*, 99 (1978), 459–61.

47. 5.1.42; Arr. 4.13.1.

48. Cf. Livy 45.6.

49. Asclepiodorus was the father of Antipater (Arr. 4.13.4); Curtius has apparently mistranslated the Greek *Antipatros Asklepiodorou*. Arr. 4.13.3–4 names the following conspirators: Hermolaus, Sostratus, Epimenes, Antipater, Anticles, and Philotas. Curtius' 'Nicostratus' may be a corruption of 'Sostratus', and Elaptonius has been emended by Hedicke to *et Aphthonius*.

50. Thus the *Oxford Latin Dictionary* interprets *attonitae mentis*, but perhaps it means only 'divinely inspired'. Arrian (4.13.5–6) says that she was 'possessed by the god' when she met Alexander, though he does add that she was originally 'a figure of fun for both Alexander and his friends'.

51. Arrian (4.13.7) mentions only Ptolemy, son of Lagus.

52. Aristobulus and Ptolemy (*F.Gr.Hist.*, 139 F31; 138 F16) both wrote that Callisthenes had urged Hermolaus to plot against the king (although this is rejected by Arr. 4.14.1); but Plut. *Alex.* 55.6 mentions a letter from Alexander to Craterus, Attalus and Alcetas in which he said that the pages confessed under torture but did not implicate anyone outside their number. In a letter to Antipater the regent, however, Alexander included Callisthenes among the conspirators (Plut. *Alex.* 55.7). It is clear that Callisthenes' own unpopularity with Alexander and some of his powerful friends, and his association with Hermolaus, led to his downfall.

For a good discussion see T. S. Brown, 'Callisthenes and Alexander', *A.J.P.*, 70 (1949), 225–48.

53. Apparently Sopolis, son of Hermodorus, commander of a squadron of the Companion Cavalry (Arr. 3.11.8).

54. For *latro* in this sense, cf. 8.2.9.

55. 7.1.5–9.

56. Perhaps a reference to Callisthenes' praise of the tyrannicides, Harmodius and Aristogiton, who assassinated Hipparchus in 514 B.C.

57. There are several versions of his death: he was tortured and crucified (Ptolemy, *F.Gr.Hist.*, 138 F17); he was kept in fetters and died of illness (Aristobulus, 139 F33); he died of obesity and a disease of lice (Chares, 125 F15). Justin 15.3.3ff. says that Alexander caged him like a beast and that Lysimachus out of pity gave him poison.

58. Arrian 4.9.7 says Alexander was consoled by Anaxarchus in this instance.

59. i.e., the Indian Ocean.

60. The Chenab.

61. Hedicke added *Iomanen*, for geographical sense. *Acesines eum auget. Ganges decursurum Iomanen intercipit* ... 'Its volume is augmented by the Acesines. The Ganges meets the Iomanes before it reaches the sea ...' See McCrindle, 184, n.1.

62. Since *erythros* is the Greek word for 'red'.

63. Oddly, Curtius nowhere records the famous self-immolation of the Indian philosopher Calanus, found in the other Alexander historians.

64. Arr. 4.22.7; 4.30.9.

65. In Greek *méros* means 'thigh'.

66. Justin 12.7.7–8; Arr. 5.2.7; for the revel in Carmania see 9.10.24ff.

67. The Choaspes is the Kunar; for Coenus at Beira or Bazira (Bir-kot) see Arr. 4.27.5ff. For Mazaga (Massaga) cf. *Metz Epitome* 39–45; Arr. 4.26.1ff.; Diod. 17.84 and Plut. *Alex.* 59.6–7 relate the treacherous slaughter of Indian mercenaries who had been allowed to leave the city under truce. Arr. 4.27.3–4 says these mercenaries had agreed to serve under Alexander but, when he learned that they planned to desert, he surrounded them and massacred them.

68. Justin 12.7.10 is less subtle: he claims the child *was* Alexander's. *Metz Epitome* 45 records only that Alexander was impressed by the beauty of Cleophis and remained some days in her town. O. Seel, *Eine römische Weltgeschichte* 181–2, following the earlier suggestion of A. V. Gutschmid, *Rh.M* 37 (1882), 553–4, believes that Cleophis was not part of the original Alexander tradition but inserted in Roman times (either by Trogus or Timagenes, both familiar to Curtius) as an allusion to Cleopatra VII of Egypt.

69. The mss. have 'Nora'; Arr. 4.27.5 calls it Ora (Udegram) and assigns command of the expedition to Attalus, Alcetas and Demetrius the hipparch.

70. Normally called Aornus (Pir-sar). Cf. Arr. 4.28.1–30.4; Diod. 17.85.1–86.1; Justin 12.7.12–13; *Metz Epitome* 46–7. See also Fuller, *Generalship*, 248ff., with map and photographs.

71. Charus and Alexander recall Nisus and Euryalus: see the Introduction, p. 8.

72. Sisicottus, Arr. 4.30.4.

73. Diod. 17.86.2 calls him Aphrices; he also had fifteen elephants.

74. Omphis is the proper rendering of the Sanskrit Ambhi (see McCrindle, 413). Diod. 17.86.4ff. and *Metz Epitome* 49–52 have 'Mophis'.

75. Abisares was king of Kashmir. Diodorus wrongly calls him Embisarus (17.87.2) and Sasibasares (17.90.4). Porus ruled the region between the Hydaspes (Jhelum) and the Acesines (Chenab) Rivers.

76. Cf. Plut. *Alex.* 59.5.

77. See 6.6.36.

78. Cf. 8.9.28. Porus' army: 4,000 cavalry, 30,000 infantry, 300 chariots, 200 elephants (Arr. 5.15.4); 50,000 infantry, 3,000 cavalry, 1,000 chariots, 130 elephants (Diod. 17.87.2); 20,000 infantry, 2,000 cavalry (Plut. *Alex.* 62.2).

79. Plut. *Alex.* 60.12 gives Porus' height as '4 cubits and a span'. Arr. 5.19.1 and Diod. 17.88.4 say he was 'more than 5 cubits'. By Tarn's calculations (*Alexander the Great*, 2. 170), if the Attic cubit (18¼ inches) is used, Porus' height ranges from 6 feet 8½ inches to over 7½ feet. But, using the shorter Macedonian cubit (13–14 inches), he measures Porus' height as about 6 feet. See Hamilton, *Plutarch, Alexander*, 166, with additional references to primary sources.

80. Actually, Alexander wanted the island to hide his *crossing* from the enemy's view (cf. Arr. 5.11.1). The location of Alexander's crossing of the Hydaspes has been much debated. Sir Aurel Stein (*Geographical Journal*, 80 (1932), 31–46) argued that the island was Admana, which was about a mile and a half wide and heavily wooded, and that Alexander crossed from Jalalpur; his main camp was at Haranpur, seventeen and a half miles downstream. For a full discussion of this and earlier views see Fuller, *Generalship*, 180ff.

81. This is an error. Ptolemy accompanied Alexander (8.14.15; cf. Arr. 5.13.1). Craterus commanded the force directly opposite Porus (Arr. 6.11.3; *Metz Epitome* 59–60). The battle took place in May, 326 B.C. (Arr. 5.19.3; though Arr. 5.9.4 dates it wrongly to the summer solstice). For the ancient accounts see Arr. 5.8.4–19.3; Diod. 17.87–9; Plut. *Alex.* 60–62; Justin 12.8.1–7; *Metz Epitome* 55–61. For the strategy see Fuller, *Generalship*, 185–99.

82. Cf. *Metz Epitome* 58. Not the son of Andromenes, who was stationed with Meleager and Gorgias half-way between the main camp and the crossing-point.

83. Ptolemy (*F.Gr.Hist.*, 138 F20 = Arr. 5.14.6) said that Porus' *son* commanded 2,000 cavalry and 120 chariots; Plut. *Alex.* 60.8 gives 1,000 cavalry and 60 chariots; according to Arr. 5.18.2, Spitaces was an Indian *nomarch* (local ruler) and apparently no relation to Porus. A different account is given by Polyaenus 4.3.2.1.

84. Plut. *Alex.* 60.13.

85. According to Plutarch (*Alex.* 60.14), Porus asked to be treated 'like a king'.

86. The Latin is ambiguous at this point. *Contra spem omnium* could be taken with what follows: e.g. 'and when he recovered Alexander surprised everyone by making him one of his friends'. But this translation is unlikely to reflect Curtius' meaning. According to Diod. 17.88.7 the rumour had spread that Porus was already dead.

BOOK 9

1. Helius, the sun, had given him the East to conquer (Diod. 17.89.3).

2. Müller, following Castiglioni, reads *Graecis sermonis eius ignaris; Indi aliud* ... ('by the Greeks who were ignorant of that language; the Indians use a different word ...').

3. Nicaea and Bucephala (9.3.23).

4. For Abisares' earlier embassy see 8.13.1; cf. Arr. 5.20.5.

5. This is the banyan tree, described also by Diodorus (17.90.5). Nearchus (Arrian, *Indica* 11.7) claimed that 10,000 men could find shade under a single tree, but Strabo (15.1.21) says that according to Onesicritus (*F.Gr.Hist.*, 134 F22) it could shade 400 horsemen; Aristobulus (139 F36) said only 50.

6. The Hydraotis (Arr. 5.21.4), modern Ravi. Alexander was at that time in pursuit

of 'Bad Porus', the cousin (or nephew) of the one defeated at the Hydaspes (Arr. 5.21.2–3; Diod. 17.91.1).

7. Sangala. Probably Lahore or Amritsar. For the battle there see Arr. 5.22.4ff., and Fuller, *Generalship*, 255–8.

8. Cf. Arr. 5.24.6. This is the first mention of Eumenes of Cardia, who was a secretary of both Philip II and Alexander. He played an important role in the age of the Successors, as a supporter of Perdiccas and opponent of Antigonus the One-Eyed, until his death in 316 B.C.

9. Sophites (or Sophytes) appears to be the correct form of his name (see McCrindle, 411); Diodorus 17.91.4–92.3 and Arrian 6.2.2 have Sopeithes. *Metz Epitome* 66–7 appears to have had 'Sophes'.

10. *eadem aestimatur in liberis.* Perhaps 'that is the characteristic admired in children'.

11. Normally the 'Hyphasis'. It is the modern Beas.

12. Arrian (5.20.8) describes the Acesines in similar terms; Diodorus (17.93.1) says the Hyphasis was 7 stades wide, 6 fathoms deep and had a violent current.

13. The Ganges was said to have been 30 stades wide (*Metz Epitome* 68; Diod. 2.37.2; at 17.93.2 Diodorus has '32 stades').

14. Diod. 17.93.2 and *Metz Epitome* 68 call the king of the Gangaridae Xandrames. Diodorus gives his forces as 20,000 cavalry, 200,000 infantry, 2,000 chariots and 4,000 elephants; Plut. *Alex.* 62.3 has 80,000 cavalry, 200,000 infantry, 8,000 chariots and 6,000 elephants.

15. Cf. Diod. 17.93.3. His low birth is alluded to by Plut. *Alex.* 62.9.

16. For the mutiny at the Hyphasis see also Arr. 5.25.1ff. and Justin 12.8.10–17; Diodorus (17.93.3–94.5) and Plut. *Alex.* 62 treat it very briefly.

17. Cf. Arr. 5.27.1ff.

18. With Müller, the translator removes the strong stop after *expeditionis suae.*

19. Diod. 17.95.1 says the altars were 50 cubits high; cf. Arr. 5.29.1; *Metz Epitome* 69.

20. Diodorus (17.95.3), Justin (12.9.1) and the *Metz Epitome* (70) all agree with Curtius that Alexander returned to the Acesines, but this is perhaps the error of their common source. The Hydaspes flowed into the Acesines and thereafter took its name. Arrian (6.2.1) places Coenus' death at the Hydaspes. E. Badian, *J.H.S.*, 81 (1961), 22, is suspicious of Coenus' fatal illness, coming so soon after his opposition to Alexander at the Hyphasis.

21. Probably 'Menon'.

22. Diod. 17.95.4: more than 30,000 infantry and just under 6,000 cavalry.

23. Diod. 17.95.5 breaks this figure down into 200 galleys and 800 transports. *Metz Epitome* 70 has 800 biremes and 300 transports. Ptolemy (*F.Gr.Hist.*, 138 F24 = Arr. 6.2.4) reported that there were nearly 2,000 ships in all; cf. Nearchus (Arrian, *Indica* 19.7), who gave the number 1,800. The most influential men of Alexander's entourage provided the funds for this by becoming *trierarchs* in the Attic sense. Many scholars have misunderstood this and assumed that these men (named by Arrian, *Indica* 18.3–8) were 'trireme-commanders'. But see Berve, *Das Alexanderreich*, 1.165; Wilcken, *Alexander the Great*, 188.

24. Cf. 9.1.6; Diod. 17.95.5. Bucephala was on the west bank of the Hydaspes, Nicaea on the east. Most writers reported that Bucephalas died of wounds in the battle at the Hydaspes (Arr. 5.14.4; Plut. *Alex.* 61.1; Diod. 17.95.5; Justin 12.8.4; *Metz Epitome* 62), but according to Onesicritus (*F.Gr.Hist.*, 134 F20 = Plut. *Alex.* 61.1) the horse died of old age *after* the battle.

25. Diod. 17.96.1; Justin 12.9.2; Strabo 15.1.8.

26. The Agalasseis (Diod. 17.96.3); Justin 12.9.2 calls them 'Accensones' or 'Agesines'. For the Sibi and the Agalasseis see McCrindle, 366-7.

27. According to Diodorus (17.96.4-5) Alexander himself, angered by the resistance of the Indians and the Macedonian losses, set fire to the city and burned its inhabitants.

28. In Diodorus' version (17.97.2-3) Alexander does jump into the river and swim to safety, battling the river as Achilles had fought with the Scamander (*Iliad* 21.228ff.).

29. Diodorus and Strabo (15.1.8) also have Sudracae, but Arrian (6.4.3) calls them the Oxydracae. According to Strabo the Sudracae claimed to be descendants of Dionysus.

30. 80,000 infantry, 10,000 cavalry, 700 chariots (Diod. 17.98.1); 80,000 infantry, 60,000 cavalry (Justin 12.9.3).

31. Arr. 6.8.4ff. calls it a town of the Mallians; cf. Plut. *Alex.* 63.3; Strabo 15.1.33.

32. He carried the sacred shield from the temple of Athena at Illium (Arr. 6.9.3).

33. Limnaeus, Plut. *Alex.* 63.5; *Moralia* 344d.

34. Only Curtius mentions Aristonus, who like Leonnatus was one of Alexander's bodyguards. Arr. 6.10.1 names a certain Abreas who was killed in the engagement.

35. See the Introduction, p. 5, for the historians Clitarchus and Timagenes. Plutarch, *Moralia* 344d includes Ptolemy among Alexander's protectors. Arr. 6.11.8 also points out that Ptolemy (by his own admission) was elsewhere, but that some writers derived Ptolemy's title, *Soter* ('Saviour'), from his alleged role in this incident. It was much later, when Ptolemy aided the Rhodians against Demetrius Poliorcetes, that he earned the title *Soter*. This is not mentioned in Curtius or the other vulgate writers – apparently because Cleitarchus wrote before Ptolemy took the title *Soter*. Ptolemy ruled Egypt from 323 to 283 B.C.; he assumed the title of king in late 305.

36. Arr. 6.11.1 calls him Critodemus, but Critobulus may be the correct form. The latter was a physician of Philip II, renowned for his surgical skill (Pliny, *N.H.* 7.37), and a 'Critobulus, son of Plato, from Cos' is attested as one of the *trierarchs* at the Hydaspes in 326 (Arrian, *Indica*, 18.7). See W. Heckel, *Mnemosyne*, 34 (1981), 396ff.

37. Nearchus (*F.Gr.Hist.*, 133 F2 = Arr. 6.13.4) claimed that Alexander was angry with the friends who criticized his recklessness.

38. It was now very late in 326. Alexander was in the eleventh year of his reign, and he was thirty years old.

39. For Semiramis, the Assyrian queen Sammuramat, see the note to 5.1.24.

40. Philip II was murdered as he walked to the theatre in Aegae in 336 B.C. His killer was Pausanias of Orestis, one of his bodyguard (cf. 7.1.6).

41. Diodorus (17.99.5) says that the Greeks had heard of Alexander's wounding in the Mallian town and supposed that he was dead.

42. It appears that 3,000 men under Biton (cf. Diod. 17.99.6) returned to Greece. The remainder (some 23,000) were massacred by Peithon on Perdiccas' orders in 323 B.C. (Diod. 17.99.6; 18.7.1-9).

43. That is, the Mallians and the Sudracae.

44. Aristobulus portrayed him as one of Alexander's flatterers (Athenaeus 6. 251a = *F.Gr.Hist.*, 139 F47; cf. Plutarch, *Moralia* 341b). For this episode see also Diod. 17.100-101; Aelian, *Varia Historia* 10.22.

45. Diod. 17.100.2 has Coragus; the correct form is probably Corrhagus (Hoffmann, *Die Makedonen*, 144. n.37; Berve, 2.146).

46. Diod. 17.100.5 compared it to a battle of gods, with the Macedonian as Ares (Mars) and Dioxippus as Hercules.

47. Diod. 17.102.1 calls them Sambastae.

48. The Sodrae and Massani (Diod. 17.102.4). Perhaps these are the Xathrians and Ossadians of Arr. 6.15.1, in which case the Sabarcae may be the Abastanes. But it is difficult to relate Diodorus and Curtius to Arrian at this point.

49. The Kingdom of Musicanus (Diod. 17.102.5; Arr. 6.15.5). Eggermont (5–9) locates Musicanus' capital at Alor.

50. Tyriespis (Arr. 4.22.5; 6.15.3).

51. Oxyartes was the father of Alexander's wife Roxane. If we may believe the *Metz Epitome* (70), she had borne Alexander a son who died (or was stillborn) just before the descent of the Indus river-system began.

52. Oxicanus (Arr. 6.16.1; cf. Berve no. 589, s.v. Oxycanus).

53. Cf. Diod. 17.102.6 and Arr. 6.16.3; Plut. *Alex.* 64.1 (Sabbas); Strabo 15.1.33 (Sabus); Justin 12.12.2 (Ambus; Orosius 3.19.11, Ambira). Eggermont (18–21) argues that he is identical with Samaxus (see 8.13.4 above; Hedicke's Damaraxus is nonsense).

54. *F.Gr.Hist.*, 137 F25.

55. Harmatelia, a town of the Brahmins (Diod. 17.103).

56. His father was Lagus, but his mother Arsinoe was believed to have belonged to the Macedonian royal family. It is not inconceivable that Ptolemy himself encouraged the rumour that he was a bastard son of Philip of Macedon.

57. For a full discussion see Eggermont, 107ff.

58. The other sources call it Pattala or Patala. Cf. Arr. 6.17.5.

59. For what follows cf. Arr. 6.18.3–19.5.

60. Nearchus was the admiral, Onesicritus the chief helmsman (Plut. *Alex.* 66.4); but Onesicritus in his history claimed that he had been the admiral, a point refuted by Nearchus (Arr. 6.2.3; cf. 6.19.5; *Indica* 20.3–8; Diod. 17.104.3). See also T. S. Brown, *Onesicritus* (Berkeley and Los Angeles, 1949) and E. Badian, 'Nearchus the Cretan', *Y.C.S.*, 24 (1975), 147–70.

61. Cf. Arr. 6.12.4 for the Arabites (or Arabitae); Diodorus 17.104.4 has 'Abrites', Strabo (15.2.1) 'Arbies'. The Horitae are normally the Oreitae. See J. R. Hamilton, 'Alexander among the Oreitae', *Historia*, 21 (1972), 603–8.

62. The *Ichthyphagi* or 'Fish-eaters': cf. Strabo 15.2.1; Arr. 6.23.3; *Indica* 29.9ff.; Diod. 17.105.3–5.

63. Diod. 17.105.7. Alexander was said to have chosen the route through the Cedrosia in emulation of Semiramis and Cyrus the Great, both of whom had suffered heavy losses returning from India (Strabo 15.1.5; Arr. 6.24.3).

64. For Leonnatus' victory see Arr. 7.5.5; Arrian, *Indica* 23.5 records that 6,000 of the Oreitae were killed, while Leonnatus lost fifteen cavalrymen, a few of his infantry. Diod. 17.105.8 says that the Oreitae attacked Leonnatus' division, inflicted heavy losses and escaped.

65. Arr. 6.27.3 names only Ordanes; whether he is identical with Curtius' Ozines cannot be determined.

66. Arr. 6.27.1–2 gives different information: Sibyrtius had been satrap of Carmania but he now ruled Cedrosia and Arachosia; Tlepolemus became satrap of Carmania. Menon had been satrap of Arachosia (7.3.5 above). Astaspes was probably the satrap of Carmania under Darius III (Berve, 2.89).

67. Cf. 8.10.18 above.

BOOK 10

1. See 7.2.19ff., where only Cleander is named.

2. Similar charges were brought against Harpalus (Diod. 17.108.4). For the great purge that followed Alexander's return from India see E. Badian, 'Harpalus', *J.H.S.*, 81 (1961), 16ff., and F. Schachermeyr, *Alexander der Grosse* (Vienna, 1973), 474ff.

3. Ozines and Zariaspes (9.10.19).

4. They reached the coastal town of Salmus (Diod. 17.106.4), but Nearchus himself (Arrian, *Indica* 33) claimed that they anchored at the mouth of the Anamis river; Arr. 6.28.5 says 'an inhabited part of the seashore in Carmania'.

5. Cf. 8.9.14.

6. For Alexander's so-called 'Last Plans' see Diod. 18.4.4; cf. E. Badian, 'A King's Notebooks', *Harvard Studies in Classical Philology*, 72 (1968), 183–204, and F. Schachermeyr, 'Die letzten Pläne Alexanders des Grossen', *J.Ö.A.I.* (1954), 118–40 (repr. in Griffith, *Main Problems*).

7. Arr. 6.27.2 calls him Eudamus (cf. Diod. 19.14.1). Eudamus later murdered Porus and joined forces with Eumenes of Cardia. He was executed by Antigonus the One-Eyed in 316 B.C. (Diod. 19.44.1).

8. Cf. 4.12.8.

9. For Bagoas see the note to 6.5.23. Plut. *Alex.* 67.8 also attests to Alexander's devotion to Bagoas at this time.

10. Plut. *Alex.* 69.3 reports that the man punished for plundering Cyrus' tomb was Poulamachus, a prominent Macedonian from Pella; but cf. Arr. 6.30.1–2 for the fate of Orsines.

11. Here, as in 6.5.21 and 8.3.17, Curtius writes Phradates for Autophradates. Curtius alone records his execution.

12. Cf. 7.1.6.

13. Perhaps Curtius has mistranslated the Greek word *koinon*, in which case the news may have come from the *koinon* of the Macedonians.

14. There is a *lacuna* in the text at this point. Curtius probably went on to discuss the flight of Harpalus to Greece. This man had been a close friend of Alexander's and had been exiled in 336 B.C. by Philip II. Because he was physically unfit for military service, Alexander employed him as his treasurer (Arr. 3.6.5–6). But Harpalus squandered the imperial treasures on his personal pleasures (Diod. 17.108.4). Not content with the sexual abuse of the native women (cf. 10.1.1ff. above, with note 2), Harpalus imported expensive courtesans from Athens, Glycera and Pythionice (Diod. 17.108.5–6; Athenaeus 13.594d–596b). When Alexander returned from India, Harpalus, afraid that he would be punished for his excesses, absconded with 6,000 mercenaries, with whom he sailed to Attica in order to incite rebellion (Diod. 17.108.7). For a good discussion of the background to Harpalus' flight see E. Badian, 'Harpalus', *J.H.S.*, 81 (1961), 16–43.

15. i.e., the Piraeus.

16. Pausanias 2.33.4 says that Alexander sent Philoxenus to demand Harpalus' extradition.

17. See Plutarch, *Demosthenes* 25; cf. *Phocion* 21–2.

18. Thibron (Diod. 17.108.8); or, perhaps, by a certain Pausanias (Pausanias 2.33.4) on Thibron's orders.

19. In the summer of 324, Nicanor of Stagira was sent to Olympia to proclaim the so-

called exiles' decree, a major cause of political unrest in Greece leading to the Lamian war (Diod. 17.109.1: 18.8.2–7). See also A. J. Heisserer, *Alexander the Great and the Greeks* (Norman, Oklahoma, 1980), and M. N. Tod, *A Selection of Greek Historical Inscriptions*, vol. 2 (Oxford, 1945), 201, 202, translated as nos. 4–5 in R. S. Bagnall and P. Derow, *Greek Historical Documents: The Hellenistic Period* (Chico, California, 1981), 5–8.

20. There were 10,000 of these: Diod. 17.109.1; Arr. 7.12.1–4. They were led by Craterus and Polyperchon, and included also Gorgias, Polydamas. Antigenes and White Clitus (Justin 12.12.8).

21. Cf. Diod. 17.109.2; Plut. *Alex.* 70.3; Plutarch, *Moralia* 339b–c; Justin 12.11.1–4.

22. The mutiny at Opis. cf. Diod. 17.109.2; Justin 12.11.5–9; Arr. 7.8.1ff. For Alexander's speech cf. Arr. 7.9–10.

23. Plut. *Alex.* 15.2: 'not more than 70 talents'. according to Aristobulus (*F.Gr.Hist.*, 139 F4).

24. Roxane.

25. Statira (Diod. 17.107.6; Justin 12.10.9); Arr. 7.4.6 calls her Barsine. Although it is difficult to see how it fits into Curtius' narrative, he must have mentioned the weddings at Susa and, possibly, the self-immolation of Calanus in the *lacuna* that follows 10.1.45. For the order of events cf. Diod. 17.107–9 and Plut. *Alex.* 69.6–71.1.

26. See now A. B. Bosworth, 'Alexander and the Iranians', *J.H.S.*, 100 (1980), 1–21.

27. The text breaks off again. J. Froben added: 'When he had made this speech, Alexander entrusted the protection of his person to the Persians and he made Persians his attendants and servants. When the Macedonians, who were the instigators of the sedition, were led by these men to their execution in bonds, they say that one of them, who commanded respect through his personal authority and advanced years, spoke thus to the king.'

28. At this point there is a large *lacuna*. The following episodes are, apparently, lost from Curtius' original: the arrival of Persian soldiers to replace the discharged Macedonian veterans (Diod. 17.110.1; Justin 12.12.1ff.), including 1,000 for his bodyguard; the addition of 20,000 Persian bowmen and slingers to the army (Diod. 17.110.2); the education of 10,000 sons of Macedonian soldiers and captive women (Diod. 17.110.3); Alexander's advance from Susa to Ecbatana (Diod. 17.110.3–7; Plut. *Alex.* 72.1); the death of Hephaestion (Justin 12.12.11–12; Plut. *Alex.* 72.2–3; Diod. 17.110.8); the campaign against the Cossaeans (Diod. 17.111.4–6; Plut. *Alex.* 12.4); Alexander's return to Babylon (Justin 12.13 1ff.; Diod. 17.112; Plut. *Alex.* 73) and prophecies of his death; embassies from all over the world, including Rome (*F.Gr.Hist.*, 137 F31 = Pliny, *N.H.* 3.57; Diod. 17.113; Justin 12.13.1); preparations for Hephaestion's funeral (and a discussion of Hephaestion's character?; Diod. 17.114–15) and his 'deification' or 'heroization' (Diod. 17.115.6; Plut. *Alex.* 72.3; Justin 12.12.12); omens of Alexander's death (Diod. 17.116.2ff.; cf. Arr. 7.22); the dinnerparty of Medius and Alexander's subsequent illness (Diod. 17.117.1–2; Justin 12.13.7ff.).

29. Cf. Diod. 17.117.3; Justin 12.15.7–12. Arrian (7.26.3), significantly, omits any mention of Perdiccas and Alexander's ring. See R. M. Errington, *C.Q.*, n.s. 19 (1969), 239–40.

30. The Greek *kratistos* (Arr. 7.26.3; Diod. 17.117.4; 18.1.4: *aristos*) can mean either 'the best man' or 'the strongest man'. and some have even seen in it a pun on the name Craterus. Justin (12.15.8) has *dignissimus*.

31. Her name was Drypetis (Arr. 7.4.4; Diod. 17.107.6). After Alexander's death she and

her sister Statira were murdered by Roxane, with the aid of Perdiccas (Plut. *Alex.* 77.6).

32. For the savagery of Ochus cf. Justin 10.3.1; Val. Max. 9.2 ext. 7. The remaining son was Oxathres (3.11.8; 3.13.13).

33. Diod. 17.118.3; Justin 13.1.5–6.

34. For a full discussion see F. Schachermeyr, *Alexander in Babylon und die Reichsordnung nach seinem Tode* (Vienna, 1970); R. M. Errington, 'From Babylon to Triparadeisos: 323–320 B.C.', *J.H.S.*, 90 (1970), 49–77.

35. Justin 13.2.5: *exacto mense octavo.*

36. Nearchus favoured Barsine's son, Hercules (cf. Justin 13.2.7), because he himself was married to the daughter of Barsine and Mentor. Cf. P. S. Brunt, *R.F.I.C.*, 103 (1975), 32.

37. Curtius appears to have the emperor Tiberius in mind; see the Introduction, p. 3.

38. Justin 13.2.6–8 ascribes this advice to Meleager himself.

39. Arrhidaeus was the son of Philip by Philinna of Larissa. He was probably born in 357 and suffered from some mental deficiency. Malicious gossip made him a bastard, the son of a Thessalian dancing-girl or prostitute and the victim of Olympias, who gave him mind-destroying drugs. If Arrhidaeus is meant to recall the emperor Claudius, then Curtius prudently overlooks these slanders. See the Introduction, p. 3.

40. One of the bodyguard.

41. Cf. Justin 13.2.14.

42. There seems to be a *lacuna* at this point.

43. Perhaps an error for Damis, a known Megalopolitan; Hedicke suggested Damyllus. These men were Greeks and were regarded as impartial; Plutarch, *Eumenes* 3.1 claims that Eumenes of Cardia helped to bring about an agreement.

44. Third, that is, after Craterus and Perdiccas. Curtius is virtually silent about Craterus' position. Arrian, *History of the Successors* Ia. 3 makes Meleager Perdiccas' lieutenant (*hyparchos*); Justin 13.4.5 treats them as equals.

45. See the Introduction, pp. 1–2.

46. For Meleager's death cf. Justin 13.4.7–8; Arrian, *History of the Successors* Ia. 4; Diod. 18.4.7, who places Meleager's death *after* the division of the satrapies.

47. Laomedon, the brother of Erigyius. He was later arrested by Ptolemy who seized his satrapy (Appian, *Syriaca* 52; Diod. 18.43.2).

48. Antigonus the One-Eyed (cf. 4.1.35); Justin 13.4.15 gives Lycia and Pamphylia to Nearchus.

49. Here, as in other sources, an error for Asander.

50. Ariarathes was defeated and killed by Perdiccas in 322 (Arrian. *History of the Successors* 1.11; Appian, *Mithridatic Wars* 8; Diod. 18.16.1–3).

51. Cf. Justin 12.14; Diod. 17.118.1–2; Plut. *Alex.* 77.2–5; *Metz Epitome* 87ff. See also A. B. Bosworth, 'The Death of Alexander the Great: Rumour and Propaganda', *C.Q.*, n.s. 21 (1971), 112–36. For a full discussion of the poisoning story see W. Heckel, *The Last Days and Testament of Alexander the Great: A Prosopographic Study*, Historia Einzelschriften 56 (Stuttgart, 1988).

52. He had been sent to replace Antipater, who was to bring reinforcements to Alexander in Asia (Justin 12.12.9; Arr. 7.12.4). See also G. T. Griffith, 'Alexander and Antipater in 323 B.C.', *P.A.C.A.*, 8 (1965), 12–17.

53. The Styx was a river of the Underworld.

54. This statement about Cassander is not exactly true. He *did* murder Roxane and Alexander IV, but he also married Alexander's half-sister Thessalonice (Diod. 19.52.1, 61.2).

APPENDIX 1

List of Variations from the Budé Text

The translation is based on Henri Bardon's Budé text rather than the superior edition of Konrad Müller (see Bibliography) for no other reason than that Müller's edition is out of print and difficult to find, whereas Bardon's is available in most academic libraries. In places, however, the translation reflects readings other than those in Bardon's text, and a list of these is given below. For the provenance of these readings the reader is referred to Bardon's *apparatus criticus* or, better, the excellent textual appendix in Müller's edition.

BARDON   PENGUIN

BOOK 3

3.2.6	†militatura idem vicies†	equitibus mille Tapuris Derbices ...
3.4.1	regionem	in regionem
3.4.11	subeuntes	in subeuntes
3.6.18	fortuna, temeritas	fortuna et temeritas
3.9.10	ex Graecia	ex Thraecia
3.10.8	deditae: bis	deditis. Ab his
3.11.9	Macedones circa regem	Macedones qui circa regem
3.12.7	in tabernaculum	ad tabernaculum
3.12.25	capio	capere (see Shackleton Bailey, *C.Q.*, n.s. 31 (1981), 175)

BOOK 4

4.1.31	agros	agros discurrunt
4.2.7	obiectum crebros	obiectum qui crebros
4.2.8	pulsu inlisa mari	pulsu inlisi maris
4.3.13	undique orsi	[undique] orsi
4.3.22	in maiore locaverant	in maiorum locaverant
4.3.24	validis asseribus harpagonas	validis asseres funibus
4.5.16	suis viribus quam	suis viribus fisi quam
4.6.19	stupens	tepens
4.7.15	cedentium iterque	ducentium iterque
4.7.20	quom (misprint?) Hammonios	quos Hammonios
4.7.21	veteres (misprint?)	veterem
4.7.26	destinaret pater	destinaretur; vates
4.8.15	bello utrimque in regem	in bellum utroque rege
4.10.4	pro seditione	prope seditionem

4.10.17	sed et	sed
4.10.23	cui nunc	qui
4.11.4	Et quid	ecquid
4.13.25	discriminis adeundi thorace	discriminis quod adeundum erat lorica
	alacres	alacrem
4.16.20	in fuga	in fugam

BOOK 5

5.1.7	causamque belli	causam belli
5.1.11	euntibus a parte laeva, Arabia	euntibus Media a parte laeva, a dextra Arabia
5.1.26	CCLXVIII	CCCLXV
5.1.38	virorum ... quos	virginum ... quas
5.2.5	Adarrhias	Atarrhias
5.5.3	nocte cum	nocte vectus cum
5.10.4	regni iis potiri	regis potiri
5.12.3	arguenti	purganti
5.12.16	deorum auspiciis ac suis honoribus cultus	deorum a suis honoribus cultus
5.13.1	quod patebat	quod petebat

BOOK 6

6.4.7	quicumque demissi	quaecumque demissa
	duos	duos equos
6.6.28	vapore torrida iam inarserat	vapore torrido iam inaruerat
6.6.29	dare	dari
6.10.9	sane ut viveret adhuc vellet	sane et vivat adhuc et velit
6.11.5	Nunc cum	nunc cur
6.11.32	dux tantus	dux [tantus]

BOOK 7

7.7.25	qui scis plus quam potes	qui † saepius quam potest

BOOK 8

8.2.22	munitas ac validas manu	munitas valida manu
8.5.8	piissimorum carminum	pessimorum carminum
8.14.10	sagittarios, tympana	sagittarios et tympana
8.14.31	tela multo ante	tela multa ante
8.14.40	compositoque	confossoque

BOOK 9

9.4.10	hinc coetu	hinc aestu
9.10.18	rerum solo	rerum sola
9.10.27	parta praeda	parata praeda

10.3.1	metu, et	

APPENDIX 2

Chronology

B.C.

359   Philip II ascends the throne of Macedon.

358/357   Birth of Arrhidaeus (Philip III: cf. 10.7.2ff.).

357   Philip marries Olympias.

356   20 July. Birth of Alexander the Great (Plut. *Alex.* 3.5).

338   2 August. Battle of Chaeronea (Plutarch, *Camillus* 19); (3.10.7; 8.1.23).

337   Early Spring. Alexander's Illyrian campaign (8.1.25).

336   Summer. Death of Philip II (6.11.26; 7.1.6). Alexander's accession.

336/335   Deaths of Amyntas, son of Perdiccas, and Attalus (6.10.24; 7.1.3; 8.1.42; 8.7.4); (Arr. 1.5.4; *Succ.* 1.22; Diod. 17.5.2).

335   Destruction of Thebes (3.10.7; 8.1.33).

334   Alexander crosses the Hellespont.
   Victory at the Granicus River (3.10.7; 4.9.22; 4.14.1, 10; 8.1.20; 9.2.23).
   Capture of Sardis (3.12.6; 5.1.44).
   Fall of Miletus (8.2.8) and Halicarnassus (5.2.5; 8.1.36).

334/333   Winter. Conquest of Lycia and Pamphylia (Arr. 1.24.5); Cleander sent to Peloponnese (3.1.1); death of Memnon (3.1.21; 3.2.1).

333   Spring. Alexander at Celaenae and Gordium (3.1.1–18).
   Death of Charidemus (3.2.10–19).

333   Summer. Alexander in Cilicia (3.4.1ff.).

333   November. Battle of Issus (3.8.22ff.).

333   Winter. Alexander reaches Marathus (4.1.6), Byblus and Sidon (4.1.15).
   Amyntas, son of Antiochus flees to Egypt (4.1.27ff.).
   Agis' brother Agesilaus campaigns on Crete (4.1.38–40; cf. Arr. 2.13.4–6; Diod. 17.48.1–2).

332   January–August. Siege of Tyre (4.2.1–4.19); (Arr. 2.24.6: Hecatombaeon 332).

332   September–October. Siege of Gaza (4.6.7–30); (Diod. 17.48.7: 'a siege of two months').

332/331   Winter. Alexander visits the oracle of Jupiter Ammon (4.7.5–32).

331   Spring. Foundation of Alexandria in Egypt (4.8.1–6).
   Amphoterus is sent to Crete (4.8.15).

331   Late summer. Battle of Megalopolis (6.1.1ff.)

331   20 September. Eclipse of the moon seen at Gaugamela (4.10.2).

331   1 October. Battle of Gaugamela (Arbela) (4.12.1ff.); (Plutarch, *Camillus* 19.5).

331   Autumn. Alexander captures Babylon and Susa (5.1.17–2.22).
   Campaign against the Uxians (5.3.1–16).

330	January–May. Alexander at Persepolis (5.6.12: 'the setting of the Pleiades'; Plut. *Alex.* 37.6); (5.6.1–7.12).
330	July. Death of Darius (Arr. 3.22.2); (5.13.16ff.).
	Trial and death of Philotas (6.7.1–11.40).
	Death of Parmenion (7.2.11–33).
330/329	Revolt and death of Satibarzanes (7.3.2ff.; 7.4.33–8).
	Capture of Bessus (7.5.19–43).
329	Summer. Alexander at the Tanais (Iaxartes); (7.6.1ff.).
	Revolt of Spitamenes (7.6.14ff.). Disaster at Polytimetus River (7.6.24; 7.7.31–9).
329/328	Winter. Alexander winters at Bactra (Arr. 4.7.1); (7.10.10ff.).
328	Spring. Capture of the Sogdian Rock (Ariamazes); (7.11).[1]
328	Summer. Death of Clitus at Maracanda (8.1.19–52).
328/327	Winter. Alexander winters at Nautaca (8.2.13ff.).
	Capture of Sisimithres' rock (8.2.19ff.)
	Deaths of Philip, brother of Lysimachus (8.2.35–9) and Erigyius (8.2.40).
	Death of Spitamenes (8.3.1–16).
	Alexander marries Roxane (8.4.21ff.).
327	Spring. Introduction of *proskynesis* (8.5.5ff.).
	Conspiracy of the Pages (8.6.7ff.).
327/326	The Swat campaign and the capture of Aornus (8.11.2–25).
326	May. Alexander at the Hydaspes (Arr. 5.19.3), battle with Porus (8.13.5–14.46).
326	Summer. Mutiny at the Hyphasis (9.1.35–3,19).
	Death of Coenus (9.3.20).
326/325	November 326–July 325. Descent of the Indus River system (Strabo 15.1.17); (9.3.21–8.30).
325	August. Alexander begins his return to the west (9.10).[2]
325/324	Winter. Alexander in Carmania (9.10.20ff.).
	Punishment of the satraps (10.1.1–42).
324	Summer. The Exiles' Decree (10.2.4ff.).
	Meeting at Opis (10.2.12–4.3).
324	Autumn. Death of Hephaestion (Arr. 7.14).
323	May. The dinner-party of Medius; Alexander falls ill.
323	10 June. Alexander's death (10.5.5).
	The political settlement at Babylon (10.5.6ff.).
321	Alexander's body taken to Egypt (10.10.20).

NOTES

1. This episode probably belongs in 327; cf. Arrian 4.18–19.
2. Curtius places the departure for the west at the end of winter 326/325 (9.10.4).

APPENDIX 3

Glossary of Personal Names

The number immediately following the name refers to Berve's catalogue in volume 2 of *Das Alexanderreich auf prosopographischer Grundlage* (Munich, 1926).

ABDALONYMUS (1): Distantly related to the Sidonian royal house, he was selected on the basis of his pure and simple life to rule in place of the deposed Strato (4.1.19ff.).

ABISARES (2): Indian ruler of the Kashmir area who submitted to Alexander in the winter of 327/326 (8.13.1); despite his fears (9.1.7–8) he was allowed to retain his kingdom until his death in 325. His son and namesake succeeded him (10.1.20–21).

ABISTAMENES (4): Alexander appointed him satrap of Cappadocia in 333 (3.4.1). Arrian (2.4.2) calls him Sabiktas (Berve 690). Nothing else is known about him under either name.

ABULITES (5): Satrap of Susiana under Darius III, he surrendered Susa to Alexander in late 331 (5.2.8). He was allowed to continue in his office under Alexander (5.2.17), but in 324, on Alexander's return to Susa, he was put to death, along with his son Oxathres, for abusing his authority (Arr. 7.4.1; Plut. *Alex.* 68).

AESCHYLUS (35): A Rhodian, left behind as overseer (along with Ephippos, Arr. 3.5.3) of the mercenaries in Egypt; Curtius (4.8.4) exaggerates his importance.

AGATHON (8): Commander of the Thracian cavalry at the Granicus and Gaugamela (Arr. 1.14.3; 3.12.4), he was apparently left behind at Ecbatana, where he was one of Parmenion's murderers (10.1.1). Together with Cleander, Sitacles and Heracon, he was charged with abuse of power and sacrilege and imprisoned (10.1.1–8).

AGATHON (9): Macedonian garrison commander of the citadel of Babylon (5.1.43).

AGIS (15): King of Sparta 338–331 B.C. He led an uprising against Macedon in 332–331, which ended with his death near Megalopolis (6.1.1–16). Most of his story is lost from our text of Curtius.

AGIS (16): An epic poet from Argos, and one of Alexander's worst flatterers (8.5.8 and Arr. 4.9.9).

ALEXANDER (37): Brother of Heromenes and Arrhabaeus, who were executed for allegedly instigating the murder of Philip. He was pardoned because he was Antipater's son-in-law and because he was the first to hail Alexander as the new king. His arrest (Arr. 1.25) was probably recounted in the lost second book. For his 'trial' and execution see 7.1.5–9.

ALEXANDER (38): King of Epirus (342?–331/330); Alexander's uncle and brother-in-law. He is alluded to by Clitus (8.1.37). He died in battle in Italy.

ALEXANDER (–): Son of Cleophis (8.10.36); some suspected that he was Alexander the Great's son.

ALEXANDER (40): A young man of 'Alexander's cohort' (hypaspist, or a page?) who, along with Charus, died a heroic death at Aornus (8.11.10–15).

AMEDINES (51): *Scriba regis* of Darius III, in 330 Alexander gave him authority over the Ariaspians (or Euergetae); nothing else is known of him (7.3.4).

AMISSUS (53): Perhaps an error for 'Damis'; from Megalopolis. He acted as a go-between in the factional strife at Babylon in 323 (10.8.15).

AMPHOTERUS (68): Brother of Craterus, he was the agent who arrested Alexander Lyncestes. In the extant books of Curtius he is known only for his conduct of the naval war in the Aegean (3.1.19; 4.5.14ff.; 4.8.15).

AMYNTAS (57): Son of Andromenes. He commanded a battalion of the Macedonian phalanx at Issus (3.9.7), but was on a recruiting mission in Macedonia (4.6.30; 5.1.40; 7.1.37ff.) and was not present at Gaugamela. Curtius does not record his death in battle shortly after the Philotas affair (cf. Arr. 3.27.3).

AMYNTAS (58): Son of Antiochus. Fled Macedonia at the time of Alexander's accession fearing reprisal for his friendship (and plot?) with Amyntas, son of Perdiccas. He escaped from Issus with some 4,000 Greek mercenaries (3.11.18; 4.1.27) and perished in an unsuccessful attempt to gain control of Egypt (4.1.27–33; cf. 4.7.1).

AMYNTAS (60): Became satrap of Bactria and Sogdiana in 328 (8.2.14), although the office had been intended for Cleitus the Black. Since he vanishes from the list of satraps in 323 B.C., it is likely that he perished in the uprising of Greek soldiers around Bactria in 325 (9.7.1–11).

AMYNTAS (61): Son of Perdiccas III and rightful heir to the Macedonian throne in 359 B.C. Philip II seized power and later married Amyntas to his daughter Cynnane. He was accused of plotting against Alexander in 336/335 and executed. Curtius mentions him only in connection with Philotas, who was on intimate terms with him (6.9.17; 6.10.24).

AMYNTAS (–): Otherwise unknown, he won fourth prize in the contest of valour in Sittacene (5.2.5).

AMYNTAS (63): A Lyncestian who won seventh prize in the contest of valour in Sittacene (5.2.5).

AMYNTAS (64): One of the conspirators named by Dymnos (i.e., in the Philotas affair; 6.7.15); probably he is identical with the son of Andromenes.

AMYNTAS (65): *Regius praetor* who spoke against Philotas at his trial (6.9.28–9). Curtius' summary of his speech is perhaps a clumsy and inaccurate doublet of the speech of Amyntas, son of Andromenes.

ANDROMACHUS (76): Left in charge of Coele-Syria in 332 (4.5.9). While Alexander was in Egypt (winter 332/331), the Samaritans rebelled and burned Andromachus alive (4.8.9).

ANDRONICUS (78): Apparently the son of Agerrus; he was sent with Artabazus, Caranus and Erigyius to deal with rebel Satibarzanes (7.3.3).

ANTICLES (88): Son of Theocritus; party to the pages' conspiracy, for which he was executed (8.6.9; 8.8.20).

ANTIGENES (83–84): Placed second in the contest in Sittacene (5.2.5); he is probably identical with the Antigenes named in the account of the Hydaspes battle (8.14.15).

ANTIGONUS (–): Finished sixth in the contest in Sittacene (5.2.5); nothing else is known about this Antigonus.

ANTIGONUS (87): Antigonus the One-Eyed (Monophthalmus). An older Macedonian officer, born *c.* 380; appointed satrap of Phrygia (Curt. 4.1.35 wrongly says Lydia) in 334/333 B.C. After the battle of Issus he defeated the remnants of the Persian army in three separate battles (4.1.35), and in late 332 he invaded and secured Lycaonia (4.5.13). After Alexander's death in 323, he was confirmed in his satrapy (10.10.2). The father of Demetrius Poliorcetes, he played an important role in the history of the Successors until his death in the battle of Ipsus in 301 B.C.

ANTIPATER (94): Regent of Macedon from 334 until his death in 319 B.C., he was the father-in-law of Alexander Lyncestes, whom he tried in vain to save from execution (7.1.7). In spring 333, he received money from Alexander to help prevent Memnon from effecting an uprising in Greece (3.1.20). Curtius' account of Antipater's victory over King Agis III of Sparta (cf. 4.1.39) is mostly lost (6.1.1–21), but it is alleged that Alexander envied his achievement and belittled it (see 6.1.18 with note). He sent reinforcements to Alexander in 331 (led by Amyntas, son of Andromenes, 5.1.40), in 330 (3,000 troops from Illyricum, 6.6.35) and again in 329/328 (8,000 Greeks,, 7.10.12). After Alexander's death Pithon recommended that Antipater and Craterus should administer Europe jointly (10.7.9). Rumour held that he poisoned Alexander (10.10.14–18).

ANTIPATER (93): Son of Asclepiodorus (satrap of Syria). One of the pages who conspired with Hermolaus against Alexander (8.6.9); he was executed (8.8.20).

ANTIPHANES (95): Scriba equitum (apparently the accountant of the Companion cavalry), who complained of Amyntas' arrogant behaviour in the trial that followed the condemnation of Philotas (7.1.15ff.).

APHOBETUS (190): One of Dymnus' co-conspirators (6.7.15); executed along with Philotas (6.11.38).

APOLLODORUS (101): Both Curtius (5.1.43) and Diodorus (17.64.5) say that Apollodorus and Menes were appointed military governors over the territories from Babylon to Cilicia; but Arrian (3.16.9) gives that authority to Menes alone and says (3.16.4) that Apollodorus commanded the garrison at Babylon.

APOLLONIDES (102): Leader of the pro-Persian faction at Chios (4.5.15); eventually captured by Amphoterus and Hegelochus (4.5.17). He was brought to Alexander in Egypt and sent to Elephantine under heavy guard (Arr. 3.2.7).

APOLLONIUS (104): Given authority over Libya by Alexander in 331 (Curt. 4.8.5; cf. Arr. 3.5.4).

ARCHELAUS (158): Commanded a garrison of 3,000 men at Susa in late 331 (5.2.16).

ARCHEPOLIS (161): One of the conspirators named by Dymnus (6.7.15); he was executed along with Philotas (6.11.38).

ARETES (109): Commander of the lancers (sarisophori), he was sent against the Scythians who were plundering the Macedonian baggage at the battle of Arbela (Gaugamela); he had only limited success (4.15.13; 4.15.18).

ARIARATHES (113): Rule of Cappadocia; in 323 B.C., Eumenes was ordered to dislodge him from that region (10.10.3).

ARIMAZES (112 'Ariamazes'): Local Sogdian baron, commander of the Sogdian rock (7.11.1ff.). Because he felt that the rock was impregnable, he refused to surrender until Alexander's climbers took the heights above him. He and his relatives were crucified (7.11.28).

ARIOBARZANES (115): Satrap of Persia, he commanded the Persians, Mardians and Sogdians at Arbela (Gaugamela) (4.12.7). He resisted Alexander at the Persian Gates (5.3.17ff.). He is probably not (pace Berve) to be identified with the son of Artabazus.

ARISTANDER (117): Alexander's seer from Telmessus, he features prominently in

Curtius' history (Tyre: 4.2.14; Gaza: 4.6.12; Arbela: 4.13.15; 4.15.27; Persian Gates: 5.4.2; at the Iaxartes: 7.7.8; 7.7.22ff.).

ARISTOGITON (123): Athenian ambassador to Darius III, captured by Parmenion at Damascus (3.13.15).

ARISTOMEDES (128): Thessalian exile in the service of Darius III; he commanded 20,000 infantry at Issus (3.9.3). Arrian (2.13.2–3) says that he joined the unsuccessful enterprise of Amyntas, son of Antiochus in Egypt.

ARISTOMENES (126): Persian fleet-commander (331/332 B.C.), defeated by Hegelochus and Amphoterus (4.1.36).

ARISTON (138): Paeonian cavalry-officer. He killed Satropates in battle and brought his head to Alexander (4.9.24–5).

ARISTONICUS (131): Tyrant of Methymna, he was captured by Hegelochus and Amphoterus at Chios (4.5.19–21). Alexander handed him back to his own people, who put him to death by torture (4.8.11).

ARISTONUS (133): One of Alexander's seven bodyguards. Curtius alone says that he helped protect Alexander in the attack on the Mallians (9.5.15–18). He was a supporter of Perdiccas in the strife that followed Alexander's death (10.6.16ff.).

ARRHIDAEUS (781 'Philip Arrhidaeus'): Mentally deficient half-brother of Alexander, promoted to the kingship by the leaders of the phalanx (10.7.1ff.), especially Meleager.

ARSACES (–): Sent to Media to replace Oxydates (8.3.17). This is probably an error for Atropates.

ARSAMES (146 'Arsaces'): Curtius (8.3.17) speaks of 'Arsames, satrap of the Drangae', though he is referring to Satibarzanes' successor in Aria. Arrian 3.25.7 calls him 'Arsaces'. See note to 7.3.1.

ARSAMES (149): Darius' satrap of Cilicia, he used Memnon's scorched-earth policy to no avail in 333 (3.4.3–5). Curtius does not mention him again; according to Arr. 2.11.8, he fell in battle at Issus.

ARTABAZUS (152): His wife and his son, Ilioneus, were captured at Damascus (3.13.13). A faithful courtier of Darius, he had once been a guest at the court of Philip II (5.9.1; cf. 6.5.2). He continued to support Darius when Bessus and Nabarzanes plotted against him (5.9.1ff.), and he later submitted to Alexander (6.5.1ff.). Artabazus campaigned with Caranus, Erigyius and Andronicus against Satibarzanes (7.3.2). In 329 Alexander appointed him satrap of Bactria (7.5.1; cf. 7.11.29), which he helped to subdue (8.1.10), but later excused him from the office because of his old age (8.1.19; cf. 6.5.3); Clitus was supposed to succeed him. His son, Cophes, negotiated with Arimazes (7.11.5). Pharnabazus and Barsine were also his children.

ASANDER (165): Alexander's satrap of Lydia from 334 to 331. In 329/328 he brought reinforcements from Lycia to Alexander at Bactra (7.10.12).

ASCLEPIODORUS (167): Satrap of Syria (Arr. 3.6.8), he brought reinforcements to Alexander at Bactra in 329/328 (7.10.12). He was the father of the page Antipater, but Curtius (8.6.9) erringly calls him one of the conspirators.

ASCLEPIODORUS (–): Member of the pages' conspiracy (8.6.9); see above.

ASSACANUS (172): Deceased ruler of the Mazagae in India, son of Cleophis (8.10.22).

ASTASPES (173): Satrap of Carmania who came to meet Alexander on his return from India in 325. Although he suspected Astaspes of wishing to rebel against him, Alexander disguised his anger (9.10.21), but kept him in his entourage until he could determine the truth. Then Astaspes was executed (9.10.29).

ATARRHIAS (178): A veteran soldier, distinguished for his valour at Halicarnassus (5.2.5; 8.1.36). The mss. at 5.2.5 have 'Adarrhias' but he is clearly the same man mentioned by Clitus at 8.1.36. He won first place in the contest in Sittacene (5.2.5). Alexander sent him to arrest Philotas (6.8.19–21), and it was he who called for the condemnation of Alexander Lyncestes (7.1.5).

ATHANAGORAS (26): Member of the pro-Persian party at Chios in 332, he was captured by Hegelochus and Amphoterus (4.5.15–17). Like Apollonides, who was captured with him, he was probably sent in chains to Elephantine in Egypt (Arr. 3.2.7).

ATHENODORUS (29): Leader of the Greek rebels who seized control of Bactra, he assumed the title of king and hoped to lead the rebels back to Greece (9.7.2–3). He was invited to dinner by a fellow-Greek, Biton, who suborned a Bactrian named Boxus to assassinate him (9.7.4ff.).

ATIZYES (179): Darius' satrap of Phrygia, he fell in battle at Issus (3.11.10).

ATTALUS (182): Uncle of Philip II's last wife, Cleopatra, and brother-in-law of Philotas (6.9.17), he was murdered on Alexander's orders by Parmenion (7.1.3; 8.1.42; 8.7.5; cf. 8.1.52; 8.7.4; 8.8.7).

ATTALUS (183): Commander of the Agrianes at Arbela (Gaugamela), 4.13.31.

ATTALUS (–): Otherwise unknown, he was similar to Alexander in appearance, and Alexander used him as a decoy at the Hydaspes (8.13.21).

ATTINAS (185): In 328 he was given 300 horsemen to deal with the Massagetae, who were harming the Bactriani, but he fell into an ambush and was killed along with his men (8.1.3; cf. Arr. 4.16.5).

BAGISTANES (193 'Bagisthanes'): A Babylonian, he brought Alexander news of Darius' impending arrest (5.13.3).

BAGOAS (–): A eunuch who murdered Ochus and was later forced by Darius to take his own poison (6.3.12; 6.4.10).

BAGOAS (195): A eunuch and a favourite of King Darius III, he surrendered to Alexander in the company of Nabarzanes, whose life he persuaded Alexander to spare (6.5.23). Through his influence with Alexander, he ruined the Persian nobleman, Orsines (10.1.22–38).

BAGOPHANES (197): Commander of the citadel and treasury at Babylon, he carpeted the road to Babylon with flowers to welcome Alexander (5.1.20ff). Alexander kept him in his entourage, but no further mention is made of him (5.1.44).

BALACRUS (203): In 332 he defeated Idarnes (Hydarnes) and recaptured Miletus (4.5.13).

BALACRUS (202): Apparently identical with the commander of the *akontistai* at Gaugamela (Arr. 3.12.3, 13.5), he conducted a scouting mission at Aornus (8.11.22).

BARSINE (206): Daughter of Artabazus and wife of Memnon, she was captured by Parmenion at Damascus (3.13.14). She became intimate with Alexander (Justin 11.10.2; Plut. *Alex.* 21.7) and bore him a son, Hercules, to whom Nearchus refers (10.6.11).

BARZAENTES (205 'Barsaentes'): Satrap of the Drangae, he was one of the murderers of Darius and fled to India (6.6.36), where he and his ally King Samaxus were arrested (8.13.3–4).

BESSUS (212): Darius' satrap of Bactria, he joined the king before the battle of Gaugamela (4.6.2), but his loyalty was suspect (4.6.4). At Gaugamela he commanded

8,000 Bactrian horse (4.12.6, also the Massagetae, 4.12.7; 4.15.2), and after the battle he fled to the upper satrapies with Darius (5.8.4), whom he plotted against, arrested and killed (5.9.2ff.). Bessus then fled in the direction of Bactria and was pursued by Alexander (6.3.9ff.); his fellow-conspirator Nabarzanes (cf. 6.4.8) fled to Hyrcania. Thereafter Bessus assumed royal dress and the title Artaxerxes (6.6.13ff.). He encouraged Satibarzanes to revolt from Alexander (7.3.2), almost killed Cobares in a drunken quarrel (7.4.1–19), and crossed the Oxus, burning the boats behind him (7.4.20–21). But Spitamenes, Catanes and Dataphernes plotted against him and turned him over to Alexander (7.5.19–26, 36–9; cf. 7.6.14–15), who gave him to Oxathres for punishment (7.5.40–43; he was sent to Ecbatana for punishment 7.10.10).

BETIS (209 'Batis'): A eunuch (Arr. 2.25.4) who governed Gaza. Alexander defeated him, sacked Gaza, and punished Betis as Achilles had Hector (4.6.7–29).

BION (217): A Greek soldier in the service of Darius. At Gaugamela he deserted to Alexander and pointed out to him traps set into the battlefield by the Persians (4.13.36–7).

BITON (216): A Greek rebel in Bactria, he brought about the death of the rebel-leader Athenodorus (9.7.4). He twice escaped execution at the hands of his fellow-Greeks and led about 3,000 of them back to Greece (9.7.5–11; cf. Diod. 17.99.5–6).

BOLON (218): An obscure Macedonian soldier, he gave a speech condemning Philotas (6.11.1–7).

BOXUS (219): A Bactrian, who on the orders of Biton assassinated Athenodorus at the banquet table (9.7.4).

BROCHUBELUS (82 'Antibelus'): Son of Mazaeus; former satrap of Syria, he surrendered to Alexander after the arrest of Darius (5.13.11).

BUBACES (221): A faithful eunuch of Darius III (5.11.4; 5.12.10–12).

CALAS (397): Probably a cousin of Harpalus the treasurer, he ruled Hellespontine Phrygia (3.1.24) and in 332 attacked Paphlagonia (4.5.13).

CALIS (398): Confronted by Philotas before the Macedonian assembly, Calis was shamed and frightened into confessing that he and Demetrius had plotted against Alexander (6.11.36–7).

CALLICRATES (401): Charged with guarding the treasures at Susa, 331/330 (5.2.16).

CALLICRATIDES (402): Spartan ambassador to Darius, captured at Damascus (3.13.15); Arrian (3.24.4), who calls him Callistratidas, postpones his capture until 330 B.C.

CALLISTHENES (408): Alexander's official historian, the nephew of Aristotle (see Introduction, pp. 5, 9). In 327 B.C. he opposed Cleon's call for the performing of proskynesis and the granting of divine honours to Alexander (8.5.13ff.). Curtius depicts him as 'the champion of public freedom' (8.5.20). Alexander, however, resented Callisthenes' outspokenness and took advantage of his friendship with Hermolaus to implicate him in the latter's conspiracy (8.6.1, 24ff.; 8.7.3ff.). He was executed along with the conspirators (8.8.21).

CARTHASIS (413): Brother of the king of the Scythians who lived beyond the Iaxartes (7.7.1ff.).

CASSANDER (414): Son of Antipater; Curtius mentions him only in connection with the alleged poisoning of Alexander by Antipater's sons (10.10.17). The reference to Cassander, satrap of Caria (10.10.2), is an error for Asander.

CATANES (415): A follower of Bessus; together with Spitamenes and Dataphernes, he arrested Bessus and delivered him to Alexander (7.5.21ff.). Because of his great skill in archery he was assigned the task of keeping the birds off Bessus' body (7.5.41–2). He persisted in his disloyalty towards Alexander and was finally killed in battle by Craterus (8.5.2).

CEBALINUS (418): Brother of Nicomachus, he brought the news of Dymnus' conspiracy and Philotas' negligence to Alexander's attention (6.7.16ff.).

CHARES (819): Athenian commander who held Mytilene with a garrison of 2,000 Persians. He was ousted by Amphoterus and Hegelochus in 332; they allowed him to go in safety to Imbros (4.5.22).

CHARIDEMUS (823): From Oreus on Euboea. Exiled from Athens on Alexander's order, he joined Darius, who put him to death for his outspokenness (3.2.10ff.).

CHARUS (826): A member of Alexander's 'cohort' (either a page or a hypaspist), he died a valiant death at Aornus (8.11.10ff.).

CHOERILUS (829): From Iasus; he was reputedly the worst poet in Alexander's entourage (8.5.8).

CLEANDER (422): Son of Polemocrates and, apparently, the brother of Coenus; in 334/333 he was sent to the Peloponnese to bring reinforcements (3.1.1), rejoining Alexander at Tyre (4.3.11). He was among Parmenion's assassins at Ecbatana (7.2.19ff.) but was later found guilty of abusing his power and imprisoned (10.1.1ff.). Arrian (6.27.4) says he was put to death.

CLEITARCHUS: See Introduction, pp. 5ff. (9.5.21; 9.8.15).

CLEOCHARES (436): Macedonian sent by Alexander to demand the surrender of Porus in 326 B.C. (8.13.2).

CLEOMENES (431): A Greek from Naucratis, in 332/331 he was appointed by Alexander the collector of taxes in Libya and Egypt (4.8.5).

CLEON (437): A Sicilian, flatterer of Alexander (8.5.8). He urged that the Macedonians recognize Alexander as a god and do obeisance to him (8.5.10ff.).

CLEOPHIS (435): Mother of Assacenus, deceased king of the Mazagae (8.10.22). She surrendered to Alexander and won a pardon, retaining her title of queen (8.10.34–5). She bore a son named Alexander, whom rumour held to be Alexander's son (8.10.36; Justin 12.7.9–11).

CLITUS (427): Commander of the 'Royal Squadron' of Alexander's cavalry (4.13.26). He saved Alexander's life at the Granicus (8.1.39), and was designated to succeed Artabazus as satrap of Bactria-Sogdiana (8.1.19). Alexander killed him after a drunken quarrel at Maracanda in 327 B.C. (8.1.20–52).

COBARES (196 'Bagodarus'): A Mede skilled in magic, who narrowly escaped to Alexander after advising Bessus to surrender to Alexander (7.4.8–19).

COENUS (439): Son of Polemocrates and, apparently, the brother of Cleander. An infantry commander at Issus (3.9.7) and Gaugamela (4.13.28), where he was wounded (4.16.32), he led his battalion in the encircling manoeuvre at the Persian Gates (5.4.20, 30; but cf. Arr. 3.18 who says he was sent to bridge the Araxes). He contributed to the fall of Philotas (6.8.17; 6.9.30; 6.11.10–11), although he had married Philotas' sister (6.9.30). He commanded one-third of the army in Sogdiana in 328 (8.1.1); besieged Beira in 327 (8.10.22); led the slower troops to Ecbolima (8.12.1); served as a cavalry commander in the battle with Porus (8.14.15ff.). At the Hyphasis he was the spokesman of the soldiers and urged Alexander to turn back (9.3.3ff.). Soon afterwards he died of illness (9.3.20).

COENUS (440): If not a mistranslation of *to koinon*, the man who informed Alexander of affairs in Europe in 324/323 (10.1.43).

COPHES (459 'Cophen'): A son of Artabazus, Alexander sent him to negotiate the surrender of Arimazes (7.11.5ff.).

CRATERUS (446): One of Alexander's leading generals. For his military activities see 3.9.8 (Issus); 4.3.1, 11 (Tyre); 4.13.29 (Gaugamela) 5.4.14–16; 5.4.34 (the Persian Gates); 5.6.11; 6.4.1; 6.4.23; 6.6.25, 33; 7.6.16; 7.7.9; 7.9.20ff.; 8.1.6; 8.5.2; 8.10.4–5; 9.8.3; 9.10.19; 10.1.9. He is not mentioned by name in Curtius' account of the battle with Porus, although he played a major role. Craterus contributed greatly to the condemnation of Philotas, whose personal enemy he was (6.8.2–9; 6.8.17; 6.11.10ff.). He urged Alexander not to risk his life (9.6.6). After Alexander's death in 323 it was proposed by Pithon that he administer Europe with Antipater (10.7.9). There was also a rumour that Alexander had sent Craterus to kill Antipater (10.10.15).

CRITOBULUS (452): A doctor from Cos, he had once been the physician of Philip II (Pliny, *N.H.* 7.37). He treated Alexander when he was wounded in the battle with the Mallians (Curt. 9.4.26 calls them the Sudracae) in 326 B.C. (9.5.25–7).

DARIUS (244): Darius III 'Codamannus', King of Persia 336–330 B.C. Books 3–5 *passim*; 6.1.21; 6.2.7–11; 6.3.9ff.; 6.4.8ff.; 6.5.1ff.; 6.6.4ff.; 6.11.29; 7.3.4; 7.4.3; 7.5.20, 25, 37, 40, 43; 7.7.8; 7.10.10; 8.1.47; 8.4.25; 9.6.10; 10.1.34; 10.3.12; 10.5.19, 21–3, 25.

DATAPHERNES (246): A Bactrian noble, together with Catanes and Spitamenes he arrested Bessus in order to hand him over to Alexander (7.5.21–2 and ff.). But he too continued to oppose Alexander until he was bound by his erstwhile allies, the Dahae, and turned over to the king (8.3.16).

DEMETRIUS (260): One of Alexander's bodyguards, he had been party to Dymnus' conspiracy (6.7.15; 6.9.5), for which he was tried and executed (6.11.35–8).

DEMOCRATES (261): An Athenian sent as ambassador to Darius. He chose suicide rather than entrust himself to Alexander's mercy after Darius' death (6.5.9).

DEMOPHON (264): A Greek seer who to no avail warned Alexander to postpone his siege of the Mallians (Sudracae) (9.4.27–8).

DERDAS (250): Probably from Elimiotis and a relative of Harpalus the treasurer. Alexander's ambassador to the Scythians (7.6.12; 8.1.7).

DIOXENUS (280): One of Dymnus' co-conspirators (6.7.15), he was stoned to death (6.11.38).

DIOXIPPUS (284): A famous Athenian boxer in Alexander's entourage (9.7.16), he defeated an armed Macedonian, Horratus (Corrhagus), in single combat although he was armed with only a purple cloth and a club (9.7.17–22). Thereafter he was falsely accused of stealing a golden drinking cup and committed suicide (9.7.24–6).

DITAMENES (718 'Stamenes'): In 328 he replaced Mazaeus, who had died, as satrap of Babylonia (8.3.17). 'Ditamenes' is probably an error for 'Stamenes' (cf. Arr. 4.18.3).

DROPIDES (291): An Athenian ambassador to Darius, captured at Damascus in 333 B.C. (3.13.15). Arrian (3.24.4) says he entrusted himself to Alexander's clemency after Darius' death in 330.

DYMNUS (269 'Dimnus'): A Macedonian who, for an unknown reason, plotted against Alexander (6.7.1ff.). He revealed his plot to his lover Nicomachus (6.7.6–16), but Nicomachus informed his brother Cebalinus, who in turn alerted the king (6.7.22ff.). Dymnus, when soldiers came to arrest him, committed suicide (6.7.29–30).

ELAPTONIUS (296): One of the pages who conspired with Hermolaus to kill the king (8.6.9); he was presumably executed (8.8.20). Hedicke perhaps rightly emended the text to *et Aphtonius* (for that name cf. Hoffmann, *Die Makedonen*, 179).

EPIMENES (300): One of the pages who conspired to kill Alexander (8.6.9). When the initial attempt was foiled (8.6.12ff.), Epimenes revealed the plot to his brother Eurylochus (8.6.20), who brought the news to Alexander and won a reprieve for Epimenes (8.6.21–6).

ERICES (191 'Aphrices'): An Indian leader who, with 20,000 men, tried to oppose Alexander *en route* to Ecbolima (8.12.1). He was murdered by his own men and his head was delivered to Alexander (8.12.3).

ERIGYIUS (302): Brother of Laomedon (see 'Leomedon' below), originally from Mytilene; one of Alexander's closest friends (cf. Plut. *Alex.* 10.4; Arr. 3.6.5). Erigyius took the baggage train through Parthiene (6.4.3) and rejoined Alexander at Arvae (6.4.23). Later he met with Alexander and several others to discuss the matter of Philotas' 'conspiracy' (6.8.17). Together with Caranus, Andronicus and Artabazus, he campaigned against the rebel Satibarzanes (7.3.2), whom he slew in single combat (7.4.32–8). In 329 he served as a counsellor of Alexander (7.7.9) and advised against crossing the Tanais (7.7.21ff.). In 328 he died, perhaps of illness (8.2.40), and was buried with due honours.

ERSILAUS (325 'Eurysilaus'): Tyrant of Eresus, he was captured by Hegelochus (cf. 4.5.19ff.; he was probably captured with Aristonicus) and taken to Alexander in Egypt in 332/331 B.C. He was sent back to Eresus where his countrymen put him to death by torture (4.8.11).

EUCTEMON (316): A Greek from Cyme and a spokesman for the 4,000 mutilated Greeks. He opposed the views of Theaetetus the Athenian and argued that they should remain in Asia rather than return in their unfortunate state. His arguments prevailed (5.5.9–16; 5.5.21).

EUDAEMON (311 'Eudemus'): A general of the Thracians; when Philippus, the satrap of north-west India, died, Eudaemon was ordered to replace him (10.1.20–21).

EUMENES (317): A Greek from Cardia and Alexander's secretary. He commanded part of Alexander's force in India (9.1.19), and was appointed satrap of Cappadocia and Paphlagonia after Alexander's death (10.10.3).

EURYLOCHUS (322): Brother of Epimenes, who had been a fellow-conspirator with Hermolaus. But when Epimenes revealed the plot to Eurylochus (8.6.20), the latter informed Alexander and won his brother's reprieve (8.6.21–6).

EUXENIPPUS (318): A handsome youth, sent in 329 B.C. on an embassy to the Sacae (7.9.19).

GOBARES (238): The Persian commander of Parsagadae; he surrendered it and the treasure to Alexander in 330 (5.6.10).

GORGATAS (232): A young Macedonian at the court of Olympias, conscripted by Amyntas, son of Andromenes, in 331 against the queen mother's wishes (7.1.38).

GORGIAS (234): Like Gorgatas, enlisted by Amyntas against Olympias' wishes (7.1.38).

HARPALUS (143): Alexander's treasurer and personal friend. Before the battle of Issus he fled to Megara, but he later returned and was reinstated as treasurer by Alexander (cf. Arr. 3.6.4–7). Curtius says that he sent 7,000 infantrymen and 25,000 suits of gold and silver armour to Alexander in India (9.3.21). When he heard of Alexander's return from India, he feared punishment for his abuse of power and fled to Athens (10.2.1–7); the details of his flight are lost.

HAUSTANES (186): Sogdian rebel, defeated and captured by Craterus in 327 (8.5.2).

HECATAEUS (293): A young Macedonian at the court of Olympias, conscripted by Amyntas, son of Andromenes, in 331 against the wishes of the queen mother (7.1.38).

HECTOR (295): Son of Parmenion, brother of Philotas and Nicanor. He drowned in the Nile after riding in an overloaded boat (4.8.7–9; 6.9.27).

HEGELOCHUS (341): Son of Hippostratus, a high-ranking Macedonian officer who, together with Amphoterus, was charged with conducting the naval war in the Aegean (3.1.19), where he effectively eliminated the forces of Pharnabazus (4.5.14ff.). In Egypt, it is alleged, he plotted against Alexander (6.11.22ff.), although this did not come to light until after his death (probably at Gaugamela).

HEGESIMACHUS (344): Apparently a member of the hypaspists, he perished in a skirmish on an island in the Hydaspes river (8.13.13–15).

HELLANICE (462 'Lanice'): Sister of Clitus, and Alexander's nurse (8.1.21); two of her sons died fighting for Alexander at Miletus (8.2.8).

HELLANICUS (298): Probably one of the hypaspists, he won eighth place in the contest of valour in Sittacene (5.2.5).

HEPHAESTION (357): Alexander's dearest friend (3.12.16), but a man of questionable military ability. He visited the Persian captives after Issus and was mistaken for Alexander (3.12.15ff.; for his good looks cf. 7.9.19); he installed Abdalonymus as king of Sidon (4.1.16ff.); and he took the fleet from Tyre to Gaza in late 332 B.C. (4.5.10). At Gaugamela he was wounded in the arm (4.16.32). Hephaestion was on at least one occasion (6.2.9) responsible for the Persian captives; later he played no small part in the fall of Philotas (6.8.17; 6.11.10–11). He was among Alexander's advisers at the Tanais in 329 (7.7.9), and he campaigned with one-third of the army in Sogdiana in 328 (8.1.1, 10). He secured provisions for the following winter (8.2.13); bridged the Indus River (8.10.2; 8.12.4); negotiated with Omphis (Taxiles) (8.12.6); served as a commander in the battle with Porus (8.14.15); and subdued a part of India east of the Hydaspes (9.1.35). Hephaestion commanded the major part of the army in the land of the Horitae (9.10.6, apparently the least mobile and the non-combatants). Drypetis, the daughter of Darius, was his grieving widow (10.5.20).

HERACON (354): One of Parmenion's murderers in Ecbatana (330 B.C.), he was imprisoned in 325/324 for abuse of power (10.1.1–6).

HERMOLAUS (305): Son of Sopolis (8.7.2); a page. He was punished by Alexander for killing a boar which the king intended to strike (8.6.7). Hermolaus then conspired with Sostratus and a number of other pages to murder the king during the night (8.6.8ff.). The plot was revealed by Eurylochus (8.6.20ff.), and Hermolaus and his supporters were arrested (8.6.27). His relationship with Callisthenes implicated the latter as well (8.6.27ff.). For his trial see 8.7.1ff. He was put to death by torture (8.8.20).

HORRATAS (445 'Corrhagus'): The form Corrhagus is found in Diodorus (17.100.1) and is probably correct (see Hoffmann, *Die Makedonen*, 144ff.). A Macedonian soldier, he challenged the boxer Dioxippus to a duel and lost (9.7.17ff.).

HYPSIDES (764): A friend of Menedemus. When the latter was killed in the ambush at the Polytimetus River, although he had the means to escape Hypsides stayed behind and shared Menedemus' fate (7.7.36–7).

HYSTASPES (763): A general and relative of Darius III (6.1.7); his wife was found among Alexander's captives in 330 B.C. (6.1.6–9). He is probably the Bactrian Hystaspes of Arr. 7.6.5.

IDARNES (759 'Hydarnes'): A satrap of Darius, he captured Miletus in 333, only to be defeated in 332 by Balacrus (4.5.13). Berve (2.376) identifies him with the son of Mazaeus (Arr. 7.6.4).

ILIONEUS (384): A son of Artabazus, he was captured at Damascus in 333/332 B.C. (3.13.13).

IOLAUS (387): One of Dymnus' fellow-conspirators (6.7.15); he was presumably executed in 330 B.C. (6.11.38).

IOLLAS (386 'Iolaus'): The youngest son of Antipater the regent; he was one of Alexander's attendants (10.10.14) and rumour held that his brother, Cassander, brought poison from Macedonia, which Iollas served to Alexander (10.10.17).

IPHICRATES (393): Son of the famous Athenian general, Iphicrates; he was an ambassador sent to Darius and captured at Damascus in 333/332 (3.13.15). Arrian (2.15.4) says that Alexander kept him in his entourage until he died of illness (apparently not long afterwards).

LEOMEDON (464 'Laomedon'): Brother of Erigyius and a personal friend of Alexander. In the division of satrapies that followed Alexander's death, he was awarded Syria and Phoenicia (10.10.2). Otherwise Curtius does not mention him.

LEONIDAS (470): The commander of the *Ataktoi* or the 'Undisciplined Squadron', which was composed of suspected malcontents after the murder of Parmenion (7.2.35).

LEONNATUS (466): Bodyguard and kinsman of Alexander (he was related to Philip's mother, Eurydice). He was sent to the captive Persian queens to tell them that Darius still lived and that Alexander would see to their needs (3.12.7ff., with note 78). He advised Alexander during the Philotas affair (6.8.17), tried to restrain him during the Clitus episode (8.1.46) and revealed the conspiracy of the pages to him (8.6.22). For his role in the battle at the Hydaspes see 8.14.15; as a bodyguard, he saved Alexander's life in the town of the Sudracae (Mallians) and was seriously wounded (9.5.15, 17). Leonnatus commanded a portion of the army in the land of the Horitae (9.10.6–7, 19). For his role in the succession struggle of 323 B.C. see 10.7.8, 20; 10.8.4. His satrapy was Hellespontine Phrygia (10.10.2).

LYSIMACHUS (480): One of the seven bodyguards of Alexander. He had once been mauled by a lion in Syria (8.1.15), and in Bazaira the king prevented him from exposing himself to a similar danger (8.1.14–16). There was a rumour that Alexander once exposed Lysimachus to a lion (8.1.17). Lysimachus attempted to restrain Alexander during the Clitus affair (8.1.46). He offered his brother, Philip, a horse when the latter accompanied Alexander on foot, but Philip refused it and eventually collapsed from exhaustion (8.2.35ff.). In the division of satrapies after Alexander's death (323), he was awarded Thrace and the adjoining Pontic peoples (10.10.4).

MAENIDAS: See MENIDAS.

MANAPIS (55 'Amminapes'): A Parthian, in 330 he became satrap of Hyrcania (6.4.25). He was soon replaced by Phrataphernes; what became of him is unknown.

MAZACES (485): Ruler of Egypt in the absence of Sabaces, who took the Egyptian contingent to Issus and fell in battle (3.11.10; 4.1.28); he defeated the disorganized forces of Amyntas, son of Antioches (4.1.32–3). In 332 he surrendered Memphis and its treasure to Alexander (4.7.4).

MAZAEUS (484): A prominent Persian commander who monitored Alexander's advance to the Tigris but unwisely failed to prevent his crossing (4.9.7ff.; esp. 4.9.22). Mazaeus resorted to burning the villages and supplies in Alexander's path (4.10.14).

Curtius implies that Mazaeus was destined to marry a daughter of Darius (4.11.20), but this may be a dramatic invention. Mazaeus fails to attack Menidas and his scouts before the battle of Gaugamela (4.12.1ff.) but he distinguishes himself in the actual battle (4.15.5; 4.16.1ff.). In late 331 he surrendered Babylon to the Macedonians, and he remained there as its governor (5.1.17ff.; 5.8.12). Alexander learned of his death in 328 and replaced him with Stamenes (see DITAMENES above; 8.3.17). Brochubelus, 'the former satrap of Syria', is named as his son (5.13.11).

MEDATES (483 'Madates'): Ruler of the Uxians and a relative of Darius and Sisigambis (her brother-in-law) (5.3.12). He put up a stiff fight against Alexander (5.3.4ff.), but through the pleas of Sisigambis he was pardoned (5.3.15) and the Uxians freed from paying tribute.

MELEAGER (494): A Macedonian phalanx commander (for his position at Issus and Gaugamela, 3.9.7; 4.13.27). In the battle at the Persian Gates, he remained in the main camp with Craterus (5.4.14). At the Tanais (Iaxartes) Meleager and Perdiccas besieged the town of the Memaceni (7.6.19, the text is corrupt; 7.6.21), which fell under Alexander's leadership. His criticism of Alexander in India was dangerous in the aftermath of the Clitus affair (8.12.17). Meleager was most famous for his role in supporting the kingship of Philip Arrhidaeus (10.6.20; 10.7.1ff.), but he was soon tricked and executed by Perdiccas (10.9.7ff.).

MELON (496): Darius' interpreter, he surrendered to Alexander after Darius' arrest (5.13.7).

MEMNON (497): Rhodian mercenary leader; husband of Barsine and son-in-law of Artabazus. For his activities see the Summary of Books 1 and 2. His death changed the complexion of the war in Asia Minor and brought Darius into direct conflict with Alexander (3.1.21; 3.3.1; 3.4.3). His wife, Barsine, and his son were captured by Parmenion at Damascus (3.13.14).

MEMNON (499): He brought reinforcements from Thrace to India in 326 B.C. (9.3.21).

MEMNON: see MENON (514).

MENANDER (501): Alexander's satrap of Lydia; he retained his satrapy in the reorganization of 323 B.C. (10.10.2).

MENEDEMUS (504): He appears only in Curtius and the Metz Epitome 13. Menedemus commanded a contingent of 3,000 infantry and 800 cavalry sent to deal with Spitamenes at Maracanda (7.6.24). But Menedemus and his men were ambushed at the Polytimetus River (7.7.31ff.) with the loss of 2,300 lives (7.7.39). Alexander saw to their burial (7.9.21).

MENES (507): A prominent Macedonian and bodyguard of Alexander; he was left in charge of Babylonia and Cilicia (5.1.43; see the accompanying note).

MENIDAS (508): Commander of the mercenary cavalry at Gaugamela (Arr. 3.12.3; cf. Curt. 4.15.12). Before that battle, he was sent ahead to reconnoitre and came upon Mazaeus' contingent (4.12.4–5). He unsuccessfully tried to protect the Macedonian baggage at Gaugamela (4.15.12) and was wounded in the engagement (4.16.32). He is apparently identical with the 'Maenidas' who brought reinforcements to Alexander at Bactra (7.10.11).

MENON (514): Son of Cerdimmas, he was given charge of Syria in 331, after the Samaritans had murdered Andromachus (4.8.11).

MENON (515): In 330 he was made governor of Arachosia by Alexander, and a garrison of 4,000 infantry, 600 cavalry was left with him (7.3.5). When he died in 325/324, he was replaced by Sibyrtius (9.10.20).

MENTOR (−): Brother of Memnon of Rhodes but already dead when Alexander's campaign began. He was the father of Thimodes (3.3.1), and his three daughters were captured by Parmenion at Damascus in 333/332 (3.13.14).

METRON (520): The page and guardian of the armoury who brought news of Dymnus' plot to Alexander (6.7.22; 6.9.7ff.).

MITHRACENES (522 'Mithrazenes'): A supporter of Darius, he surrendered together with Orsilus to Alexander after Darius' arrest by Bessus (5.13.9).

MITHRENES (524): Commander of Sardis, he surrendered the city to Alexander (3.12.6; 5.1.44; 5.8.12). Alexander placed him in charge of Armenia in late 331 (5.1.44).

MOERIS (536): King of the Indian Patalii, he fled to the hills on Alexander's arrival (9.8.28).

MULLINUS (542): *Scriba regis*, he was placed in charge of the light-armed at Aornus (8.11.5).

NABARZANES (543): Darius' *chiliarchos*; his seal was on the letter which led to Sisenes' death (3.7.12ff.). Nabarzanes commanded the cavalry and about 20,000 slingers and archers on the Persian right at Issus (3.9.1). With Bessus, he plotted to arrest and murder Darius (5.9.2ff.; 5.12.14; 5.13.18; cf. 6.4.8). Thereafter he fled into Hyrcania (6.3.9), but soon surrendered to Alexander along with Bagoas, who secured his immunity from punishment (6.5.22–3).

NEARCHUS (544): Alexander's personal friend and fleet-commander. He was ordered to sail with Onesicritus down the Indus to the Ocean and westward to the Euphrates (9.10.3; 10.1.10). In the debate that followed Alexander's death Nearchus argued for Hercules, son of Barsine, as Alexander's successor (10.6.10–12).

NICANOR (554): Son of Parmenion and commander of the hypaspists (3.9.7; 4.13.27). He died shortly before the Philotas affair in 330 (6.6.18; 6.9.13, 27).

NICANOR (558): One of Dymnus' fellow-conspirators (6.7.15); he was apparently stoned to death (6.11.38).

NICANOR (560): A courageous young Macedonian − perhaps one of Alexander's hypaspists. Along with Hegesimachus and several others, he was killed on an island in the Hydaspes shortly before the battle with Porus (8.13.13ff.).

NICARCHIDES (563): Macedonian commander of the citadel of Persepolis (5.6.11).

NICOMACHUS (569): Lover of Dymnus (6.7.2ff.; 6.8.1; 6.9.7; 6.10.5ff.; 6.11.37–8).

NICOSTRATUS (570): A member of the pages' conspiracy (8.6.9), unless his name is an error for Sostratus.

OCHUS (833): Son of Darius III and Statira. Alexander admires his courage after the battle of Issus (3.12.26). Darius offers him to Alexander as a hostage in return for a peaceful settlement (4.11.6), but his offer is rejected. In his speech to his troops before Gaugamela, Darius laments the captivity of his son (4.14.22).

OLYMPIAS (581): Married Philip II in 357 B.C. Mother of Alexander and Cleopatra (cf. 5.2.22). Alexander wished her to be deified after his death (9.6.26; cf. 10.5.30). She opposed Cassander after Alexander's death, brought about the deaths of Arrhidaeus and Eurydice, and was finally executed by Cassander's agents in 316 B.C. (cf. 10.10.19).

OMPHIS (739 'Taxiles'): Omphis is the Greek rendering of the Sanskrit Ambhi. He was king of Taxila and cooperated with Hephaestion (8.12.4ff.). He surrendered to Alexander and was given lavish gifts including 1,000 talents (8.12.7ff.). Omphis then took the name of his kingdom ('Taxiles') (8.12.14). Alexander turned over to him thirty elephants captured with Barsaentes (8.13.3–5). Curtius relates that Taxiles' brother was killed by Porus (8.14.35–6). When Alexander sailed south he left Porus and Taxiles (former foes) as friends (9.3.22; cf. 10.1.20).

ONESICRITUS (583): Onesicritus of Astypaleia was Alexander's chief helmsman and author of a work entitled *How Alexander was Educated* (see T. S. Brown, *Onesicritus: A Study in Hellenistic Historiography*, Berkeley, 1949). In 325 B.C. he and Nearchus were ordered to take the fleet to the Ocean and sail westward to the Euphrates (9.10.3; cf. 10.1.10). Curtius does not mention his literary achievements.

ONOMAS (538 'Monimus'): A Spartan ambassador to Darius, captured by Parmenion at Damascus (3.13.15). The mss. read *omaio*, which Hedicke emended to Onomas; but Berve (2.266, n.2) argues for Monimus, since Onomas in Arr. 3.24.4 is a short form of Curtius' Onomastorides. Arrian dates his capture to 330 B.C.

ONOMASTORIDES (584 'Onomastoridas'): A Spartan ambassador captured by Parmenion at Damascus in 333/332 (3.13.5); Arrian 3.24.4 dates his capture to 330 B.C. Cf. 'Onomas' above.

ORONTOBATES (594 'Orontopates'): Together with Ariobarzanes he commanded the Persians, Mardians and Sogdiani at Gaugamela (4.12.7).

ORSILUS (595 'Orsillus'): After the arrest of Darius by Bessus, Orsilus and Mithracenes surrendered to Alexander (5.13.9). Orsilus *may* be a familiar form of Orxines (Orsines; see below).

ORSINES (592 'Orxines'): A descendant of Cyrus and of the 'Seven Persians' (4.12.8; 10.1.23), Orsines had supreme command of the Persians, Mardians and Sogdiani at Gaugamela (4.12.8). When Alexander returned to Parsagada he found that Orsines had taken over the satrapy of Persia on Phrasaortes' death, without Alexander's orders (Arr. 6.29.2). Curtius claims (10.1.24ff.) that Orsines gave splendid gifts to Alexander and his friends but disregarded the eunuch Bagoas, who poisoned Alexander's mind against him and brought about his death (10.1.24–38).

OXARTES (–): Alexander's ambassador to Sisimithres, he convinced the latter to surrender (8.2.25ff.). Arrian (4.21.6) calls him Oxyartes (the father of Roxane), but in Curtius' account Oxyartes had not yet surrendered to Alexander (see 'Oxyartes' below).

OXATHRES (586 'Oxyathres'): The brother of Darius III, he fought gallantly at Issus (3.11.8). In 330 he was found among the prisoners (presumably captured after Darius' death, 6.2.9) and added to the number of Alexander's 'Friends' (*Hetairoi*) (6.2.11). Darius' murderer Bessus was handed over to him for punishment (7.5.40–41). His daughter was captured by Parmenion at Damascus in 333/332 (3.13.13).

OXYARTES (587): A Sogdian baron (Curtius makes him a satrap, but does not name the territory he is supposed to have ruled) who surrendered to Alexander in 327 B.C.; two of his sons served as soldiers (hostages) with Alexander (8.4.21). According to Alde's emended text (but see the Glossary s. v. SISIMITHRES), he gives a banquet at which Alexander is so impressed by the beauty of his daughter Roxane that he chooses to marry her (8.4.22–30; cf. 10.3.11). Ruler of Bactriana (9.8.10).

OXYDATES (588): A Persian noble, imprisoned by Darius and marked out for execution, he was released by Alexander and made satrap of Media in 330 B.C. (6.2.11). In 328/327 he was recalled and replaced by Atropates (see 8.3.17, with accompanying note).

OZINES (579): A rebel Persian noble who, along with Zariaspes, was defeated and captured by Craterus in 325 B.C. (9.10.19). For his punishment see 10.1.9.

PARMENION (606): Alexander's foremost general until 330 B.C. Father of Philotas,

Hector and Nicanor. Captured Tarsus (3.4.14–15); warned Alexander against the supposed treachery of Philip of Acarnania (3.6.4ff.); secured Issus (3.7.6ff.); his command at Issus (3.9.7ff.; 3.11.3, 13); captured Damascus (3.12.27–13.17); governed Coele-Syria (4.1.4) and then handed it over to Andromachus (4.5.9). His son Hector drowned in the Nile (4.8.7–9); advised Alexander not to read out Darius' letters to the Greek troops (4.10.17); urged Alexander to accept Darius' peace-terms (4.11.11ff.; cf. 4.12.21); advocated a night attack on the Persians at Gaugamela (4.12.21); his command at Gaugamela (4.13.4ff.; 4.15.6–7; 4.16.2ff.); took the heavily-armed troops and baggage train along the wagon-road from Susa to Persepolis (5.3.16); left behind with Craterus at Persepolis (5.6.11). His son Nicanor died in Aria (6.6.18); his son Philotas was summoned to Alexander's tent (6.7.18). Parmenion in relation to the Philotas affair (6.7.18; 6.8.7ff.; 6.9.4ff.; 6.10.34; 6.11.20ff.; 7.1.27); Parmenion's death (7.2.11ff.); Curtius' eulogy of Parmenion (7.2.33–4). See also 7.3.4; 8.1.33; 8.1.38; 8.1.52; 8.7.4–5; 8.8.5; 10.1.1; 10.1.6.

PASAS (608): Thessalian who acted as a go-between for the cavalry and infantry in the succession struggle after Alexander's death (10.8.15).

PASIPPUS (617 'Pausippus'): A Spartan ambassador to Darius, captured by Parmenion at Damascus in 333/332 B.C. (3.13.15); Arr. 3.24.4 dates his capture to 330.

PATRON (612): Commander of the Greek mercenaries who remained with Darius after Gaugamela (5.9.15). He tried in vain to protect Darius from the treachery of Bessus (5.11.1ff.; cf. 5.12.4, 7).

PAUSANIAS (614): Assassin of Philip II (7.1.6).

PERDICCAS (627): A prominent commander and trusted friend of Alexander, Perdiccas was the most powerful individual in Babylon at the time of Alexander's death. He was an infantry commander at Issus (3.9.7) and was entrusted with the siege of Tyre in Alexander's absence (4.3.1); later he was wounded at Gaugamela (4.16.32). With Meleager he besieged the town of the Memaceni on the Iaxartes river (7.6.19ff.). He tried to restrain Alexander during the quarrel with Clitus (8.1.45, 48). Perdiccas and Hephaestion were sent ahead to bridge the Indus (8.10.2), and played major roles in the battle with Porus (8.14.15). See also 9.1.19 for Perdiccas' independent mission in India. Before he died, Alexander gave Perdiccas his signet ring, but Perdiccas did not seize the throne, hoping instead to secure it through Roxane's child (10.5.4ff.). He eliminated his opponent Meleager by trickery (10.9.7ff.) and was *de facto* the leading man in Babylon in 323 (10.10.4). He was murdered by his own officers two years later. Cf. 6.8.17 for his role in the Philotas affair.

PERILAUS (630 'Perillus'): Macedonian. Acted as a go-between for the cavalry and infantry in the succession struggle after Alexander's death (10.8.15).

PEUCESTES (635 'Peucestas'): Commander of the troops left by Alexander in Egypt in 332/331 B.C. Curtius (4.8.4) exaggerates his role.

PEUCESTES (634 'Peucestas'): Saved Alexander's life in India in 325 (9.5.14ff.); for this he was appointed an extraordinary eighth bodyguard (Arr. 6.28.4).

PEUCOLAUS (637): A fellow-conspirator of Dymnus (6.7.15; 6.9.5). He was presumably stoned to death (6.11.38).

PHARASMANES (765): Ruler of the Chorasmians. Curtius (8.1.8) erringly calls him Phrat1aphernes.

PHARNABAZUS (766): Son of Artabazus, he took command of the war in the Aegean when Memnon died (3.3.1) and gave Thimodes Greek mercenaries to take to Darius in 333 (3.8.1). In 333/332 he exacted money from Miletus, and garrisoned Chios,

Andros and Siphnos (4.1.37). Later, in 332, he was captured at Chios by Amphoterus and Hegelochus (4.5.14ff.), though he later escaped (Arr. 3.2.7).

PHEGUS (770): Indian king. Informed Alexander of the Ganges and the tribes east of the Hyphasis river (9.1.36; 9.2.2).

PHILIP (788): Doctor from Acarnania. He had been a long-time associate of Alexander, whom he healed after his collapse in the Cydnus River in Cilicia (3.6.1ff.). Parmenion charged that Philip had been bribed by Darius to poison Alexander (3.6.4; cf. 6.10.34). Philip also treated Alexander for the wound sustained at Gaza (4.6.17).

PHILIP (778): Son of Balacrus. He led an infantry battalion at Gaugamela (4.13.28). Arrian (3.11.9) gives this command to Simmias, son of Andromenes. See Bosworth, Arrian, 300–301.

PHILIP (779): Son of Menelaus. Commander of the Thessalian cavalry (4.13.29; 6.6.35); he replaced Alexander Lyncestes.

PHILIP (774): Son of Agathocles, brother of Lysimachus. He accompanied Alexander on foot for 500 stades in pursuit of Sogdian rebels. After fighting at his side, Philip expired in Alexander's arms (8.2.35–9).

PHILIP (780): Son of Machatas, brother of Harpalus. Alexander's satrap of India; he was killed in 325 and replaced by Eudaemon (Eudemus) (10.1.20–21).

PHILIP (781 'Philip Arrhidaeus'): See ARRHIDAEUS.

PHILOTAS (806): When Alexander moved southward to Egypt in 332, he left Philotas in charge of the area around Tyre (4.5.9).

PHILOTAS (802): Son of Parmenion and commander of the Companion cavalry. For his command at Gaugamela, see 4.13.26. He argued that Alexander should place his feet on Darius' table (5.2.15); encircled Ariobarzanes at the Persian Gates (5.4.20, 30); performed the funeral rites for his brother, Nicanor, who died in Aria in 330 (6.6.19). Soon afterwards, he learned of Dymnus' conspiracy from Cebalinus but did not report it to Alexander (6.7.18ff.), and it was assumed that Philotas suppressed the information because he was party to the plot (6.8.1ff.). He was tried and executed (6.8.20–11.40). For further references see 7.1.1, 5; 7.1.10–11; 7.1.30, 32; 7.2.4, 16, 34; 8.6.21; 8.8.5.

PHILOTAS (807): From Augaea (or Aegae?). A winner in the contest of valour in Sittacene (5.2.5).

PHILOTAS (801): Son of Carsis. A member of the pages' conspiracy (8.6.9). He was presumably executed (8.8.20).

PHILOTAS (804): Satrap of Cilicia in 323 B.C. (10.10.2).

PHRADATES (189 'Autophradates'): Curtius consistently calls him Phradates. He commanded 50 chariots and the Caspians at Gaugamela (4.12.9); satrap of the Tapurians, he surrendered to Alexander after Darius' death and retained his post (6.4.24–5; cf. 6.5.21). 'Phradates' at 8.3.17 is an error for Atropates. He was suspected of aiming at royal power, arrested and executed in 324 (10.1.39).

PHRATAPHERNES (814): Satrap of the Hyrcanians, he surrendered to Alexander after Darius' death (6.4.23), but did not immediately retain his satrapy (6.4.25, see MANAPIS), though it was later awarded to him (8.3.17). Alexander ordered him to bring provisions as he approached Gedrosia (9.10.17).

PHRATAPHERNES: See PHARASMANES (8.1.8).

PITHON (619 'Peithon'): Son of Agenor. Alexander sent him to deal with the rebellious Musicani in 326/325 (9.8.16).

PITHON (621 'Peithon'): Son of Crateuas. One of Alexander's seven bodyguards. He opposed the acclamation of Philip Arrhidaeus in 323 (10.7.4) and supported Perdiccas (10.7.8). He was named satrap of Media in 323 (10.10.4).

PLATON (Berve 2.429, no. 67, thinks he is fictitious and Curtius' error for Socrates; see 4.5.9 with note 35). Brought reinforcements to Alexander from Cilicia (5.7.12).

PNYTAGORAS (642): King of Salamis on Cyprus. He brought ships to aid Alexander in the siege of Tyre (4.3.11).

POLEMON (646): Son of Theramenes. Alexander's fleet-commander in Egypt; ordered to protect the mouths of the Nile with 30 triremes (4.8.4).

POLEMON (644): Son of Andromenes. Brother of Amyntas. He fled from Alexander's camp after Philotas' arrest (7.1.10), and was arrested and returned for trial (7.2.1ff.).

POLYDAMAS (648): Sent by Parmenion to Alexander during the battle at Gaugamela with orders to fetch help (4.15.6ff.). He later took the message to Cleander that led to Parmenion's murder (7.2.11ff.).

POLYPERCHON (654): A prominent Macedonian infantry-commander, he supported Parmenion's strategy at Gaugamela and incurred Alexander's anger (4.13.7ff.). Curtius seems to say that he commanded the 'foreign troops' at Gaugamela (4.13.28 – the text is corrupt). He led his battalion against Ariobarzanes (at the Persian Gates) by a third route (5.4.20, 30). He subdued the region of Bubacene in Sogdiana(?) (8.5.2). And he fell briefly into disfavour for mocking *proskynesis* (8.5.22–6.1).

POLYSTRATUS (655): The soldier who found Darius just before he died (5.13.24).

PORUS (683): Indian king who opposed Alexander at the Hydaspes River (8.12.13ff.). Porus was heavily wounded in the defeat (8.14.31–2), but he survived and entered into a friendly alliance with Alexander, retaining his kingdom. See further 9.1.7; 9.2.5ff.; 9.3.22; 10.1.20.

PTOLEMAEUS (670): Son of Seleucus. An infantry-commander at Issus (3.9.7), where he fell in battle (Arr. 2.10.7).

PTOLEMAEUS (673): Commander of the Thracians. In 329/328 he brought reinforcements to Alexander at Bactra (7.10.11).

PTOLEMY (668: 'Ptolemaeus'): Macedonian officer and friend of Alexander; king of Egypt 305–283 B.C. Attempted to restrain Alexander during his quarrel with Clitus (8.1.45, 48); learned from Eurylochus the details of Hermolaus' conspiracy (8.6.22); his exploits in India are exaggerated (8.10.21); his activities at the Hydaspes River (8.13.18–19; 8.13.23, 27; 8.14.15); his history refutes Cleitarchus and Timagenes (9.5.21; cf. Introduction, p. 5); near death at Harmatelia (9.8.22ff.); opposed Perdiccas' plan to await the birth of Roxane's child (10.6.13ff.); awarded Egypt in 323 (10.10.1); transported Alexander's body to Memphis and then to Alexandria (10.10.20).

RHEOMITHRES (685 'Rheomitres'): Persian commander who died in the battle of Issus (3.11.10).

RHOSACES (687 'Rhoisaces'): Tried to kill Alexander at the Granicus River in 334, but Clitus cut off his arm with his sword (8.1.20). According to Arrian (1.15.8), this was Spithridates, Rhosaces' brother.

ROXANE (688): Daughter of Oxyartes, she married Alexander (8.4.23ff.). Her as yet unborn son was favoured by Perdiccas as Alexander's successor (10.6.9ff.).

SABACES (689): Satrap of Egypt. He fell in battle at Issus (3.10.11; cf. 4.1.28).

SAMBUS (693): Indian king who surrendered to Alexander (9.8.13, 17).

SAMAXUS (692): An Indian ruler who gave shelter to the regicide Barsaentes. He was captured and brought to Alexander in chains (8.13.4).

SATIBARZANES (697): Satrap of Aria, he brought news to Alexander that Bessus had assumed the tiara and the title Artaxerxes (6.6.13); he retained his satrapy but soon rebelled (6.6.21ff.). Alexander sent Caranus, Erigyius, Artabazus and Andronicus against him (7.3.2), and Erigyius killed him in single combat (7.4.33–40).

SATROPATES (699): His name is perhaps correctly 'Atropates'. A cavalry commander of Darius, (4.9.7) he was killed in hand-to-hand combat by Ariston (4.9.25).

SEUTHES (702): King of the Odrysians, revolted from Macedon (10.1.45).

SIBYRTIUS (703): Satrap of Carmania (Arr. 6.27.1); Curtius says he was given authority over Arachosia, Gedrosia and the territory of the Oreitae (9.10.20).

SISENES (710): A Persian in Alexander's entourage, Nabarzanes had urged him in a letter (which Alexander intercepted) to betray the king. When Sisenes appeared to conceal the letter Alexander had him murdered (3.7.11–15).

SISIGAMBIS (711): Mother of Darius III, Oxathres and, apparently, Statira (721). She appeared in the Persian procession (3.3.22), accompanied Darius to Issus (3.8.2), where she was captured (3.11.24ff.) and visited by Leonnatus, Alexander and Hephaestion (3.12.7ff.; she mistook Hephaestion for the King, 3.12.13–17). She was not fooled into thinking that the Persians were victorious at Arbela (4.15.10–11); Alexander insulted her by suggesting she learn to work with wool (5.2.18ff.; though Alexander honoured her as a second mother, 5.2.20–22). Medates had married her niece (5.3.12) and asked Sisigambis to intercede with Alexander on behalf of the Uxians (5.3.13); in this she was successful (5.3.13–15). When Alexander died in Babylon, she ceased eating and died five days later (10.5.19–25).

SISIMITHRES (708): Sogdianian baron who took refuge on the Rock of Paraetacene together with his mother and children (8.2.19, 33). Alexander sent Oxyartes to him in order to induce Sisimithres to surrender (8.2.5). Seeing that Alexander's men had scaled the cliffs above him Sisimithres agreed to surrender (8.2.30–32) and gave as hostages two of his sons, who served in Alexander's army (8.2.33). This appears to be all that Curtius has to say about Sisimithres, but comparison with Arrian and the Metz Epitome suggest that he and Chorienes (apparently unknown to Curtius) are identical. Berve had concluded rightly that Chorienes was the official (regional, i.e. ruler of Choriene: cf. the case of Taxiles, whose personal name was Omphis or Ambhi) name of Sisimithres. This suggests too that the MS reading at 8.4.21, 'Cohortandus' may in fact be a reference to Chorienes (= Sisimithres). Alde corrected the reading to Oxyartes, since the passage that follows refers to Oxyartes' daughter Roxane. It apears that something has gone wrong with Curtius' text and that the banquet at which Alexander met the daughter of Oxyartes was hosted by Chorienes (cf. Metz Epitome 28–29). Simple emendation of the text will not solve all the difficulties. For discussion see W. Heckel, 'Chorienes and Sisimithres', Athenaeum 74 (1986) 223–6.

SISOCOSTUS (707 'Sisicottus'): Alexander left him as commander of Aornus (8.11.25).

SITALCES (712): One of Parmenion's murderers (10.1.1). He was punished for abuse of power while Alexander was in India (10.1.1–8).

SOCRATES (732): Son of Sathon. A regiment commander in the Companion cavalry (Arr. 1.12.7). Given a military command in Cilicia in 332 (Curt. 4.5.9 is vague).

SOPHITES (734 'Sopeithes'): Indian king who ruled territory between the Hydraotis and the Hyphasis (9.1.24ff.). Arrian and Diodorus call him Sopeithes. But see McCrindle, 411.

SOPOLIS (736): Father of the page Hermolaus, he feared that Hermolaus' crime and his outspokenness would bring about his own death as well (8.7.2). Berve (2.368–9) identifies him with the cavalry-commander and son of Hermodorus (against this view see Bosworth, *Arrian*, 58).

SOSTRATUS (738): Son of Amyntas. A page and lover of Hermolaus, he conspired against Alexander (8.6.7–8) and was presumably executed (8.8.20).

SPITACES (716): According to Curtius (8.14.2) Spitaces was a brother of Porus. He commanded the advance force sent to attack Alexander, who had just crossed the Hydaspes. Arrian (5.18.2) says Spitaces perished in the battle.

SPITAMENES (717): Bactrian noble who, together with Dataphernes and Catanes, arrested Bessus (7.5.19–26) and delivered him to Alexander (7.5.36ff.). But when Alexander summoned Spitamenes and his followers to Bactra in 329, they feared treachery and continued to oppose him (7.6.14ff.). Alexander sent Menedemus against Spitamenes at Maracanda, but Spitamenes caught him in an ambush at the Polytimetus River, destroying almost his entire force (7.7.31–9). On Alexander's approach he fled to Bactra (7.9.20). In 328/327 he was murdered by his own wife, who delivered his head to Alexander (8.3.1–16). Arrian (4.17.7) claims that the Massagetae murdered Spitamenes in order to avert Alexander's hostility from themselves.

STASANOR (719): Cypriot from Soli, satrap of the Drangae (8.3.17).

STATIRA (721 'Stateira'): Not named by Curtius, she was the sister and wife of Darius, and also reputed to be the most beautiful woman in Asia (3.12.22). In 333 B.C. she accompanied Darius to Issus, along with her mother, her two daughters and her son Ochus (3.8.12; cf. 3.3.22), where they were captured after the battle (3.11.24ff.) and visited by Alexander (3.12). Darius tried unsuccessfully to ransom her (4.1.8) and she died before Alexander reached Gaugamela (4.10.18–19). News of her death was brought to Darius by the eunuch Tyriotes (4.10.25ff.).

STATIRA (722 'Stateira'): One of Darius' daughters, she was captured at Issus (3.11.24ff.). Darius offered her in marriage to Alexander before the battle of Gaugamela (4.5.1; 4.11.5), but Alexander rejected the offer and claimed that Statira had been destined to marry Mazaeus (4.11.20). In 324, however, Alexander did marry Statira at Susa (10.3.12); her sister Drypetis had married Hephaestion (cf. 10.5.20).

STRATO (727): King of Aradus (4.1.6).

STRATO (728): King of Sidon and a supporter of Darius, he was deposed by Alexander (4.1.16; cf. 4.1.26). Abdalonymus was chosen to replace him (4.1.19–26).

TAURON (741): Son of Machatas and, apparently, the brother of Harpalus. He commanded 1,500 mercenaries and 1,000 Agrianes in the skirmish with the Uxians (5.3.6ff.). He appears again in the battle against Porus (8.14.15).

TAXILES (739, see also above under OMPHIS): Formerly known as Omphis, with Alexander's consent he became ruler of Taxila and took the name Taxiles (8.12.14). Alexander assigned to him the 30 elephants captured with Barzaentes and Samaxus (8.13.5). His brother was killed in battle by Porus (8.14.35–6), and Alexander argued that Porus ought to have seen in Taxiles himself an example of Alexander's clemency (8.14.41). Taxiles made a marriage alliance with Porus (9.3.22); later he reported to Alexander the deaths of Philip and Abisares in India (10.1.20).

TERIOLTES (758 'Tyriespis'): Governor of Parapanisadae, accused of misrule and executed on Alexander's order (9.8.9).

THAIS (359): An Athenian courtesan, later the mistress of Ptolemy, she induced Alexander to burn the palace at Persepolis to avenge Xerxes' destruction of Athens (5.7.3ff.).

THALESTRIS (Berve 2.419, no. 26): Queen of the Amazons, she met Alexander in Hyrcania and spent thirteen days of intimacy with him in the hope of having a child by him. Convinced that she had conceived, she returned to her kingdom (6.5.25–32).

THEAETETUS (360): An Athenian, spokesman for the mutilated Greeks who met Alexander before Persepolis. He argued in favour of returning to Greece (5.5.17–20), but few accepted his arguments (5.5.21).

THEODOTUS (361): One of the victors in the contest of valour in Sittacene; he was placed seventh (5.2.5).

THERSIPPUS (368): A Greek who carried a letter to Darius from Alexander at Marathus in 333/332 (4.1.14).

THIMODES (380 'Thymondas'): Son of Mentor (3.3.1) and commander of the Greek mercenaries on the Aegean seaboard; he brought these to Darius at Issus (3.8.1). His advice that Darius withdraw to the plains of Mesopotamia was rejected (3.8.2ff.). He commanded 30,000 Greeks on the right wing in the battle of Issus (3.9.2).

TIMAEUS (474 'Limnaios'): He died shielding Alexander's body in the town of the Sudracae of India (9.5.15–16).

TIMAGENES (–): Historian (1st cent. B.C.) from Alexandria. See Introduction, p. 7 (9.5.21).

TIRIDATES (754): Persian commander of the citadel of Persepolis, which he surrendered with its treasure to Alexander in 330 (5.5.2); Alexander allowed him to retain his position (5.6.11).

TYRIDATES (756 'Tiridates'): Alexander handed over his estate to Eurylochus as a reward for revealing the details of Hermolaus' conspiracy (8.6.26).

TYRIOTES (742 'Teireos'): The eunuch who brought Darius news of his wife's death and of Alexander's grief (4.10.25–34). Plutarch (*Alex.* 30) calls him Teireos.

XENOPHILUS (578): Left by Alexander as commander of the citadel of Susa (5.2.16).

ZARIASPES (335): A rebel Persian noble who, along with Ozines, was defeated and captured by Craterus in 325 B.C. (9.10.19). For his punishment see 10.1.9.

ZOILUS (339): Brought 500 soldiers from Greece to Alexander in 330 B.C. (6.6.35).

ZOPYRION (340): Governor of Thrace, conducted disastrous expedition against the Getae (10.1.44).

APPENDIX 4

Index of Mythical, Historical and Literary Figures

Achilles: 4.6.29; 8.4.26
Aesculapius (Asklepios): 3.7.3
Agenor: 4.4.19
Amazons: 6.4.17; 6.5.27
Apollo: 4.3.21–2
Belus (Baal): 3.3.16; 5.1.24
Bucephalas (Alexander's horse): 6.5.18; cf. 9.3.23
Castor: 8.5.8
Croesus: 3.4.1
Cyrus (the Great): 3.4.1; 4.12.8; 4.14.24; 5.6.10; 6.3.12; 7.3.1, 3; 7.6.11, 20;
    10.1.23; 10.1.30, 34
Darius I: 3.10.8; 4.1.10; 5.6.1
Erythrus: 8.9.14; 10.1.13
Euripides: 8.1.28
Father Liber (Dionysus): 3.10.5; 3.12.18; 7.9.15; 8.2.6; 8.5.8, 11; 8.5.17; 8.10.1,
    11–12; 8.10.17; 9.2.29; 9.4.21; 9.8.5; 9.10.24
Furies (Erinyes): 6.10.14
Gordius: 3.1.14
Hercules (Heracles): 3.10.5; 3.12.27; 4.2.2, 4, 17; 4.3.22; 4.8.16; 8.5.8, 11; 8.5.17;
    8.10.1; 8.11.2; 8.14.11; 9.2.29; 9.4.2, 21; 10.1.17
Jupiter (Zeus): 3.1.14; 3.3.11; 3.12.27; 4.7.5, 8; 4.7.24–5; 4.7.28, 30; 4.13.15; 5.5.8;
    6.9.18; 6.10.26–7; 6.11.5–7; 6.11.23; 8.1.42; 8.5.5; 8.7.13; 8.8.14; 8.10.1, 12;
    8.10.29
Mardonius: 4.1.11
Midas: 3.1.11, 14
Minerva (Athena): 3.7.3; 3.12.27
Minerva Victoria (Athena Nike): 4.13.15; 8.2.32; 8.11.24
Mithras: 4.13.12
Neptune (Poseidon): 4.2.20; 4.4.5
Ninus: 3.3.16
Perdiccas III (King of Macedon, 365–359 B.C.): 6.11.26
Philip II (King of Macedon, 359–336 B.C.): 3.7.11; 3.10.7; 4.1.12; 4.7.27;
    4.10.3; 4.15.8; 6.4.25; 6.5.2; 6.6.9; 7.1.3, 6; 8.1.20, 23, 25, 27, 30, 33, 36, 52;
    8.7.13; 9.8.22; 10.2.23; 10.5.30
Pollux (Polydeuces): 8.5.8
Prometheus: 7.3.22
Saturn (Cronus): 4.3.23
Semiramis: 5.1.24; 7.6.20; 9.6.23

APPENDIX 5

Index of Peoples

APPENDIX 6

Geographical Index

Acadira: 8.10.19
Acesines: 8.9.8; 9.3.20; 9.4.1, 8
Achaea: 4.5.14
Aeolis: 4.5.7; 6.3.3
Africa: 4.3.20; 4.4.19; 4.8.5; 4.9.1; 8.9.17; 10.1.17; 10.10.1
Alexandria (in India): 9.8.8
Alexandria (in the Caucasus): 7.3.23
Alexandria (in Egypt): 4.8.2, 5; 10.10.20
Alexandria (on the Tanais): 7.6.25
Alps: 10.1.18
Amanic Gates: 3.8.13
Ancyra: 3.1.22
Andros: 4.1.37
Aornis: 8.11.2
Arabia: 4.3.1; 4.3.7; 5.1.11
Arabus: 9.10.6
Aradus: 4.1.5
Araxes: 4.5.4; 7.3.19
Arbela: 4.9.9; 4.16.9; 5.1.2–3, 10; 6.1.21; 9.2.23
Armenia: 4.9.14; 4.12.12; 5.1.13, 44; 6.3.3; 7.3.20
Artacana: 6.6.33
Arvae: 6.4.23
Asia: 3.1.13, 16; 3.3.5; 3.7.11; 3.10.4; 4.1.13, 20, 38; 4.3.11; 4.4.1; 4.5.14; 4.10.34;
    5.1.1, 39; 5.4.9; 5.5.9; 5.9.4; 5.10.3; 6.2.14; 6.6.6; 6.11.29; 7.1.3; 7.3.19, 21;
    7.7.2, 4, 14; 7.8.13, 30; 7.9.17; 7.11.10; 8.1.26; 9.1.3; 9.2.15, 24; 9.6.20–21;
    10.1.37, 43; 10.2.8, 11–12, 23, 25; 10.3.7, 13; 10.5.13, 18
Athens: 3.2.10; 10.2.2–3
Attica: 10.2.1
Babylon: 3.2.2; 3.3.3; 4.9.6; 4.16.7; 5.1.7, 17; 5.1.35, 43–5; 5.6.9; 10.1.16, 19;
    10.6.1; 10.8.11
Babylonia: 4.6.2; 4.9.2; 5.1.43; 8.3.17
Bactra: 3.10.5; 4.5.4, 8; 4.11.13; 5.8.1; 5.9.5, 8, 16; 5.10.6, 9; 5.11.6; 5.13.2, 18;
    6.3.9; 6.6.22; 6.11.32; 7.4.31; 7.7.4; 7.8.21, 30; 7.9.20; 7.10.10; 9.7.1, 11; 10.10.4
Bactriana: 8.2.13
Bactrus (river): 7.4.31
Bazaira: 8.1.10
Beira: 8.10.22
Boeotia: 3.10.7; 4.4.19; 6.3.2

Ganges: 8.9.5, 8; 9.2.3; 9.4.8, 17, 20
Gaza: 4.5.10; 4.6.7; 4.7.2
Gazaba: 8.4.1
Gordium: 3.1.12
Gordyaean Mountains: 5.1.14
Granicus River: 3.1.9; 3.10.7; 4.9.22; 4.14.1, 10; 8.1.20; 9.2.23
Greece: 3.10.8; 4.1.11; 4.1.36, 38; 4.5.11; 5.5. 10; 5.5.22; 5.7.4, 8; 5.8.16; 5.11.6;
   6.2.5; 6.6.35; 7.4.32; 7.5.28; 8.1.30; 9.1.2; 9.6.20; 10.1.45; 10.10.18
Halicarnassus: 3.7.4; 5.2.5; 8.1.36
Halys River: 4.5.1; 4.11.5
Hammon (oracle of): 4.7.5; 4.7.22; 4.8.1; 6.9.18; 10.5.4
Hecatompylos: 6.2.15
Hellespont: 3.1.19–20; 3.5.7; 3.12.18; 4.1.10, 36; 4.5.1, 7; 4.11.5; 4.14.9; 6.3.3, 15;
   9.2.24; 9.6.20; 10.10.2
Hiarotis: 9.1.13
Hiberia: 10.1.18
Hiberus: 10.1.18
Hister: 4.11.13 (cf. Ister)
Hypasis: 9.1.35
Hyrcania: 4.5.4; 5.13.11, 18; 6.3.9; 6.4.2–3; 6.4.19, 25; 6.5.1, 11; 6.5.22, 24;
   8.3.17
Hyrcanian Sea: 7.3.21
Illyricum: 6.6.35
Imbros: 4.5.22
India: 3.10.5; 4.11.13; 5.2.10; 6.2.18; 6.4.19; 6.6.36; 7.1.24; 7.4.20, 39; 7.8.19;
   7.11.8; 8.2.27; 8.5.1; 8.9.1–2; 8.9.9, 13; 8.13.4; 9.1.8; 9.2.3, 12; 9.3.8; 9.4.8, 16;
   9.7.1; 9.8.4, 11; 9.10.21; 10.1.43
Indus River: 8.9.4, 6; 8.10.2; 8.11.7; 8.12.4; 9.4.8
Ionia: 4.5.7; 6.3.3
Ister: 7.7.4 (cf. Hister)
Italy: 8.1.37; 10.1.18
Lesbos: 3.1.19
Libanus: 4.2.18; 4.2.24; 10.1.19
Lycaonia: 4.5.13
Lycia: 3.1.1; 5.4.9; 7.10.12; 10.10.2
Lycus River (in Phrygia): 3.1.5
Lycus River (in Armenia): 4.9.9; 4.16.8, 16
Lydia: 3.4.1; 4.1.34–5; 4.5.7–8; 4.11.5; 6.3.3; 6.6.35; 7.8.19; 10.10.2
Lyrnesus: 3.4.10
Macedonia: 3.6.1; 3.7.8; 4.1.8, 39; 4.6.30; 4.11.13; 5.1.42; 5.2.18; 5.8.16; 6.2.15;
   6.6.10; 6.9.17; 7.1.37; 7.8.30; 8.8.3; 9.1.2; 9.3.20; 9.6.8, 19–20; 10.5.12;
   10.10.16; 10.10.18
Maeotis (Lake): 6.4.18
Mallus: 3.7.5
Maracanda: 7.6.10; 7.6.24; 7.9.20; 8.1.7, 19; 8.2.13
Marathus: 4.1.6
Mareotis: 4.7.9; 4.8.1
Margiana: 7.10.15

INDEX TO MAPS

THE CAMPAIGNS OF ALEXANDER THE GREAT (334 – 323 B.C.)

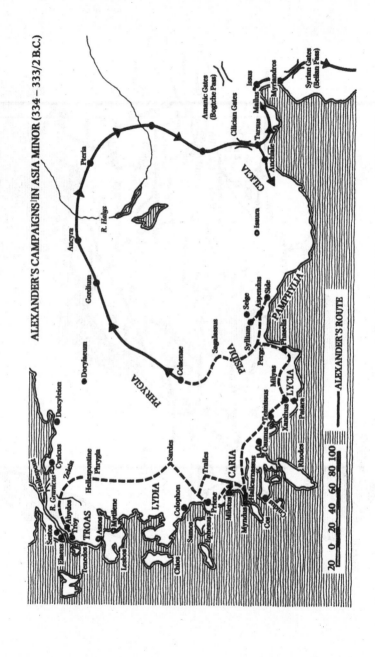

ALEXANDER'S CAMPAIGNS IN ASIA MINOR (334 – 333/2 B.C.)

——— ALEXANDER'S ROUTE

20 0 20 40 60 80 100

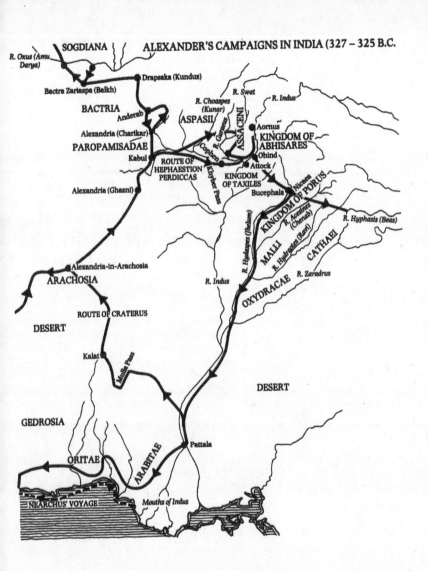

ALEXANDER'S CAMPAIGNS IN INDIA (327 – 325 B.C.

SOGDIANA

R. Oxus (Amu Darya)

Bactra Zariaspa (Balkh)

Drapsaka (Kunduz)

BACTRIA

Anderab

R. Swat

R. Choaspes (Kunar)

R. Indus

Alexandria (Charikar)

ASPASII

PAROPAMISADAE

ASSACENI

Aornus

Kabul

R. Garoaea

KINGDOM OF ABHISARES

ROUTE OF HEPHAESTION PERDICCAS

Cophen

Ohind

Khyber Pass

Attock

Alexandria (Ghazni)

KINGDOM OF TAXILES

Nicaea

Bucephala

KINGDOM OF PORUS

R. Hyphasis (Beas)

R. Acesines (Chenab)

Alexandria-in-Arachosia

MALLI

R. Hydraotes (Ravi)

CATHAEI

ARACHOSIA

R. Hydaspes (Jhelum)

R. Indus

R. Zaradrus

ROUTE OF CRATERUS

OXYDRACAE

DESERT

Kalat

Mulla Pass

DESERT

GEDROSIA

Pattala

ORITAE

ARABITAE

NEARCHUS' VOYAGE

Mouths of Indus

READ MORE IN PENGUIN

In every corner of the world, on every subject under the sun, Penguin represents quality and variety – the very best in publishing today.

For complete information about books available from Penguin – including Puffins, Penguin Classics and Arkana – and how to order them, write to us at the appropriate address below. Please note that for copyright reasons the selection of books varies from country to country.

In the United Kingdom: Please write to *Dept. EP, Penguin Books Ltd, Bath Road, Harmondsworth, West Drayton, Middlesex UB7 0DA*

In the United States: Please write to *Consumer Services, Penguin Putnam Inc., 405 Murray Hill Parkway, East Rutherford, New Jersey 07073-2136.* VISA and MasterCard holders call 1-800-631-8571 to order Penguin titles

In Canada: Please write to *Penguin Books Canada Ltd, 10 Alcorn Avenue, Suite 300, Toronto, Ontario M4V 3B2*

In Australia: Please write to *Penguin Books Australia Ltd, 487 Maroondah Highway, Ringwood, Victoria 3134*

In New Zealand: Please write to *Penguin Books (NZ) Ltd, Private Bag 102902, North Shore Mail Centre, Auckland 10*

In India: Please write to *Penguin Books India Pvt Ltd, 11 Community Centre, Panchsheel Park, New Delhi 110017*

In the Netherlands: Please write to *Penguin Books Netherlands bv, Postbus 3507, NL-1001 AH Amsterdam*

In Germany: Please write to *Penguin Books Deutschland GmbH, Metzlerstrasse 26, 60594 Frankfurt am Main*

In Spain: Please write to *Penguin Books S. A., Bravo Murillo 19, 1°B, 28015 Madrid*

In Italy: Please write to *Penguin Italia s.r.l., Via Vittorio Emanuele 45/a, 20094 Corsico, Milano*

In France: Please write to *Penguin France, 12, Rue Prosper Ferradou, 31700 Blagnac*

In Japan: Please write to *Penguin Books Japan Ltd, Iidabashi KM-Bldg, 2-23-9 Koraku, Bunkyo-Ku, Tokyo 112-0004*

In South Africa: Please write to *Penguin Books South Africa (Pty) Ltd, P.O. Box 751093, Gardenview, 2047 Johannesburg*